DEFICITS AND THE DOLLAR

DEFICITS AND THE DOLLAR: THE WORLD ECONOMY AT RISK

Stephen Marris

INSTITUTE FOR INTERNATIONAL ECONOMICS
WASHINGTON, DC
DECEMBER 1985. Revised AUGUST 1987

Stephen Marris is a Senior Fellow at the Institute for International Economics and a member of the Group of Thirty. He was formerly Economic Adviser to the Secretary-General of the Organization for Economic Cooperation and Development, where he was also the first editor of the OECD Economic Outlook and a major contributor to numerous OECD studies. He was a Visiting Professor at the Brookings Institution (1969–70).

INSTITUTE FOR INTERNATIONAL ECONOMICS

C. Fred Bergsten, *Director*
Ann L. Beasley, *Director of Publications*

The Institute for International Economics was created by, and receives substantial support from, the German Marshall Fund of the United States.

Library of Congress Cataloging-in-Publication Data

Marris, Stephen
    Rev. ed. of: Deficits and the dollar. 1985.

    (Policy analyses in international economics ; 14)
    References: p. 335
    1. Budget deficits—United States.   2. Dollar, American.   3. Balance of payments—United States.   4. Saving and investment—United States.   I. Marris, Stephen. Deficits and the dollar.
II. Title.   III. Series.
HJ2052.M37   1987   332.4'973   87–29887
ISBN 0–88132–067–6 (pbk.)

To Margaret

Contents

vii

ix

xi

xii

xiii

Technical Notes

Discussion of the more technical points in this study has been relegated to a set of Technical Notes at the end. These are referred to in the text as TN1, TN2, etc. Figures, tables, and boxes are numbered, with decimal notation, by chapter.

Glossary

. .	Not available
BIS	Bank for International Settlements
CBO	Congressional Budget Office
D&D	Deficits and the Dollar
EC	European Community. The short-form designation of adherents to the treaties forming the European Coal and Steel Community (ECSC), the European Economic Community (EEC), the European Atomic Energy Community (Euratom), and the treaties amending those treaties. Members are Belgium, France, Denmark, Federal Republic of Germany, Greece, Ireland, Italy, Luxembourg, the Netherlands, and the United Kingdom. Spain and Portugal are to accede January 1, 1986.
ECU	European Currency Unit, the EMS unit of currency
EMS	European Monetary System
GATT	General Agreement on Tariffs and Trade
Group of Five	Finance ministers of France, Germany, Japan, the United Kingdom, and the United States
Group of Seventy-seven	The developing-country members of the United Nations
Group of Ten	Finance ministers and central bank governors of countries participating in the General Arrangements to Borrow which provide a line of credit to the IMF: Belgium, Canada, France, Germany, Italy, Japan, the Netherlands, Sweden, the United Kingdom, and the United States. The Swiss National Bank is also a participant.
Group of Twenty-four	Finance ministers and central bank governors of the developing countries currently members of the Intergovernmental Group of 24 in International Monetary Affairs
MERM	The Multilateral Exchange Rate Model developed by the International Monetary Fund
n.a.	Not applicable
NIC	Newly industrializing (developing) country
OECD area	The countries comprising the membership of the Organization for Economic Cooperation and Development, i.e. the United States, Canada, Japan, Australia and New Zealand, and all the West European countries including Turkey
OPEC	Organization of Petroleum Exporting Countries
ROECD	The rest of the OECD area, i.e. all member countries, but the United States
ROW	The rest of the world, i.e., in principle all countries but the United States
SDR	Special Drawing Right. A monetary reserve asset established by the IMF. Its current value is based on a basket of the five major industrial countries' currencies.

Acknowledgments

David D. Johnson was responsible for constructing the D&D model, and much else besides. Laura J. Knoy did a valiant job on the figures and the bibliography. Nicolas Plessz gave invaluable help, especially on the portfolio balance analysis in chapter 3. Paul S. Armington helped with the analysis of exchange rates and budget deficits in chapter 6, and Paula R. Demasi researched the impact of the strong dollar on the structure of the US economy. Kathleen A. Lynch much improved the style. Julie K. Harris did the typing, with outstanding competence and devotion to duty.

I am grateful for the comments made by participants in many meetings at which preliminary results of this study were discussed on both sides of the Atlantic and Pacific. Barry P. Bosworth, Richard N. Cooper, Edward M. Truman, Masaru Yoshitomi, and several of my colleagues at the Institute made helpful comments on the penultimate draft. C. Fred Bergsten provided constant encouragement and constructive criticism throughout.

Preface

In December 1985, the Institute published *Deficits and the Dollar: The World Economy at Risk* by Stephen Marris. It remains the most comprehensive analysis of the rise of the dollar and the American trade deficit in the first half of the 1980s, of the implications of these developments for both the United States and the world economy, and of the policy alternatives for responding to the problem. This new edition includes an update which brings the story up to August 1987, reviews the predictions of the original volume in light of subsequent events, and suggests a policy course for the coming months and years.

Two elements in this update stand out. One is the almost precise degree to which the decline of the dollar envisaged in the original study has eventuated over the past two-and-a-half years. The other is the juxtaposition, during the early part of 1987, of a further fall in the dollar with a sharp increase in American interest rates—perhaps a harbinger of the much more serious "hard landing" envisaged by Dr. Marris. The issues addressed in this study clearly remain of central importance to both policymakers and markets around the world, and this updated edition of *Deficits and the Dollar* seeks to expand understanding of them and provide a foundation for constructive responses by both the public and private sectors.

In conducting the study, Stephen Marris has drawn on the unique perspective of his experience of nearly thirty years at the Organization for Economic Cooperation and Development in Paris. During that period Dr. Marris observed closely—and often participated actively in—the evolution of economic policies throughout the industrial world and the halting, erratic, but occasionally fruitful efforts to coordinate them. Few, if any, students of international economic affairs are as well placed to address this complex of macroeconomic, monetary, and trade issues across the entire range of major nations.

The Institute for International Economics is a private nonprofit research institution for the study and discussion of international economic policy. Its purpose is to analyze important issues in that area, and to develop and communicate practical new approaches for dealing with them. The Institute is completely nonpartisan.

The Institute was created by a generous commitment of funds from the German Marshall Fund of the United States in 1981, and continues to receive substantial support from that source. In addition, major institutional grants are now being received from the Ford Foundation, the William and Flora Hewlett Foundation, and the Alfred P. Sloan Foundation. A number of other foundations and private corporations are contributing to the increasing diversification of the Institute's financial resources. The original project which produced *Deficits and the Dollar: The World Economy at Risk* was partially funded by the Andrew W. Mellon Foundation, whose support is deeply appreciated.

The Board of Directors bears overall responsibility for the Institute and gives general guidance and approval to its research program—including identification of topics that are likely to become important to international economic policymakers over the medium run (generally, one to three years) and which thus should be addressed by the Institute. The Director, working closely with the staff and outside Advisory Committee, is responsible for the development of particular projects and makes the final decision to publish an individual study.

The Institute hopes that its studies and other activities will contribute to building a stronger foundation for international economic policy around the world. Comments as to how it can best do so are invited from readers of these publications.

C. FRED BERGSTEN
Director
August 1987

Deficits and the Dollar Revisited: August 1987

Deficits and the Dollar: the World Economy at Risk was published in December 1985. The computer runs on which the analysis was based go back to March 1985. This postscript brings the story up-to-date. How far have events over the last two years conformed to the prognosis? Where they have not, why not? The conclusion reached is that both the dollar and the world economy are still on track for the predicted "hard landing," even though several important developments were not anticipated.

The Hard Landing

There were two key features of the hard landing predicted in *Deficits and the Dollar*. The first was that the dollar would fall very sharply, and in the end too far. The second was that, as confidence in the dollar ebbed, strong upward pressures on US interest rates would lead to a recession in the United States. This recession, combined with the weak dollar, would have a very negative impact on growth both in Europe and Japan, and in the indebted developing countries, and hence would spread out through the world economy.

The dollar has, indeed, fallen very sharply; but so far the second half of this prediction has not come to pass. Indeed, critics have asked why the correction of a US trade deficit, amounting to around 3½ percent of GNP, should have such dire consequences. A summary of the three main reasons that led to this prediction in the first place may thus be helpful.

The first reason is simply that the starting position was so bad. In 1986, US merchandise exports "paid for" only 61 percent of US imports.[1] This is significantly worse than the position of the seven major developing-country

---

1. If imports and exports of nonfactor services are included, this figure rises to 66 percent.

debtor countries in 1982, when their exports covered 78 percent of their imports. It means that:

In relation to its export earnings, the United States is going into debt faster than any major developed country since World War II, and faster than the average of the seven major developing-country debtors on the eve of the debt crisis. (p. 94)[2]

Put starkly: eliminating the US merchandise trade deficit will require either a 39 percent reduction in US imports from their 1986 level, or a 64 percent increase in US exports, or some combination of both.

This bad starting position creates two "adverse gap factors." First, if exports are much smaller than imports, they have to increase much faster than imports just to prevent the trade deficit from widening still further:

This may seem an odd piece of arithmetic. But it reflects a reality that other countries have discovered to their cost, especially recently in Latin America: once a large trade deficit . . . has opened up, it takes a very sharp reduction in the growth of imports *relative* to exports to start a move back toward equilibrium. (p. 86)

Second, as long as imports exceed exports, the United States has to make increasing interest payments on the money it borrows to finance the current account deficit. Together, these two adverse gap factors added over $20 billion a year to the current account deficit in 1985, and would have added over $45 billion by 1990 had the dollar stayed at its early 1985 level (table 3.3).

The second reason why correcting the US trade deficit will be unusually difficult is simply that the US economy is so large. If a small country corrects a trade deficit equivalent to several percentage points of GNP, it will have little impact on the world economy as a whole. The United States, however, is the world's single largest export market, and a major competitor in other countries' markets. Thus, correcting a large US trade deficit is bound to have a strongly negative impact on trade balances, and hence growth rates, in other countries. This phenomenon, already apparent in the second half of 1986, makes the adjustment that much more difficult by slowing down the growth of US export markets.

It also means that other countries have a strong incentive to resist a correction of the US trade deficit. Smaller countries can do so by letting their currencies fall with the dollar. Larger countries may decide they would

---

2. Page, table, and chapter numbers are references to *Deficits and the Dollar*, pp. 1–343.

prefer to finance the US deficit rather than accept the necessary change in trade balances. Both phenomena have been evident since the dollar started going down, as discussed later.

There is a third, unique, feature of the present situation. By the end of 1986, the United States had become the world's largest debtor nation, with a net negative foreign investment position of $263 billion. Even so, the United States was still very largely able to borrow in its own currency.[3] This means that foreigners carry the exchange risk when lending to the United States. At the same time, moreover, foreigners are exposed to an exchange risk on their uncovered portfolio of dollar-denominated debt issued by *other* countries, estimated at around $800 billion at the end of 1984 (p. 371):

As long as things go well, there is an advantage in being the issuer of the world's leading vehicle currency. Increasing demand . . . provides a more or less automatic source of finance. If things go wrong, it is a different matter. People will try to sell off dollar-denominated assets that originated outside the United States and for which the United States is in no way responsible. The United Kingdom learned this lesson from bitter experience . . . . (p. 96)

To sum up: because the starting position was so bad, and the US economy is so large, further large current account deficits are bound to be incurred and will have to be financed, even if the dollar goes down a long way. Because of the enormous exchange rate losses:

A time is bound to come . . . when foreigners' willingness to invest their savings in the United States dries up faster than the US economy's need for them. This may not happen until the dollar has gone quite a long way down. But when it does, a "crunch" will develop in US financial markets, and the economy will be headed for trouble. (p. xxvii)

The Dollar

How far have events conformed to this prognosis? As can be seen from figure 1, the dollar has gone down at quite close to the *rate* projected in the

3. Since the dollar began to go down, however, borrowing in foreign currencies by US corporations has risen sharply. New bond issues denominated in foreign currencies placed directly abroad by US borrowers, for example, rose from $800 million in 1984 to $10.5 billion in 1986, or from 7 percent to 24 percent of all such issues (*Survey of Current Business*, March 1987, table M, p. 41).

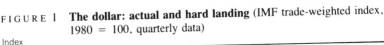

FIGURE 1   **The dollar: actual and hard landing** (IMF trade-weighted index, 1980 = 100, quarterly data)

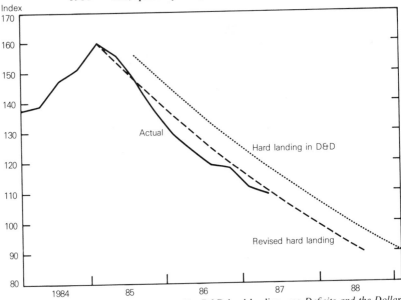

Note: For revised hard landing, see text. For D&D hard landing, see *Deficits and the Dollar*, table 4.5.

hard-landing scenario, in line with the assumption that it "will not go down very much faster than it came up" (p. 130). The decline started six months earlier than assumed, however—in the second quarter of 1985, rather than the fourth quarter. Allowing for this, the dollar had by 24 August 1987 declined by 32.6 percent from the first quarter of 1985, close to the 34.2 percent projected for the third quarter of 1987 in a revised hard-landing scenario, as measured by the trade-weighted index of the International Monetary Fund (IMF).

The movement of each of the major currencies against the dollar has been broadly in line with past behavior (table 1, third column). With the liberalization of Japanese financial markets, the yen has appreciated somewhat more—and the deutsche mark and Swiss franc somewhat less—than predicted on the basis of past relationships, as anticipated (pp. 165–69).

There have nevertheless been a number of new developments. First, Canada has suffered a serious deterioration in its terms of trade since 1985, so that it no longer seems reasonable to expect a further significant appreciation of the Canadian dollar vis-à-vis the US dollar. As a result, for any given decline in the dollar's trade-weighted index, other key currencies are now projected to appreciate more against the dollar. Second, events since 1985 have underlined the importance to the United States of the currencies of a number of developing countries not covered in the traditional trade-weighted indices for the dollar—for example, the Korean won, the Taiwan dollar, and the Mexican peso, which have generally gone down with the dollar.[4] According to a new index produced by the Morgan Guaranty Trust Company, which includes these currencies, the dollar dropped by 24.7 percent in real terms between the first quarter of 1985 and the second quarter of 1987, i.e., by only about three-quarters as much as shown by the IMF index.

The Dollar and the US Current Account Deficit

Events since February 1985 have amply confirmed what was described as the "single most striking result of this study," namely, "that the dollar would have to drop a long way simply to stop the US current account deficit from getting worse" (p. xxvi). By August 1987 the dollar had, however, gone down enough to produce, according to most projections, at least some improvement in the US current balance. Thus, according to the D&D model, with the dollar at its present level, the deficit could drop back to around $100 billion by 1989 (figure 2).[5] Although not good enough, this is an enormous improvement compared with what would have happened had the dollar stayed at its early 1985 level—a projected current account deficit in 1990 of over $300 billion!

---

4. In spring 1987, the Korean won, and, in particular, the Taiwan dollar, began to appreciate against the US dollar, by 6 percent and 14 percent, respectively, between January and mid-August 1987. (This brought the rise in the Taiwan dollar to 27 percent from the first quarter of 1985.) This was a desirable development, as advocated by Bela Balassa and John Williamson, in *Adjusting to Success: Balance of Payments Policy in the East Asian NICs*, POLICY ANALYSES IN INTERNATIONAL ECONOMICS 17 (Washington: Institute for International Economics, June 1987).
5. This is a somewhat more favorable outcome than suggested by other forecasters. In its June 1987 *Economic Outlook*, the OECD Secretariat forecast a current account deficit of $120 billion in the second half on 1988 (annual rate).

FIGURE 2   **The dollar and the US current account deficit** (billion dollars)

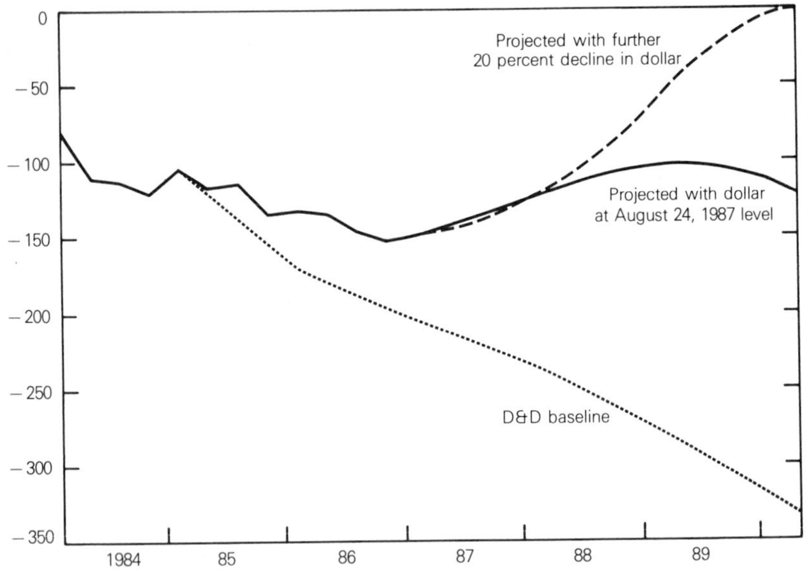

Note: Projections made using the D&D model, assuming a 2.5 percent growth rate in both the United States and in Europe and Japan. For D&D baseline, with the dollar at its early 1985 level, see *Deficits and the Dollar*, table 3.2.

Nevertheless, there was virtually no improvement in the current account, measured in current dollars, through the second quarter of 1987 (figure 3). Measured at constant 1982 prices, however, the deficit in *volume terms* shrank at an annual rate of $40 billion to $45 billion between the third quarter of 1986 and the second quarter of 1987. The rise in the volume of exports accelerated to an annual rate of 14 percent, much faster than the growth of world trade during this period, while the dramatic surge in imports since 1981 was halted. While this pace of adjustment may not be sustained, and there is a long way still to go, it is clear that a major improvement is under way.

Absent a US recession, however, almost all projections show the current account balance beginning to deteriorate again after only two or three years. This is because, as long as the United States continues to run a large deficit, the adverse gap factors will reassert themselves after the benefits of the dollar's decline have worked through.

FIGURE 3   **US exports and imports of goods and nonfactor services in constant 1982 dollars, 1975:Q2–1987:Q2** (billion dollars)

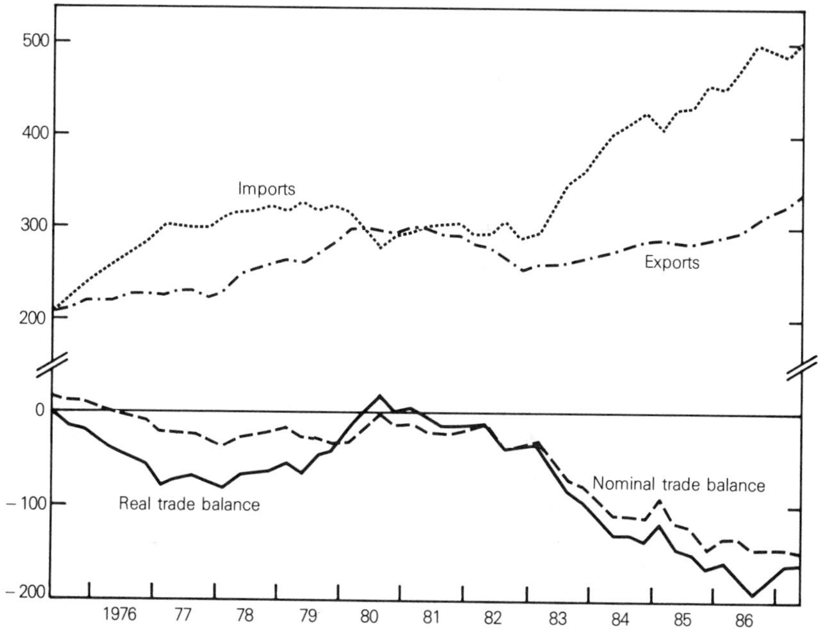

Source: US Department of Commerce, *National Income and Product Accounts.*

If, however, the current account deficit were eliminated—by either a further drop in the dollar or a US recession, or a combination of both—these adverse gap factors would cease to operate. Thus, it is by no means as implausible as it may seem in the summer of 1987 to suggest that the United States might be running a current account surplus by the early 1990s, as projected in the hard-landing scenario (pp. 130–43). On present policies, however, this is only likely to happen because the dollar goes down too far and there is a recession in the United States.

Financing the US Current Account Deficit

Until the autumn of 1986, the US current account deficit was financed largely through the world's private sector, with remarkable ease. Indeed, during this period the United States experienced the congenial and relatively unusual combination of a sharp decline in the dollar with a sharp decline in interest rates, and a narrowing of the interest-rate differential against the other major currencies (figure 6).

At first sight, it may seem odd that foreigners went on lending to the United States at an annual rate of over $100 billion, even though they were losing on the exchange rate nearly every month. ''Surely, nobody could be that stupid.'' But:

> The record suggests that indeed they can: that at almost every point some people will be prepared to bet that the dollar has, at least temporarily, gone down too fast or too far—and lose.'' (p. 126)

Two additional factors, however, helped to cushion the dollar's decline. First, the sharp drop in oil prices more than offset the inflationary impact of the declining dollar on US import prices through most of 1986, so that for over a year US inflation declined, even though the lower dollar was pushing other import prices up. Second, a remarkably strong bull market on Wall Street meant that, for most foreign investors, exchange rate losses were offset by capital gains on stocks and bonds (figure 4).

Already in 1986, however, there was some change in the nature of the capital inflow. Thus, while the current account deficit rose to $141 billion, the inflow of private capital dropped to $108 billion, leaving $33 billion to be financed by changes in official reserve assets (figure 5). But the situation changed much more dramatically in the early months of 1987. Indeed, from the figures now available it is clear that *in the first five months of 1987 the net inflow of private capital fell to zero.*

This was not immediately apparent from US balance of payments statistics for the first quarter of 1987, which showed an increase in official reserve assets equal to only about one-half of the current account deficit, with the remainder apparently financed by a still sizable inflow of private capital. But during this quarter, there was an unusually large discrepancy between the increase in official reserve assets held by foreign central banks in dollars in the United States as reported in the US balance of payment statistics ($15.5 billion), and the increase in these banks' foreign-exchange reserves as reported to the International Monetary Fund ($47 billion). While various factors can account for such a discrepancy, the main explanation seems to be that foreign central banks placed an unusually large fraction of their increased dollar

FIGURE 4   **The yen, the dollar, and the Dow–Jones Index** (semi-log scale, monthly averages, February 1985 = 100)

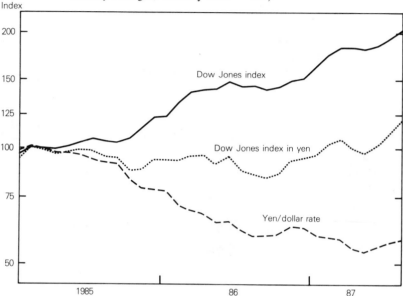

Source: New York Stock Exchange, Inc.; IMF, *International Financial Statistics.*

holdings in the Eurodollar market, where yields were higher.[6] Such deposits do not, however, appear in the statistics of US liabilities to foreign official holders. Thus, total official financing for the US current account deficit was very much larger than suggested by US balance of payments statistics.

The IMF figures point to continued central bank intervention at a very high level through April and well into May. For the first five months of the year, the rise in foreign-exchange reserves held outside the United States was a phenomenal $73 billion. During the same period, the US current account deficit was probably about $55 billion to $60 billion. The reported increase in foreign-exchange reserves overstates the increase in foreign official

6. Identified official holdings of Eurocurrencies accounted for 29 percent of total official holdings of foreign exchange at the end of 1985, of which 60 percent were denominated in dollars (IMF, *Annual Report 1986,* Washington, appendix 1, table 1.4).

FIGURE 5   **Financing the US current account deficit** (billion dollars, annual rate)

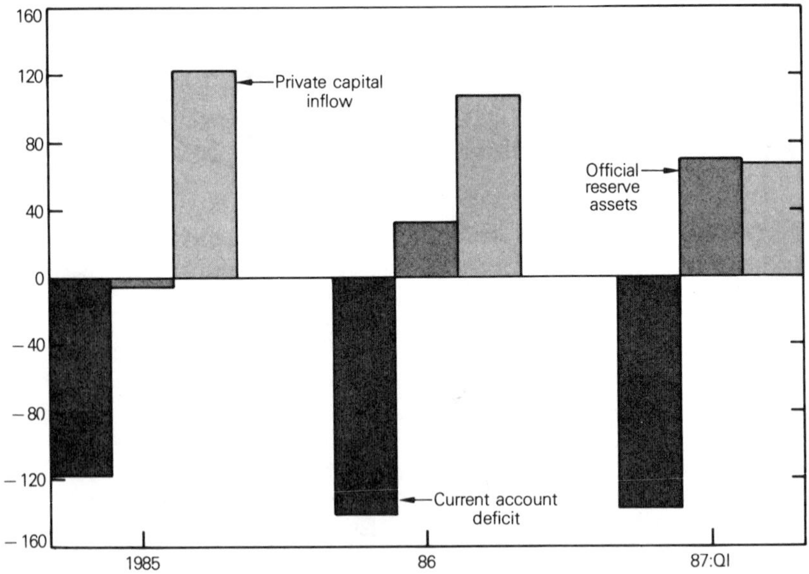

Note: Not seasonally adjusted. Private capital is defined as the difference between the current account deficit and the change in official reserve assets (and hence includes nonreserve official capital transactions).
Source: Survey of Current Business, US International Transactions, tables 1 and 2.

dollar holdings.[7] But even allowing for this, the figures suggest that there was no *net* inflow of private capital on average over this five-month period.

---

7. The increase in foreign-exchange reserves reported to the IMF overstates the increase in central bank dollar holdings for a number of reasons. First, the share of dollars in all countries' foreign-exchange holdings was only 65 percent at the end of 1985 (IMF, *Annual Report 1986,* appendix 1, table 1.2). During the period of heavy intervention, it is likely that the reported increases were mainly dollars, because converting the proceeds of intervention into other currencies would have defeated its purpose. Some of the smaller central banks, however, may have been shifting out of dollars to avoid exchange rate losses. Second, since about one-third of world reserves are held in currencies that have been appreciating against the dollar, the figures as reported *in dollars* will include an upward valuation effect. This could, indeed, account for more than half of the rise in foreign-exchange reserves between February 1985 and December 1986, shown in figure 7. A rough estimate suggests that it could have accounted for around $10 billion of the increase reported in the first five months of 1987.

Large gross inflows continued as Japanese investors, for example, continued to acquire US financial and real assets. But the global figures tell us that other people—be they Japanese, Europeans, or Americans—were shifting out of dollar-denominated assets on a similar or somewhat larger scale. Exactly what form these outflows took we do not know, and to some extent never will. Past experience suggests that in part they will only turn up in the "statistical discrepancy" in the US balance of payments, which, significantly, turned sharply negative in the first quarter of 1987 (minus $11.9 billion,[8] compared with a quarterly average of *plus* $6.1 billion from 1981 to 1986).

Thus, during this period it was the world's central banks that financed the US current account deficit—and, directly or indirectly, most of the US budget deficit.[9] This sudden drying up of the inflow of private capital happened despite a sharp widening of the interest-rate differential in favor of the dollar—for US and Japanese 10-year government bonds, from 170 basis points in January to a peak of nearly 500 in mid-May (figure 6).

This sequence of events led to a growing awareness of the possibility of a negative reaction between US financial markets and foreign-exchange markets. As described in *Deficits and the Dollar*:

• In the domestic financial markets, the combination of upward pressures on interest rates and accelerating inflation will be taken as evidence that all the long-felt fears about the inevitable consequences of excessive budget deficits were coming true with a vengeance: this would add to upward pressure on interest rates.

• In the foreign exchange market, the combination of a strongly positive interest-rate differential and a falling dollar will be taken as evidence that the long-held view that the size of the US external current deficit was unsustainable was also coming true: this would add to the downward pressure on the dollar.

---

8. After deducting the seasonal adjustment discrepancy.

9. Foreign central banks financed the US budget deficit directly insofar as they invested the dollars they bought in the foreign-exchange markets in US Treasury bills. More broadly, a country's external current account *equals* its current expenditure *less* its current income, which in turn *equals* the sum of private savings *less* private investment *plus* the budget deficit (pp. 37–40). Thus, by financing a US current account deficit of around $140 billion to $150 billion (annual rate), the world's central banks directly or indirectly financed almost all of the federal budget deficit which was running at around $160 billion to $170 billion. If they had not done so, with no foreign savings to finance the budget deficit, private investment would have been crowded out by rising interest rates, bringing it down to the level that could be financed by domestic savings.

FIGURE 6   **The yen and the US-Japan bond-yield spread** (monthly averages)

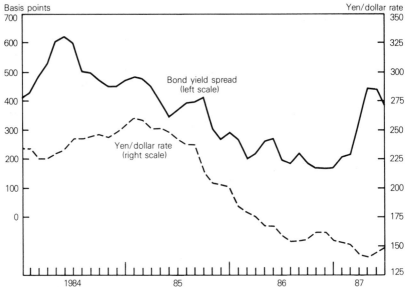

Note: Bond-yield differentials are computed using the United States 10-year Treasury-bond yield and the Japanese government 10-year interest-bearing bond yield.
Source: Federal Reserve Bulletin; NIKKEI.

● These psychological reactions in the two markets will feed on each other. The fall in the dollar will unsettle the domestic financial markets. Accelerating inflation and falling bond prices will unnerve foreign investors. Strengthening downward pressure on the dollar will put further upward pressure on interest rates, pushing bond prices down further. And so on (pp. 146–47).

Slow Growth in Europe and Japan

Perhaps the most striking development outside the United States since 1985 is the sharp slowdown in growth in Japan and Europe even before the US trade balance had improved significantly (from 3.3 percent in 1985 to 2 percent in the first half of 1987). This came as a surprise to the national authorities and to the major international organizations, which had to steadily reduce their forecasts for growth in 1986 and 1987, since it was widely held that the drop in oil prices would boost world growth. Basically this overoptimism reflected a widespread failure to recognize how much growth in Europe and Japan since the beginning of the 1980s had depended on external demand (pp. 64–74).

It was unduly simplistic to believe that because higher oil prices had led to recession, lower prices would lead automatically to faster growth. First, companies did not pass on the full benefits from lower energy costs to consumers, preferring instead to raise profit margins. This boost to profits, moreover, tended to be invested in financial rather than real assets, because of mediocre growth prospects and high real interest rates. Second, when oil prices rose in the 1970s, some of the most important oil producers simply could not, at first, spend all the money they were earning. But they soon learned, and by 1982 the oil producers as a group were already running a current account deficit. So when oil prices collapsed, they had no option but to cut back imports sharply—by an estimated 45 percent in volume terms from 1984 to 1987[10]—with devastating consequences for Europe's and Japan's exports to those markets.

But that was not all. The prices of primary commodities other than oil were also very soft, and, from mid-1984 to early 1987, the terms of trade between nonoil commodities and manufactured products deteriorated by over 30 percent, cutting at least $50 billion from the purchasing power of the exports of producers of these products in the developing world.[11] Since most of these countries were in financial difficulties, they also had to slash their imports.

Only in the latter part of 1986 did growth in Europe and Japan begin to be hit by a third negative external shock—the deterioration (in volume terms) in their trade balance with the United States. This still has a long way to go, since by the second quarter of 1987, the US trade deficit had only been cut back by about one-fifth in volume terms from its peak in the third quarter of 1986 (figure 3). As analyzed in *Deficits and the Dollar* (chapter 6), this negative shock is likely to continue for several years, and in a hard-landing scenario could amount to 3.5 percent of the GNP of Europe and Japan, before allowing for multipliers—or to over 5 percent of GNP adding the three shocks together.

---

10. *OECD Economic Outlook* (June 1987), table 58.

11. The rise in commodity prices, mainly metals, in the first half of 1987 had, up to mid-year, reversed about one-fifth of this shift.

Events have shown, moreover, the strong negative multiplier effects on domestic demand in export-oriented economies such as those of Japan and Germany. Thus, despite quite buoyant consumer demand at home, Japanese and European exporters to the US market, seeing their profit margins evaporate as the dollar went down, began to scale back their investment plans, in some cases even before their US sales actually fell.

So far, the main policy response has been a widespread easing of monetary policy. Investment demand has weakened, however, despite lower interest rates, because of the poor outlook for exports. Indeed, one of my prophecies has already been partially fulfilled. Europe and Japan:

. . . may start intervening in the exchange markets on a significant scale to slow down the appreciation of their currencies against the dollar. For the same reasons, and partly as the direct result of such intervention, their monetary authorities may begin to tolerate excessive rates of growth of monetary expansion. In other words, it could be the central banks of the other OECD countries that end up printing the money needed to finance the US budget and current account deficits. . . . Indeed, the uncomfortable fact is that periods of US balance of payments weakness (under fixed rates) or a falling dollar (under flexible rates) have almost always been associated with excessive rates of monetary expansion in the world, and to a subsequent burst of world inflation. (pp. 249–50)

So far, this danger seems to have been avoided (see below). But, given this lesson from history, the easing of monetary policy in Europe and Japan has probably gone about far enough. What is needed is a sizable, albeit temporary, fiscal stimulus. Indeed, there is:

. . . the potential for a "Reagan miracle" in Europe and Japan of the kind enjoyed by the United States in 1983–84. They could take a strong dose of fiscal expansion, and set off a strong rise in domestic demand, while inflation would be held down because their currencies would be appreciating, and budget deficits would not push up interest rates because their savings would be flowing back from the United States. (p. 220)[12]

Up to mid-1987, however, there had been only slow movement on the fiscal front. The two expansionary fiscal packages announced by the Japanese government in 1986 turned out to be quite small, and the FY1987 budget approved by the Diet was actually restrictive. On 29 May 1987, however, a

---

12. More accurately, a strong ex ante desire to get out of dollars would put downward pressure on domestic interest rates, as happened in March–April 1987.

new "fiscal stimulus" package was announced—on paper amounting to ¥6 trillion, or $40 billion. About one-third of this amount will give a genuine boost to the economy, split about equally between increased investment in public works and net tax cuts. This should suffice to prevent growth from slowing down still further, at least temporarily. But it falls far short of what will be needed, since most of the necessary correction of the US trade deficit is still to come and will fall particularly heavily on Japan (pp. 320–21).

In Europe, fiscal policy was quite expansionary in the United Kingdom in the run-up to the elections in June 1987, financed in part out of the proceeds of privatization. As a result, the United Kingdom became the "locomotive" of Europe. How long this can last is open to some doubt, given the underlying weakness of its balance of payments, and a rate of inflation well above that of its main competitors.

In Germany, the government has stuck doggedly to its policy of fiscal consolidation, despite a marked slowdown in the economy that started in the autumn of 1986 as the weakness of export demand began to make itself felt in earnest. There has been widespread support in Germany for a more active response to the changed situation, from both business and academic circles, and from the major international organizations, generally in the form of stronger action to cut subsidies and improve the supply side, coupled with larger tax cuts to give a significant net fiscal stimulus.[13] The Commission of the European Communities has recommended that Germany bring forward not only the tax cuts planned for 1988, but also some of those planned for 1990, as well as stepped-up infrastructure investment and a temporary 10 percent reduction in income and corporate tax rates under the provisions of the 1967 Stability Law.[14] So far, however, the government has rejected all such proposals.[15]

This reluctance to adopt more expansionary fiscal policies persists despite the fact that events have confirmed the analysis in chapter 6 suggesting that

---

13. See, in particular, the *OECD Economic Survey, Germany,* parts III and IV, Paris, July 1987.

14. *The economic outlook for 1988 and budgetary policy in the Member States,* Communication of the Commission of the European Communities, Brussels, 3 July 1987, p. 36.

15. Part of the problem lies in divergent views about the form the fiscal stimulus should take. The Länder governments, for example, object to the planned tax cuts because they reduce the tax revenue they receive from the federal government. The trade unions feel that too much of the benefits from the tax cuts go to upper income groups, and believe that an increase in public investment would give a stronger boost to employment.

after the efforts made to bring budget deficits under control in the early 1980s there is now scope for fiscal easing in Europe and Japan, especially as the ''deficit-debt calculus would be improved . . . when, as the dollar declines, their interest rates become decoupled from US rates'' (p. 189)—as has happened.

Thus, in July 1987 the Commission of the European Communities concluded that in Germany, the United Kingdom, France, and Denmark, accounting for over 60 percent of Community GNP:

The medium-term evolution of the borrowing requirement and the public debt can be considered satisfactory. Some temporary deterioration in the budget balance should not affect financial equilibrium . . . (p. 35)

Passive acceptance of the low growth rates now prevailing will, however, lead to a worsening of the fiscal position. As the Commission put it:

The progressive weakening of final demand in the Community leaves it bogged down on a low growth path. Low growth increases the dangers of returning to a budgetary vicious circle, with the room for maneuver created by the control of current expenditure being wiped out by a weak increase in receipts. (p. 28)

By mid-1987 both the IMF and the Organization for Economic Cooperation and Development (OECD) were forecasting continued slow growth in Europe and Japan in 1988. National authorities, however, appeared to believe that the worst was over, and that growth would pick up progressively from then on. This seems unlikely:

If the other major OECD countries stick to their present policies, a hard landing for the US economy will have unpleasant consequences. The stimulus from external demand, which was directly or indirectly responsible for up to one-half of their growth during the recovery, will go into reverse. (pp. xxix) There would be a severe growth recession in 1987–88; by 1990, . . . GNP would be around 6 percent below the level assumed in the baseline, and unemployment would have risen sharply. (p. 164)

What Happens Next?

Early in 1987, when the dollar was weak and US interest rates were rising, the possibility that this combination could lead to a US recession became more widely recognized. But after mid-May, the markets calmed down, US interest rates declined, the dollar recovered somewhat, and the inflow of private capital resumed. Thus, by August the feeling was widespread that the dollar might have bottomed out, and that the US economy would continue to grow through 1988 at around 2.5 percent, boosted by a rise in net exports.

I am doubtful. The crucial question remains whether continuing large US trade and current account deficits can be financed without renewed upward pressure on US interest rates.

On one hand, the trade figures—with the usual fluctuations from month to month—are likely to go on disappointing the markets. First, while exporters to the US market were initially slow to put up their prices, the rise in US import prices began to accelerate in the first quarter of 1987. This trend could continue for some time considering how drastically exporters' profit margins have been squeezed. So even with a further improvement in volume terms, the trade deficit in current dollars will continue to be pushed up by rising import prices (the delayed J-curve). Second, unless and until there is a "crunch" in US financial markets, there could be a "wrong way" growth gap, with the US economy growing as fast or faster than those of the other OECD countries, rather than the other way around as postulated in a "cooperative" scenario (pp. 204–209).[16]

The adverse consequences of such a "wrong way" growth gap on the US trade deficit could, moreover, be more important than many observers seem to realize. First, past experience suggests that as the dollar goes down, foreign consumers will be less likely to switch over to buying US products, and foreign exporters more determined to hang on to their US markets, if demand is sluggish and there is excess capacity in their own domestic markets—and vice versa.

Second, as noted earlier, nonoil commodity prices have declined sharply in real terms largely because of slow growth in the industrial countries since mid-1984. In the present context, it is important to realize that the value of European and Japanese imports of nonoil commodities is five times that of the United States ($186 billion against $37 billion in 1983). Thus, faster growth in Europe and Japan would give a disproportionately strong boost to commodity prices, and the resultant improvement in the position of the commodity-exporting countries, many of whom are important markets for US exports (Latin America and Canada), would feed back to benefit the US

---

16. In its June 1987 *Economic Outlook*, the OECD Secretariat forecast a GNP growth rate averaging 0.5 percent faster in the United States than in Europe and Japan in 1987–88; in terms of domestic demand, however, there was a slightly larger gap in the opposite direction.

trade balance. Moreover, since Europe and Japan are net importers of nonoil commodities ($72 billion in 1983), while the United States is a net exporter ($11 billion in 1983), the resultant shift in the terms of trade would also help to move trade balances in the right direction.

Private Capital Flows

If the improvement in the trade figures continues to be disappointingly slow, the next question is whether the recent resumption of private capital inflows is likely to continue on a sustained basis, given a reduced, but still significant interest-rate differential in favor of the dollar. After all, since the dollar has now gone down a long way, is not now a good time to start buying dollar-denominated assets?

Here, the point that most observers seem to miss is that the time at which the pressures spill over from the foreign-exchange markets into the *domestic financial markets* usually only comes after the currency has gone most of the way down. The last time the dollar went down a long way, for example, in 1978–79, it reached what turned out to be its trough in the third quarter of 1979. But US interest rates continued to rise and the interest-rate differential in favor of the dollar only reached its peak in the first quarter of 1980. Subsequently, the dollar continued to be weak until the fall of 1980, even though the current account deficit had begun to shrink two-and-a-half years earlier, and had moved into surplus by 1980.

Why? Because expectations in foreign-exchange markets are "adaptive" (pp. 117–23). And once market operators become convinced that a further decline in the currency is a one-way bet, then even if they think the currency has gone most of the way down and may only have a few percentage points to go, they are well aware that even a small further fall would wipe out the gains from a very large interest-rate differential. If one looks, for example, at the record since 1973, one finds:

A nearly 90 percent chance that the dollar-DM rate could move in *one month* by an amount which—if it were downwards—would wipe out all the benefits to be gained from a 5 percent annual interest differential, and *a 50 percent chance that it could move enough to wipe out a 20 percent interest differential.* (p. 123)

At the time of writing, however, the exchange markets seem to feel that the central banks have it in their power to stabilize exchange rates at their present level. And, indeed, there have been suggestions the Group of Five countries have agreed on fairly specific "reference" ranges for the key currencies. If so, the strength of their determination to defend these levels is likely to be severely tested as confidence in the dollar ebbs and flows over the long period ahead during which the United States continues to run large current account deficits.

Such deficits in themselves generate an excess supply of dollars. More fundamentally, it is widely felt that, with the growth rates currently foreseen in the United States and elsewhere, the dollar has not yet gone down far enough to correct the US trade deficit. Thus, virtually all forecasts suggest that with the dollar at its present level the United States would run very large current account deficits indefinitely into the future. A simulation of the D&D model, for example, suggests that with both the United States, and Europe and Japan growing at 2.5 percent, the IMF dollar index would have to decline by something like another 20 percent to eliminate the current account deficit and stop the United States from going further into debt by the early 1990s (figure 2). Since a number of important currencies, including especially the Canadian dollar, would be likely to move with the dollar, the dollar would have to drop by more than this against the yen and the major European currencies—for example, to about 115 yen by the first quarter of 1988 (table 1).

This is a smaller decline in the dollar than several observers have suggested would be needed to eliminate the US current account deficit.[17] It reflects the fact that as the current deficit shrinks, the adverse gap factors diminish, and the dynamics of adjustment are such that:

The exchange rate becomes an increasingly powerful instrument in restoring equilibrium. It is like pushing an automobile up and over a hill. Once the brakes are off, it takes a great deal of effort to stop it from rolling backwards and get it moving uphill. Once it is moving, things get easier. And once it is over the top— i.e. the current balance moves into surplus—gravity starts working the other way. (p.106)

Central Bank Intervention

Absent a major change in policies, however, it is clear that as of August 1987 the dollar had not gone down enough, even if there is a substantial

---

17. Rudiger Dornbusch, "Why the Dollar Must Fall Another 30%," *New York Times,* 10 May 1987.

TABLE 1   **Selected dollar exchange rates: actual, predicted, and with further 20 percent decline in the dollar** (national units per dollar)

	25 Feb 1985	24 Aug 1987		With further 20 percent decline	
		Actual	Predicted[a]	1988:Q1	1990:Q1
Yen	263	142	148	114	107
Deutsche mark	3.44	1.82	1.69	1.23	1.17
Pound sterling[b]	1.05	1.63	1.53	1.85	1.71
French franc	10.54	6.08	6.01	4.55	4.77
Canadian dollar[b]	0.71	0.75	0.75[c]	0.75[c]	0.75[c]
IMF-MERM	100	67.4	67.4	88.4	88.4
1985:Q1 = 100					

a. Predictions based on past relationships, given the decline in the dollar's trade-weighted index from 1985:Q1 to 24 August 1987.
b. Dollars per national unit.
c. Set exogenously.
Notes: Dollar exchange rates for selected currencies are predicted and projected using the technique described in *Deficits and the Dollar* (pp. 317–19):
● The projection shown in the last two columns assumes a 2.5 percent growth rate in the United States and in Europe and Japan. The trade-weighted dollar falls by a further 20 percent from August 1987 to the first quarter of 1988, and then levels out. Subsequent changes in individual currencies reflect their time trends against the dollar.
● The assumption made about the Canadian dollar has been changed. Instead of appreciating further it is assumed to stay at its August 1987 level, which is close to the "fundamental equilibrium exchange rate" calculated by John Williamson (after allowing for the recent deterioration in Canada's terms of trade) in his appendix to Paul Wonnacott's *The United States and Canada: The Quest for Free Trade*, POLICY ANALYSES IN INTERNATIONAL ECONOMICS 16 (Washington: Institute for International Economics, March 1987).
● With the Canadian dollar appreciating less, the other currencies have to appreciate more to produce the same overall trade-weighted decline in the dollar.
● These cross-rate projections are based on historical relationships 1973–84. As discussed in *Deficits and the Dollar*, they probably understate the likely appreciation of the yen and overstate the likely appreciation of the European currencies.

margin of uncertainty as to how much further it will have to go. It is thus probable that the central banks will find that, if they try to maintain the dollar at its present level, they will end up having to intervene to support it massively (albeit with the same sort of ups and downs that occurred in 1978–80). Indeed—partly as a result of such intervention—they may well find they are financing not only the US current account deficit, but also substantial outflows of private capital.

This is what happened in 1970–72; and again in 1977–78, when over a two-year period intervention amounted to around $65 billion against a US current account deficit of $30 billion, with private capital outflows of $35 billion. It is anybody's guess how large the private capital outflow could be this time around. But it is a sobering thought that if the same quantitative relationship between the current and capital account were to hold as in 1977–78, the central banks could find that they had to intervene at an annual rate of up to $300 billion!

How long would their nerves hold? By the end of May 1987, the foreign-exchange reserves of the major holders had risen by $127 billion, *57 percent*, from the beginning of 1986 (figure 7). Even excluding Taiwan, the rise came to $90 billion, of which $58 billion came in the first five months of 1987. Japan, Germany, and the United Kingdom were the main players among the industrial countries, but reserve increases were widely spread among most of the others (figure 8 and table 2).

What is the likelihood that the central banks would be prepared to resume intervention on this scale to support the dollar should this prove necessary? The United States' contribution has up to now been relatively modest. In the three months February to April 1987, intervention purchases of dollars by the US monetary authorities came to $4.1 billion, all of which was financed by drawing down foreign currency balances.[18] Thus, the foreign central banks took on almost all the exchange risk involved in buying dollars on a falling market, and also had to try to mop up (''sterilize'') the domestic liquidity created when they buy up dollars with their own currencies.

Up to mid-1987 central banks did not seem to find it too difficult to sterilize most of their intervention. True, monetary growth targets were exceeded in many countries, including, notably, Germany and Japan. This reflected, to an important extent, efforts to bring down short-term interest rates and ease upward pressure on their currencies. But it cannot be taken as evidence of great difficulty in sterilizing intervention, since it was already happening in 1986 before intervention started on a large scale.

One reason why central banks have so far been able to sterilize most of their intervention is that they started off from a relatively good position. In Japan the ratio of foreign-exchange reserves to total assets of the monetary authorities peaked at 34 percent during the last period of heavy intervention in 1977–78. By 1985 this ratio had dipped to under 20 percent, and by March 1987 it had only risen to 24 percent (it probably rose further by

---

18. *Federal Reserve Bulletin* (July 1987), pp. 552–57.

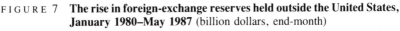

FIGURE 7   **The rise in foreign-exchange reserves held outside the United States,
January 1980–May 1987** (billion dollars, end-month)

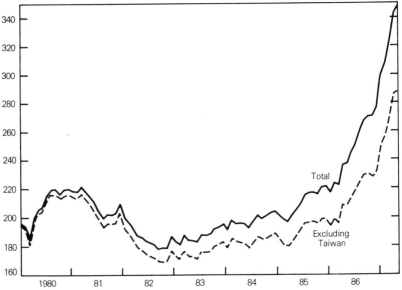

Note: See note, table 1.

Source: IMF, *International Financial Statistics;* Central Bank of China Financial
Statistics.

several percentage points in April when foreign-exchange reserves increased
by over $10 billion). Similarly, in Germany, foreign-exchange reserves were
equal to only 27 percent of all Bundesbank assets at the end of April 1987,
compared with previous peaks of 44 percent in 1978 and 50 percent in 1973.
Equally, with financial deregulation and liberalization, central banks have a
wider range of instruments available to them.[19]

Despite the seeming ease so far in preventing intervention from leading to
excessive monetary creation, this would no longer be the case if the central
banks found that they had to finance a large outflow of private capital from

19. See David Hale, "Will Currency Intervention Trigger a Resurgence of World Inflation?"
(paper for the National Business Economic Issues Council, San Francisco, 3–4 August 1987;
processed).

FIGURE 8   **The rise in foreign-exchange reserves held outside the United States, January 1986–May 1987** (billion dollars)

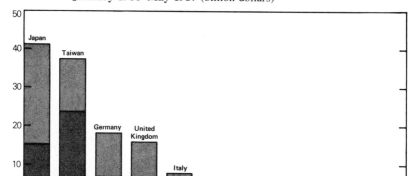

Note: See notes, table 2.

Source: IMF, *International Financial Statistics;* Central Bank of China Financial Statistics.

the United States, as suggested earlier. From the figures just quoted, it seems likely that sterilization would become increasingly difficult as and when renewed intervention moved into the $100 billion to $200 billion range. In that case, as David Hale put it, "the next phase of the dollar's devaluation could produce an explosion in global monetary reserves which would produce rising inflation in goods markets and not just financial asset prices" (op. cit. at n. 19 p. 12).

Reagan Bonds?

It is perhaps not surprising that during the period of strong pressure on the dollar we began to hear calls, especially from Tokyo, for the US Treasury to issue bonds denominated in foreign currencies.

T A B L E 2   **Foreign-exchange reserves held outside the United States,**
1980–May 87 (billion dollars, end-period)

	1980	1982	1984	1985	1986	May 1987	Dec 86–May 87 change
Japan	24.6	23.3	26.4	26.7	42.3	68.8	26.5
Taiwan	0.2	0.5	15.7	22.6	46.3	60.0ᵃ	13.7
Germany	48.6	44.8	40.1	44.4	51.7	63.4	11.6
United Kingdom	20.7	12.4	9.4	12.9	18.4	29.1	10.7
Italy	23.1	14.1	20.8	15.5	20.0	24.1	4.1
Saudi Arabia	23.4	29.5	24.7	25.0	18.3	20.5	2.2
Netherlands	11.6	10.1	9.2	10.8	11.2	13.2	2.0
Sweden	3.4	3.5	3.8	5.8	6.6	8.4	1.8
Canada	3.0	3.0	2.5	2.5	3.3	4.9	1.6
Belgium	7.8	3.9	4.6	4.8	5.5	6.8	1.3
Australia	1.7	6.4	7.4	5.8	7.2	8.3	1.1
Spain	11.9	7.7	12.0	11.2	14.8	15.5ᵇ	0.7
France	27.3	16.5	20.9	26.6	31.5	31.5	0.1
South Korea	2.9	2.8	2.8	2.9	3.3	3.4	0.0
Venezuela	6.6	6.6	8.9	10.3	6.4	5.7	−0.7
Brazil	5.8	3.9	11.5	10.6	5.8	4.0ᵇ	−1.8
Switzerland	15.7	15.5	15.3	18.0	21.8	19.8	−2.0
Total	238.5	204.5	236.1	256.2	314.3	387.4	73.0
Total, ex Taiwan	238.2	204.0	220.5	233.7	268.0	327.4	59.3

Note: Covers only major holders of foreign exchange reserves, ranked by change from Dec 1986–May 1987.
Source: International Financial Statistics, and Central Bank of China Financial Statistics.
a. 19 June 1987.
b. end-February 1987.

Theoretically, this could solve many of the problems just discussed. First, since the US Treasury would convert the foreign currency proceeds of these issues into dollars, it would be taking over the exchange risk from both foreign central banks and the private sector. Second, such Treasury paper would be very attractive, since it would be denominated in a "strong" currency while being backed by the creditworthiness of the US Treasury. Strong private demand for such bonds could thus ease the upward pressure on US interest rates, and, as long as the bonds had a sufficiently long maturity, would help to mop up excess liquidity in the foreign markets where they were issued.

But both political and economic question marks surround this option. At the political level, President Ronald Reagan would have to agree to issue what everybody would recognize as ''Carter bonds.'' This would obviously not appeal to him—although it also seems probable that in a crisis, faced with a choice between raising taxes or issuing yen-denominated bonds, he would choose the latter, given his strong opposition to tax increases.

More fundamentally, a decision by the US Treasury to borrow in foreign currencies could well be interpreted by the markets as a sign of weakness— that the United States would resort to any gimmick to enable it to go on with its present borrowing spree, rather than face up to the unpleasant decisions needed to put its house in order. Treasury Secretary James A. Baker III used this argument when he turned down the idea ''for the time being'' in April 1987.

Conventional wisdom has it that a decision by a government to embark on large-scale foreign borrowing to finance an external deficit is likely to work only if it is part of a package that includes other more basic measures to deal with the problem. The decision to issue Carter bonds, for example, was preceded by an agreement at the 1978 Bonn summit on collective action by several countries to reduce payments imbalances, and by a new US anti-inflation program. It was also accompanied by a one-point rise in the discount rate and the mobilization of $30 billion to support the dollar, of which the Carter bonds accounted for only one-third.

The Dollar and the US Budget Deficit

There is still some confusion about interrelations between the budget deficit, the dollar, and the trade deficit. True, it is now widely understood that large budget deficits, by sucking in foreign capital, were a major factor behind the dollar's rise. But then the question is asked: ''How come the dollar has gone down so far, despite continuing large budget deficits?''

The first part of the answer is that the value of the dollar in the foreign-exchange markets is determined not only by capital flows, but also by the net balance of supply and demand for dollars resulting from current transactions. Thus, the strong dollar generated by large budget deficits could not last indefinitely because it led to a rising trade and current account deficit which, in itself, generated a steadily increasing excess supply of dollars (pp. 16–19).

A full answer to the question is, however, more tricky. There are complex interrelations between the current account deficit, the inflow of foreign savings, the budget deficit, and the savings balance of the private sector (pp. 110–17). By the fall of 1986, the dollar had come down enough, and for long enough, to start reducing the US trade deficit in real terms. To maintain the overall investment-savings balance, something else had to give. In the event—and more by luck than good management—it was the budget deficit, which was expected to come down by around $60 billion between FY1986 and FY1987, i.e., somewhat faster than the improvement in the real trade balance.

Yet despite this somewhat fortuitous equal and offsetting shift in these two elements of the investment-savings balance, there was nevertheless upward pressure on US interest rates.[20] Why? Because the current balance and the capital balance are not inexorably linked, ex ante. Even with a continuing large current account deficit, it is perfectly possible for the inflow of private capital to fall off, ex ante—and if there is large-scale official intervention, also ex post. This was what happened in the first five months of 1987.

What happens next? The sharp drop in the budget deficit in FY1987 primarily reflected action taken by Congress to slow the rise in defense expenditure back in 1985, and a temporary boost to revenues from the transitional arrangements in the 1986 Tax Reform Act which will be reversed in subsequent years. Thus, the latest projections from the Congressional Budget Office show that the "current services" budget deficit (the deficit assuming no change in present legislation) will rise again in 1988 and 1989. On the political front, the deadlock between the President and Congress continues, and it is widely felt that nothing much will be done about the budget deficit until after the November 1988 elections.

Given this, some observers have argued that if the budget deficit does not come down, then neither will the trade deficit, since these two elements both

---

20. Only in real terms did the budget deficit and trade deficit drop at roughly the same rate, with offsetting effects on aggregate real demand. In nominal terms, the budget deficit fell while the trade deficit was flat. Other things being equal, this should have led to *downward* pressure on US interest rates.

enter into the investment-savings balance, which, ex post, must balance.[21] This is by no means necessarily the case, although in one scenario it could be. If the authorities manage to convince the markets that the dollar will not go down any further, then—with large budget deficits continuing to put upward pressure on US interest rates—large private capital inflows could resume. In this case the large budget deficits would, in time, halt and reverse the improvement in the trade deficit by pushing up the dollar again.

This could be a possible scenario—at least for a time. But it would be both highly undesirable and, in the end, unsustainable. It is extremely important that the dollar should go down far enough, and stay down long enough, to undo the serious damage done to the US economy by the strong dollar in the first half of the 1980s (pp. 54–60). This is important not only for the United States but also for the rest of the world. Some "reindustrialization" of the US economy is needed to reverse the rising tide of protectionism, enable the United States to service its growing foreign debt, and put the world's key currency on a sounder footing. Even now, with the dollar in the 140 to 150 yen range, there is a risk that the structural changes needed to improve US competitiveness, and make the Japanese economy less dependent on external demand, may be slowed down or halted before they have gone far enough to reestablish the basis for a healthy trading relationship between the world's two largest industrial countries.

There are several paradoxes here. If nothing is done about the budget deficit, growing confidence that central banks had put a floor under the dollar could push the dollar up again, with the undesirable consequences just described. But the political realities are such that nothing much may be done about the budget deficit until the electorate really feels the pinch. Thus, by helping to restore confidence in the dollar, and hence easing the upward pressure on US interest rates, the world's central banks may actually facilitate inaction on the budget. Equally, if the dollar remained too strong and the US trade position began to deteriorate again, the markets would eventually lose confidence in the authorities' ability to defend the dollar and the stage would be set for an even harder landing.

This brings us back to a second scenario in which the ex post identity between investment and savings is maintained by a quite different mechanism. If confidence in the dollar remains fragile, then, as and when the monetary authorities reach the limits of noninflationary support for the dollar, the

---

21. Ronald I. McKinnon, "The US nutcracker," *Financial Times*, 12 May 1987, p. 23.

continuation of large budget deficits would at last lead to serious crowding out in US financial markets. Instead of being maintained by a rise in the dollar leading to a renewed deterioration in the trade deficit, the investment-savings balance would be maintained by a rise in interest rates forcing down private investment—in other words, by a recession:

> What few people seem to realize . . . is that at some point, when the dollar's decline has gathered momentum, people's ex ante willingness to increase their exposure in dollars will fall to zero—and, indeed, turn negative. At that point, crowding out will become inevitable *unless, by then, the structural [budget] deficit had been reduced to close to zero.* (p. 146)

Events in the early months of 1987 brought this home vividly, but for the time being the world's central banks came to the rescue.

Could there be some middle way out between these two equally unpleasant scenarios? With present policies, it seems unlikely. According to the projection in table 1, with a growth rate of 2.5 percent in the United States and the other industrial countries, the dollar would have to decline immediately by another 20 percent to eliminate the US current account deficit by the early 1990s. But such a sharp decline in the dollar would be likely to set in motion the forces making for a US recession and would have an extremely negative impact on growth in Europe and Japan. In other words, the assumption of steady 2.5 percent growth made in this projection is unrealistic, unless it is assumed that significant further action is taken to reduce the US budget deficit and to boost domestic demand in Europe and Japan.

The upshot is that as of August 1987 the US economy was poised on a knife edge between two equally undesirable outcomes. The culprit remains the excessively large budget deficit. As long as large budget deficits continue, then either misplaced confidence in the dollar will push it, and the trade deficit, up again or, more likely over time, loss of confidence in the dollar will at some point push up interest rates again and generate a recession. The answer remains as simple—and as elusive—as it has been since 1984: the budget deficit should be cut as quickly as possible (pp. 151–59).[22] But:

---

22. To complicate matters, some observers argue that cutting the budget deficit would, by improving confidence, *strengthen* the dollar. This question was discussed in *Deficits and the Dollar* where the conclusion reached was that, "in the short term, a determined effort to cut the budget deficit might strengthen the dollar; in the slightly longer run it would probably weaken the dollar by lowering interest rates; but beyond this point . . . it would be crucially important in helping to prevent the dollar from going down . . . too far" (p. 159).

The political realities are such that decisive action quite probably will only be taken when . . . crowding out begins to be felt in earnest in US financial markets. (p.213) [And] experience from other countries is painfully relevant. There is a great deal of difference between the confidence-building impact of action to cut an excessive budget deficit *before* the markets lose confidence, and the impact of the same measures after the markets have begun to "speak." (p. 147)

From the Plaza to the Louvre

Looking back, it is remarkable to realize how much, under the pressure of events, official attitudes to exchange rates, and to macroeconomic cooperation more generally, have changed since *Deficits and the Dollar* was written. Indeed, two years later we were already some way into the world prefigured in the last section of the book on "Making Constructive Use of a Crisis," especially after the Louvre agreement of 22 February 1987.

It is hard not to feel schizophrenic about these developments. On the one hand, it is encouraging to see the progress that has been made toward better management of the exchange rate system. The official slogan in the early 1980s was that if countries got the "fundamentals" right—in particular, their monetary and fiscal policies—exchange rates would look after themselves. But now the pendulum has swung the other way and, somewhat ironically, considerable effort and ingenuity is being devoted to stabilizing exchange rates, while the fundamentals, especially fiscal policies, are still not right.

The political trigger for the change in official attitudes was concern about rising protectionist pressures in the United States, which became intense in the summer of 1985. Since this concern was shared by the US administration and its major trading partners, it provided a strong mutual incentive to do something about the excessively strong dollar. Building on this, Treasury Secretary Baker embarked on a series of initiatives designed not only to deal with the immediate situation but also to develop a more formal institutional framework for macroeconomic policy cooperation based on an agreed set of "objective indicators."[23]

---

23. Described in more detail, together with proposals for a better designed system, in John Williamson and Marcus H. Miller, *Targets and Indicators: A Blueprint for the International Coordination of Economic Policy*, POLICY ANALYSES IN INTERNATIONAL ECONOMICS 22 (Washington: Institute for International Economics, September 1987).

A first step was taken at the Plaza meeting in New York in September 1985. In retrospect this clearly marked an important change in the philosophy underlying official attitudes toward macroeconomic cooperation. This change was most obvious for the United States. For the first time, the Reagan administration acknowledged that markets were not always right—especially foreign-exchange markets—and that government action was needed to bring the dollar down to a more sensible level. But it was also significant that the other countries acknowledged that this was not a matter just for the United States, but would require cooperative action on their part. It was disquieting to note, however, that there was little evidence of a willingness to make the necessary policy changes. Thus, in a series of "policy commitments" appended to the communiqué, the United States merely reiterated its oft-repeated promise to reduce the budget deficit, while the other participants essentially reaffirmed their commitment to their existing policies.

It would nevertheless be fair to say that the Group of Five was quite skillful in its attempts to "talk" the dollar down. In part it was a matter of luck since some key factors were moving in the right direction (notably an improved outlook for the US budget deficit). But the Group of Five was also on the whole quite successful in giving the markets the impression that they knew what they were doing, while remaining sufficiently vague to avoid losing credibility as, inevitably, the dollar kept on going further down. And following their successful, if expensive, defense of the dollar in April–May 1987, they appeared to have convinced the markets, at least temporarily, that they could stabilize the dollar at the then prevailing level.

A key factor was the definite shift that has occurred since the Plaza meeting toward giving exchange rate objectives a more important role in the conduct of national monetary policies. The lead came from the Bank of Japan. In October 1985 it clearly signaled to the markets its readiness to give a high priority to yen appreciation by raising interest rates. Then, as exchange rate expectations shifted, the bank moved aggressively to lower interest rates despite its concern about the high level of liquidity in the domestic economy. The United Kingdom has also moved fairly explicitly toward targeting the exchange rate as an important element in its conduct of monetary policy.

The Bundesbank was, at first, more recalcitrant. Indeed, at one moment in the summer of 1986 it seemed to be saying: "We might have lowered interest rates if only you Americans had not insisted on telling us to do so!" But as the negative effects of the appreciation of the deutsche mark on German growth became increasingly apparent, the Bundesbank facilitated a decline in interest rates and turned a blind eye to a substantial overrun in the growth of the monetary aggregates.

Even more significant, when the dollar came under pressure in the early months of 1987, the Federal Reserve Board acquiesced in, and to some extent actively promoted, a substantial rise in US interest rates, even though the economy was quite weak, and when, on purely domestic grounds, lower interest rates would have been more appropriate. If the Fed continues this new approach under the leadership of Alan Greenspan, as seems likely, then:

The main operational features of a new regime of monetary cooperation between the major central banks can already be discerned:

● First, they would try to ensure that taken together they maintained an appropriate anti-inflationary stance.

● Second, they would stand ready to deviate in opposite directions from their medium-term domestic monetary objectives if the exchange rate between their currencies was moving out of line with the "fundamentals." (p. 259)

It seems, moreover, that the meeting of the Group of Five at the Louvre in February 1987 may have marked another important step in the right direction. Although there has not, as yet, been any official confirmation, it appears increasingly probable that the participants agreed on some quite specific "reference ranges"—or "target zones," to use the terminology of one of the inventors of this idea, John Williamson[24]—for the major currencies. So indeed:

There is the fascinating possibility that, in responding to the crisis, the two key and closely interrelated ingredients of a new regime for the major currencies might emerge, de facto, and in a pragmatic way:

● agreement between the governments concerned on the desirability of keeping the dollar rate against the deutsche mark and the yen within a certain range, and,

● a demonstration to the markets that they were both able and willing to do so. (p. 254)

---

24. John Williamson, *The Exchange Rate System*, POLICY ANALYSES IN INTERNATIONAL ECONOMICS 5 (Washington: Institute for International Economics, rev. ed. June 1985). The post-Louvre regime—insofar as it exists—appears to differ from Williamson's proposals in several respects: the target ranges have not been made public; they appear to be narrower than Williamson's plus or minus 10 percent; and seem likely to have been fixed in nominal rather than real terms.

Too Little, Too Soon?

As we have seen, in the three months following the Louvre agreement, the participants first successfully demonstrated their ability and willingness to maintain the present pattern of exchange rates. It is hard to decide, however, how much comfort should be drawn from this. It has certainly shown that governments possess considerable power to influence exchange rates. But the clear lesson from history is this will only continue for as long as they use such power wisely. It all depends, therefore, on one's assessment of whether the necessary adjustment is now well under way and whether, where further policy changes are needed, they will be made in a timely manner.

If an optimistic view is taken on this, it can be argued that the central banks have provided a useful breathing space to the markets, and, more important, given more time to governments concerned to overcome the political obstacles to taking the further action needed. More specifically, it can be argued that a further attempt by the US administration to pressure Europe and Japan to change their fiscal policies by "talking the dollar down" would not only have risked setting off a full-fledged dollar crisis, but would also have been counterproductive because of resentment against being "pushed around by the Americans." And it can be further argued that, as long as policies are on track, it should not be too difficult for the Group of Five to revise downward their reference range for the dollar if, as seems likely, this proves necessary, without undermining their credibility in the markets.

An alternative view is that policies have not changed enough to support an orderly adjustment with anything like the present pattern of exchange rates, and that, on the evidence to date, the necessary changes in policy are unlikely to be made in time to prevent a hard landing. In this case there is a real danger that the attempt to establish reference ranges for the major currencies could break down under the pressure of a series of further runs on the dollar. If so, not only would the central banks find that they had used up valuable ammunition in vain, but this whole approach to better management of the exchange rate system, highly desirable in itself, might also become discredited.

The jury is still out. But I very much doubt whether a sensible pattern of exchange rates can be defended for long unless and until the divergent trend in fiscal policies between the United States, and Europe and Japan, has been more decisively reversed, since this was the basic cause of the disequilibrium in the first place. The United States has not yet taken convincing action to reduce its budget deficit sharply over the next few years. Europe and Japan have not yet taken expansionary fiscal action on the scale needed to offset the inevitable negative drag on their growth as the US trade deficit is eliminated.

If this assessment is correct, the world is in a no-win situation. Absent a further timely change in fiscal policies, neither the present attempt to maintain the dollar at an unsustainable level nor the alternative of pushing it down further, is viable. The former has the advantage of putting off the time when the chickens come home to roost, but at the cost of easing pressures on governments to make the necessary policy changes. The latter would intensify these pressures but could well precipitate an inflationary recession in the United States, and a hard landing for the world economy. Perhaps it is only natural for the authorities to play for time, especially with US elections coming up in November 1988. Whether they are right to do so is a difficult question, on which views can and do differ. Where there is—or should be— a wide measure of agreement, is on the need for futher policy changes.

In the end, events will no doubt *force* a change in policies. At some point the United States will find that there is:

. . . little option but to cut the budget deficit . . . even if the US economy is already weakening. . . . Under these conditions the Fed would have little or no scope to fend off recession by stepping up the money supply because this would aggravate both inflationary expectations at a time when inflation was accelerating, and negative exchange rate expectations at a time when the dollar was falling. (p. 150)

As for Japan and Europe, there may be some limited scope for a further reduction in interest rates, although under present circumstances it would not do much either to relieve pressures on the dollar or to stimulate domestic demand. Eventually, therefore, the governments concerned will be forced to take substantial expansionary fiscal action. But considerable delays will occur before the political obstacles are overcome, before the programs are implemented, and before they begin to significantly affect domestic demand. Thus it may already be too late for such a shift in policies to do much to prevent a US recession from spreading out through the world economy.

Based purely on historical analogy, the trough in the hard-landing scenario set out in *Deficits and the Dollar* was assumed to be reached three-and-a-half years after the dollar started going down. This would put it in the third quarter of 1988, just before the November elections. History is unlikely to repeat itself with that much precision, but in August 1987 there seemed no obvious reason to change this time scale.

As ever, trying to foresee the events that could trigger the next run on the dollar is hazardous. It could be bad news on inflation, a sharp drop on Wall Street, political or military events abroad, or simply a continuing string of bad trade figures. A strong candidate could be a new outbreak of trade frictions, as in April 1987, when the US administration announced its intention to retaliate against Japan for what it considered breaches in an agreement on semiconductors. Subsequent events in the world's foreign exchange and financial markets showed only too clearly how protectionist action—or simply the threat of such action—can undermine the confidence of both foreign and domestic holders of dollar-denominated assets. With pending trade legislation and continuing massive US trade deficits, protectionist sentiment is likely to remain strong, and will play an important role in the election campaign, creating unsettling uncertainty about the future course of US trade policy.

To conclude, in *Deficits and the Dollar* I set out "the reasons why, on present policies, a hard landing has become inevitable for the dollar and the world economy. The dollar will, over time, go down too far and there will be an unpleasant world recession" (p. xxi). Regrettably, this conclusion still holds, since the key policy changes needed to avoid such an outcome have not been forthcoming.

Summary

This study sets out the reasons why, on present policies, a hard landing has become inevitable for the dollar and the world economy. The dollar will, over time, go down too far and there will be an unpleasant world recession. Chapter 7 sets out the major changes needed in the fiscal, monetary, and exchange rate policies by both the United States and its major allies to avoid such an outcome.

As this study neared completion, there were some signs of movement in the right direction. The Group of Five held an important meeting in New York on September 22. In October, a new effort to cut the US budget deficit got underway, and some modest expansionary action was announced in Japan. The dollar declined, and by October 31, 1985, was 11.4 percent below the baseline level used in this study. But this was not nearly enough. If the dollar were to stay at that level, the US current account deficit would rise to $250 billion by 1990, and US external debt would rise to over $1 trillion.

Since it still seems quite likely that the action taken will be too little and too late, chapter 8 considers how constructive use might be made of a crisis to promote desirable changes in the international monetary system.

The Dollar and the World Economy

The phenomenal rise in the dollar from 1980 to early 1985 was both a cause and symptom of a major and growing disequilibrium in the world economy. The basic reason was a strong rise in investment demand relative to domestic savings in the United States, largely because of a massive increase in the structural budget deficit, at a time when there were ample surplus savings in the rest of the world, where structural budget deficits were being reduced (figures 1.1 and 1.2). The United States sucked in foreign savings at a rapidly increasing rate, rising to a level greater than at any time since just after the Civil War. The rest of the industrial world swung sharply from importing savings in 1979–80 (largely from OPEC) to exporting savings on a large scale, mainly to the United States. And the nonoil developing countries— quite contrary to normal historical experience and their domestic needs— experienced a net outflow of real resources in 1984 (table 1.1).

These shifts in the flow of world savings were accompanied by equivalent shifts in the international flow of goods and services, and hence a dramatic deterioration in the US trade and current account balance. Roughly two-thirds of the deterioration through 1984 can be attributed to the rise in the dollar (table 1.2).

This is, however, only half the story. A rising current account deficit should, in time, depress the dollar. Although this relationship appeared to break down in 1984, it will reassert itself in time. One of the main reasons why the present exchange rate system has got locked into a cycle of "overshooting" is that the lags in this two-way relationship between the dollar and the US current balance add up to three years or more (figure 1.4), and that this is too long a time horizon to generate stabilizing speculation in the exchange markets.

High US interest rates boosted the dollar. But the influence of interest rates on exchange rates is less obvious than it seems because foreign investors are primarily interested in the value of their interest earnings in their own currencies. Exchange rate expectations thus play a key role. Positive interest-rate differentials in favor of the United States can strengthen the dollar; at other times they can be a symptom of a loss of confidence in the dollar (figure 1.5). It is not particularly helpful to analyze the dollar's strength in terms of real interest-rate differentials (box 1.5).

Foreign investors are not directly interested in the rate of inflation in the United States. A country's inflation performance has nevertheless come to be regarded as a good barometer of its overall economic health, and the

1980–83 improvement in US relative inflation performance was certainly a factor behind the dollar's rise. At the same time, however, the rise in the dollar explains a not unimportant part of the improvement in the United States' relative inflation performance (figure 1.6).

Since the early 1970s there have been three major shocks to the world's investment-savings balance of roughly the same magnitude (figure 1.8). The two oil crises created a large surplus of world savings almost overnight. The shock from US budget deficits has been building more slowly and is creating a shortage of world savings. Had other countries followed the same course there would have been a strong world boom leading rather quickly to a new outbreak of world inflation. But the other major industrial countries took a diametrically opposite course, cutting their structural budget deficits enough to offset most of the expansionary shift in the United States. The root cause of the disequilibrium thus lies not simply in US policies but in the interplay of quite opposite policies—based on quite different views of how policy works—being followed by the United States and its major allies.

Strong Recovery in the United States

In terms of domestic demand, the 1983–84 US upswing was the strongest since the 1950s (table 2.1). Investment rose by over 4 percentage points as a share of GNP to about the same level as in 1978–79, but because of the rising structural budget deficit nearly three-fifths of this increase had to be financed by foreign savings (table 2.2). Had it not been for these capital inflows, interest rates would have had to have risen sharply to choke off the rise in interest-sensitive demand—perhaps by 5 percentage points or more (box 2.1).

The 1981 Economic Recovery Tax Act raised the after-tax rate of return on new investment in real assets and made it easier for US investors in real assets to live with higher interest rates on financial assets (table 2.3). But higher interest rates and fiscal incentives did not lead to a significant increase in the supply of private savings (box 2.2). What the tax changes did was to make it possible for the US economy to grow strongly at higher interest rates than in the past, helping to attract foreign capital.

Large capital inflows were responsible for two other unusual features of the recovery: actual inflation was significantly lower than domestically generated inflation because of the rising dollar; and domestic spending rose 20 percent faster than domestic output. Over 1980–84, these two factors helped to raise an indicator of the economy's "wellbeing" well above its "performance," to a postwar peak more than 7 percentage points above its 1960–82 average in 1984 (table 2.4).

This refers to the wellbeing of Americans as consumers; as producers the story has been very different. Inevitably, sectors of the economy exposed to foreign competition at home and abroad have not done nearly so well as those sheltered from such competition by the nature of their markets. Agriculture has been especially hard hit. By early 1985, profits in the "exposed" sector of the economy were $20 billion—around 20 percent— lower than might have been expected on the basis of past relationships (figure 2.4). Strong protectionist pressures have been generated that the administration has not always been able to resist.

Structural change involves costs: skills become redundant, plant is written off, people have to move. Normally these costs are well worth the benefits. But much of the structural change generated by the prolonged overvaluation of the dollar will have to be reversed when the time comes to restore the US trade balance to a sustainable level. There is no satisfactory way of measuring these costs. But they will have been heavy, will have served no good purpose, and could have been avoided by more internationally consistent macroeconomic policies and a better functioning international monetary system.

Weak Recovery in Europe and Japan

In sharp contrast to US experience, the recovery in the other OECD countries has been the weakest since World War II: unemployment continued to rise, and there was virtually no pickup in the share of investment in GNP, which remained 20 percent below its 1972–73 peak.

Explanations for the weak recovery in the other OECD countries based on structural problems and rigidities—real as these may be—are largely beside the point, since an explanation based on the major macroeconomic factors at work on the demand side fits the facts reasonably well (figures 2.6 and 2.7). It seems that the net impact of US policies on GNP growth in other countries has, on balance—and up to now—been positive (table 2.6). Thus, the major reason for slow growth in the rest of the OECD (ROECD) area must be found in its own macroeconomic policies, and in particular in the restrictive stance of fiscal policy, notably in Japan, Germany, and the United Kingdom.

There is an important sense in which the controversy about how US policies have affected growth in other countries is also beside the point. A rise in GNP generated by rising net exports obtained at the cost of a deterioration in the terms of trade is not a particularly good bargain (table 2.7). The other OECD countries would have been unambiguously better off, in welfare terms, if their recovery had been based more on domestic demand and less on exports. A less expansionary fiscal policy in the United States, coupled with less restrictive fiscal policies in other major countries—and hence less appreciation of the dollar, could well have produced a stronger recovery in the ROECD area with a lower rate of inflation.

As it was, the divergence in economic policies and performance, as it persisted, affected expectations and behavior and created a psychological climate that accentuated and prolonged the disequilibrium. This was a vicious circle: the larger the disequilibrium, the more difficult and costly it will be to correct.

How Long Can It Go On?

Neither history nor recent trends suggest that—having been a capital exporter since the late nineteenth century—the United States has suddenly become a structural capital importer (table 3.1). Tax changes will not have a permanent impact. The logical destination for excess Japanese savings lies not in the United States but in the newly industrializing and resource-rich countries, especially in the Pacific basin. Looking to the 1990s, the United States seems most likely to resume its traditional role as a capital exporter.

Analysis of a hypothetical baseline case for the dollar and the world economy on present policies shows that the US current account deficit—and hence the capital inflows needed to keep the dollar from going down—would go on rising indefinitely into the future, reaching over 5 percent of GNP by 1990 (table 3.2). The impact on the US external investment position would be devastating (figure 3.2). From being the world's largest net creditor nation in 1982, it would become the world's largest debtor by 1986, and by 1990 its external debt, at over $1 trillion, would substantially exceed the total debt of the developing countries.

The basic reason is that the starting position is so bad: strong adverse "gap" factors are at work because the existing large deficit means that exports have to increase much faster than imports both to close the gap and cover rising interest payments (table 3.3).

In the 1970s, large US current account deficits were more than financed by inflows of official capital (figure 3.3). A major difference now is that, as long as the major countries' central banks stick to their present intervention policies, the US current account deficit will have to go on being financed by massive inflows of private capital.

If the dollar were to stay at its present level, the external debt indicators for the United States, as conventionally measured, would signal the danger of sovereign risk before the end of the decade (figure 3.4). Because, however, the United States borrows largely in its own currency, the limits on its external indebtedness will be determined more by the exchange rate risk than by illiquidity or sovereign risk.

In the baseline case, foreigners' uncovered dollar portfolio, estimated at around $800 billion at end-1984, would have to rise to over $2 trillion, equivalent to 30 percent of ROECD GNP, by 1990 (table 3.5). This ratio rose from 8 percent to 18 percent from 1980 to 1984, mainly because of the rising value of the dollar, but there is little reason to suppose that this apparent increase in the demand for dollars would be maintained when the dollar goes down. Moreover, the share of the rest of the world's savings needed to sustain the dollar at its early 1985 level would have to rise to a quite improbable level by 1990 (table 3.6).

What Happens When the Dollar Goes Down?

Perhaps the single most striking result in this study is that the dollar would have to drop a long way simply to stop the US current account deficit from getting worse (figure 4.1). The reason for this is that the benefits from a lower dollar, which take time to come through, are swamped by the adverse "gap" factors (table 4.1). This is why a "super-soft-landing" scenario suggested by some economists, in which the dollar declined no faster than could be covered by a reasonable interest-rate differential, is highly implausible (box 4.3).

Because of the time it will take to correct the "real" imbalances in the US economy—the excess of investment over savings and imports over exports—the brunt of a decline in the capital inflow will fall heavily on the financial markets, generating upward pressure on US interest rates and downward pressure on the dollar (figure 4.2).

Unfortunately, the stabilizing forces at work in the exchange markets have weakened as the majority of operators increasingly concentrate on what is likely to happen over the next few hours or days rather than the next months or years. Their longer term view, moreover, tends to "adapt" to what happens in the short run, so that once an exchange rate begins to move, this itself changes expectations about its future level (figure 4.4).

Even with a rapid drop in the dollar, further large current account deficits are bound to be incurred and will have to be financed. Indeed, the fragility of the US position is vividly illustrated by the fact that even in a hard-landing scenario involving rapid external adjustment, asset holders would have to go on increasing their exposure in dollars by up to $400 billion while the dollar declined by over 40 percent.

The enormous exchange rate losses this implies (table 4.3) means that a time is bound to come, as the dollar's decline gathers momentum, when foreigners' willingness to invest their savings in the United States dries up faster than the US economy's need for them. This may not happen until the dollar has gone quite a long way down. But when it does, a "crunch" will develop in US financial markets, and the economy will be headed for trouble.

In a soft-landing scenario, this crunch is avoided, and the US economy continues to grow at a satisfactory rate, because the capital inflow declines only slowly and is offset by cuts in the budget deficit. This scenario looks implausible, because even with capital inflows still as high as 1.5 percent of GNP in 1990, the dollar would have to come down by 36 percent from the baseline to cut the current account deficit to this level (figure 4.5), while US external debt would go on rising indefinitely into the future, reaching $1 trillion in 1992 (figure 4.8).

In a hard-landing scenario, the dollar overshoots, going down by over 40 percent from the baseline, and the US current account goes into a surplus equivalent to 1.5 percent of GNP by 1990. The inflation rate doubles. If the economy were not already in recession, interest rates would have to rise by enough to generate one. Because of what would be, for the United States, an unusual combination of a recession accompanied by a sharp drop in the dollar and accelerating inflation, the wellbeing indicator would fall to minus 7 percent, its lowest level since the Great Depression (figure 4.7). Unemployment would rise to over 10 percent.

This is a measure of the macroeconomic costs of allowing an external disequilibrium to become so large. The microeconomic costs will also be heavy as the structural distortions in the US economy created by the overvalued dollar are reversed. The all-important counterpart would be that the rise in foreign debt would be halted by 1988, and by 1993 the United States would have regained its status as a creditor nation.

Policy Options Facing the United States

Cutting the budget deficit is the only certain way to increase US savings to make up for a reduced supply of foreign savings. What few seem to realize is that at some point, when the dollar's decline has gathered momentum, people's *ex ante* willingness to increase their exposure in dollars will fall to zero (and, indeed, turn negative). At that point, crowding out in US financial markets will become inevitable unless the structural budget deficit has been reduced to around zero. But that point may be only a year or two away, and obviously the budget deficit cannot be cut that quickly.

Thus, once the decline in the dollar gathers momentum, the stage will be set for what, in other countries, has been called a "stabilization crisis." In order to restore confidence, there may be no option but to cut the budget deficit even if, as seems probable, the US economy is already weakening because of normal cyclical forces. Nevertheless, no matter how determined the efforts to reduce the deficit, interest rates will stay high for some time because of foreigners' attempts to get out of dollars.

Under these conditions, the Fed would have little or no scope to fend off recession by stepping up the money supply because this would aggravate both inflationary expectations at a time when inflation was accelerating, and negative exchange rate expectations at a time when the dollar was falling.

In the hard-landing scenario, persistent crowding out even after the dollar had gone down could be avoided only if the structural deficit were cut by 5½ percent of GNP or more by 1990 (table 5.1). Seen in this light, much of the current debate about cutting the budget deficit sounds like Alice in Wonderland. The truth is that US public finances are getting out of control in the same basic political sense as happened in many other countries in the 1970s. And their experience shows that even when governments became convinced of the need to make major cuts in the budget deficit, and had clear parliamentary majorities, they greatly underestimated the intrinsic political difficulties involved.

The window of opportunity in 1983–84, when strong action to cut the budget deficit would have put the US recovery on a sustainable course, has long since closed. Proposals for gradually reducing the deficit over a period of years accompanied by an offsetting switch to a more expansionary monetary policy are unrealistic. The deficit should be reduced as quickly as possible, so as to give the Fed more room for maneuver either—according to the circumstances—to ease policy to counter recessionary tendencies and reduce the risk of a financial crisis, or to tighten up to prevent a bandwagon against the dollar from developing (table 5.2).

Policy Options Facing Europe and Japan

If the other major OECD countries stick to their present policies, a hard landing for the US economy will have unpleasant consequences. The stimulus from external demand, which was directly or indirectly responsible for up to one-half of their growth during the recovery, will go into reverse (figure 6.1 and table 6.1). Growth would fall off sharply, and unemployment could rise to over 14 percent in Europe. The competitive position of Germany and Japan would be the most adversely affected by the dollar's decline, but, by the same token, they should also benefit most in terms of reduced inflation (table 6.3). Exchange rate losses would be particularly heavy for investors whose ''bread currency'' was the deutsche mark, yen, or Swiss franc, which would appreciate by 100 percent or more from their trough against the dollar (table 6.4).

For the developing countries, the hard-landing scenario would involve a replay of the 1981–83 debt crisis (figure 6.2). As then, the purchasing power of their available export earnings would be severely hit by slow OECD growth, deteriorating terms of trade, and high US interest rates. There would, however, be one major difference: the dollar would be falling, not rising. This would do little to alleviate the squeeze on their export earnings, but would improve their debtor status and reduce the real resource cost of debt servicing (box 6.2).

The adverse impact on the world economy could be mitigated by a shift to more expansionary policies in the ROECD area. But as of late 1985, the governments of the key countries involved remained extremely reluctant to consider such a shift. They are committed to steady-as-you-go monetary and fiscal policies based on medium-term considerations, and believe that more expansionary policies would involve serious inflationary risks and be subject to important budgetary constraints. Europe may be caught in an ''expectations trap'': expansionary policies are needed to achieve faster growth, but are thought likely to have such adverse effects on confidence in financial and foreign exchange markets as to be self-defeating.

However, the inflation risk for countries accounting for nearly 50 percent of ROECD GNP appears to be small, and, in the event of a sharp decline in the dollar, nonexistent, because of lower import prices. In most countries, moreover, there appears to be little constraint on more expansionary fiscal policies arising from the size of budget deficits in relation to current *flows* of private savings and investment. The extent to which there may be a constraint because of the level of the *stock* of public debt in relation to GNP is complex and controversial (figure 6.4). To the extent that there is such a constraint, it appears to vary greatly from country to country: Japan, Germany, and the United Kingdom are in a relatively comfortable position (figure 6.5).

The budget deficit and public debt calculus would be improved for all ROECD countries when, as the dollar declines, their interest rates become fully decoupled from US rates. It would be much further improved in a cooperative scenario because, with faster growth, deficits would be reduced by the automatic stabilizers. In this scenario, Germany, Japan, and the United Kingdom could take expansionary fiscal action equal to several percentage points of GNP while at the same time stabilizing their public debt-GNP ratios at roughly the present level.

Faster growth in Europe would help solve its "real wage" problem by creating sufficient excess demand in product markets to enable prices to be raised relative to wages, and provide a strong incentive to shift from capital-deepening to capital-widening investment. This approach, which would have been risky earlier, should now be adopted given the progress made in restoring profits and the changing international environment (figure 6.6).

Japan's structural problems are very different; they arise primarily from the chronic excess savings in the private sector (figure 6.7). Correcting the US external imbalance will require both a reduction in the shortfall of savings in the United States *and* a rise in investment relative to savings in Japan, given the importance of trade relations between the two countries.

The Right Answer

The right answer to the present disequilibrium in the world economy is to correct its basic cause: the divergent trend in investment demand relative to domestic savings in the United States and the rest of the world. This can and should be achieved by a major change in the mix of fiscal and monetary policy by the United States and its major allies.

THE COOPERATIVE SCENARIO

The US structural budget deficit should be reduced to around zero by 1990. The cuts should be front loaded to minimize the risk of a stabilization crisis. The other OECD countries should take expansionary monetary and fiscal action sufficient to offset the negative impact coming from the United States and reduce unemployment during a period of "catch-up" growth. Cooperative action by the major central banks should aim to bring down the dollar and stabilize it at a level consistent with rough balance in the US current account by 1990.

Cooperative action along these lines would generate positive feedbacks yielding significant benefits to all concerned. For the United States, the costs of rectifying the present disequilibrium would be reduced in terms of both inflation and growth (figure 7.1). Inflation would rise less because the dollar declines by under 30 percent instead of over 40 percent. Export demand would be stronger, despite the smaller drop in the dollar, because of faster growth in the rest of the world.

The other OECD countries would grow faster and unemployment in Europe might be brought down to 8 percent to 9 percent. The ROECD area would enjoy several more years of steadily improving economic wellbeing in terms of both lower inflation and a fast rise in domestic spending (figure 7.2). This should greatly help to dissipate "Europessimism."

There would also be major gains for the developing countries. By 1990, the purchasing power of their export earnings could be 40 percent higher than in the hard-landing scenario. With sustained growth in the OECD area and a return to normal levels for the dollar and interest rates, the debt-export ratio of the seven major developing-country debtors would be halved between 1984 and 1990 to well below its 1977 level (box 7.1). In other words, by 1990 the accumulated damage to the creditworthiness of the developing countries since the mid-1970s would have been reversed—essentially by a reversal of the factors that caused it.

This scenario may sound too good to be true (figure 7.3). But before dismissing it out of hand, it should be borne in mind that the underlying conditions for a period of sustained growth in the world economy are better today than at any time since the 1960s.

It would, nevertheless, be far from easy to pull off, because of the difficulty of breaking out of several forms of an expectations trap. Two major departures from current conventional wisdom would be required: the governments of the other major OECD countries would have to become convinced that a temporary fiscal stimulus would, in the present international context, be highly beneficial; and the US administration would have to demonstrate that it had become genuinely converted to the idea that an active and cooperative policy toward the dollar was not only desirable but would work. And in both cases, the conversion from present attitudes would have to be sufficiently convincing to convince the markets as well.

A satisfactory outcome for the United States requires both a sharp cut in the budget deficit *and* a substantial decline in the dollar. Either without the other would severely depress the economy: if the deficit was cut but the dollar remained strong, domestic output would be crowded out by the exchange rate; if the deficit was not cut but the inflow of foreign savings dried up, investment demand would be crowded out by rising interest rates.

A prompt but manageable decline in the dollar can be brought about only by both a shift to fiscal restraint in the United States *and* a shift to fiscal stimulus in the rest of the OECD area. By itself, significant fiscal restraint in the United States could simply lead to a worldwide slowdown: absent any upward shift in investment demand relative to savings in the rest of the world, the dollar could remain strong and the damage to the structure of the US economy and the fabric of the world trading system would go on building up. Equally, however, a substantial fiscal stimulus in the ROECD area without a corresponding cut in the US budget deficit would, in time, lead to worldwide crowding out.

FASTER GROWTH IN EUROPE AND JAPAN

Paradoxically, by provoking such a strong and unsustainable rise in the dollar, Reaganomics has created the potential for a "Reagan miracle" in Europe and Japan of the kind enjoyed by the United States in 1983–84. They could take a strong dose of expansionary action, and set off a strong rise in domestic demand, while inflation would be held down because their currencies would be appreciating, and budget deficits would not push up interest rates because their savings would be flowing back from the United States.

Once the dollar's decline gathered momentum, ROECD central banks should be prepared to raise their monetary targets by enough and for long enough to bring about a significant decline in interest rates. A sizable, albeit temporary, fiscal stimulus would also be needed. The multiplier effects of fiscal action would be higher than suggested by conventional estimates because of the international context in which it was being taken. Allowing for this, the necessary cumulative shift in ROECD fiscal stance might be on the order of 3 percent of GNP, raising the ROECD structural budget deficit by 2 percent of GNP from the 1984 position by 1988. The increase in actual budget deficits would be very much smaller because of the automatic stabilizers.

Scope for taking expansionary action would be greatest for countries with currencies that would attract investors trying to move out of the dollar, including, in particular, Germany and Japan. If they took the lead, scope would open up for others to follow suit, though on a more modest scale. Prompt and skillful realignments within the European Monetary System would be necessary. The United Kingdom is in a somewhat special position and could have more to gain than most from a cooperative approach.

Such a strategy could only succeed, however, if Europe and Japan did not make the same monumental mistake as the Reagan administration. What is needed is a substantial but *temporary* fiscal stimulus. Once the share of private investment in GNP began to rise to more normal and satisfactory levels, prompt action would be needed to make room for it by cutting back the public sector's demands on domestic savings.

Europe's general strategy should be to cut taxes now, while at the same time putting in place programs to cut expenditures and restore the appropriate structural budget balance over a period of years. Tax cuts should be directed primarily to reducing the wedge between the cost of labor to employers and the after-tax incomes of employees resulting from income taxes and, especially, high social security charges. These cuts should be substantial and permanent. If there is a need to make up for lost revenue as recovery gathers momentum, the yield from indirect taxation should be increased.

On the expenditure side, once the decision has been made to go for faster growth, plans should be made in advance to phase out programs whose main or only justification has been slow growth and high unemployment, for example, subsidies to lame-duck industries and labor market programs serving as palliatives for high unemployment. Further adjustments may be needed to bring the future evolution of social benefits into line with countries' ability to finance them. On the other hand, a good case can be made for some increase in public infrastructure investment, which has borne too much of the brunt of budgetary restraint.

For Japan, the situation is different. The main domestic consideration is how best to use the present surplus of domestic savings to prepare for the expected scissors movement—as the rapid aging of the population gathers momentum in the 1990s—between rising demands on public expenditure and declining private savings. It makes sense to export part of these savings to build up income-earning assets abroad, but there are limits to the size of the current account surpluses that can be run without provoking destructive trade tensions. Given the aging problem, maximum use should be made of the present surplus of domestic savings to finance improvements in the economic and social infrastructure, including housing, transport, health care, and cultural, leisure, and recreational facilities.

In the field of company taxation, this could be done by granting more favorable investment tax credits or depreciation schedules for domestically oriented investment. Outside the corporate sector, there is considerable scope for fiscal incentives and other action to encourage home ownership, as well as the provision of social and cultural amenities by the private sector, or jointly by the public and private sector at the local level. The tax treatment of interest payments and receipts should be reconsidered (box 7.5).

These tax changes would not, however, provide enough stimulus to the economy in the short run, since Japan will be hit particularly hard by the necessary correction of the dollar and the US current balance. This will require some combination of more public investment and income tax cuts.

ELIMINATING THE US SAVINGS DEFICIENCY

The basic fiscal problem facing the United States is that the existing tax base is too narrow to support the level to which federal expenditure has risen and is likely to continue. Other countries have reacted to this problem by introducing a value-added tax, but this might prove too easy a way to raise too much revenue. One possibility would be a hefty rise in the gasoline tax, phased in in stages over the five years to 1990, which could provide a good part of the revenue needed, while providing time to adapt the automobile stock and driving habits (box 7.6). If legislated in advance, with an element of front loading, it would be the kind of clear-cut measure most likely to convince the financial markets that definitive action was being taken to deal with the deficit problem on a permanent basis.

MONETARY COOPERATION AND EXCHANGE MARKET INTERVENTION

Monetary cooperation and coordinated intervention would have an important role to play in managing the dollar's decline. In a first phase, the aim would be to prod the dollar down. The United States should follow a somewhat easier monetary policy, and the other major OECD countries somewhat tighter monetary policies, than would be appropriate on purely domestic grounds. In a second phase, the aim would be to slow the dollar's decline and stabilize it at a level compatible with the longer run evolution of the US current and capital account. This would require a tighter US monetary policy and easier ROECD monetary policies than would be appropriate on purely domestic grounds. Large-scale intervention—or at least the threat of it—would also be needed to prevent the dollar from overshooting downwards because of the size of the present disequilibrium and the lags involved in correcting it.

This runs directly counter to much of today's conventional wisdom. In terms of achieving the key domestic objectives of low inflation and growth, however, keeping the exchange rate within a sensible range is just as important as keeping the growth of the money supply within a sensible range. Indeed, recent experience with floating exchange rates has shown that the exchange rate has become just as powerful a channel of transmission from monetary policy to the level of domestic output and prices as the traditional channels of liquidity, wealth, and interest rates.

The central issues involved here are not technical, but political in the broadest sense. The postwar record shows clearly that the extent to which it is necessary to deviate from domestic monetary objectives or to intervene in the exchange market to achieve a given impact on the exchange rate depends, above all, on the market's perception of the degree of the government's political commitment to achieving a given outcome for its exchange rate. In other words, governments can have a strong influence on the exchange rate—as long as they do not abuse it. But for the United States to acquire this influence, after years of benign neglect, would require not only a fundamental change in present attitudes, but also a demonstration to the markets over an extended period of time that it was prepared to act accordingly. A first step was taken in the right direction at the meeting of the Group of Five in New York on September 22, 1985, but much remains to be done to follow it up.

Crisis Management

With growth slowing down in both the United States and the rest of the world, we may see a "soggy scenario" with the dollar remaining in a state of suspended animation. If so, protectionist pressures in the United States could become irresistible, and could prove to be the trigger setting off the crisis.

If, as events unfold, the action taken is too little, too late, and quite possibly misguided, then a crisis may become inevitable. This need not necessarily be a pessimistic conclusion. History shows that genuine reform—or simply change—in the untidy and amorphous entity constituting "the international monetary system" has often taken place only as the result of a crisis and has then sometimes happened quite quickly. So, to be realistic, perhaps the most important issue is how constructive use might be made of a crisis.

What must be hoped is that at some point a window of opportunity opens up during which the United States has become sufficiently worried about the situation to be fully converted to the need for cooperation, and be prepared to pay the price, while the other major OECD countries are still sufficiently unworried about the situation to be able to respond constructively and collectively to US requests for help. By this point the question of intervention in the exchange markets to stem the dollar's decline would probably have come very much to the fore. The immediate issue would be whether a sufficiently close linkage could be established between agreement on arrangements for large-scale coordinated intervention with firm commitments from both sides to take the fiscal and monetary policy actions needed to make such intervention effective.

THE EXCHANGE RATE REGIME AND MONETARY COOPERATION

It is possible that in trying to prevent the dollar from going down too far, the two key and closely interrelated ingredients of a new regime for the major currencies might emerge, de facto, in a pragmatic way: agreement between the governments concerned on the desirability of keeping the dollar rate against the deutsche mark and the yen within a certain range; and a demonstration to the markets that they were both able and willing to do so. This might just be a flash in the pan, with the participants reverting to benign neglect as the crisis receded. But it could lead to some formalization of a new regime, either quite quickly, or progressively over time.

Suppose that the consensus favored a managed float, but that gradually the markets began to get the upper hand again. The question could then arise as to whether it might not be sensible to make a "jump" to a more formal regime in order to cash in on its stabilizing impact on exchange rate expectations (box 8.2). The establishment of the EMS in March 1979—after quite a long period of trial and error—provides an interesting precedent. It was greeted with much skepticism, but in the event has worked better than expected by most experienced observers at the time.

All OECD countries other than the United States have for some time allowed exchange rate considerations to play a significant role in the implementation of monetary policy. If, under the pressure of events, this were to become true for the Fed, the main operational features of a new regime of monetary cooperation between the major central banks can be discerned. First, they would try to ensure that taken together they maintained an appropriate anti-inflationary policy stance. Second, they would stand ready to deviate in opposite directions from their medium-term domestic monetary objectives if the exchange rate between their currencies was moving out of line with the "fundamentals."

The governments concerned might decide to signal such a new approach to monetary cooperation through institutional innovation, which might lead to the emergence of a de facto triumvirate of the Federal Reserve Board, the Bundesbank and the Bank of Japan, with responsibility for the day-to-day management of the dollar-deutsche mark-yen nexus.

SUMMITS AND OTHER INSTITUTIONAL ISSUES

The issues involved in achieving greater exchange rate stability extend, however, well beyond the competence of central banks, so any institutional innovation in the monetary sphere would have to be paralleled by changes in the broader institutional framework for economic cooperation between the major countries.

There is widespread disillusionment with summit meetings, even—or especially—among those most closely involved. Here again, a crisis might be useful. If the imminence of a hard landing led to a decision to hold an "emergency" summit, various opportunities for institutional innovation could open up. Participation could be updated to bring it more in line with economic and political realities. Linkage with the existing international bodies could be strengthened. It might be agreed that meetings in a new format should be held regularly, perhaps twice a year, while retaining the existing annual format as a more political and media-oriented event dealing with foreign policy and defense issues.

It is to be hoped that, in responding to the crisis, some thought would also be given to tidying up the present institutional mess and paving the way to longer term reform (box 8.3). A joint secretariat, composed of officials from national capitals and the relevant international organizations, might be established to service the "new format" summits. This could help to break down the excessive compartmentalization of departmental interests—although this would also require progressive rationalization and reform of the existing international institutions. Something should be done to lessen the political pressures from the largest countries on the international organizations and strengthen their independence and objectivity (box 7.2). More input should be sought from the private sector, parts of which have become extremely knowledgeable about the issues involved in intergovernmental economic cooperation and have a strong self-interest in its success.

The agenda for change in present international arrangements will remain blocked as long as nothing goes seriously wrong. But under the pressure of unpleasant events this could change quite quickly. One of the great strengths of the United States is its capacity to respond to new problems; it is a "fix it" country. With US leadership much could be done to improve the management of the world economy that now seems out of the question. The ideas canvassed here ane not meant as a blueprint for reform. They are put forward simply in the hope of stimulating some more imaginative thinking in official and private circles.

1 The Dollar and the World Economy

Let us look . . . at the country of my dear mother. I rejoice at what Reagan is doing. He has broken all the rules, and all the economists are furious . . . Five million new jobs . . . and at the same time inflation has been kept quite low. It is a miracle; the House should know how it has been done. I think I know how it has been done: it is because they have had the sense to make somebody else pay for it . . . In a word Reagan (to reverse Keynes) has called in the resources of the old world in order to finance the expansion of the new.[1]

The exchange value of the dollar is not only the most important, but probably also the least understood price in the world economy.[2]

As an economist it is very hard to understand the concept of an overvalued dollar.[3]

The phenomenal rise in the dollar from 1980 to early 1985 was both a cause and symptom of a major and growing disequilibrium in the world economy. International flows of both savings and goods and services have been increasingly distorted. For the United States, the most dramatic consequences were that, by the first half of 1985:

---

1. The 90-year-old Earl of Stockton (formerly Harold Macmillan), maiden speech to the House of Lords, 13 November 1984.

2. Former President of the Deutsche Bundesbank, Otmar Emminger (1985a).

3. Paul Craig Roberts, former Treasury Assistant Secretary for Economic Policy, *National Journal*, 23 February 1985, p. 412.

1

• Inflows of foreign savings were financing over 45 percent of US net private investment, whereas in 1980 US domestic savings had more than sufficed to finance domestic investment.

• Americans were spending 40 percent more abroad than they were earning, whereas in 1980 they were earning more than they were spending.

This shift in the flow of savings and goods still has some way to go. It is already equivalent to over 3 percent of US GNP ($120 billion at 1985 prices). Because the US economy is so large, it has had, and will continue to have, a major impact on the flow of savings in the world economy as a whole, of the same magnitude as—but of a quite different nature from—that created by each of the two oil price shocks of the 1970s.

This chapter first examines the most fundamental reason for this growing disequilibrium: a strong rise in investment demand relative to domestic savings in the United States at a time when there were ample surplus savings in the rest of the world, to a large extent because fiscal policy was moving in opposite directions. The fairly complex ways in which this has affected economic activity, inflation, interest rates, trade and capital flows, and exchange rates in and between different parts of the world are then discussed. Quantitative estimates are given of how changes in these variables have produced a dramatic deterioration in the US trade and current account balance. The various interrelated reasons for the unusually strong and prolonged rise in the dollar are analyzed and summarized.

A final section examines the nature and magnitude of the imbalance created in the pattern of savings and investment in the world economy as a whole, and compares it with that generated by the two oil price shocks of 1973–75 and 1979–81. The shock from the US budget deficit is of the same magnitude, but is building up more slowly, and is creating not a surplus but a shortage of world savings. The main conclusion reached is that the root cause of the disequilibrium lies not simply in US policies, but in the interplay of quite opposite policies—based on quite different views about how economic policy works—being followed by the United States and its major allies. Without a major change in these policies, which seems unlikely for political reasons, the disequilibrium will continue to gather momentum until, at some point, the United States reaches the limits of its international creditworthiness.

The Analytical Approach Adopted

When a country invests more than it saves, it also, by definition, consumes more than it produces, and thus spends more abroad than it earns. Indeed, after the event, a country's domestic investment-savings balance will be identically equal to its external current balance.[4] There is thus a basic macroeconomic relationship between the deficiency of savings in the United States, resulting largely from the federal budget deficit, and its very large trade and current account deficits. They are two sides of the same coin. The many different relationships at work in many different markets to bring about this ex post identity lie at the heart of this study, and are described in some detail in an appendix to this chapter.

To understand what has been happening, one would like to quantify all these relationships using a set of simultaneous equations. This can be done using one of the integrated world models now available.[5] For this study, however, a different approach has been adopted. Experience shows that the relationships at work in "real" markets—affecting output, employment, imports, exports, prices, wages, etc.—can be quantified with some degree of accuracy and are comparatively stable. However, the relationships at work in financial markets, in particular those affecting interest rates and exchange rates, are both difficult to measure and often unstable. This is painfully evident from the fact that none of the existing world models were able to predict at all accurately the size and duration of the rise in the dollar. Nor, when used to simulate the future, would they produce a dollar decline of the speed and magnitude which the analysis in this study suggests is inevitable.

The approach adopted is thus as follows. A model has been developed for the US trade and current balance which only attempts to track, quantitatively, the relationships in the "real" markets at work in the United States, in the rest of the OECD (ROECD) area (treated as a single entity), and, in less detail, the developing countries. It will be referred to as the D&D model (box 1.1), and is described in TN1. This does not mean that what happens in the financial markets will be ignored—far from it. In putting forward possible scenarios for the future, the likely movements in exchange rates and

---

4. The current balance, unfortunately a much less familiar concept than the trade balance, is equal to the sum of the merchandise trade balance and any surplus or deficit on imports and exports of services, investment income, workers' remittances, and unilateral transfers.

5. OECD (1983a); Federal Reserve Board (1984); Yoshitomi (1984).

BOX 1.1   **The D&D (Deficits and the Dollar) model**

The relationships quantified in the model are the effects of:
- rising US incomes (GNP) on US imports, and of rising ROW incomes on US exports (the income elasticities)
- a rising US dollar in lowering the (dollar) price of US imports and raising the (foreign currency) price of US exports (the pass-through factors)
- lower US import prices in increasing US imports, and of higher export prices in reducing US exports (the price elasticities)
- lower US import prices in lowering the US cost and price level, and of higher US export prices in raising the cost and price level in the ROECD (the price level feedbacks)
- lower US exports and higher US imports in reducing incomes and output in the US and raising them in the ROW (the trade multipliers)
- the capital inflows corresponding to a deficit in the current balance in reducing the US net stock of foreign assets, and hence the net current income from interest and dividends on them.

The coefficients used (income elasticities, pass-through factors, etc.) have not been estimated by fitting the model to the past. Instead, they have been selected, after examining the relevant properties of the better known existing models, so as to give "middle of the road" values for each coefficient. As a check, the model has been "backcast" to see that it tracks reasonably well what happened to imports and exports when the dollar was rising very strongly from 1980 to 1984 (TN1, table C).

---

interest rates are quantified and fed into the D&D model on the basis of a close look at how they moved in the past *at times of strong pressures in financial markets and major changes in exchange rate expectations.* These are precisely the periods that the complete world models, incorporating financial market behavior, are unable to track.[6]

---

6. As Kindleberger put it: "A synthesis of Keynesianism and monetarism, such as the Hansen-Hicks IS-LM curves . . . remains incomplete . . . if it leaves out the instability of expectations,

Shifts in the Pattern of World Investment and Savings

Let us first consider the reasons for the major shift in investment demand relative to domestic savings in the United States and the rest of the world in the 1983–84 upswing. The starting point is an approach widely shared by both Keynesian and monetarist economists.[7] Over the short run, an acceleration in the growth of money incomes and output is set off by—and accompanied by—a rise in the private sector's desire to invest in relation to its willingness to save. This can be seen very clearly for the United States in figure 1.1.[8] In each of the three upswings of 1970–73, 1975–77, and 1983–84 (bottom panel), there was a strong rise of 3 to 5 percentage points in the private sector's propensity to invest (top panel). Private savings, however, fluctuated erratically in a narrower range, sometimes even falling when investment was rising strongly. In consequence, the "surplus" savings of the private sector fall sharply during upswings and rise sharply in recessions (1970–71, 1974–75, 1980, and 1982).

By far the major counterpart is to be found in opposite swings in the position of the public sector. This close inverse relationship between the private sector's surplus savings and the public sector's dissavings—observable in all countries—arises because there is a powerful causal relation between the two in both directions (box 1.2).

Because of this strong two-way relationship, a large part of fluctuations in the private sector's surplus savings are offset by opposite swings in the budget deficit. Normally, in an open economy, the offset is not complete: at some point during the upswing the private sector's financing needs begin to rise faster than the cyclical decline in the budget deficit. In a closed economy,

---

speculation, and credit. The omissions under particular circumstances may be so critical as to make both Keynesianism and monetarism misleading." (Kindleberger 1978, p. 23)

7. The analysis in this study broadly follows the IS-LM-BP curve framework as used by both Keynesian and monetarist economists (see, for example, Parkin and Bade, 1982, chapters 20–32). The terminology used, however, is often rather loose in an effort to help those unfamiliar with this framework. Thus, terms such as "surplus" or "deficient" savings, or a "rise in investment relative to savings" are used to describe situations that can exist only ex ante and not ex post. Equally, for ease of exposition, the discussion is often limited to partial equilibrium conditions, when one or more of the IS, LM, or BP relationships is considered to be of secondary importance in the context of the point being made.

8. For the definitions and sources used in the analysis of investment-savings balances in this study, see TN4. For the United States, state and local governments have been included in the private sector for reasons discussed in TN5.

BOX 1.2   **The two-way relationship between budget deficits and the private sector**

One chain of causation runs from the private sector to the public sector. In the 1980 recession, for example, when surplus private savings rose by about 2.5 percent of GNP, the budget deficit rose by nearly as much, because of lower tax revenues and higher transfer payments. In this instance, the increased budget deficit was largely a *result* of the recession, i.e., the "automatic stabilizers," and the increased deficit did not stimulate the economy. Lower tax payments do not leave more income to spend if they result from lower private incomes. Neither does increased public expenditure (for example, on unemployment insurance) increase total income and spending if it is the result of job and income losses.

An opposite chain of causation runs from the federal deficit to the private sector. This is illustrated for the United States in figure 1.1 by events between mid-1974 and mid-1976. Large income-tax cuts, amounting to 2 percent of disposable income in May 1975, strongly boosted private incomes and savings (black line, top panel). People began to spend more, stimulating the economy. But once the recovery gathered momentum, the private sector's surplus savings—and the budget deficit via the automatic stabilizers—declined dramatically.

To distinguish between these two chains of causation, an estimate has to be made of what would have happened to the budget deficit at an unchanged level of economic activity and in the absence of any changes in tax or expenditure policies. Despite important conceptual and empirical difficulties (TN6), this can be calculated in a number of different ways, and is variously known as the "cyclically adjusted," "high-employment," "mid-cycle," or "structural" deficit. The latter term will be used in most places in this study. The impact of the large 1975 tax cuts in raising the US structural budget deficit and providing a spur to the economy shows up clearly in figure 1.1.

this would not be possible and interest rates would have to rise by enough to choke off the excess investment demand. In an open economy, savings can be sucked in from abroad to make up for the deficiency of domestic savings (red shading). But, *the ease with which savings can be attracted from abroad depends crucially on what is happening to investment demand relative to the supply of savings in other countries* (box 1.3).

Shifts in the investment-savings balance in the rest of the industrial world over this period are shown in figure 1.2. In 1971–73, the strong cyclical upswing in the United States coincided roughly with an almost equally strong upswing in the ROECD area. Investment rose just as strongly as in the United States, and surplus savings declined more sharply. This left little scope for the United States to attract savings; inflows rose to a peak equivalent to 0.5 percent of GNP in 1972, but quickly turned into outflows as the US economy moved into recession a year earlier than the ROECD area.

The story was very different in the 1983–84 upswing:[9]

• In the United States, investment rose strongly and thus, despite a small rise in the savings rate, *surplus private savings fell by $125 billion, or over 3 percentage points of GNP*. This was fairly typical for a cyclical upswing, but was offset much less than usual by a drop in the public sector's absorption of private savings because of a sharp increase in the federal government's structural budget deficit.

• In the ROECD area, however, the share of investment in GNP hardly rose, and *surplus private savings remained at a postwar peak of around $300 billion, or 5 percent of GNP*. Equally striking, the ROECD public sector deficit only rose from 1979 to 1982 by $50 billion, or just over 1 percentage point of GNP during its most severe postwar recession, while in the United States it rose by $130 billion, or 5.5 percentage points. The reason was that, since 1979, most other OECD countries have been making strenuous efforts

---

9. The impact of the two oil shocks on the pattern of world savings and investment is discussed below. It suffices to note here that OPEC's excess savings, after intermediation in world financial markets, ended up mainly in the nonoil developing countries and the ROECD area, rather than the United States. In 1976–78, however, with a very steep drop in the US private sector's surplus savings, at a time when they were still rising in the rest of the OECD area, there was an inflow of foreign savings peaking at 1 percent of GNP early in 1978.

FIGURE 1.1. **Investment-savings balances in United States, 1970–84**

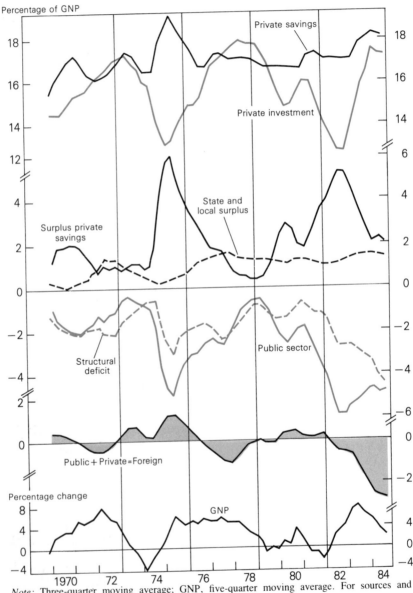

Note: Three-quarter moving average; GNP, five-quarter moving average. For sources and definitions, see TN4.

FIGURE 1.2   **Investment-savings balances in rest of OECD area, 1970–84**

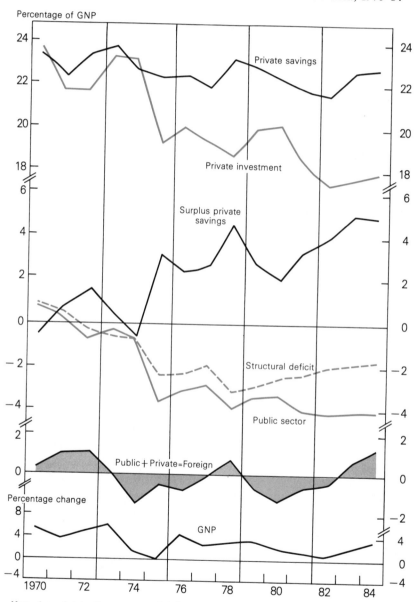

Note: Annual data. For sources and definitions, see TN4.

B O X 1.3   **The US investment-savings balance**

The regression analysis in TN7 confirms that whether the United States can attract foreign savings depends heavily on its cyclical position *relative* to rest of the world.

Using only US variables, the results suggest that, without any change in the structural budget deficit, a recovery-induced reduction in the cyclical component of the budget deficit, equivalent to 1 percent of GNP, is normally associated with a decline in the private sector's surplus savings equivalent to 1.36 percent of GNP. The difference is made up by a reduced outflow, or increased inflow, of foreign savings. But when a term for the cyclical position of the United States relative to the rest of the world is introduced, this coefficient falls to around 1.0. These results thus suggest that the United States can only attract foreign savings to fill the gap between rising investment demand and a cyclical reduction in the budget deficit when US domestic demand rises faster than domestic demand in the rest of the world, as in 1983–84 (figure 1.7).

---

to reduce their structural budget deficits. Thus, at a time when an unusually large savings deficiency was developing in the United States because of the rising structural budget deficit, there was a ready supply of savings available in the ROECD area, both because of the weakness of investment demand and because of a sharp reduction in structural budget deficits.

These divergent trends become even more marked when account is taken of what was happening in the nonoil developing countries (figure 1.3).[10] After the first oil shock, they were able to make good use of the rise in world savings (Zaidi 1985). Investment as a share of GNP rose by about 3 percentage points from 1973 to 1979; two-thirds was financed by a rise in their own savings and the remainder by attracting savings from abroad. After the second

---

10. For conceptual and statistical reasons, it is much more difficult to distinguish between the I-S balances of the public and private sectors in most developing countries. In addition, the coverage in figure 1.3 is less complete.

FIGURE 1.3 **Investment-savings balances in developing countries, 1960–84**

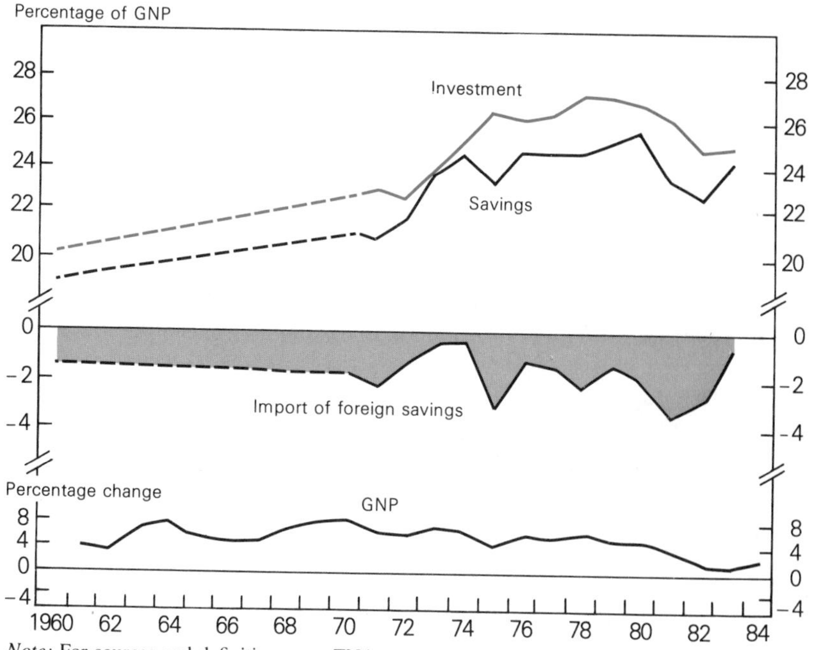

Percentage of GNP

Note: For sources and definitions, see TN4.

oil shock, however, it was a different story, largely, but by no means entirely, because of the—necessarily—more strongly anti-inflationary policy response in the industrial countries. Investment demand declined sharply relative to domestic savings because of both the slowdown in economic activity and energetic measures, under IMF adjustment programs, to cut budget deficits— which, in turn, contributed to the slowdown. There was a substantial outflow of private "flight" capital, mainly to the United States. The net inflow of capital dropped by $70 billion, or 3 percent of GNP between 1981 and 1984, and was no longer sufficient to cover net interest payments (table 1.1).

These trends in investment and domestic savings in the rest of OECD area and the nonoil developing countries, though partly offset by a decline in OPEC's savings, resulted in a substantial surplus of domestic savings in the

TABLE 1.1   **Current balances of nonoil developing countries: 1973–84**
(billion dollars)

	1973–75 average	1976–79 average	1980	1981	1982	1983	1984
Current balance	−32	−42	−88	−109	−86	−52	−38
Net investment income	−7	−12	−26	−40	−51	−49	−50
Current balance excluding investment income	−25	−30	−62	−68	−35	−3	+12
Import of foreign savings (percentage of GNP)	−0.3	−1.5	−2.3	−3.2	−2.5	−0.7	..

Source: IMF, *World Economic Outlook,* April 1985, table 37. Last line, World Bank, *World Development Report,* 1985, table A.7. All developing countries.

rest of the world as a whole. The consequences can be seen very clearly in figures 1.1, 1.2, and 1.3. The United States was able to suck in foreign savings at a rapidly increasing rate, rising to a level three times greater than at any time since the early 1870s (table 3.1). The ROECD area swung sharply from importing savings in 1979–80 (largely from OPEC) to exporting them on a large scale (largely to the United States). There was a dramatic decline in the flow of savings to the nonoil developing countries, and—contrary to normal historical experience and their domestic needs—they experienced a small net outflow of real resources in 1984.[11]

To sum up: the extent to which a deficiency of domestic savings can be mitigated by importing foreign savings depends on the *relative* strength of the rise in investment demand in relation to the supply of domestic savings at home and abroad. In this case, the shift was unusually strong because:

● The private sector's "animal spirits" revived more strongly in the United States than in the rest of the world, especially Europe, bedeviled as it is by

11. In other words, they had a surplus on current account, excluding net interest and dividend payments (table 1.1).

Europessimism; and also the developing world, borne down as it is by the debt crisis.

• In the public sector the divergent trend was greatly strengthened because most other countries were reducing structural budget deficits while the United States was doing the opposite.

The US Trade and Current Balance

These shifts in the flow of world savings were, of necessity, accompanied by a dramatic deterioration in the US current balance, as capital inflows pushed up the dollar, and domestic demand rose more strongly in the United States than in the rest of the world. Table 1.2 presents estimates of the quantitative importance of the different factors at work using the D&D model.

• Between 1980 and 1984, the dollar rose in nominal terms by 44 percent against its trading partners' currencies (IMF index, box 1.4). During this period, inflation in other countries, weighted according to their importance as competitors for US goods and services, was somewhat higher than in the United States; in real terms, the dollar rose by about 35 percent. According to the D&D model, this appreciation was responsible for about $70 billion—or two-thirds—of the net deterioration in the US current balance from 1980 to 1984.[12] Because, moreover, changes in the dollar go on affecting the current balance for quite some time, there would be a further lagged negative impact from the previous rise in the dollar—of about $40 billion in 1985–86 had the dollar stayed at its average level in the six months to March 1985 (table 3.3).

• The US current balance has also been adversely affected by a "growth gap." Faster US growth sucked in imports while slower growth in the rest of the world curbed US exports. In 1982, with a more severe recession in the United States than abroad, this factor worked the other way. But for the period as a whole it accounted, according to the D&D model, for about $25 billion of the deterioration in the US current balance.

• This phenomenon was aggravated by the debt crisis. The imports of many heavily indebted countries fell by more than could be attributed to their

---

12. If the period covered were extended to include 1985, when US growth slowed down while the dollar remained strong, this share would rise to over three-quarters.

BOX 1.4   **Which dollar exchange rate?**

There is no single exchange rate for the dollar; there is a whole series of rates between it and every other currency. Unfortunately, there is no uniquely right way of weighting these together to measure changes in "the" dollar, and different methods produce significantly different results. A good deal of confusion is caused by the fact that speakers and authors often do not specify to which index they are referring. Between 1980:3 and 1985:1, for example, the nominal dollar indices published by the Morgan Guaranty Trust Company, the International Monetary Fund, and the Federal Reserve Board rose by 51, 63, and 83 percent, respectively. Regression analysis shows a strong and systematic relationship between the three indices; for a 1 percent change in the IMF index the Morgan Guaranty index will change by around 0.86 percent and the Fed's index by 1.18 percent. All quantitative analyses in this study use the IMF index, for reasons discussed in TN8. This is important when comparing these results with those in other studies.

slower growth because they had to impose import controls or carry through sharp real devaluations, or both. This is estimated to have cut US exports by $10 billion to $15 billion more than can be explained by slow or negative growth rates in the debtor countries.

• US investment income fell by $12 billion because of slow growth in the rest of the world, the strong dollar, and the decline in the US net investment position (chapter 3).

• These negative factors were offset to the tune of about $20 billion by a decline in the volume and price of US oil imports.

Various estimates have been published of the contribution the dollar's rise made to the deterioration in the US current account.[13] Most are not directly

---

13. For example: Wallich (1985, p. 6); CEA (1984, pp. 42–55); McNamar (1984a); Morgan Guaranty (1984b, p. 5); and DRI (1983, pp. 30–31).

TABLE 1.2   **Factors affecting US current balance, 1980–84**
(changes from previous year, billion dollars)

	1981	1982	1983	1984	Cumulative from 1980
The strong dollar	−4	−25	−21	−18	−68
Growth gap[a]	−5	+16	−7	−29	−25
Debt crisis[b]	n.a.	−4	−8	−1	−13
Net investment income	+4	−6	−4	−5	−12
Oil imports[c]	+1	+17	+7	−3	+22
Residual[d]	+8	−13	+1	−4	−8
Actual	+4	−15	−32	−60	−103

Note: Based on a "backcasting" exercise using the D&D model (see TN1, table C).

a. The impact of differences in GNP growth rates between the United States and the rest of the world, including, in 1984, an add factor of $10 billion for the impact of unusually strong inventory accumulation.

b. Measured by the amount by which US exports to developing countries fell below the level predicted on the basis of past relationships.

c. Reflecting both reduced volume and lower dollar prices.

d. Difference between the sum of the factors quantified above and the actual change, including transfers and military transactions.

comparable with table 1.2 because of differences in timing and definition. A rough comparison has, however, been made by using the D&D model to estimate the dollar's contribution with the definitions and time periods used in these studies. The results suggest that the D&D estimates are similar to those of the Federal Reserve Board and the Council of Economic Advisers. Although they are at the upper end of the range of some other estimates, it was decided that the parameters built into the D&D model in this respect provide the best basis for the purposes for which the model is used in this study. A model with parameters that gave a *smaller* contribution from the dollar's rise to the deterioration of the current balance since 1980 would also require a *larger* decline in the dollar for a given improvement in the future, i.e. it would make most of the problems of correcting the present disequilibrium even more difficult to resolve than this study suggests.

Why Did the Dollar Rise So Much?

Having set out the most fundamental feature of the present disequilibrium in the world economy, we can trace the reasons for the unusually strong and prolonged rise in the dollar.

THE CURRENT BALANCE

Over the last four years, the change in the value of the dollar has been the single most powerful force driving the US current account. In fact, analysis covering a longer period suggests that this has been true ever since the move to more flexible exchange rates. Thus, the results of the regression analysis shown in the top panel of figure 1.4 imply that, by themselves, changes in the dollar since 1971 can, with a lag of one year, explain an important part of the changes in the US current balance.[14]

   This is, however, only half the story. A rising current account deficit should, in time, *depress* the dollar. Indeed, the results of the regression analysis given in the bottom panel of figure 1.4 show that there has been a fairly consistent tendency for the dollar to begin to depreciate two years after the current balance has begun to deteriorate, and vice versa.[15] What is striking, however, is that this relationship appears to have broken down, beginning in 1983, but most dramatically in 1984 and early 1985.[16]

   This experience has led many observers to conclude that there has been a systemic change in the way the exchange rate system works. It is argued that because capital flows have become so very much larger than trade flows, the trade balance (and hence the current balance) no longer plays a significant

---

14. $\bar{R}^2 = 0.63$. This contrasts sharply with experience prior to 1971 when, with nominal exchange rates mostly fixed and real exchange rates changing only slowly, the dominant influence came from changes in the "growth gap" between the United States and other countries.

15. $\bar{R}^2 = 0.45$.

16. The current account deteriorated by $11 billion over the two years to 1982 (figure 1.4, top panel, black line). According to the regression, the dollar should have depreciated by 3.5 percent over the following two years to 1984 (bottom panel, red line), whereas actually it appreciated by 14 percent (black line). These regression results are presented here for expositional purposes, not for their predictive value (TN9).

FIGURE 1.4   **The two-way relationship between dollar and US current balance, 1972–86**

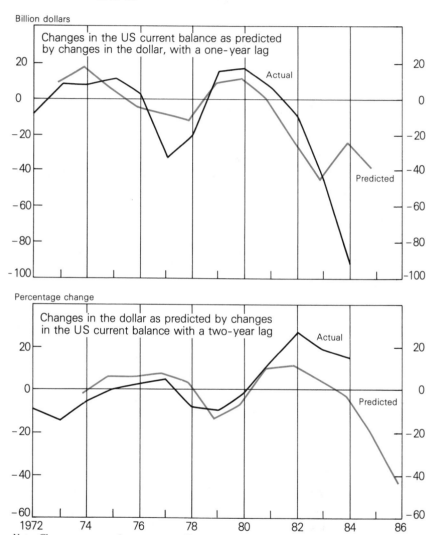

Note: Changes over previous two years. For sources and methodology, see TN9.

role in determining the level of the dollar. Recent experience, not only for the United States, can be cited to support this view.[17]

It is, however, a common but serious mistake to assume that the underlying relationship between exchange rates and current balances could cease to operate altogether. When the US current balance is in deficit, it means that more dollars are being sold on the exchange markets to buy foreign goods and services than are being bought by foreigners to buy US goods and services. This, in itself, is *bound* to put downward pressure on the price of the dollar. If the dollar does not go down, it can only be because this pressure is being fully offset, or more than offset, because more dollars are being bought by foreigners to purchase dollar-denominated financial or real assets than are being sold by Americans to buy foreign currencies to purchase assets denominated in other currencies. This is what was happening in 1983–84. But it is unlikely that the United States has become a structural capital importer. Looking five years ahead and more, there is little reason to expect a persistent positive *net* demand for dollar-denominated assets; and at some point before then such demand will (ex ante) become insufficient to finance the current account deficit and could well turn negative (chapter 3). A time is thus approaching when a continuing US current account deficit will inevitably depress the dollar.

The two-way relationship shown for the United States in figure 1.4 illustrates graphically why the flexible exchange rate system has been working much less well than had been hoped. If the current account responded *quickly* to a change in the exchange rate, and if the exchange rate responded *quickly* to a change in the current account, a rise in the dollar would quickly generate a force to depress it. Strong self-stabilizing forces would be at work to dampen fluctuations in nominal (and real) exchange rates. For the United States, however, the total average lag between these two relationships is three years or longer: a year for the exchange rate to affect the current balance, and then two years or more for the current balance to affect the exchange rate. This is too long a time horizon to generate stabilizing speculation in the exchange markets (chapter 4). Thus, *when, for whatever reason, the dollar begins to move in one direction, it normally takes at least three years before the self-stabilizing force from the current account begins to operate.* In the meanwhile, with greatly increased mobility of private

---

17. For Germany, for example, see Micossi and Padoa-Schioppa (1984, p. 17).

capital, the resultant shifts in current balances are quite easily financed by opposite shifts in capital flows. In the process, however, the exchange rate "overshoots" the level at which it would produce a current balance roughly equal (with opposite sign) to the sustainable level of the capital balance over the longer run.[18]

Initially, it was thought that, as exchange markets gained experience with the flexible rate system, traders would increasingly realize that a current account deficit greater than the sustainable level of capital inflows would in time cause a currency to depreciate, and that, by anticipating this, traders would engage in stabilizing speculation that would dampen, if not eliminate, overshooting. For a time, it looked as if it might work this way. Since 1976, however, the markets have seen that the relationship between current balances and exchange rates can be very elastic with long and unpredictable lags. The markets have thus tended to increasingly ignore the current balance and concentrate on variables with a shorter time horizon such as interest rates. With erosion of the self-stabilizing mechanism from the current balance, the flexible-rate system appears to be headed for continuing cycles of overshooting of increasing amplitude and duration. The increasing costs for the "real" economy are discussed in chapter 2; the policy implications, in chapters 7 and 8.

INTEREST RATES

The influence of interest rates on exchange rates in a flexible rate system appears obvious at first sight but is actually rather complex. That the relationship is not straightforward emerges clearly from figure 1.5: in 1978–79, US interest rates were higher than foreign rates but the dollar went down; in 1980–82 they were also higher, but the dollar went up. Why?

Most foreigners who invest in US financial assets do not intend to spend either their capital or their interest earnings in the United States, but in their own countries. They are therefore primarily interested in the value of their investment, and earnings from it, *expressed in their own currencies*.[19] This

---

18. Academic economists began to develop models with these properties, emphasizing the rapid adjustment of asset markets relative to goods markets, from the mid-1970s onwards, starting with Dornbusch (1976, pp. 1161–76).

19. Apparently the first question a Swiss banker asks a new foreign client is "What is your bread currency?"

BOX 1.5   **Nominal or real interest rates?**

A more meaningful economic argument can be made linking high real interest rate differentials with the dollar. (Sprinkel 1984, p. 5)

International investors alter exchange rates by shifting their portfolio preferences towards investments in countries where the after-tax, real rate of return from investments is higher. (McNamar 1984b, p. 8)

Discussing the rise in the dollar in terms of high *real* interest rates or *real* rates of return can be misleading. The layman, trying to understand the reasons for the strong dollar, may get the impression that real rates of interest are more real—and hence more meaningful—than nominal rates, and that real rates of interest are more or less the same thing as real rates of return.

The first point is that most of the capital flows that finance current balances are financial in nature (chapter 3 and figure 3.3). Financial investors are not directly interested in real rates of return or real interest rates because they are not investing in real assets. They are interested in *two* variables, nominal interest rate differentials and future exchange rates.

Why then do economists so often work out their models and present their results in terms of real interest rates? The first reason is that real interest rates *are* highly relevant to what is happening in the domestic economy. Second, when building models of exchange rate behavior, economists necessarily *have* to make assumptions about how nominal interest rates move in relation to domestic inflation and how nominal exchange rates move in relation to inflation differentials.

Once this has been done, it becomes both possible and often convenient to work in terms of real interest rates. In a very simple model, for example, in which it is assumed that the purchasing power parity condition holds at all times, the two variables concerned can both be measured. Between two countries, *A* and

B, where the nominal interest rate differential is $(i_A - i_B)$, the expected change in the exchange rate is given by the inflation differential, $(p_A - p_B)$. The exchange rate changes only if these two terms, with opposite signs, do not equal each other. The condition for exchange rate stability can therefore be rewritten $(i_A - p_A) = (i_B - p_B)$, i.e., a zero real interest-rate differential.

Even in much more sophisticated models *some* assumption has to be made as to how past and expected future rates of inflation (as well as other factors) influence exchange rate expectations. So far, however, there has not been much success in developing realistic models of the determination of exchange rate expectations, despite intensive efforts (starting, in particular, from Dornbusch 1976 and Frenkel 1976). For so long as this remains the case, discussion of the relationship between interest rates and exchange rates has to come back to the two variables, nominal interest rates, which are easy to measure, and exchange rate expectations, which are the joker in the pack (chapter 4).

True, a rise in after-tax rates of return can, if the supply of domestic savings is inelastic, lead to a rise in nominal interest rates (chapter 2), and if it does, it may attract *temporary* inflows of financial capital. Such inflows will, however, be sustainable only if there has been a major and permanent rise in US real rates of return relative to the rest of the world, which seems improbable (chapter 3).

means that *two* variables always enter into their investment decisions: the difference between interest rates in the United States and in their own country *and* the expected future exchange rate at which they could convert their US investment or interest earnings back into their own currencies. Moreover, what is directly relevant is the nominal interest rate, *not* the real interest rate (box 1.5).

This provides a simple explanation for the odd behavior noted above. In 1978–79, the dollar had been declining since early 1977. Foreigners were not tempted to take advantage of the higher US interest rates lest they lose

more from a further decline in the dollar than they would gain from higher
interest rates. In 1981–82, on the other hand, the dollar was well into a
strong rise that had started in mid-1980. Dollar-denominated assets thus
seemed attractive not only because of higher US interest rates, but also
because of the prospect of gains from a rising dollar.

This dual role of interest rates and exchange rate expectations has two
important consequences.

• In the short run—while little happens to change exchange rate expectations—there can well be a strong positive correlation between interest rates
and exchange rates. Moreover, because of this short-term relationship, the
markets may for a time get into an interest rate "mode" when actual and
expected changes in interest rates play a determining role.

• But once something *else* happens to change exchange rate expectations,
this relationship can break down; and, at times, go completely into reverse.
The exchange markets then shift into a different "mode," concentrating their
attention, for example, on a rising current account deficit or accelerating
inflation.

The important point is that a major change in exchange rate expectations
can reverse the direction of causality between interest rates and the exchange
rates. In 1978–79, people wanted to get out of the dollar because they
expected it to go down. They sold US financial assets, tending to push up
US interest rates, and bought, for example, DM assets, tending to push down
German interest rates. Thus, adverse exchange rate expectations, in themselves, helped to *generate* the positive interest-rate differential.[20] The moral
is clear. *Positive interest-rate differentials in favor of the United States will
at times strengthen the dollar; at other times they can be a symptom of a
loss of confidence in the dollar* (box 1.6).

INFLATION

Inflation is the other main variable entering into models of exchange rate
determination. Here again the relationship is not as obvious as it may seem

---

20. This is, of course, only part of the story. Among other things, the response of monetary
policy in both countries to the declining dollar and appreciating deutsche mark also tended to
generate a positive interest differential.

FIGURE 1.5   **The dollar, interest rates, inflation, and US current balance, 1970–84**

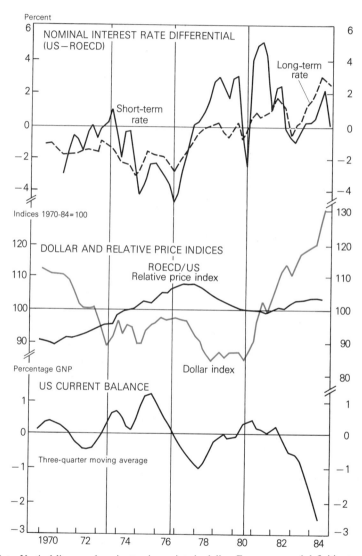

Note: Vertical lines mark major turning points in dollar. For sources and definitions, see T10. US current balance is on NIPA basis.

B O X 1.6   **The dollar, interest rates, and the US Treasury**

Given the inherent instability of the relationship between interest rates and exchange rates, it is possible to prove almost anything by a judicious choice of time periods. The Under Secretary for Monetary Affairs at the US Treasury from 1981 to early 1985, Beryl W. Sprinkel, liked to tell his foreign colleagues that in his native Missouri, a favorite saying is "show me," and then proceed to show them they were wrong to attribute the strength of the dollar to high US interest rates. Thus, ". . . we are told that the dollar has been driven up by an excessive budget deficit and high US interest rates . . . [but] on balance, over the last three years, the dollar appreciated substantially against all major currencies—yet interest rates differentials moved *against* the dollar" (1984, p. 4).

Mr. Sprinkel was speaking in March 1984, about four years after the dollar's rise began. Working with quarterly data, as in figure 1.5, the interest-rate differential in the first quarter of 1984 could have been compared with any of the preceding 16 quarters. In 8 such comparisons the differential, using short-term rates, moved against the dollar, in 8 it moved in favor; using long-term rates, it moved in favor in all 16. Mr. Sprinkel's conclusion was thus 25 percent right—and 75 percent wrong—depending on the choice of interest rate and time period. For the relationship between budget deficits and interest rates, see chapter 6 and TN25.

---

at first sight. Foreign investors are not directly interested in the rate of inflation in the United States, since they do not normally intend to spend their capital or interest income in the United States. They may be indirectly interested, however, insofar as they have grounds for believing that what happens to US inflation relative to inflation in their own country provides some guide to what is likely to happen to the exchange rate of their currency against the dollar.

Why should relative inflation rates provide a guide to future changes in nominal exchange rates? The logic goes back to the proposition discussed above that current balances cannot, over an extended period of years, differ from the sustainable level of capital inflows or outflows, which changes only slowly. Suppose one makes the further—heroic—assumption that a country's competitive strength changes only when its rate of inflation is higher or lower than abroad. Then it would follow that, over a period of years, the exchange rate of a country whose inflation rate was, say, 1 percent higher than its trading partners' should decline at an average rate of 1 percent a year.

The historical record shows that there is at least some truth in this hypothesis: changes in exchange rates, corrected for inflation differentials ("real" exchange rates) have tended to move a good deal less than exchange rates without such a correction. But the record also shows that, especially since the move to flexible exchange rates, significant and prolonged departures from this "purchasing power parity" condition have become the rule rather than the exception:

The failure of purchasing power parity to hold under floating rates has been particularly marked over the short to medium term—i.e., month to month or quarter to quarter, or even two-year to three-year periods. . . . Thus, only over long periods and only when relative price changes among countries have been quite large, has purchasing power parity served as a useful rule of thumb for explaining actual exchange rate movements.[21]

The validity of this conclusion as applied to the United States emerges vividly from the second panel of figure 1.5. During the first period, to mid-1973, there was a significant improvement in the US relative inflation performance but, since other factors were at work, the dollar went down. During the second period, to end-1976, continuation of a better US inflation performance was associated with a modest rise in the dollar. And, in the next two periods, there was a positive relation between movements in the dollar and, first deteriorating, then improving, US inflation performance. The striking thing, however, is that the *amplitude of the movements in the dollar was many times greater than could be justified by the assumption of purchasing power parity.*

Models have been developed that attempt to explain this phenomenon. Suppose, for example, that nominal interest rates are higher in the United

---

21. IMF (1984, p. 5). This is perhaps the best recent survey of how the floating rate system has been working.

States than in, say, Germany and Japan (as they have been for some years). Suppose, moreover, that people do believe that purchasing power parity holds, but takes, say, five years to assert itself. This means that they can enjoy the benefits of higher US interest rates for five years before all the inevitable exchange rate loss is incurred. Suppose further that the difference in nominal interest rates reflects solely differences in expected rates of inflation. Formalized into a model it can then be shown that a 1 percent change in the expected inflation differential should produce a 5 percent change in the exchange rate.[22]

In practice, the relation between exchange rates and inflation performance is almost certainly both broader and looser than suggested by such models. A country's inflation performance has come to be regarded—particularly after the unpleasant experiences of the 1970s—as a good barometer of its overall economic health. For a whole variety of reasons, a country where inflation is falling, or is already better than average, is regarded as a better bet than countries where the reverse is true.

The improvement in US relative inflation performance was thus almost certainly one factor behind the strong rise in the dollar. There is, however, a fascinating circularity here. While improved US inflation performance helped to push up the dollar, the dollar's rise has at the same time been reducing US inflation and adding to inflation in other countries. Indeed, the rise in the dollar explains a not unimportant part of the *relative* improvement in US inflation performance. This can be seen from figure 1.6, which compares actual inflation in the United States and the ROECD area from 1980 to 1984, with an estimate from the D&D model of what might have happened to inflation had the dollar been constant, in real terms, at its 1980 level (called here "domestically generated" inflation: see TN11). Actual inflation rates in 1980 were somewhat higher in the United States than in the rest of the OECD area. By 1984, the US rate had been cut by as much as two-thirds, the ROECD rate by only one-quarter. In terms of domestically generated inflation, however, the US rate fell by just over one-half, the ROECD rate by over one-third.

This provides another graphic illustration of how, under a floating system, exchange rate deviations from longer run equilibrium levels can develop considerable momentum before the forces generating them go into reverse. Perceptions of an improved US inflation performance were one reason for

---

22. Isard (1980).

FIGURE 1.6 **Comparative inflation performance in United States and rest of OECD area, 1980–84**

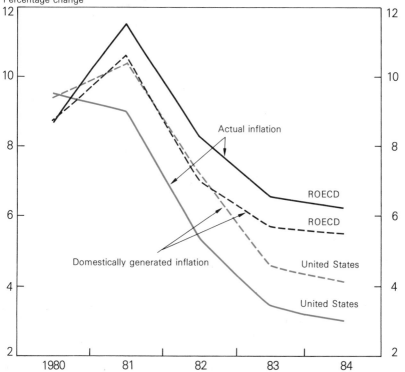

Note: For sources and definitions, see TN11. For data, see tables 2.4 and 2.7.

the strong rise of the dollar; subsequently, the dollar's strong rise made a significant contribution to the improvement in the US relative inflation performance. At first sight, this is a helpful virtuous circle. But as a result, the dollar's real exchange rate rose sharply, generating large current account deficits that will in time depress the dollar, reversing the process and setting off a vicious circle. Once the dollar starts going down, this will tend to push up US inflation and push down inflation in the countries whose currency is appreciating, leading to a sharp deterioration in US inflation performance *relative* to countries into which money is trying to move out of the dollar.

TABLE 1.3   **Flow of private foreign capital into United States, 1975–84**
(billion dollars, annual averages)

	1975–78	1979–80	1981–82	1983–84
Recorded	18	48	84	83
Adjustments[a]	n.a.	n.a.	−52	−19
Errors and omissions[b]	7	25	25	20
Total (adjusted)	25	73	57	84
Percentage of GNP	1.3	2.7	1.9	2.4

Source: Survey of Current Business.
a. Proposed by Isard and Stekler (1985) to allow for the way the recorded figures were affected by the introduction of international banking facilities (IBFs) in 1981, and borrowing abroad by US companies through Eurobonds issued by their Netherlands Antilles affiliates.
b. To an important extent, errors and omissions are thought to reflect inflows of foreign capital (TN12).

THE SAFE HAVEN

A popular—but tricky—explanation for the rise in the dollar is that the United States is the world's "safe haven." Anything that makes people feel insecure about their future is likely to generate flows of money (and people) to the United States, the world's richest and most powerful country. A first point to note, however, is that people are just as likely—indeed more likely—to feel insecure when the United States appears *weak* as when it appears strong. Thus, for example, perceptions that the Carter administration was weak and that the Russians were increasingly taking advantage of it could have been expected to generate capital flows to the United States. Indeed, inflows of foreign capital (including errors and omissions) nearly tripled from an average of $25 billion in 1975–78 to an average of $73 billion in 1979–80 (table 1.3). Turning this argument around, perception that the Reagan administration would strengthen US defenses and take a stronger line with the Russians could be expected to make people living outside the United States feel more secure and *reduce* their desire to put their savings into a safe haven.

There was, however, a cluster of events, mainly in 1979–81, that created a sense of insecurity in the rest of the world: the Iranian revolution (September 1979) and the Iraq-Iran war (September 1980); the Russian invasion of Afghanistan (December 1979); Polish unrest (1980–81); the election of a socialist government in France (May 1981); and the "missile crisis" in

Europe (which lasted into 1983). These enhanced the attraction of the "safe haven" and help to explain why, in 1981–82, with the developing-country debt crisis gathering momentum, foreign capital inflows remained at a relatively high level.

Even here, however, there is a "danger of using the term safe haven as a vague label for unexplained shifts in the investors' portfolios."[23] Other events should have helped to strengthen investors' confidence in Europe: the election of a conservative government in West Germany (March 1983), the over-whelming reelection of British Prime Minister Margaret Thatcher (June 1983), and a fairly general shift to the right in many smaller countries in northern Europe. Despite the strength of the US recovery and the growing talk of an "American renaissance," inflows of foreign capital were at much the same level in 1983–84 as in the last two years of the Carter administration (table 1.3). [24, 25]

The Dollar: A Wrap-Up

The reasons for such a strong and prolonged rise in the dollar can now be summarized—at least with the benefit of hindsight (box 1.7).

Starting from a trough in the third quarter of 1980, when the dollar was widely thought to be undervalued, the rise in 1981 and 1982 can be largely explained in conventional terms. The current balance had been improving for the previous two-and-a-half years. With the United States going into recession earlier than the rest of the world, its relative inflation performance started to improve sharply, and this was subsequently accentuated by the rise

---

23. Council of Economic Advisers (1984, p. 54).

24. There was, however, a sharp rise in foreign purchases of US securities following the abolition of the withholding tax in mid-1984.

25. A problem with the safe-haven argument is the difficulty of distinguishing exogenous factors affecting confidence from those that resulted from—and were thus endogenous to—economic trends and policies. There can be little doubt that the consequences of the divergent macroeconomic policies being followed created a psychological climate that accentuated the tendency for money to flow into the United States, and hence helped to perpetuate the disequilibrium that they created (chapter 2). From the analytical point of view, however, this cannot really be regarded as an independent explanation for the strength of the dollar; neither can it be expected to continue to operate when trends and policies begin to change.

BOX 1.7   "Modes" in the exchange markets

Economists are still trying to recover from the loss of face when Meese and Rogoff tested the out of sample predictive power of many of the then existing models of exchange rate behavior and showed that they all did worse than a simple model in which it is assumed that the exchange rate in twelve months' time will be the same as it is now (Meese and Rogoff 1983). With this in mind, some economists have tried to demonstrate that it is "news," or *unpredictable* economic events, that are the main determinant of exchange rates (Dornbusch 1980; Frenkel 1981).

But, are we "really as ignorant about the causes of exchange rate fluctuations as might be argued on the basis of such evidence"? (Black 1984, p. 1). Black goes on to present the results of a piece of empirical analysis using rolling regressions of monthly data from 1973 to 1982 for the key factors discussed here—interest rates, inflation, and current balances—and demonstrates that "each of them . . . played some role at different times, but none uniformly over the entire period" (p. 25).

This tends to confirm that exchange markets, like haute couture, are subject to changes in fashion and at times switch quite quickly from one "mode" to another. Once this is accepted, it is easier to explain the behavior of exchange rates—at least after the event—if not to predict them. Perhaps the most promising line of research, as suggested by Black, is to try to get a better understanding of the circumstances under which these shifts take place.

in the dollar itself. The Federal Reserve Board, following a major switch in emphasis to monetary aggregates in October 1979, imposed what turned out to be an unexpectedly restrictive monetary policy, and until late 1982 US interest rates (with a brief interruption in mid-1980) were very much higher than in the ROECD area. In addition, a number of geopolitical events in Europe and the Middle East enhanced the attractiveness of the United States as a safe haven.

By 1983, and especially in 1984, the key factor was that an unusually

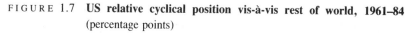

FIGURE 1.7   **US relative cyclical position vis-à-vis rest of world, 1961–84**
(percentage points)

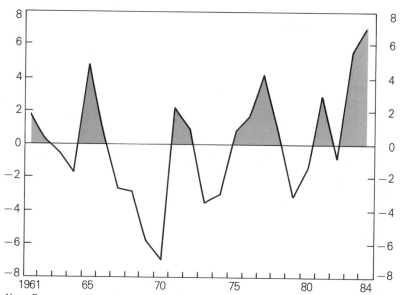

Note: Percentage change in US domestic demand less percentage change in ROW domestic demand. Average differences 1961-84 are normalized to zero. ROW aggregate using 1982 weights.

Source: World Bank and OECD data bases.

marked divergence had developed between a strong rise in investment relative to domestic savings in the United States—essentially due to the deterioration in the structural federal budget deficit—and weak investment relative to domestic savings in the rest of the world. Foreign savings were sucked into the United States through the financial markets faster than the US economy's need for them to finance its growing current account deficit.

There is nothing new about this. Wallich and Friedrich (1982) have shown that ever since World War II, whenever the US economy has been cyclically strong *relative* to the rest of the world, its private capital balance has improved, ex ante or ex post, more than its current balance deteriorated.

With fixed exchange rates, this meant that the sum of its current and private capital balance (then called the "balance on official settlements") went into surplus. With floating rates it meant that the dollar appreciated. Moreover, as Wallich and Friedrich point out, Bloomfield (1943, 1950) showed earlier that the same phenomenon can be traced back as far as World War I. What *is* new is that the cyclical position of the United States relative to the rest of the world—and more particularly the divergence in investment-savings behavior—was stronger in 1983–84 than at any time since World War II (figure 1.7).

One, but only one, of the mechanisms by which this divergent investment-savings behavior was transmitted through the financial markets worked through interest rates (themselves influenced by tax changes as discussed in chapter 2). Equally important, the sheer strength of credit demand in the United States relative to the rest of the world helped to reduce capital outflows and pull in foreign money; the more so since, during this period, measures were being taken to deregulate financial markets in Europe, and especially in Japan (Frankel 1984).

The flexible exchange rate system in itself helped to accentuate and prolong the disequilibrium. Divergent trends in investment and savings in different parts of the world will gather more momentum and go farther under a flexible exchange rate system than under a fixed or adjustable-peg system because, with flexible rates, trade flows adjust more rapidly and fully to changes in capital flows (TN13). This is not necessarily bad. It provides a useful shock absorber to cushion unexpected shocks, like the two oil crises. But, by the same token, it gives countries a longer rope to hang themselves in the event of prolonged policy errors. Regrettably, this is just what has been happening.

A Policy-Induced Disequilibrium

Since the early 1970s, there have been three major shocks to the world's investment-savings balance: the two oil crises of 1973–74 and 1979–80, and the progressive deterioration of the US structural federal budget position starting in 1981. The size of each of these shocks, in terms of the world economy as a whole, has been of roughly the same order of magnitude, equivalent to 1.5 percent to 2.0 percent of OECD GNP (figure 1.8).[26] The

---

26. Measured ex ante, the oil shocks were larger than shown in figure 1.8 (TN14).

FIGURE 1.8 **Major shocks to world's investment-savings balance, 1970–90** (percentage of OECD GNP)

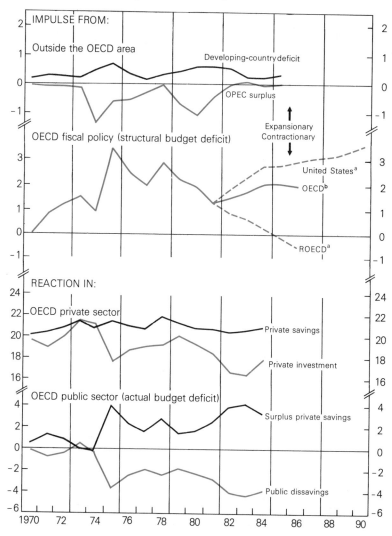

Note: For sources and notes, see TN14.
a. Cumulative change from 1981.
b. Cumulative change from 1970.

BOX 1.8   **The two oil shocks and the world investment-savings balance**

Much higher oil prices acted like a tax on oil consumers, the proceeds from which the oil producers could not, in important cases, spend immediately because of their small populations and underdeveloped infrastructure. For the world economy as a whole the impact was demand depressing (figure 1.8, top panel) and cost inflationary—a particularly unpleasant combination. The ensuing inflationary recession led to a sharp drop in OECD investment demand and created surplus private savings within the OECD area (bottom panel). The counterpart was a massive deterioration in the structural savings position of the public sector, from rough balance in the 1960s and early 1970s, to deficits averaging about 3 percent of GNP since 1974 (bottom panel). See Llewellyn (1983) and Price and Chouraqui (1983).

   The unique feature of the two oil crises was the *suddenness* of the shock to the world's investment-savings balance. Once they had happened, however, powerful market forces were set in motion reducing the imbalances they had created. The oil producers quite quickly found ways to spend their new riches. In oil-consuming countries, demand for oil dropped sharply because of recession and slower growth and the increasingly powerful effect of higher prices in reducing oil consumption. Moreover, the nonoil developing countries were able to borrow and make good use of the world's surplus savings, thus boosting the world economy. Together, these factors were sufficient to eliminate OPEC surpluses each time in about three years.

---

timing and nature of the latest shock is, however, totally different.

   The two oil crises created almost overnight a large surplus of savings by raising world savings and depressing investment (box 1.8). The shock from US budget deficits has been building up much more slowly. It is, moreover, creating, not a surplus, but a *shortage* of savings. This means that, in itself, it has been demand expansionary. Up to a point, this was appropriate because the US economy was best placed to lead the world economy out of the 1981–

82 recession. But not only did the United States overdo it, the other major OECD countries took the diametrically opposite course, cutting their structural budget deficits by an amount which, for the OECD area as a whole, offset most of the expansionary policy shift in the United States (figure 1.8).

The persistence of the disequilibrium in the world's investment-savings balance should not, therefore, be attributed solely to US policies; *it has resulted from the interplay of quite opposite policies followed by the United States and the other major OECD countries.* Had the United States followed the others, there would have been a continuing world recession. Had the others followed the United States, there would have been a strong world boom, leading rather quickly to a new outbreak of world inflation. As it is, we had neither. Instead, we have had a world recovery which in aggregate has been reasonably satisfactory, but which, because of its uneven distribution, is generating a massive disequilibrium between the United States and its major allies that is fraught with danger for the world economy.

How did this rather extraordinary divergence in policies come about? Its origins can be traced back to the breakdown of the Keynesian consensus of how economic policy works in the 1970s.[27] The subsequent tug-of-war between Keynesian and monetarist ideas, plus the advent of supply-side economics, has left policymakers confused and generally suspicious of advice from their economic advisers. To simplify a complicated story, many governments became convinced that the way out of recession and stagflation was to cut budget deficits, while the new Reagan administration came to power convinced that the right answer was to cut taxes at a time when it also saw a need to raise defense spending. This is thus *a policy-induced disequilibrium, in which the policies being pursued are founded on quite different views of how policy works.* Moreover, the governments concerned have invested a great deal of political capital in the rightness of their (opposite) approaches. Prime Ministers Yasuhiro Nakasone and Margaret Thatcher and Chancellor Helmut Kohl have committed their political fortunes just as firmly to giving overriding priority to reducing budget deficits as President Ronald Reagan has to cutting taxes even if expenditure has not been reduced.

A number of important conclusions can be drawn from this chapter. The analysis of the factors behind the strong and prolonged rise in the dollar

27. See Marris (1984) for a more detailed discussion of how this came about.

showed that (in contrast to the two oil crises) the market forces working to correct the investment-savings imbalance created by large and rising US structural budget deficits have been slow to come into operation because of the way the flexible exchange rate regime has been working.[28] As long as this is the case, the growing disequilibrium could be halted and reversed only by a major change in policies by both the United States and its major allies. Such a change seems unlikely, however, because on both sides the governments concerned are politically committed to the rightness of their present policies. If so, the disequilibrium will continue to build up until, at some point, the United States reaches the limits of its international credit-worthiness. Market forces will then start working to correct the investment-savings imbalance in an extremely unpleasant way. But since the United States is the world's richest and most powerful country, it is hard to judge when this moment will come. This question is discussed in chapter 3. What will happen when the crunch comes is the subject of chapter 4. Before turning to these questions, we will take a closer look at what happened in the United States and the other OECD countries in 1980–84.

---

28. *Political* forces are, however, growing to do something about the disequilibrium—in the worst way possible—through increasing protectionism (chapter 8).

Appendix   GUIDE TO KEY RELATIONSHIPS ANALYZED IN THIS STUDY

The basic ex post identity underlying this study is:

$$(X - M) = (S - I) + (T - G),$$

where X and M are exports and imports of goods and services, S is private savings, I is private investment, T is government revenue, and G is public expenditure including public investment; $(X - M)$ is the external current balance (excluding transfers), $(S - I)$ is referred to in this study as "surplus private savings," and $(T - G)$ is the budget surplus (usually a deficit). Treating the rest of the world (ROW) as an entity we have:

$$(X - M)_{US} = (S - I)_{US} + (T - G)_{US}$$
$$= (M - X)_{ROW} = -[(S - I)_{ROW} + (T - G)_{ROW}].$$

This identity brings out clearly how the final outcome depends on what is happening to private investment-savings (I-S) balances, budget deficits, and trade flows in both the United States *and* in the rest of the world. As always, however, such an identity tells us nothing about the direction of causality, or about the mechanisms that ensure that an ex ante inequality becomes an ex post identity, which are central to the analysis in this study.

Figure 1.9 thus summarizes most of the more important relationships involved, and the direction in which they have been working as investment demand rose more strongly relative to the supply of domestic savings in the United States than in the rest of the world. The relationships quantified in the D&D model are marked with an asterisk. Most of the others are discussed at various points in chapters 1 to 6.

When the dollar begins to go down, many of these relationships will go into reverse. The way in which the identity between the investment-savings balance and the current account balance will be maintained in the US economy under these conditions is discussed in chapter 4 and summarized in figure 4.2.

The top panel in figure 1.9 shows the impact of the strong rise in investment relative to savings in the United States on the relevant US variables. The second panel shows the impact of the weakness of investment demand in the rest of the world on these same US variables. Line 10 summarizes the net impact on the US economy of these factors at work in both the United States and the rest of the world. The bottom panel shows the impact of these developments in the US economy on the rest of the world.

Line 1. The rise in investment demand relative to savings in the United States boosted domestic demand (line 1, column 1). Some part of this increase went abroad in the form of higher imports, but the remainder went into GNP (line 1, column 2). The rise in investment demand relative to domestic savings, combined with the Federal Reserve's anti-inflationary stance, raised interest rates (line 1, column 4). Faster growth of domestic demand and GNP raised imports* and worsened the current account balance (line 1, column 6).

Line 2. The net impact on the price level was negative (line 10, column 3). At the prevailing levels of capacity utilization, upward pressures from domestic demand (line 1, column 3) were more than offset by lower import prices resulting from the rise in the dollar* (line 4, column 3) and the impact of increased competition from imports on domestic prices (line 5, column 3). The weaker-than-normal recovery in the rest of the world and the strength of the dollar also depressed world commodity prices (line 8, column 3).

The net downward impact on prices helped to lift domestic demand through real incomes and real money balances (line 2, column 2). It also helped to lower inflationary expectations, hence interest rates (line 2, column 4), and to strengthen confidence in the dollar (line 2, column 5).

Line 3. US nominal interest rates declined because of declining inflationary expectations (line 2, column 4). But real interest rates remained high, and hence nominal rates stayed higher than they would have been (line 10, column 4), because of the strong rise in investment demand relative to domestic savings. This was only partially mitigated by capital inflows (line 6, column 4) and lower than normal ROW interest rates because of weak ROW investment relative to the supply of domestic savings (line 9, column 4).

Line 4. The net impact of positive and negative pressures on the dollar was strongly positive (line 10, column 5). The positive pressures came from the improved inflation performance (line 2, column 5) and high real interest rates (line 3, column 5) which attracted large capital inflows (line 6, column 5). These inflows were further encouraged by lower than normal ROW interest rates (line 9, column 5). Against this, the deterioration in the current balance increased the supply of dollars in the exchange markets, putting downward pressures on the exchange rate (line 5, column 5). Nevertheless, the dollar rose. In principle, the consequences of the rise in the dollar on the dollar itself are ambiguous (line 4, column 5); it may create expectations of a subsequent decline or further rises, as seems to have been the case on this occasion.

FIGURE 1.9 **Factors at work when investment demand rises more strongly relative to domestic savings in the United States than abroad**

Impact on United States →							
Of change in US	(1)	GNP (2)	Price level (3)	Interest rates (4)	Exchange rate (5)	Current balance (6)	Capital balance (7)
1. Domestic demand	+	+*	+	+		−*	+
2. Price level	−	+		−	+	+*	
3. Interest rates	+	−			+		+
4. Exchange rate	+		−*		?	−*	?
5. Current balance	−	−	−		−		
6. Capital balance	+			−	+		
Impact on United States →							
Of rest of world							
7. Domestic demand	Weaker					−*	+
8. Commodity prices	Weak		−				
9. Interest rates	Lower			−	+		+
10. Net change in United States		+	−	+	+	−*≡	+
Impact of above US changes on rest of world →							
Net impact							
11. GNP	+			−		+*	
12. Price level	+				+*		
13. Interest rates	+			+			+

* Quantified in D&D model.

The rise in the dollar had a negative impact on the price level* (line 4, column 3), and on the current balance through higher imports and lower exports* (line 4, column 6).

Line 5. Both the strong rise in domestic demand* (line 1, column 6) and the rise in the dollar* (line 4, column 6) caused a deterioration in the current balance which swamped the positive contribution to US competitiveness from lower inflation* (line 2, column 6). In addition, the relatively weak recovery in the rest of the world adversely affected US exports* (line 7, column 6).

Line 6. The forces working on the capital balance were all positive (column 7). They came from both relatively strong investment demand (line 1, column 7) and higher interest rates (line 3, column 7) in the United States and relatively weak investment demand (line 7, column 7) and lower interest rates (line 9, column 7) in the rest of the world.

Line 10. This line summarizes the net impact of all the above relationships on the US variables listed in columns 2 to 7. Since, on the whole, central banks were not intervening on a significant scale, the changes in the US current and private capital balance were approximately equal with opposite signs (line 10, columns 6 and 7).

Lines 11 through 13. These lines show how the changes in the US variables shown in line 10 affected the rest of the world. The growth of ROW domestic demand was curtailed by upward pressure on interest rates from the United States (line 11, column 4), but the impact of this on GNP was increasingly more than offset by rising US demand for imports* (line 11, column 6). The depreciation of ROW currencies against the dollar raised their import prices and price level* (line 12, column 5). And, as noted, high US interest rates and large capital outflows to the United States put upward pressure on ROW interest rates (line 13, column 7).

2 The Present Disequilibrium Between the United States and Its Major Allies

In Europe, they're calling it the "American miracle." Day by day we are shattering accepted notions of what is possible.[1]

The bottleneck to faster economic growth [in Europe] . . . is not inadequate demand, but an inelastic supply . . . due to deeply rooted structural rigidities at the microeconomic level.[2]

This chapter examines the origin and nature of the growing disequilibrium between the United States and its major allies.[3] It starts with the reasons for the strong recovery of investment demand in the United States, including the role of "supply-side" tax changes in the 1981 budget. It considers both the contribution that the rising dollar and increasing capital inflows have made to the "wellbeing" of the US economy as a whole, and the pain inflicted on those sectors most exposed to foreign competition. It examines the reasons for the significantly weaker recovery in the countries of the rest of the OECD area; in particular, how much this was due to their own policies and circumstances, and how much to the indirect impact of US policies and economic developments. It is suggested that a vicious circle has been at work, whereby the longer the present disequilibrium lasts, the longer it could

---

1. President Reagan (State of the Union address, 6 February 1985).

2. Juergen Donges in Layard et al. (1984, p. 62).

3. Readers primarily interested in the outlook for the future may wish to skip to chapter 3.

41

last—but also the more dangerous and damaging it has become, both to the United States and to the rest of the world.

Strong Recovery in the United States

The reasons for the strength of the 1983–84 recovery in the US economy are not hard to find—at least with the benefit of hindsight. From mid-1981, the rapid increase in the structural budget deficit gave a strong push to the economy. From August 1982, monetary policy was significantly eased as the Federal Reserve allowed M1 to rise by 13 percent over the next 12 months. Together, this was quite enough to set off a strong recovery, especially since after the prolonged 1980–82 recession there was a considerable backlog of demand for consumer durables and new investment to take advantage of rapid technological change.

Why then was the strength of the recovery not foreseen by the vast majority of observers, who could not see how it could happen with real interest rates so abnormally high? The answer is twofold. First, virtually nobody foresaw the ease with which the United States would be able to attract savings from abroad. Second, few observers correctly anticipated—or rather saw the full consequences of—the changes in company taxation made in the Economic Recovery Tax Act of 1981 (ERTA).

THE INVESTMENT-SAVINGS BALANCE

> *It is more a fiscal bust than an investment boom that has commandeered foreign capital for domestic use.*[4]

In terms of GNP growth the 1983–84 recovery was, by a small margin, the strongest since the 1950s. In terms of domestic demand, however, which rose 20 percent faster than GNP, it thoroughly beat the record (table 2.1). Domestic demand—often referred to in this study as "domestic spending"—is a relatively unfamiliar concept to most Americans. It equals GNP plus imports, less exports. The influence of monetary and fiscal policy is felt first

---

4. Bergsten and Cline (1985, p. 30).

TABLE 2.1   **Physiognomy of 1983–84 upswing**
(percentage change in volume, annual rates)

	Past recoveries		1983–84 recovery[c]
	Typical[a]	Strongest[b]	
Final domestic demand	4.6	5.5	5.9
Contribution of change in inventories[d]	+0.7	+0.4	+1.4
Total domestic demand	5.4	5.9	7.3
Contribution of net exports[d]	−0.1	0.0	−1.3
GNP	5.3	5.8	6.0
Personal consumption	5.1	6.0	5.0
Residential construction	13.2	21.5	20.5
Other fixed investment	6.9	7.4	15.0
Producer durables	9.4	10.7	18.6
Public expenditure	1.2	0.2	1.6
Exports	6.4	8.3	3.7
Imports	8.5	9.2	19.4

Source: Survey of Current Business.
a. Average over the first eight quarters of the recoveries starting in 1954:2, 1958:2, 1961:1, 1970:4, and 1975:1. The recovery starting in 1949:4 has been excluded because it was of a different nature, driven by a massive build-up of defense expenditures.
b. Over the eight quarters starting in 1970:4.
c. First eight quarters from 1982:4 recession trough.
d. As percentage of GNP in previous period, annual rate.

on domestic demand, not GNP; the consequent changes in imports and exports determine what happens to GNP.[5]

The domestic demand components that rose more rapidly than in a typical recovery were business investment, especially producers durable equipment, and additions to inventory: the share of total investment in GNP rose by over 4 percentage points (table 2.2). In retrospect, it has become clear that what was unusual was the *speed* of the pickup in investment rather than the level it reached. As a share of GNP, it began to flatten out by early 1985 at a level no higher than the previous cyclical peak (figure 1.1), leaving net investment slightly below its 1960–82 average (table 2.2).

---

5. As long as foreign trade was relatively unimportant to the US economy, and real exchange rates relatively stable, there were only quite small differences between the growth of domestic demand and GNP.

BOX 2.1   **How much did the inflow of foreign savings keep down US interest rates in 1983–84?**

The massive rise in capital inflows into the United States in 1983–84 was possible only because of an ample supply of surplus savings available in the rest of the world (chapter 1). What would have happened if, as in 1971–73, a strong and *simultaneous* upswing had occurred in the United States and the rest of the OECD area? Had there been *no* increase in capital inflows, then other things being equal, investment would have had to have risen by 18 percent less than it did; had capital inflows risen by 1 percent of GNP (as between 1970 and 1972), it would have had to have risen 12 percent less. How much would interest rates have had to have risen to hold investment down to these lower levels?

After reviewing the evidence, the CBO suggests that the average elasticity of investment with respect to interest rates, after all the effects have worked out, may be around 0.3 (1984b, table 1, weighted average of mid-range elasticities). A simulation reported by Bosworth (1984, p. 109) also suggests an elasticity of around 0.3 over five years. Combining this elasticity with the needed reduction in investment gives a range of between 3.5 to 5.5 percentage points for the necessary rise in real interest rates. These, however, are long-run elasticities. In the shorter run, expected sales have a stronger influence on investment demand than interest rates. Thus, it seems likely that if the recovery had started off as strongly as it did, interest rates would initially have had to rise by a good deal more than these figures suggest, but would have then fallen back as higher interest rates slowed down the recovery and led to a downward revision of sales expectations.

Uncertainties abound in calculations of this kind. But it seems fair to suggest that without the ample supply of surplus savings in the rest of the world, US interest rates would, for a while, have been at least 5 percentage points higher than they were at their peak.

TABLE 2.2   **US investment-savings balance during the 1983–84 upswing**
(percentage of GNP)

	1960:1 to 1982:4	1983:1	1985:1	Change, 1983:1 to 1985:1
1. Private savings	16.7	17.1	17.4	+0.3
Household savings	4.6	3.8	3.1	−0.7
Corporate savings	12.1	13.2	14.3	+1.1
2. State and local savings	0.5	1.3	1.4	+0.1
3. Private investment	15.6	12.7	17.0	+4.3
4. Surplus private savings[a]				
(1 + 2 + 7 − 3)	+1.6	+5.6	+1.6	−4.0
5. Federal deficit	−1.3	−5.8	−4.3	+1.5
6. Inflow of foreign savings				
− (4 + 5)	−0.3	+0.2	+2.7	+2.5
Memorandum items				
7. Statistical discrepancy	0.0	0.0	−0.2	−0.2
8. Capital consumption	9.4	11.7	11.0	−0.7
9. Net investment (3 − 8)	6.3	1.0	5.9	+4.9

Source: Survey of Current Business.
a. Includes state and local savings and statistical discrepancy (TN5).

The rise in investment demand was not matched by an equivalent rise in domestic savings. The household savings rate dipped in the first year of the recovery as consumers stepped up their purchases of durables; by the end of 1984 it had recovered to just under its 1960–82 average, but then began to slip again. Corporate savings, as a share of GNP, rose sharply in the first year of the recovery, but then leveled out. State and local governments ran up record surpluses to mid-1984, but then began to increase expenditures and cut taxation. The federal deficit fell, but much more slowly than in a typical recovery because of the increasing structural component in the deficit, and it began to rise again as the economy slowed from mid-1984. Taken together, this increase in domestic savings was quite insufficient, so that nearly *three-fifths of the increase in gross investment had to be financed by a rapidly rising inflow of foreign savings which, by early 1985, were financing 45 percent of US net investment* (table 2.2). Had it not been for these capital inflows, interest rates would have had to have risen sharply to choke off the rise in interest-sensitive demand—perhaps by 5 percentage points or more (box 2.1).

THE 1981 ECONOMIC RECOVERY TAX ACT

We intend . . . to bring the tax rates of every American further down, not up. If we bring them down far enough . . . the world will beat a path to our door. . . .[6]

Turning to the role of the ERTA in encouraging capital inflows, the changes made in company taxation significantly, and intentionally, raised the after-tax rate of return on new investment in real assets. This was done mainly by reducing the number of years over which such assets could be written off for tax purposes (the ACRS), but also by increasing investment tax credits for equipment. These benefits were somewhat reduced by the Tax Equity and Fiscal Responsibility Act of 1982 (TEFRA), but remained substantial.

Economists commonly analyze the impact of changes in company taxation in terms of what happens to the "user cost" of capital.[7] This is a composite measure of the cost to a company of borrowing or using its own resources to invest in a real asset, taking into account all the relevant factors such as the rate of interest, the life of the asset, tax rates, and the expected rate of inflation. Despite many conceptual and empirical problems involved in measuring user costs, different estimates of the effect of a given set of tax changes are generally of the same order of magnitude. According to the Congressional Budget Office (CBO), the combined effect of the ERTA and TEFRA was to reduce the user cost of capital by about 2 percentage points (CBO 1984b, figures 2 and 4). Bosworth (1984, figure 4-1), drawing on work by Hulten and Robertson (1983), arrived at a somewhat lower figure.

If companies can earn more from real assets, they may be prepared to pay a higher rate of interest on the money they borrow. Indeed, a suggestive piece of analysis by the CBO shows that since 1981 the reduction in user costs resulting from tax changes has been roughly offset by the subsequent rise in real interest rates (table 2.3).[8] Benderly and Zwick (1984) carry this line of reasoning a step further. Assuming full arbitrage, i.e. that after-tax

---

6. President Reagan (acceptance address, the Republican National Convention, Dallas, Texas, 23 August 1984).

7. Also often called the "rental price" of capital in the investment literature.

8. Other studies have produced a similar result. The outcome depends, however, on the method used to estimate the cost of funds, which involves serious conceptual and empirical difficulties (Bosworth 1985).

TABLE 2.3 **Sources of change in user cost of capital,**[a,b] **1980–84**
(percentage change in user cost of capital from 1980)

	1981	1982	1983	1984
Tax changes	− 12.0	− 10.0	− 10.0	− 10.0
Interest rate changes	+ 14.5	+ 12.0	− 0.5	+ 15.0
Combined effect	+ 2.5	+ 2.0	− 10.5	+ 5.0

Source: Derived from CBO (1984c), figure II-3.
a. Producers durable equipment and nonresidential structures.
b. Assuming 100 percent debt finance. For a discussion of the difficulties that arise in measuring the cost of funds when this assumption is relaxed, see Bosworth (1985).

returns on interest-bearing assets are equal to after-tax returns on real assets, they suggest that, taking into account tax changes affecting investors in both interest-bearing and real assets, changes in tax laws since the 1970s could be expected to have raised the "normal" level of the Treasury bill rate by 2.5 to 3 percentage points.

In theory, however, one might expect that as interest rates rose because of higher after-tax rates of return on real assets, savings would increase and help to dampen the rise of interest rates. But, in the context of what has been happening to world investment and savings over the past few years, perhaps the most important conclusion to be drawn from empirical research is that *there is little evidence that higher rates of return have a significant positive impact on the private savings rate,* either over the short- or longer run, in the United States or in other countries (box 2.2). Differences in the rate of return on savings in different forms and in different countries do, however, have a significant impact on the *distribution* of the flow of new savings into different uses and between different countries.

This provides the missing clue to the unexpected features of the 1983–84 upswing. One-half of the supply-side game plan worked; the other did not. Investment demand rose rapidly[9] but was not matched by a rise in domestic savings. In a closed economy, this could not have happened. Interest rates rose, but this did not bring forth a significant increase in US private savings.

9. There is, however, a continuing controversy as to just how far the changes in company taxation were responsible for the strength of the recovery in investment demand. See, for example, the discussion by Shoven, Summers, and others on Bosworth (1985) in the *Brookings Papers on Economic Activity* 1, 1985. Bosworth found no correlation between growth in specific categories of investment and the magnitude of the tax gains.

BOX 2.2   Savings, interest rates, and tax incentives

Surprising though it may seem, there is very little solid evidence
that higher interest rates or tax incentives for savings lead to
increased savings. A priori, the influence of a higher rate of
return on savings is ambiguous. With a higher rate of return,
people may save more and consume less (substitution effect), or
they may save less because they will need less savings to provide
them with a given income in the future (income effect). Empirically, results showing a positive correlation between rates of
return and savings are generally very sensitive to model specifications and periods covered, so much so that after reviewing
recent work on the subject, Bosworth (1984) concluded: ''As-
sertions that an increase in the rate of return on capital will or
will not raise the overall private saving rate must be based on
personal beliefs, because the existing empirical evidence must be
judged as inconclusive.''

Recent events have provided a historically unique test of the
proposition that higher rates of return will lead to increased
savings, with largely negative results. Since 1979, the rate of
return on savings in the United States has risen dramatically
owing to a rise of several percentage points in real interest rates,
and to numerous tax incentives introduced by the first Reagan
administration (reduction in the top marginal tax rate from 70
percent to 50 percent, enhanced IRAs, etc.). But, while the
private sector's savings rate has risen somewhat, it is still within
its historical range of fluctuation (figure 1.1).

Tanzi and Sheshinski (1984) have recently put forward an
additional explanation for this disappointing result. Higher interest
rates raise income on past as well as new savings; and retired
people living on past savings are most likely to respond to higher
income by spending more rather than saving more. This thesis
gains support from the fact that the share of interest income
reported to the Internal Revenue Service by those over 65 years
of age rose from 20 percent to 51 percent between 1973 and
1982.

> International studies confirm the impression that a country's savings rate is determined by factors deeply imbedded in its economic, demographic, sociological, and institutional structure and is little influenced by differences in rates of return (Sturm 1983). The savings rate may, however, show secular changes, as, for example, in Japan, and be subject to somewhat erratic short-term fluctuations within a relatively narrow range, as, for example, in Europe (figure 6.7). Changes in real rates of return do, however, appear to be a significant factor in countries suffering from hyperinflation when, following a stabilization program, real interest rates swing from strongly negative to strongly positive.

The tax changes did, however, make it easier for US investors in real assets to live with higher interest rates on financial assets and made it possible for investment demand—and the US economy—to recover rapidly at a higher level of interest rates than in the past, thus making it easier to attract an inflow of foreign savings.

Difficulties abound in comparing company tax rates across countries. Recently, however, a painstaking collective effort has been made to compare the effective tax rates on new investment in four countries (King and Fullerton 1984). The main results are summarized in figure 2.1.[10] Three points are of interest:

• All four countries have been cutting the effective tax rate on new investment, most notably the United Kingdom.[11]

• The combined effect of the ERTA and the TEFRA did no more than move the US effective marginal tax rates down into the middle of the four-country range.

---

10. This study attempts to measure the influence of all forms of taxation on the effective marginal tax rate on income from capital. The results shown are for the overall economy based on actual inflation, actual depreciation, actual weights, and assuming a common pretax real rate of return in the four countries (King and Fullerton 1984, table 7.1).

11. Although Japan was not included in this study, recent work along similar lines by Noguchi (1985) shows that the reverse has been true there. See the discussion of Japan in chapter 7.

FIGURE 2.1   **The Economic Recovery Tax Act and marginal rates of company taxation, four countries, 1960–82**

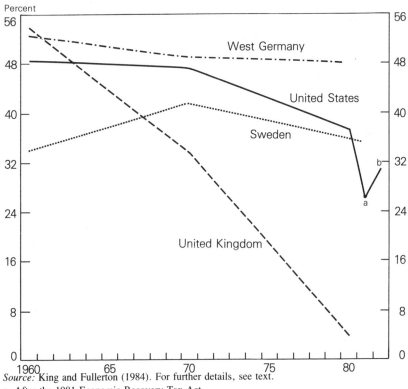

Source: King and Fullerton (1984). For further details, see text.
a. After the 1981 Economic Recovery Tax Act.
b. After the 1982 Tax Equity and Fiscal Responsibility Act.

• It did, however, represent a rather sudden change; other countries phased in such changes over a number of years.

It will be argued in chapter 3 that changes in company taxation of this kind are unlikely to have a significant *lasting* impact on the flow of savings between countries. But they may well have played a role in 1982–84 because they involved a rather *sudden* change in US company taxation, and because they occurred at a time when there was an ample supply of surplus savings in the rest of the world.

"PERFORMANCE" VERSUS "WELLBEING"

The large capital inflow was responsible for two other unusual features of the recovery:

- It both generated and was encouraged by a strong rise in the dollar. This helped to reduce the price of imports and also put strong downward pressure on prices in industries competing with imports in the US market and with foreign competitors in US export markets (figures 2.3 and 2.4). In the D&D model, following the results of other studies, each rise of 10 percent in the IMF index of the nominal effective value of the dollar lowers the US price level by around 1.5 percent.[12] Simulations with the model thus suggest that the US annual inflation rate would have been about 1.5 percentage points higher in 1981–84, and the US price level in 1984 would have been 5.5 percent higher, if the dollar had remained at its 1980:3 level. This is broadly in line with several other estimates.[13]

- The rising inflow of foreign savings enabled Americans to buy more than they were producing; thus, domestic spending rose 20 percent faster than GNP over the first two years of the recovery.

It seems reasonable to suppose that people's sense of economic well-being is determined more by what they spend than what they produce.[14] Equally, it seems reasonable to suppose that, when people assess the adverse impact of inflation on their economic wellbeing, they do not take account of the way an appreciating exchange rate has been holding down prices. Thus, in these two ways, the inflow of foreign savings has created a sense of economic well-being in the United States not fully justified by the performance of the economy, as measured by the growth of *domestically produced* output and *domestically generated* inflation.[15]

For the purposes of this study, indicators of "performance" and "wellbeing" have been devised (table 2.4 and box 2.3). Different methods of calculation would produce somewhat different results, but the message is

12. TN1, paragraph 27.

13. See, for example, Solomon (1985c, table 5).

14. At least as long as they do not have to pay back the borrowed money and can borrow more to cover the rising interest costs—which is, for the moment, the position of the United States vis-à-vis its foreign creditors.

15. As defined in TN11.

BOX 2.3   **The contribution of external factors to economic wellbeing**

Table 2.4 illustrates the important contribution that external factors made to economic wellbeing in the United States in 1981–84. These benefits accrue to the overall economy. A strongly rising real exchange rate has, as discussed in the text, a sharply differentiated impact *within* the economy, benefiting those sectors not exposed to foreign competition much more than those that are.

The method of constructing and normalizing the wellbeing and performance indicators is described in a footnote to the table. Using a different norm would alter the *level* of the two indicators but not the relation between them. The performance indicator has been constructed giving the same weight to a 1 percent above or below norm growth of GNP (positive) as to 1 percent above or below norm domestic inflation (negative), and similarly for the "wellbeing" indicator. Different people may well give different weights to growth and inflation in making such an evaluation. Again, however, while this would change the figures for the performance and wellbeing indicators, it would not greatly alter the relation between them.

As constructed, the "performance" indicator will differ from the "wellbeing" indicator only if either the exchange rate or the current balance (or both) change in real terms. Thus, averaged out over the cycle, there should be little difference between the two indicators unless the underlying structure of the country's balance of payments position has changed (for example, because of a major natural resource discovery, rapid industrialization, or a permanent shift in the terms of trade).

The present system of flexible exchange rates appears to be prone, however, to large swings in real exchange rates of an essentially cyclical nature (chapter 1). The result has been far larger and more persistent divergences between performance and wellbeing than in earlier periods. This has been equally true for the ROECD area (table 2.7).

TABLE 2.4   **Economic performance and wellbeing in US economy, role of external factors, 1980–84**
(percentage change and percentage deviation from "norm")

	1981	1982	1983	1984	1980–84 average
1. Output (GNP)	2.5	−2.1	3.7	6.9	2.8
2. Domestic inflation[a]	10.5	7.4	4.7	4.3	6.7
3. *"Performance"* (1 − 2 + 2.0)	−6.0	−7.5	+1.0	+4.6	−2.0
4. Domestic spending	3.1	−1.2	5.0	8.7	3.9
5. Actual inflation	9.1	5.5	3.5	3.2	5.3
6. *"Wellbeing"* (4 − 5 + 2.0)	−4.0	−4.7	+3.5	+7.5	+0.6
7. Contribution of external factors (6 − 3)	+2.0	+2.8	+2.5	+2.9	+2.6

Note: The performance indicator is calculated by subtracting domestic inflation from the growth of output and adding the amount by which inflation exceeded GNP on average over the years 1960–82 (2.0 percentage points). A positive figure indicates that the "performance" of the economy was better than the historical average, and vice versa. The wellbeing index is constructed in the same way using actual inflation and the growth of domestic spending. For definitions, see TN11. See also box 2.3.
Source: OECD data base.
a. An estimate, derived from the D&D model, of what the rate of inflation would have been if the exchange rate had remained constant in real terms at the 1980 level (TN11).

clear. Over 1981–84, external factors related to the inflow of foreign savings have made a major contribution to raising the wellbeing indicator well above the performance indicator, by an average of 2.6 percentage points. In the first two years, this external contribution to wellbeing was more than offset by below normal domestic performance, in particular the high rate of inflation. But in 1983, and especially 1984 with the sharp drop in inflation, rapid output growth, and a continuing strong positive contribution from external factors, the wellbeing indicator rose to a postwar peak, more than 7 percentage points above its 1960–82 average. Correction of the present US internal and external savings deficiency will, however, involve a major swing from a positive to a negative contribution from external factors at some point in the future, as discussed in later chapters (figures 4.6 and 4.7).

THE DAMAGE DONE BY THE STRONG DOLLAR

The dollar's strength . . . is altering the character of the American economy in a basic and, in my view, undesirable way.[16]

Our basic position is that the dollar is not overvalued, and the dollar is not undervalued. We happen to believe in markets here.[17]

To this point, we have been concerned with the wellbeing of Americans as consumers; as producers the story has been very different. Borrowing from Disraeli, it would hardly be going too far to talk about: "Two nations . . . dwellers in different zones . . . not governed by the same laws"[18]—who compete against foreigners, or do not.

Since 1980, when the dollar began its vertiginous rise, the volume of US imports of goods and nonfactor services rose 48 percent by 1984, while the volume of US exports fell by nearly 10 percent. Imports on this definition rose from 7.5 percent to 10 percent of GNP, while the export share fell from 11 percent to 9 percent; the trade balance deteriorated by the equivalent of 4.4 percent of GNP.[19]

This is a totally new experience for the United States. True, a small fraction of domestic demand has typically spilled abroad early in an upswing, but normally this has been reversed by the end of the second year as recovery picked up steam in the rest of the world. This time there has been a massive and steadily increasing spillover (figure 2.2).

Inevitably, sectors of the economy exposed to foreign competition at home and abroad have fared very much less well than those sheltered from such competition by the nature of their markets. Among the hardest hit have been:

• Farm and other primary and intermediate products, such as chemicals and base metals, where US producers are price takers and have had to adjust

---

16. Secretary of State George P. Shultz (1985).

17. Richard W. Rahn, vice president and chief economist at the US Chamber of Commerce, the *National Journal*, 23 February 1985, p. 412.

18. Benjamin Disraeli, *Sybil: Or the Two Nations*, vol. 1, ch. 3 (London: Henry Colburn, 1845).

19. All figures in constant 1972 prices. The deterioration in the US current balance has been greater in volume terms than at current prices (as shown elsewhere in this study) because of the improvement in the terms of trade resulting largely from the appreciation of the dollar.

FIGURE 2.2   **Spillover abroad of US domestic demand, 1982–85**

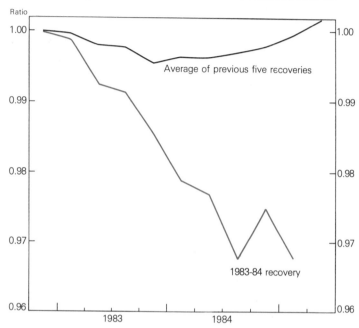

Note: Ratio of index of GNP to index of domestic demand, 1982:4 = 100.
Source: Survey of Current Business.

their export (and, frequently, also domestic) prices to the fall in dollar-denominated world market prices. Agriculture provides a vivid illustration. Exports, accounting for 31 percent of production in 1981, are projected by the Department of Agriculture at \$33.5 billion in 1985, a drop of 23 percent from 1981. Despite a sharp rise in Commodity Credit Corporation loans and payments, bankruptcies have been mounting rapidly as farmers have been unable to service debt incurred during the 1970s. Although other factors have been at work, it seems clear that the strength of the dollar has played a key role in this dismal performance by what is, after all, the world's most efficient farm economy.[20]

---

20. According to a study by the US International Trade Commission, 88 percent of the decline in farm exports in the years 1981 and 1982 was due to the appreciation of the dollar.

TABLE 2.5   **Deterioration in US trade balance, 1980–84[a]**
(percentage change and billion dollars)

	Exports (percentage change)	Imports (percentage change)	Trade balance (billion dollars)		
	1980–84		1980	1984	Change
Total trade	−1	+33	−24.6	−107.9	−83.3
Selected categories					
Agricultural products	−10	+14	+23.9	+18.0	−5.9
Manufactured goods	−1	+77	+18.8	−78.4	−97.2
Capital goods	−1	+102	+43.0	+12.2	−30.8
Electrical machinery and parts	+31	+126	+2.4	−4.5	−6.9
Computers and office machines	+68	+272	+5.8	+3.8	−2.0
Automotive products	+30	+97	−11.2	−32.9	−21.7
Consumer goods	−18	+74	−18.2	−46.7	−28.5
Clothing	−33	+111	−5.2	−12.7	−7.5
"High technology" goods[b]	n.a.	n.a.	28.0	9.0	−19.0

Source: NAM (1985), figures 1C and 1D.
a. At current prices; imports, customs value.
b. Commerce Department definition no. 3. Includes products included in other categories.

• Many traditional industries have also fared badly. The list of those whose output at the end of 1984, after two years of strong recovery, was still *lower* than in 1980 includes railroad and farm equipment, paint, leather products, cotton fabrics, carpeting, major electrical equipment, and basic chemicals.[21] The traditional industries would, in any case, have had to face strong competition from the newly industrializing countries (NICs). Several of these industries—notably textiles and clothing, automobiles, and steel—benefited from a significant degree of protection. Even with protection against Japan, however, the trade balance in automotive products deteriorated by $22 billion between 1980 and 1984, while the balance for consumer goods, excluding automobiles, deteriorated by $28 billion (table 2.5).

• More surprising have been the inroads made in sectors where the United States is traditionally highly competitive in world markets. In 1980, exports

21. Morgan Guaranty World Financial Markets (1985, table 7).

FIGURE 2.3 **Impact of price competition from imports, 1981–85**
(indices 1981:1 = 100)

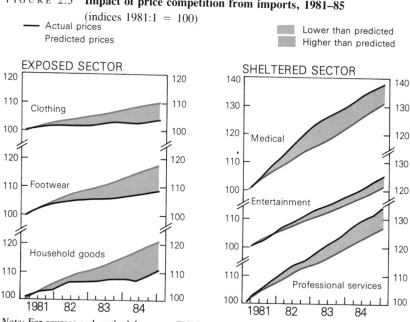

Note: For sources and methodology, see TN15.
Source: DRI data base.

of capital goods were more than double imports; by 1984, the positive balance had shrunk from $43 billion to $12 billion and, according to the Commerce Department, may have become negative in 1985.[22] In products classified as "high technology," an export surplus of $28 billion had dwindled to $9 billion. Exports of electrical equipment and parts (including semiconductors), for example, were up 31 percent, but imports had more than doubled; exports of office, computing, and accounting machines were up 68 percent, but imports had risen 272 percent. As evidenced in company reports, in these highly competitive sectors the rise in the dollar has been a powerful factor shifting sourcing and production abroad.[23]

---

22. NAM (1985, p. 6).

23. Capital expenditure by majority-owned US affiliates abroad in manufacturing, which dropped 30 percent between 1980 and 1983, rose by 6 percent in 1984 and is planned to rise 22 percent in 1985 (*Survey of Current Business*, March 1985, p. 24).

The cutting edge dividing the "two nations" was price competition from foreign suppliers. This emerges vividly from figure 2.3. By the fourth quarter of 1984, for example, consumer prices for clothing, household goods, and footwear—all exposed to strong foreign competition—appear to have been from 6 percent to 10 percent lower than if they had followed their normal historical relationship to the general rise in consumer prices since 1981. On the other hand, with little or no foreign competition, prices for entertainment, professional, and medical services appear to have been from 3 percent to 6 percent higher than predicted on the same historical basis.

The structural distortions in the US economy resulting from the strong dollar also show up clearly, albeit less dramatically, at a broader level of disaggregation. In general terms, most goods are exposed to foreign competition while most services and construction activities are not.[24] Dividing the economy into two sectors along these lines, and comparing what has actually happened since 1980 with what might have been predicted on the basis of historical relationships (TN24), we find that:

• Somewhat surprisingly, there is little evidence that the share of the exposed sector in the *volume* of total output has been adversely affected.[25]

• There is, however, clear evidence of the impact of foreign price competition. By the first quarter of 1985, prices in the exposed sector were 2 percent below and in the sheltered sector 2 percent above the predicted levels (figure 2.4).

• This price competition had a magnified impact on profits which were as much as $20 billion—or around 20 percent—above and below projected levels in the two sectors by early 1985.

• There is little evidence that the exposed sector was able to mitigate this profit squeeze by holding down wages (TN24). But it appears to have been

---

24. There are important exceptions that tend to blur the analysis. As noted, automobiles have been sheltered from Japanese competition, and defense and space spending should probably also be treated as largely sheltered. In both these sectors production was up 37 percent in 1980–84, while total industrial ouput rose only 11 percent. Within industry, utilities, building materials, petroleum refining, etc., benefit from considerable "natural" protection. On the other hand, some services—for example, tourism and transport—are subject to varying degrees of foreign competition. Using a more sophisticated disaggregation would no doubt show more sharply divergent trends.

25. A similar finding has been reported by Lawrence (1984) and Solomon (1985c). In part, however, it reflects the strong performance of automobiles and defense-related industries.

FIGURE 2.4   **The dollar and structure of US economy, 1981–85**

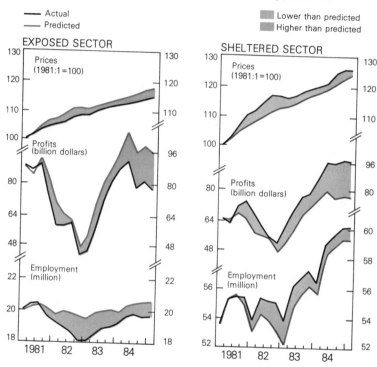

Note: For sources and methodology, see TN15.

able to get some relief by shedding labor and raising productivity. By early 1985, employment in the exposed sector was around 4 percent lower, and productivity 4 percent higher, than predicted. Labor shedding accelerated the longer term trend decline in the exposed sector's share in total employment, leaving it with about 1 million fewer jobs—and the sheltered sector with 1 million more jobs—than could have been expected on past behavior.

There have thus been both pluses and minuses from the strong dollar at the microeconomic level. Foreign competition has prompted productivity gains in the exposed sector that may well persist. It may have helped to bring about some desirable changes in relative wages within the exposed sector. On the other hand, it has generated strong protectionist pressures that the administration has not always been able to resist. Moreover, the strong adverse impact on profitability is bound, over time, to have a negative impact on investment, innovation, and productivity in the exposed sector and lead to irreversible decisions to locate new production facilities abroad. This will make it all the more difficult to boost exports and compete more effectively with imports when the dollar goes down.

Structural change always involves costs: skills become redundant, plant is written off, people have to move. Normally, these costs are well worth the benefits. But much of the structural change generated by the prolonged overvaluation of the dollar will have to be *reversed* when the time comes to restore the US trade balance to a sustainable level. In the scenarios discussed in later chapters, this would require the creation of something like 0.5 million to 1.5 million new jobs in the exposed sectors (compared to job losses of 0.75 million in 1980–84). Growth in the sheltered sectors would, on the other hand, slow down sharply.[26] In other words, many lost jobs will have to be recreated, while many recently created jobs will be lost; closed factories will have to be reopened, while new companies in the service sector go broke; families that moved and bought homes will have to sell out and move on again.

There is no satisfactory way of measuring the many economic and social costs involved. All that can be said is that they will have been very heavy, will have served no good purpose, and could have been avoided by more internationally consistent macroeconomic policies and a better functioning international monetary system.

Weak Recovery in Europe and Japan

> *As we continue to draw so heavily on world savings there is a drag on internally generated expansion elsewhere . . .*[27]

The main features of recovery in the ROECD area have been in most respects exactly the obverse of those in the United States:

---

26. In the "hard-landing" scenario discussed in chapter 4, domestic spending is no higher in 1988 than in 1984, compared with a 14 percent rise in 1982–84.

27. Volcker (1985a, p. 10).

FIGURE 2.5 **Unemployment in United States and rest of OECD area,
1970–84** (percentage of total labor force)

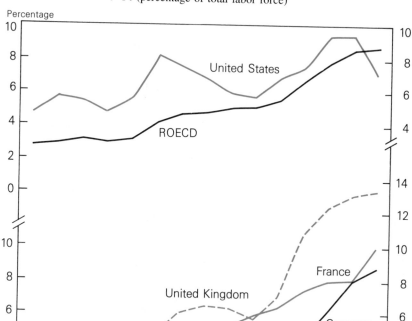

Note: 1984 figures are fourth quarter, seasonally adjusted. Figures for France, Germany, and the United Kingdom have been adjusted by the OECD to preserve continuity through time and conform to the definitions of the International Labor Organization.

Source: OECD Economic Outlook, no. 37, June 1985.

• It has been the weakest recovery since World War II. Domestic demand rose by under 6 percent over the three years following the 1981 trough, compared with nearly 12 percent during the recovery following the first oil shock—which was itself less robust than the previous postwar recoveries.

• ROECD unemployment rose by 1.2 percentage points, to 8.8 percent between 1982 and the second half of 1984, whereas in the United States it fell by 2.5 points to 7.3 percent (figure 2.5). Indeed, using US terminology, it could best be described as a "growth recession" rather than a recovery—unemployment was higher in 1984 than in 1982 in all ROECD countries except Sweden.

• There was virtually no recovery in the share of investment in GNP which, in 1984, was still 10 percent below its 1979–80 level—and as much as 20 percent below its 1972–73 peak (figure 1.2). The only really dynamic source of demand was net exports (figure 6.1).

• With the sharp decline in ROECD currencies against the dollar adding to inflation, and domestic spending rising less fast than GNP, the contribution of external factors to the "wellbeing" of the rest of the OECD area was strongly negative (table 2.7). Thus, while ROECD performance measured in terms of GNP growth and domestically generated inflation improved steadily, and was slightly above its 1960–82 average by 1984, the wellbeing index was extremely negative in 1981–83, and still 1 percent below this norm in 1984.

It is no doubt partly because of the persistence of such stark contrasts that many observers have sought to find the explanation in some fundamental differences between the United States and other economies. Thus, it was increasingly argued that the US economy is intrinsically more dynamic and flexible than most others, and it is this, combined with tax incentives and new leadership, that explains why it has enjoyed such a strong noninflationary expansion, and left the others so far behind. As President Ronald Reagan put it:

The American economy is like a race horse that has begun to gallop out in front of the field. Other nations, hobbled by high tax rates and weighed down by oversized government spending, have been slow to catch up.[28]

In less colorful language, the International Monetary Fund, in seeking to discount the importance of fiscal stimulus, has argued:

In the United States, expansion has owed much to declines in inflation and in interest rates, as well as to improvements in fiscal incentives and in the flexibility

---

28. Remarks on the trading floor of the New York Stock Exchange, 28 March 1985.

with which US markets have functioned. In Europe, by contrast, recovery has been retarded by structural factors, including high wage costs (relative to output prices) and other market rigidities.[29]

These are dubious arguments. Inflation dropped sharply in other OECD countries and was lower in Germany and Japan than in the United States; so were nominal and real interest rates. The fiscal incentives may have done more to help the US economy live with high real interest rates than to stimulate investment (as discussed above). Market flexibility does not, in itself, create demand; neither do market rigidities (or high wage costs) inhibit demand. They do, however, affect the *response* of the economy to increased demand. Could they therefore explain the much weaker recovery of investment demand in other OECD countries than in the United States? In theory, yes. In practice, it is surprising that there was not an even sharper dichotomy in investment behavior. Most research shows that rising demand is a key determinant of investment; but, from 1982 to 1984, domestic demand in OECD Europe rose by less than 3 percent, and in Japan by only 6 percent, whereas in the United States it rose by nearly 15 percent.[30]

Moreover, in assessing explanations for what happened based on the dynamism of the US economy, it is well to remember that, as recently as 1983, it was widely suggested that the United States had serious structural problems, was suffering from poor management, and was losing its technological leadership. That views on this subject should have swung around so sharply in the short span of two years suggests that present admiration for the good features of the US economy is as exaggerated as the earlier denigration. We are, after all, trying to explain striking differences in such basic macroeconomic phenomena as domestic demand, unemployment, and inflation over a relatively short period. It seems far more plausible that it is these macroeconomic differences which largely explain the changing views about the dynamism or lethargy of the respective economies, rather than the other way around. This is not to deny that there are structural problems, especially in Europe (chapter 6). These cannot, however, explain the weakness

---

29. IMF (1985, p. 9).

30. In terms of total demand, the divergence was somewhat less marked. It has been suggested, however, that business in Europe and Japan hesitated to invest in response to strong export demand from the United States because it was thought to be based on an unrealistically strong dollar and was not likely to last long (and, in Japan's case, because of fear of US protectionism).

of domestic demand, not only in Europe, but also in Japan whose economy can hardly be thought to be less dynamic than that of the United States.

FISCAL AND MONETARY POLICY

The crowning irony of this first recovery of the post-Keynesian era is that the sharply divergent performance between the United States and its major allies can be explained quite easily in terms of conventional Keynesian demand analysis. Measured by changes in structural budget deficits, fiscal policy has been steadily moving in a restrictive direction in the ROECD area since as far back as 1979. For the ROECD area as a whole, this shift amounted to 2 percent of GNP by 1985. Taking Japan, Germany, and the United Kingdom together, it amounted to as much as 4 percent of GNP, i.e. more than the shift in the opposite direction in the United States (figure 2.6).

It is a remarkable measure of the present state of confusion about macroeconomic policy that this obvious explanation has been so steadfastly rejected by the governments principally concerned. It is also fascinating that this clear confirmation of the impact of fiscal policy on demand has occurred at a time when economists who claim that it has no such impact have been gaining a wider audience, and when econometricians have been steadily revising downward their estimates of fiscal multipliers (TN16).

The divergence in fiscal policy was not, however, the whole story. Figure 2.7 compares the performance of the ROECD area in the two post-oil shock recoveries starting in 1975 and 1981. From the second panel it can be seen that, in contrast to the restrictive stance since 1979, fiscal policy was strongly expansionary in 1975 and to a lesser extent again in 1978. But from the bottom panel it can be seen that there was also a major difference in monetary policy, at least as measured by real long-term interest rates: in 1981–84, they were strongly positive and rose to over 5 percent as inflation subsided, whereas, in 1975–78, they were initially negative, and only rose to around 2 percent as inflation subsided.

Fiscal restraint and high interest rates together, applying typical fiscal and monetary multipliers (TN16), could more than explain the weakness of domestic demand in 1981–84 compared with 1975–78. At the same time, however, the rest of the OECD area benefited from a stronger stimulus from external demand in the more recent recovery: in terms of net exports, the direct boost to GNP amounted to around 3.5 percent of GNP over the five

FIGURE 2.6 **Fiscal policy on opposite courses, 1979–85**

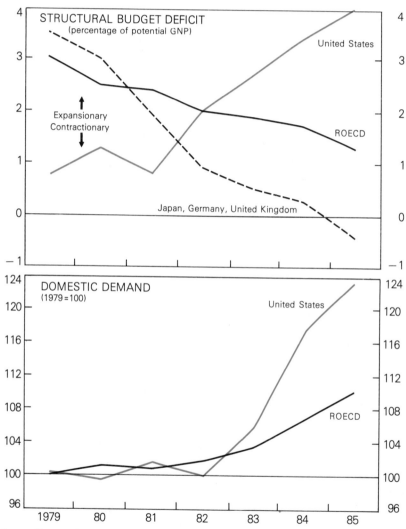

Source: Top panel, see TN6; bottom panel, OECD data base.

TABLE 2.6   Factors affecting growth in rest of OECD area, 1980–84

	1980	1981	1982	1983	1984	1980–84
External demand[a] from						*Cumulative*
United States	−0.1	+1.2	+1.0	+0.4	+1.2	+3.7
Other	+0.8	0.0	−1.0	+0.2	−0.2	−0.2
Fiscal policy[b]	−0.5	−0.1	−0.3	−0.3	−0.5	−1.7
						Average
High interest rates[c]	+0.7	+4.0	+5.1	+5.7	+6.0	+4.3

a. Estimated change in net exports in volume terms from previous year as percentage of GNP. Changes in total ROECD net exports were derived from estimates of changes in ROECD GNP and domestic demand given in *OECD Economic Outlook*. The change vis-à-vis the United States was estimated by applying the ROECD share of changes in the US trade balance at current prices, taken from US trade statistics, to the volume change in US net exports as a percentage of GNP estimated by the OECD, and scaling this to ROECD GNP. "Other" was obtained as a residual.

b. Change in structural budget deficit from previous year as percentage of GNP (TN6).

c. Deviation of real long-term interest rates from their average in the previous upswing, 1975–1979 (TN10).

years from the onset of the second oil shock (table 2.6), compared with 2.0 percent following the first. Applying typical multipliers for the feedback from external demand to domestic demand, and combining this with the fiscal and monetary impact, gives a reasonably good quantitative explanation of the difference between strengths of the two recoveries in terms of these three factors.

True, however, depending on exactly how one does the sums, one is left with the impression that domestic demand was, if anything, weaker than can be explained by this arithmetic. The most uncertain and controversial element is the weight to be given to high real interest rates. Some would argue, drawing especially on US experience, that earlier estimates of the negative impact of interest rates on investment demand should be revised downward. The difficulty is that there is strong evidence that the deterrent effect of high interest rates depends to an important extent on expected sales. In other words, a good case can be made that high interest rates did have a significant negative impact in the rest of the OECD area precisely because of the weakness of overall—and especially domestic—demand. Weighing the dif-

FIGURE 2.7 **Rest of OECD area, two recoveries compared, 1975–78 and 1981–84**

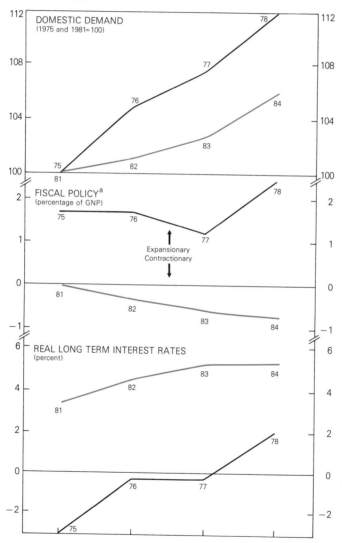

Source: Top panel, *OECD Economic Outlook;* middle, see TN6; bottom, see TN10.
a. Cumulative change in structural budget position from 1974 and 1980.

ferent arguments, it would seem that the main reason for the weakness of the recovery was that the growth of demand never reached the threshold at which a strong pickup in investment demand could have been expected; and that the main reason for this was both the restrictive stance of fiscal policy and the high level of interest rates.

This brings us to the most controversial question: why were real interest rates so high? And, in particular, was this mainly due to domestic factors or, rather, to the impact of high US interest rates transmitted to other countries through the international financial markets?

There was one domestic factor of importance: the greater emphasis most countries gave to monetary restraint in trying to contain inflation after the second oil shock.[31] But this shift in monetary policy does not explain why real interest rates *remained* high, and indeed rose further, in 1983–84. By that time, with inflation coming down quite fast, but with unemployment still rising, there was a fairly widespread tendency for the monetary authorities to operate at the upper end of their monetary targets.

This has led a number of observers to try to explain the persistence of high interest rates in terms of the persistence of large budget deficits; a line often taken by the governments concerned. At its most general, the argument is that high real interest rates reflected a worldwide shortage of savings, to which the large budget deficits in the industrial countries have made an important contribution (de Larosière 1982). This argument presents a number of serious difficulties. In the first place, it is hard to talk about a worldwide shortage of savings at a time when there has been an unusually large margin of surplus private savings in the rest of the OECD area and, more recently, in many parts of the developing world (chapter 1). Second, actual ROECD budget deficits were not much larger, as a percentage of GNP, than they had been after the first oil shock (figure 1.2) when interest rates were unusually low (figure 2.7). More important, ROECD *structural* budget deficits were—in contrast to 1975–78—being reduced; and since this, in itself, helped to improve the domestic investment-savings balance, one would have expected to see lower, not higher, real interest rates.

It has been further argued, however, that the explanation for high interest rates lies not so much in large current budget deficits as in the rapid rise in

---

31. Indeed, there would probably be a fair measure of agreement that, whatever the reason for high interest rates after the second oil shock, the low and often negative real interest rates in 1975–77 after the first oil shock can be seen, at least in retrospect, as evidence that monetary policy was too easy during this period.

public debt resulting from previous deficits.[32] This raises complex and controversial issues discussed further in chapter 6. The main point that should be noted here is that it is hard to disentangle the possible impact of the buildup of public debt from the influence of high US interest rates and the rising dollar.

Other domestic explanations for high interest rates in ROECD countries have been put forward based on improved profitability of new investments, reduced risk premiums, and deregulation. Blanchard and Summers, however, concluded that the empirical evidence on the importance of these factors was "mostly inconclusive" (1984, p. 315), and a similar conclusion was reached by Atkinson and Chouraqui (1985, p. 41).

THE IMPACT OF US POLICIES

This brings us to the arguments that would explain abnormally high ROECD real interest rates largely in terms of the high level of US interest rates and the strength of the dollar.

Some US observers have argued that whether or not this was actually the case, it need not have been. In their view, in a floating exchange rate system, other countries could have "decoupled" their interest rates from US interest rates by allowing their currencies to depreciate to the point where stabilizing speculation would have quite quickly halted the decline. This view was not, however, shared by the monetary authorities of these countries. They were concerned about the possibility of a vicious circle in which currency depreciation led to higher inflation, and higher inflation to further currency depreciation.[33] This concern, moreover, appears to have been well grounded, given the increasing tendency for floating exchange rates to overshoot (chapter 1). As James Tobin put it: "The U.S. always has a big weight in the determination of the world interest rates. These days our weight is the lion's

---

32. Muller and Price (1984b, table 11), for example, attribute more to this factor than to monetary policy, current budget deficits, or high US interest rates. Wyplosz (1984) also attributes considerable weight to a world public debt variable in trying to explain high real interest rates in six OECD countries. But see TN25, paragraph 5.

33. In Japan, the authorities were, by 1983, less concerned about inflation, but very much concerned by the protectionist pressures being generated in the United States by the undervaluation of the yen vis-à-vis the dollar.

share, because our policy-makers don't care what the exchange rate is while others do.''[34]

There remains, however, a good deal of controversy as to how far this *policy response* to the strength of the dollar can explain the abnormally high level of real interest rates in other countries. Circumstantial evidence is provided by a series of clear-cut episodes when central banks responded to weakness of their currencies by raising policy-controlled interest rates and slowing monetary growth (the Bank of Japan in March 1980; the Bundesbank in February 1981; the Bank of England in October 1981, July 1984, and January 1985). But it is less easy to marshal quantitative evidence to show that, over the period as a whole, monetary policy was significantly tighter than it would otherwise have been because of the strength of the dollar. Looking at German monetary policy, for example, the Bundesbank did operate at or below the lower end of its target range for the growth of central bank money in 1981, but in 1982 central bank money was allowed to rise a bit above the mid-point of the target range, and in 1983, it overshot the upper end of the range by a significant margin through most of the year.

It is not surprising, therefore, that econometric analysis of the various factors that might explain high ROECD interest rates have not picked up an important influence from tight monetary policies.[35] But this is by no means the end of the story. The financial markets were well aware that central banks were concerned about the weakness of their currencies, and were prepared to act on the basis of that concern. They therefore had good reason to *expect* that currency weakness would lead to higher interest rates—either because of an immediate response by the central bank or because of the inevitable response later on as inflation began to accelerate. And, since these are asset markets, such expectations tend to be self-fulfilling. In other words, a good case can be made that, as long as the dollar was expected to rise, *this expectation could itself have caused interest rates to be higher for a given rate of domestic monetary expansion than they would have been without it.*

Similar reasoning has been used to explain the high level of US interest rates, albeit in a different context. Thus, it has been argued that the persistence of high real interest rates in the United States, despite normal rates of monetary growth, can be explained at least in part by self-fulfilling expectations that future budget deficits would be so large as to force up interest rates

---

34. Tobin (1983, p. 22).

35. Wyplosz (1984), Muller and Price (1984b).

(Blanchard 1984). If this argument is accepted, however, an equally good case can be made that ROECD real interest rates were abnormally high, despite normal rates of monetary growth, because of the *expected* consequences for ROECD interest rates of the strong dollar—which, in turn, was *expected* to continue because of the *expected* consequences for US interest rates of continuing large US budget deficits. As Blanchard and Summers (1984, p. 307) put it: "It is the *divergence* in fiscal policies together with its implications for the real exchange rate and . . . monetary reaction functions that leads to high real rates."

This leads directly to the question of how far the high level of real interest rates in the industrial world as a whole should be attributed to large US budget deficits. At first sight, this is not as obvious as is often suggested. For the OECD area as a whole, the stance of fiscal policy has been broadly neutral (figure 1.8). Thus, in a world of capital mobility, upward pressure on world interest rates from rising US structural budget deficits should have been roughly offset by the impact of declining structural budget deficits in other countries. But, as just argued, a good case can be made that it was precisely this divergence in fiscal policies, together with the actual and expected response of the monetary authorities, that levered up the whole level of OECD real interest rates.

It seems likely, moreover, that the *distribution* of these high interest rates between the United States and the other OECD countries was influenced by the key role of the dollar in the international financial system. Most international intermediation transits, directly or indirectly, through US financial markets. There are thus good reasons for believing that every other currency is, in general, a closer substitute for the dollar than for any other currency. (This is, for example, a characteristic of the coefficients used in the OECD's FINLINK model.) If so, a US budget deficit attracts a larger capital inflow than deficits of similar size in other countries, and hence the equal and opposite shift in fiscal policies has not only raised OECD interest rates overall but has also resulted in higher ROECD interest rates and lower US rates than would otherwise have been the case.

To recapitulate: the most striking difference between 1975–78, when ROECD interest rates were low, and 1981–84, when they were abnormally high, is that in the first period the dollar was weak, whereas in the second US real interest rates were abnormally high and the dollar was extremely strong. There are good reasons for believing that this reflects a causal relationship running through monetary policy response, expectations, and the key role of the dollar in world financial markets. This conclusion is strengthened by the fact that other relevant factors were—with the exception of public debt to GNP ratios—either similar (for example, decelerating inflation) or could have been expected to work in the opposite direction (for example, reduced structural budget deficits).

What then has been the overall impact of US monetary and fiscal policy on the ROECD area since 1980? As might be expected, the US administration has tended to emphasize the positive impact of rising US import demand, while outside the United States more weight has been given to the negative impact of high US interest rates. Unfortunately, there is no way of giving a definitive answer. The rise in ROECD net exports to the United States (and the gains made in third markets at its expense) are measurable and have been large. Different analysts have concluded that this factor alone could have accounted for between one-third and one-half of the ROECD's GNP growth over this period.[36]

But what about high interest rates? When Hooper (1985) tried to simulate the effects of US fiscal expansion on ROECD countries using the Fed's MCM model, he found that the outcome depended entirely on the assumption made about monetary policy reaction functions in these countries. Assuming that ROECD interest rates were tied to US interest rates, the impact of US fiscal expansion on ROECD GNP was negative; assuming they were not, it was quite strongly positive.[37] Perhaps the most that can be said is that, in the early phase of the recovery, the negative impact probably outweighed the positive, but that the reverse became increasingly true in 1983–84, so that for the period as a whole the net impact was probably positive—and will remain so as long as the present stance of US policies can be maintained.

To sum up: explanations for the weak recovery in the ROECD area based on structural problems and rigidities—real as these may be—are largely beside the point, since an explanation based on the major macroeconomic factors at work on the demand side fits the facts reasonably well. It seems that the net impact of US policies on GNP growth in other countries has, on balance—and up to now—been positive. It follows that the major reason for slow ROECD growth must be found in its own macropolicies, and in particular in the restrictive stance of fiscal policy, notably in Japan, Germany, and the United Kingdom.

---

36. Applying a typical foreign trade multiplier to the net export figures shown in table 2.6 would yield a higher figure.

37. Hooper (1985) presents evidence suggesting that the linkage was quite loose, and therefore concludes that the overall impact was moderately positive.

TABLE 2.7   **Economic performance and wellbeing in rest of OECD area, role of external factors, 1980–84**

(percentage change and percentage deviation from ''norm'')

	1981	1982	1983	1984	1980–84 average
1. Output (GNP)	1.2	1.0	1.8	3.5	1.9
2. Domestic inflation[a]	10.7	7.1	5.8	5.6	7.3
3. ''Performance'' (1 − 2 + 2.5)	−7.0	−3.6	−1.5	+0.4	−2.9
4. Domestic spending	−0.2	0.8	1.2	2.7	1.3
5. Actual inflation	11.5	8.3	6.6	6.3	8.2
6. ''Wellbeing'' (4 − 5 + 2.5)	−9.2	−5.0	−2.9	−1.1	−4.5
7. Contribution of external factors (6 − 3)	−2.2	−1.4	−1.4	−1.5	−1.6

Note: The performance indicator is calculated by subtracting domestic inflation from the growth of output and adding the amount by which inflation exceeded GNP on average over the years 1960–82 (2.5 percentage points). A positive figure thus indicates that the ''performance'' of the economy was better than the historical average, and vice versa. The wellbeing index is constructed in the same way using actual inflation and the growth of domestic spending. For definitions, see TN11. See also box 2.3. *Source:* OECD data base.

a. Estimate, derived from the D&D model, of what the rate of inflation would have been if the exchange rate had remained constant in real terms at the 1980 level (TN11).

Going beyond this, in an important sense the whole controversy about how US policies have affected *growth* in other countries is beside the point. In terms of economic *welfare*, a rise in GNP generated by rising net exports obtained at the cost of a deterioration in the terms of trade is not a particularly good bargain. This stands out vividly from a comparison between the United States and the rest of the OECD area's ''performance'' and ''wellbeing.'' The performance of the ROECD countries, measured by GNP growth and domestically generated inflation, improved steadily and by 1984 was slightly above its 1960–82 norm (table 2.7). This performance, it is true, was less impressive than in the United States in 1984, which enjoyed an exceptional (and unrepeatable) year. But, equally important, in contrast to the United States, it was based to a large extent on rising net exports and depreciating currencies, so the ROECD's wellbeing index was still 1 percentage point below its 1960–82 norm while for the United States it was a phenomenal 7 points above (table 2.4).

The ROECD area would thus have been unambiguously better off in welfare terms if its recovery, weak as it was, had been based more on domestic demand and less on net exports.[38] Against this, it can be argued that deliberate action to boost domestic demand would have been more inflationary than an export-led recovery because of adverse effects on confidence in financial and exchange markets. This problem of an "expectations trap" is discussed in chapter 6. But the fact is that, according to virtually all existing models, increased overall demand *resulting from currency depreciation* is at least five times more costly in terms of inflation than a similar increase in domestic demand (box 4.7). In other words, a less expansionary fiscal policy in the United States, coupled with less restrictive fiscal policies in other major countries—and hence less appreciation of the dollar, could well have produced a stronger recovery in the ROECD area with a *lower* rate of inflation.

The Vicious Circle

> The market seems to be impervious to bad news when it comes from America, but skittish about any from anywhere else.[39]

> Bandwagons could be defined loosely as sustained uni-directional movements which seem to feed on themselves and are (or become) detached from actual economic conditions.[40]

The upshot of this chapter is that the striking divergence since 1982 between the excellent performance of the US economy and the disappointing performance of most other OECD economies can be largely explained by:

- the diametrically opposite stance of fiscal policy, and

- the way this has been amplified, under a flexible exchange rate system, by the interactions on exchange rates, interest rates, and inflation.

---

38. As Samuel Brittan put it, in a slightly different context: "Ministers who refuse to stimulate their own economies, but fight like tigers and tigresses for export contracts, or subsidize export credit, or try to find back-door methods of deterring imports, are being inconsistent as well as mercantilist" (Layard et al. 1984, p. 55).

39. The *Economist*, 5 May 1984, p. 72.

40. Jurgensen Report (1983, p. 10, n. 2).

But, if the explanation is this straightforward, why did it catch so many observers by surprise? Looking back, it seems likely that the main reason is that the divergence in macroeconomic performance, as it persisted, increasingly affected expectations and behavior in all sorts of unanticipated ways that tended to accentuate and perpetuate the initial divergence.

In Europe, the continuing rise in unemployment has strengthened "Europessimism" and been grist to the mill of those who believe that, because of structural rigidities, Europe has already lost out in the competitive race with Japan, the United States, and the NICs. Labor has been increasingly on the defensive, pressing claims for worksharing and shorter hours. In Germany, this led to a damaging strike in the automobile industry in May–June 1984. In the United Kingdom, the length and bitterness of the miners strike can be explained in part by the fact that, with unemployment at 13 percent, miners at uneconomic pits had no hope of finding another job. Similarly, because of high and rising unemployment, even conservative governments found themselves continuing to pay large subsidies to lame-duck industries, acquiescing in increased protectionism, introducing make-work (or "training") schemes to keep down registered unemployment, and being tempted by interventionist policies to encourage high technology industries. Against this background, it is hardly surprising that the business community was discouraged and looked longingly across the Atlantic; or that it became more interested in investing in the United States than at home.

Finally, poor economic performance had political consequences in Europe. It created generalized dissatisfaction with governments in power, of whatever complexion,[41] and hence raised doubts about the continuity of economic policies. In some countries, there has been rising concern about the possibility of a political sea-change in favor of much more interventionist and autarkic policies.

All these things helped to weaken European currencies and strengthen the dollar. And the resultant flow of savings across the Atlantic helped to sustain a strong and noninflationary recovery in the United States. Thus, by mid-1984 European newspapers and journals were flooded with articles about the superdollar and the American renaissance.[42] Even such a sober observer as

---

41. As evident, for example, in local election results in France, the United Kingdom, and Germany in the early months of 1985.

42. For example, the special issue of *L'Expansion*, "Les Etats-Unis: la puissance retrouvée," no. 247 (October/November 1984).

Fritz Leutwiler was quoted as saying: "The United States is seen by investors as young, flexible, and dynamic and Europe as old, sclerotic, and much less flexible. It is not just psychological. I think the reasoning . . . is quite correct."[43] Coming from a former President of the Swiss National Bank and the Bank for International Settlements, this judgment on a country running record budget and trade deficits was, to say the least, surprising. In the private sector, European euphoria about the US economy was more uninhibited: "Reagan's new slogan—'America is back'—is true . . . the U.S. is *numero uno* again."[44]

The same sort of vicious circle can be observed elsewhere. In the developing countries, recovery from the debt crisis has been hampered by weak commodity prices which can be traced back in part to high US interest rates and the lopsided nature of the recovery (box 6.1). High US interest rates and euphoria about the US economy also no doubt inhibited the hoped for reflux of flight capital. Enforced austerity in the debtor countries raised doubts about their social and political stability. This, in turn, has enhanced the attraction of the United States as a safe haven.

Many other examples of such economic, psychological, and political feedbacks could be given. The key point is that, in these and many other ways, the unbalanced mix of fiscal and monetary policies—both in and between the major industrial countries—created a psychological climate that accentuated and prolonged the disequilibrium they created in the world economy.[45] By the time of President Reagan's reelection in November 1984, this had generated a "bandwagon" in favor of the dollar, and the US economy more generally, that had acquired a life of its own, and began to fade only quite slowly in 1985. Thus, a constellation of macroeconomic policies which, as will be argued in the rest of this study, cannot be sustained much longer, nevertheless proved sustainable for much longer than might have been expected. This was a vicious circle: the larger the disequilibrium becomes, the more difficult and costly it will be to correct.

---

43. *Business Week*, 8 October 1984, p. 167.

44. Max Sonderegger, Director, Clarinden Bank, Zurich, Switzerland. Quoted in the *Wall Street Journal* (European edition), 15 March 1984.

45. Economic performance has been much better in Japan. Even there, however, confidence has been adversely affected by realization that a recovery based so heavily on exports is vulnerable to rising protectionism in the United States (as evidenced by the tendency of the yen to depreciate when new protectionist measures have been under discussion).

3 How Long Can It Go On?

It is very probable that the dollar will remain strong for the rest of the decade.[1]

Portfolio holder's asset preferences . . . are rarely based on any single, long-term consideration but rather on ever-shifting hopes, fears and assumptions.[2]

How much longer can the United States go on importing savings from abroad on such a massive scale? This chapter examines the characteristics of countries that have imported capital to the tune of several points of GNP over periods of five years or more. The conclusion reached is that the United States of today exhibits none of these characteristics; and that, looking to 1990 and beyond, it is likely to again become a capital exporter rather than a capital importer.

Analysis of a hypothetical baseline case shows that the capital inflows needed to keep the dollar at its level in the six months to March 1985 would have to go on rising indefinitely into the future, reaching well over 5 percent of GNP by 1990. This would have a devastating impact on the US external investment position. From being the world's largest net creditor nation in 1982, it would become the world's largest debtor nation in 1986, and by 1990 its external debt, at $1.3 *trillion*, would substantially exceed the total debt of the developing countries. Would the rest of the world be willing to lend such vast sums to the United States? The conclusion reached is that

---

1. Donald T. Regan, former Secretary of the Treasury, *Business Week*, 8 October 1984, p. 165.

2. Rimmer de Vries in Morgan Guaranty Trust Company (1984a, p. 5).

capital inflows could not possibly be large enough to maintain the dollar at its early 1985 level. And as the dollar goes down, foreigners will be exposed to severe exchange rate losses, not only on their claims on the United States, but also on their large holdings of dollar-denominated claims on other countries.

A Capital Importer or Capital Exporter?

> From . . . 1790 to 1875 this country . . . ran a trade deficit. And in those years we were becoming the great economic power that we are in the world today.[3]

The United States was a capital importer for much of the first hundred years following independence. The peak inflows were in 1866–73, immediately after the Civil War, when the ratio of external debt to GNP and debt to exports both peaked at around 25 percent.[4] This foreign borrowing was closely linked to the building of canals and railroads and the opening up of the West (Solomon 1985b). However, after another period of smaller capital inflows in the 1880s, the United States became a capital exporter before the end of the nineteenth century, and remained one for the next 75 years, becoming a net creditor nation during World War I.[5] The position began to change only in the 1970s when there were substantial inflows and outflows of capital, which just about canceled out between 1971 and 1982. Since then, the situation has changed dramatically, and by 1985, the capital inflow was approaching 3 percent of GNP, equaling the highest levels reached in the nineteenth century (table 3.1).

---

3. President Reagan, news conference, 17 September 1985.

4. Solomon (1985b), using data from Simon (1960), estimates the ratio of debt to mechandise exports at 23 percent in 1868–69, and the ratio of debt to GNP at about 25 percent at end-1873.

5. Interestingly, there was a minor exception in the mid-1930s when, with sharply rising economic and political tensions in Europe, there was a substantial inflow of private capital into the United States. This led mainly to an increase in the gold stock, rather than a large current account deficit, as the dollar was to a varying extent pegged (and imports were restrained by protectionism).

TABLE 3.1   **Historical examples of large-scale capital importers and exporters** (current account surplus or deficit as percentage of GNP)

Capital importers			Capital exporters		
		Pre-1914			
United States	1.5–2.0	(1831–39)	United Kingdom	4.0	(1860–1910)
	2.5–3.0	(1866–73)	Germany	1.6	(1870–1913)
Canada	8.0	(1890–1910)			
Australia	7.1	(1812–1910)			
Norway	3.2	(1875–1914)			
Japan	2.6	(1904–13)			
		Interwar years			
Norway	5.5	(1915–24)	United States	2.0	(1919–23)
Canada	3.5	(1920–30)	United Kingdom	2.3	(1921–29)
Australia	2.1	(1920–39)			
Italy	2.2	(1921–30)			
Japan	2.0	(1921–28)			
		Postwar years			
Korea	9.3	(1953–62)	United States	1.0	(1955–65)
Greece	5.3	(1973–85)	Netherlands	1.5	(1960–83)
Norway	11.4	(1975–78)	Germany	1.4	(1967–78)
Australia	2.8	(1960–83)	Italy	2.4	(1965–72)
Mexico	3.4	(1970–82)	Japan	1.3	(1981–84)
Brazil	4.1	(1970–82)	Saudi Arabia	30.2	(1970–81)

Source: United States, pre-WWII: Solomon (1985b). Other countries and interwar years: Kuznets (1966, table 5.3). Japan, pre-WWII: Ohkawa and Shinohara (1979, table A1). Post-WWII industrial countries: OECD data base; developing countries, IFS data base.

The US experience can be compared with that of other significant capital exporters or importers shown in table 3.1. Countries that have imported substantial amounts of capital over a period of years have tended to exhibit one of two characteristics. They have been:

• either sparsely populated countries with large unexploited natural resources, such as the United States in the the nineteenth century, Canada, Australia, and Norway

• or countries with a ready supply of good quality cheap labor in the early to middle phase of rapid industrialization such as Japan before and just after World War II, and, more recently, Korea and Brazil.

The corresponding capital outflows have tended to come from the countries that were the most industrially advanced at the time: Britain and Germany in the nineteenth century, the United States since World War I, and, more recently, Germany (again), and Japan.[6] Indeed, putting the two sides of the story together, there is a fairly well established "life cycle" whereby countries at an early stage of natural resource and industrial development start off as "young debtors" and then, as they become increasingly rich and developed, turn into "mature creditors."[7] This historical pattern was, however, temporarily interrupted in the 1970s, when there was a large shift in world savings to the OPEC countries, most industrial countries became capital importers, and the United States ceased to be a capital exporter.

These general implications from the historical record are strengthened—albeit in a somewhat roundabout way—by the results of recent research on the relationship between international capital movements and domestic propensities to save and invest. As Wallich (1984) stresses, the surprising thing is that *net* flows of savings between countries in response to differences in real rates of return on investment and propensities to save have been so small in relation to the domestic magnitudes involved. Thus, after reviewing and updating earlier work,[8] Penati and Dooley (1984, p. 22) conclude that "changes in the propensity to save or invest on the part of residents of an industrial country result in changes in that country's investment or saving share, while current account balances act as temporary shock absorbers." They confess that they cannot explain why this should be so because "a substantial part of the barriers to international mobility of goods and factors of production, which existed in the 1950s, has been phased out."

The explanation does not seem so hard to find. Contrary to the assumptions made in much academic work, there is still a strong institutional and psychological bias toward investing domestic savings in domestic assets. Moreover, as between countries at roughly the same level of development and the same endowment of labor, capital, and natural resources, differences

---

6. Major natural resource discoveries may initially generate capital inflows (for example, oil in Norway in 1975–78) but then generate surplus savings as in the Netherlands (gas) and Saudi Arabia (oil).

7. See the World Bank's *World Development Report, 1985*, pp. 47–48.

8. By Harberger (1980), Sachs (1980), Feldstein and Horioka (1980), and Feldstein (1983a).

in real rates of return are too small to overcome this bias. Only when there are major differences in factor endowments—such as unexploited agricultural or mineral potential or cheap labor—are differences in rates of return sufficient to generate sustained capital inflows.[9]

The upshot is that the United States today exhibits none of the features that have characterized persistent capital-importing countries in the past. From this broad historical perspective, it seems improbable that the United States, in a growing world economy, and in the absence of major economic or political disturbances, could or would go back to its nineteenth century status as a structural capital importer.

This conclusion would be hotly contested in some quarters, especially by staunch supporters of supply-side economics. At the broadest level, they would argue that the major change in policies and psychology brought about by the Reagan administration has significantly—and they hope permanently—raised real rates of return in the United States relative to the rest of the world. In making this case, they would emphasize such things as deregulation; increased incentives to work, save, and invest; the downplaying of environmental and income distribution concerns; the weakened position of labor unions (the PATCO effect),[10] and so on. The unexpectedly good performance of the US economy in 1983–84 lent credence to this belief in an "American renaissance"[11] both in the United States and abroad.

In rebuttal, the first point to be stressed is that, in the short and medium term, real rates of return are relevant only for direct investment, not for *financial* capital flows. Longer run changes in real rates of return can,

---

9. Thus, as a matter of fact, Penati and Dooley found that countries such as Australia, Canada, Norway, New Zealand, and Iceland were exceptions to their general rule. If their analysis was extended to include developing countries, the list of exceptions would be a lot longer, especially in the 1970s. It is true that the 1970s were unusual in that the rise in oil prices generated a sharp increase in the supply of internationally mobile savings. Significantly in the present context, however, after a temporary adjustment period, by far the larger part of these savings ended up in the more dynamic developing countries, not in the industrial countries—although they were intermediated through their capital markets.

10. After the abortive strike by the Professional Air Traffic Controllers Organization in August 1981.

11. "Rewarding hard work and risk-taking has given birth to an American renaissance. Born in the safe harbor of freedom, economic growth has rolled out on a rising tide that has reached distant shores." President Reagan (remarks to the Annual Meetings of the IMF and the World Bank, Washington, 25 September 1984).

FIGURE 3.1 **Profits, before and after taxes, five countries, 1962–83**
(percentage and percent)

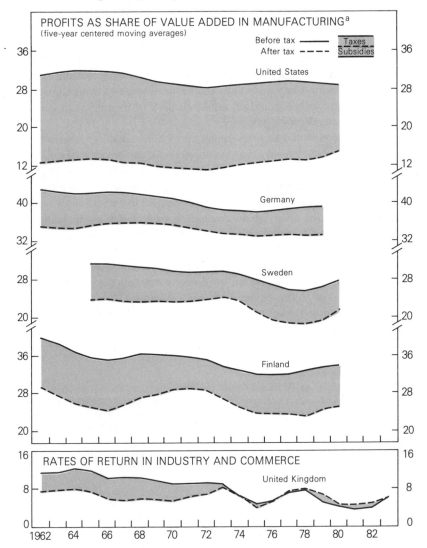

Source: OECD *National Accounts,* vol. II, and Bank of England *Quarterly Review.*

however, permanently affect the rates of interest a country can pay for imported capital. A marked increase in real rates of return, relative to other countries, could therefore make the inflow of savings sustainable over the longer term.

It is in this longer term context, however, that recent developments need to be seen in a wider historical perspective. Ever since the industrial revolution, the US economy has been more flexible, dynamic, and enterprising than most others. It may have gone through a bad patch during the 1970s and may now be heading back again. But the historical record does not suggest that such transitory fluctuations in national policies and ethos could permanently change real rates of return enough to reverse the more basic forces arising from different factor endowments. In other words, it seems unlikely that five years of Reaganomics have reversed the course of nearly a hundred years of economic history.

Another related argument is that the United States has become a "high tech NIC" riding the crest of the microchip wave. True, the application of new technologies did accelerate during the 1983–84 recovery. But postwar history offers one clear lesson, going back to the transistor radio: production based on new technology is highly mobile and gravitates quickly to countries whose factor endowments (particularly labor cost and quality) enable them to compete most efficiently in world markets. It thus seems unlikely that the recent spurt in US technological prowess could have, in macroeconomic terms, a significant and enduring effect in raising its real rates of return relative to the rest of the world.

At first sight, another strand in the "American renaissance" case carries more weight. It seems likely that the major reduction in taxes on income from new investment, enacted in the ERTA of 1981, played a role in attracting foreign savings to the United States (chapter 2). It is thus argued, in particular by McNamar (1984b) and Niskanen (1984), that the United States should and can import savings from abroad as long as these tax changes are maintained.

The record shows, however, that such tax changes can set off economic or political forces tending to erode them. In Europe, where "after-tax" wage bargaining is common, tax breaks for profits often become a target for higher wage claims—unless unemployment is very high or there is a social consensus that higher profits are desirable. In the extreme case of the United Kingdom, after-tax rates of return fell to very low levels in 1980–81 despite tax changes which by then were actually subsidizing profits (figure 3.1). Pressures on profitability from wages have been less in the United States (table 6.6), but it remains to be seen to what extent "catch-up" wage claims might eat into pretax profits if the US economy were to experience an extended period of full employment.

More important, it remains to be seen how strong the political reaction may be to these fairly radical tax changes, which reduced the share of corporate taxes in total tax revenue from 12.5 percent in 1980 to 8.5 percent in 1984. President Reagan's proposals for tax reform would reverse this trend. Supply-siders and the special interests affected have objected strongly. But the political reality is that all public opinion polls show that a large majority, asked how the budget deficit should be reduced, favors raising corporate taxes (chapter 5, footnote 14).

There is also the possibility that other countries will follow the US example. Just as their US proponents were slow to realize that the main consequence would be to help turn the United States into a large-scale importer of foreign savings, so too were foreign governments slow to realize that these changes were one reason for the unpleasant combination of high interest rates and weak currencies they have experienced since 1981. Slowly the light has begun to dawn, and other countries are considering similar tax changes. After all, if it is so easy to finance recovery with other people's savings, why not follow suit? This could, however, only lead to a "savings war" with the United States (box 7.4).

One further argument is used to justify the United States' new role as a capital importer. It is that there is no reason why America, a low-saving country wishing to grow faster, should not import capital from another country in the opposite situation, Japan. The problems posed for Japan by its high savings are discussed in chapter 6. The relevant point for the United States is that capital flows from a high-saving to a low-saving country make economic sense, and hence are sustainable over the long run, only if real rates of return are significantly higher in the United States than in Japan. But the reverse is true (Chan-Lee and Sutch 1985, and figure 6.6). In other words, the logical destination for excess Japanese savings would seem to lie not in the United States, but either at home or in the NICs and resource-rich countries, especially in the Pacific basin.

To conclude: neither history nor recent trends in the pattern of world savings and investment suggest that—having been an exporter of capital since the late nineteenth century—the United States has suddenly become a structural capital importer. The present large capital inflows mainly reflect short-term shifts in investment-savings balances likely to be reversed because they are unsustainable. Looking to 1990 and beyond, it would be surprising if the United States, as the world's richest country with a highly developed infrastructure, did not revert to its role as net supplier of savings to the rest of the world on average over the course of the cycle.[12]

The Capital Inflow Needed to Sustain the Dollar

Whatever these longer term prospects, the fact remains that the United States is currently importing savings on an unprecedented scale. How long can this go on?

As a first step, the D&D model has been simulated to give an estimate of the current account deficits that would have to be financed by capital inflows in a hypothetical "baseline case" in which the dollar stays strong, but the other negative factors cease to operate (table 3.2). In this simulation the dollar is assumed to stay at its average level in the six months to March 1985, while the growth gap between the United States and the rest of the world is assumed to be reversed, with US growth, at 3 percent, lower than hoped for by the administration.[13]

This simulation is not a forecast, simply a projection of the magnitudes involved under certain assumptions. It is nevertheless something of a shock to see that it shows a further dramatic and accelerating worsening in the US position, with the current account deficit tripling from $102 billion in 1984 to about $320 billion in 1990 (table 3.2). The basic reason for this continuing rapid deterioration is that *the starting position is so bad*. In fact, the results shown in table 3.2 depend little on the specific properties of the model used; they are mainly a matter of simple arithmetic.

In the first half of 1985, US current expenditure abroad exceeded current income by 40 percent.[14] This generates two adverse "gap" factors for the future (table 3.3):

---

12. This judgment is based on the arguments in the text. Some would argue that it would also be a desirable outcome on normative grounds; i.e. that it is appropriate for a rich developed country to export savings to poorer less developed countries.

13. For the other assumptions, see TN2. For the outcome on the assumption that the dollar stayed at its level on October 31, 1985, see note to table 3.2.

14. Goods and nonfactor services and net income from capital. Merchandise imports alone exceeded exports by 58 percent (balance of payments basis).

TABLE 3.2 **The US current balance and external indebtedness in a hypothetical baseline case, 1984–90** (billion dollars)

	1984	1985	1986	1987	1988	1989	1990
Exports of goods and nonfactor services[a]	265	270	285	315	345	375	415
Imports of goods and nonfactor services[a]	370	395	445	490	535	590	650
Net interest payments	6	−3	−16	−30	−48	−69	−94
Current balance[b]	−102	−125	−170	−205	−235	−275	−320
Net external indebtedness[c,d] (end year)	+28	−100	−270	−470	−710	−990	−1,310
Memorandum items							
Merchandise trade balance[a,e]	−108	−120	−150	−170	−185	−200	−225
GNP (current prices)[d]	3,660	3,890	4,160	4,460	4,790	5,140	5,520
Current balance as percentage of GNP	−2.8	−3.3	−4.1	−4.6	−5.0	−5.4	−5.9

Note: Simulation of D&D model, assuming the dollar stays at its average level in the six months ended March 1985. On October 31, 1985, the dollar was 11.4 percent below this baseline. If it were to stay at this level, the current account deficit would rise to $250 billion by 1990, and net external indebtedness would rise to over $1 trillion. For the other assumptions, see TN2.
a. Projections rounded to the nearest $5 billion.
b. Includes net direct investment income, military transactions, and transfers.
c. For definitions and method of projection, see TN1, paragraphs 16–19.
d. Projections rounded to the nearest $10 billion.
e. On a balance of payments basis; on the Census basis, imports c.i.f., the 1984 merchandise trade deficit was $123 billion.

● Even if current expenditure and income begin to increase at the same *rate*, instead of expenditure rising much faster than income, the gap between them continues to widen. Thus, in the baseline case, with both rising by around 10 percent from 1987, the gap between them also rises by about 10 percent— by $15 billion in 1987 and over $20 billion in 1990. This may seem an odd piece of arithmetic. But it reflects a reality that other countries have discovered to their cost, especially recently in Latin America: once a large trade and current account deficit has opened up, it takes a very sharp reduction in the growth rate of imports *relative* to exports to start a move back toward equilibrium.

TABLE 3.3 Adverse factors at work on current balance in baseline case
(change from previous year, billion dollars)

	1985	1986	1987	1988	1989	1990
The "gap" factors						
Existing deficit	−14	−13	−15	−16	−19	−22
Net interest payments	−9	−13	−14	−18	−21	−24
Lagged impact of rise in dollar						
1982–84[a]	−21	−18	−4	0	0	0
Total[b]	−44[c]	−44	−33	−34	−40	−46

Note: Simulations of D&D model.
a. Assumes dollar at 1984:4–1985:1 level and full effects felt in three years.
b. Excludes net direct investment income, transfers, and military transactions.
c. The projected deficit rises by only $25 billion in 1985 because the gap factors are offset by adjustments for the cessation of some other adverse factors thought to have been at work in 1984 (TN1).

• As long as current expenditure exceeds current income, the United States is running down its net assets and hence losing investment income from abroad. By 1990, the loss would be as much as $100 billion compared with 1984 (table 3.2, third line).[15]

• A third factor aggravates the operation of these gap factors: the lagged adverse effect on the trade balance still to come from the appreciation of the dollar in 1983–84, estimated using the D&D model at around $40 billion in 1985–87 (table 3.3). This, in turn, adds to the gap factors, which by their nature grow at a compound rate.[16]

The upshot is that the current account deficit rises to over $300 billion by 1990. What would be the capital inflow needed to sustain the dollar at its present level until then? The answer can be found in line 5 of table 3.2: *capital inflows over the six years from end-1984 to end-1990 would have to total as much as $1.3 trillion.* Readers interested in how much this hypothetical

---

15. Investment income from financial assets. Income from direct investment is projected separately (TN2).

16. In 1985 the trade balance benefits, however, from the cessation of some abnormal adverse factors thought to have been at work in 1984. See TN1, paragraph 9.

outcome depends on each of the various assumptions built into the simulation may wish to refer to the sensitivity analysis in TN3.

What would happen to the overall balance between investment and savings in the US economy in this hypothetical baseline case? To anticipate the discussion in chapter 5, it can be seen from table 5.1 that, with such massive capital inflows, the federal government could run a structural budget deficit of 6 percent of GNP in 1990 without any risk of crowding out in the financial markets—in other words, there would be no need to cut the budget deficit at all! It is no doubt fanciful to suggest that the dollar rose so much because the exchange markets were aware of this arithmetic and were acting on the assumption that nothing would ever be done to cut the deficit; especially since, if so, it would mean that they were also assuming that the world's appetite for dollars was virtually inexhaustible—a dubious proposition to which we now turn.

The United States as a Debtor Nation

> The United States has by now become a debtor country—frittering away its position as the world's largest creditor country, accumulated over 65 years, in just two years. By the end of 1985, it will be the largest debtor country in the world . . .[17]

> I think this has been exaggerated, and it isn't a case of us being a debtor nation.[18]

At the end of 1984, the reported figures showed the United States was a net creditor nation to the tune of $28 billion (table 3.4).[19] The US net investment position is basically driven by the US current balance. Thus, since the United States recorded a current account deficit of over $60 billion in the first half of 1985, it has been widely suggested that it has become a debtor nation for the first time since World War I.

---

17. Bergsten (1985, p. 5).

18. President Reagan, news conference, 17 September 1985.

19. There are various reasons for believing that the reported figures both understate and overstate the true position. See TN1, paragraph 16.

TABLE 3.4 **US net international investment position, end-1984**
(billion dollars)

	Assets abroad	Foreign assets in United States	Net
Official assets	120	199	−79
Direct investment	233	160	+73
Private financial	562	527	+35
Total	915	886	+28

Source: Survey of Current Business, June 1985, p. 26.

The relationship between the US current account and its net investment position since 1970 is shown in figure 3.2. During this period, changes in the net investment position have been relatively small; it rose from a trough equal to 3.1 percent of GNP in 1972 to a peak of 4.9 percent in 1976, which was reached again in 1982 (when it was $147 billion), followed by a sharp decline. And, as emerges clearly from figure 3.2, if anything like the hypothetical baseline-case materialized, the United States would have become a debtor nation on a massive scale by 1990—to an increasing extent because of rising interest payments.[20]

What form might such large-scale capital inflows take? Figure 3.3 summarizes the story so far. For private capital:

• There has been a net inflow of direct investment since 1981 (top panel). But it seems unlikely that direct investment could contribute much to financing increases in current account deficits on the scale foreseen in the baseline case (TN2, paragraphs 11 and 12).

• So far the deficit has been financed to an important extent by the cessation of the previous rapid buildup of US financial assets abroad (bottom panel). Since these are still large ($550 billion, end-1983) and since investment prospects in the rest of the world seem poor, it is often suggested that a

20. Making projections of the US net investment position involves serious statistical problems, related in particular to the large errors and omissions in the US balance of payments, and the existence of a large statistical discrepancy in the world's balance of payments. These are discussed in TN1, paragraphs 16 to 19, and TN12.

FIGURE 3.2   **US current account and net investment position in baseline case, 1970–90**

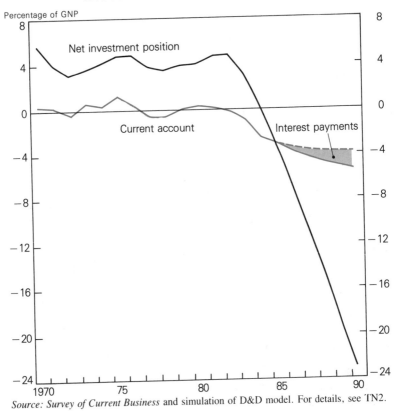

Source: *Survey of Current Business* and simulation of D&D model. For details, see TN2.

continuing rundown of US foreign assets could provide a relatively easy source of finance.[21]

In terms of the basic market forces at work, however, this distinction between assets and liabilities is largely beside the point. What matters is

21. Kubarych (1984), Morgan Guaranty (1985), and Solomon (1985a). For statistical reasons and because of institutional changes, some part of the apparent repatriation of US assets seems to reflect increased liabilities to foreigners. See table 1.3 and the discussion in Isard and Stekler (1985).

whether enough people somewhere in the world's financial system are willing to increase their exposure in dollars. This is the case when foreigners are happy to increase their holdings of dollar-denominated assets because they think the dollar will remain strong. But it is also the case, in a slightly different sense, if they decide to reduce their dollar-denominated liabilities; it means that they are paying off debt now which, if the dollar were to go on up, would cost them more to pay off later. Thus, the counterpart to the recent rundown of US bank assets abroad has been a willingness on the part of foreigners to run down their dollar liabilities.[22] This makes sense as long as—but only as long as—they expect the dollar to go up. Once they began to think that the dollar might go down, they would try to *increase* their dollar liabilities, and US banks' foreign assets would rise, not fall, as was the case, for example, when the dollar went down in 1977–78.

The most important point to emerge from figure 3.3, however, is that *when the US current account was in deficit in the 1970s it was entirely financed—indeed more than financed—by official capital,* mainly intervention in exchange markets by foreign central banks. These inflows cumulated to as much as 4.1 percent of GNP in the three years 1970–72, and to 2.5 percent ($70 billion) from mid-1976 to mid-1978. In both periods the willingness of central banks to buy up the dollars that private investors were trying to unload facilitated private capital outflows from the United States which, in the event, were of the same order of magnitude as the current account deficit, i.e. they roughly doubled the total deficit on private transactions.

Since the late 1970s, however, there has been a major change. The conventional wisdom—preached until recently especially by the United States—has been that central banks should only intervene to maintain "orderly conditions" in the exchange market. There has been some reconstitution of dollar reserves by debtor countries, and this may continue unless their situation deteriorates.[23] But the key point is that *as long as the major countries'*

---

22. To the extent that US banks have been lending less to debtor developing countries, this reflects a forced rather than a "willing" slowdown in the growth of foreign dollar-denominated liabilities. By the same token, however, the debtor countries are unlikely to be able to *reduce* their dollar liabilities over the next few years, much as they might like to, and thus US bank assets corresponding to these liabilities are in this sense "frozen."

23. Thus far, official transactions have made no contribution to financing the US current account deficit. Official capital in figure 3.3 includes outflows on US official lending. Taking reserve assets alone, there was a small outflow of $6 billion over 1981–84.

central banks stick to their present intervention policies, inflows of official capital are unlikely to play more than a minor role in financing US current account deficits. This is one of the most crucial differences between the situation in the 1960s and 1970s and the one the United States now faces. How long central banks *would* stick to their present intervention policies if the dollar dropped sharply is, however, another matter (chapter 8).

To sum up: as long as central banks stick to their present policies, continuing large current account deficits will have to be financed by large-scale inflows of private financial capital responding to relative cyclical conditions, interest rate differentials, exchange rate expectations—and the complex of economic and noneconomic ''news'' which itself strongly affects such expectations (chapter 4).

When Will Foreigners Have Had Enough?

> *What makes the U.S. debt build-up unique is that, for the first time in history, a country with large and persistent deficits has managed to avoid bearing any of the exchange risk itself.*[24]

The longer run implications of becoming a debtor nation are relatively straightforward. At some point, to service these debts, production will have to be increased or spending reduced. The key question in this relatively long time frame is whether foreign borrowing is being used to raise US productive potential above its previous trend so as to provide the output needed to service and eventually repay the debts incurred. This is open to doubt, given that private investment is no higher than its previous cyclical peak, and that the main counterpart to the capital inflows has been large federal budget deficits. The strong dollar is, moreover, doing a lot of damage to the internationally competitive sector of the economy (chapter 2). Concern has also been expressed as to how much the increase in private investment is adding to productive potential, given its rather unusual composition.[25] Quite

---

24. Anatole Kaletsky, *Financial Times,* 7 February 1985.

25. Over 90 percent of the growth in business investment since 1979 is due to a rise in outlays on office equipment (including personal computers), business automobiles, and commercial structures (Bosworth 1985, p. 34).

FIGURE 3.3 **Capital flows into and out of United States, 1970–84**
(percentage of GNP, five-quarter moving averages)

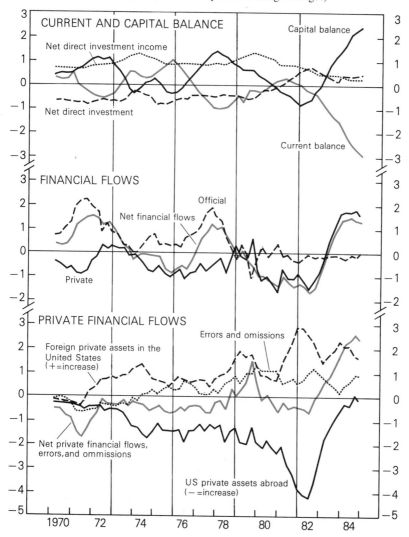

Source: DRI data base.

apart from these longer term concerns, however, it will be argued below that the dangers for the United States in going into debt at the speed and on the scale implied in the baseline case have a much shorter time horizon.

The conventional measure of the rate at which a country is going into debt in relation to its ability to earn the money needed to service this debt is the ratio of its current account deficit to its total exports of goods and services. For the United States, this ratio had risen to 40 percent by the first half of 1985. For comparison, it rose to a peak of 10 percent for France in 1982 following the socialist government's ill-fated attempt to reduce unemployment by fiscal reflation (box 7.3). For Italy, running large and rising budget deficits since the early 1970s, this ratio peaked at 20 percent in 1974. For the seven major developing-country debtors, as classified by the IMF,[26] it peaked at 29 percent in 1982 (figure 3.4, top panel). Thus, in relation to its export earnings, the United States is going into debt faster than any major developed country since World War II, and faster than the average of the seven major developing-country debtors on the eve of the debt crisis.

How long can this go on? This is an extremely difficult question to answer. The United States is by far the richest and most powerful country in the world; and there is what Armin Gutowski (1984, p. 102) calls the ''rich man's effect'': people seem happy to lend to the rich without asking too many questions.

US net external debt of $1.3 trillion by 1990 in the hypothetical baseline would compare with total developing-country debt in 1984 of roughly $730 billion net and $900 billion gross. Figure 3.4 shows what would happen to the conventional debt indicators for the United States, compared to what happened to the seven major developing-country debtors in 1978–84 using a somewhat different and less favorable definition of net debt.[27] On these commonly used but different definitions, the US debt to export ratio would rise much faster than that of the developing-country debtors and would, already by 1988, have gone above the 2.0 level often regarded as a danger signal. The US external debt to GNP ratio would rise very fast, reaching nearly 25 percent by 1990. This would still be quite low in comparison with

---

26. Brazil, Mexico, Argentina, Venezuela, Korea, Indonesia, and the Philippines.

27. The concept used for the developing countries in figure 3.4 is gross financial debt, i.e. including all financial liabilities but excluding direct investment by foreigners. In contrast to the United States, private foreign assets are not treated as a plus factor—indeed they are often not known.

FIGURE 3.4 **Debt indicators: United States in baseline case, 1984–90, versus seven developing-country debtors, 1978–84**

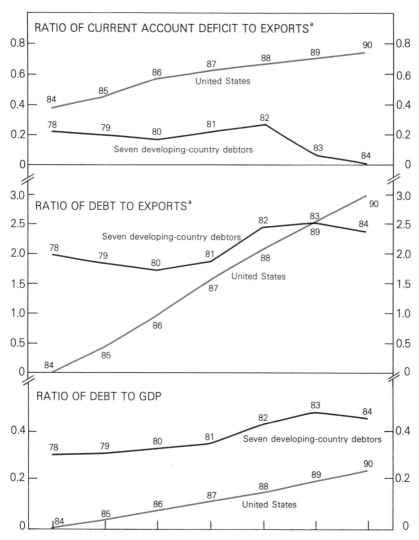

Source: Debtors, see TN23; United States, *Survey of Current Business* and simulation of D&D model.
a. Exports of goods and nonfactor services.

the developing-country debtors, but would equal the nineteenth century peak for the United States, when it was at the height of its most rapid phase of economic development.

These comparisons, though fascinating, may not be a good guide to the sustainability of the present situation. In the first place, most US assets and liabilities are denominated in dollars. Thus, the United States cannot run out of the money needed to service its debts because it can always print more, i.e. there is no danger of illiquidity. Second, foreigners will probably feel little risk that their assets might be frozen because of the strong free market traditions in the United States.

Two important considerations go in the opposite direction. First, precisely because the United States lends and borrows mainly in its own currency, *foreigners carry the exchange rate risk.* For a currency that has fluctuated as widely as the dollar has over the past 14 years, this risk is obviously considerable. In other words, the limits on the ability of the United States to go into external debt are likely to be determined more by people's willingness to incur exchange rate risk than by their assessment of its liquidity position or creditworthiness as a sovereign borrower.

Second, because of the dollar's role as the world's leading currency, *foreigners are already exposed to an exchange risk on a large existing stock of dollar-denominated assets* which do not, at the end of the line, represent claims on the United States, but on other countries that have issued liabilities denominated in dollars. As long as things go well, there is an advantage in being the issuer of the world's leading vehicle currency. Increasing demand for working balances and wealth-holding in dollars provides a more or less automatic source of finance. If things go wrong, it is a different matter. People will try to sell off dollar-denominated assets that originated outside the United States and for which the United States is in no way responsible. The United Kingdom learned this lesson from bitter experience:

I come from a country that has experience from the past of the advantages—and also of the risks and the responsibilities—of operating a reserve currency. The availability to borrow abroad in one's own currency gives opportunity and time which would not otherwise be available, to some extent at the expense of the rest of the world. But we also have experience of the consequences that occur when this special privilege is abused.[28]

28. Nigel Lawson, Chancellor of the Exchequer of the United Kingdom (Statement to the IMF-World Bank Joint Annual Meetings, Washington, 24 September 1984, p. 5).

In light of these considerations, one way to assess the situation and prospects is to try to estimate how much foreigners' holdings of dollar-denominated assets would have to increase, and what would happen to the dollar share of their total financial portfolio, in the baseline case. This kind of portfolio analysis involves major conceptual and statistical difficulties. The most that can be claimed for what follows is that it tries to clarify some of the conceptual issues and put forward very rough estimates of some of the magnitudes involved.[29] We will consider first the factors likely to affect the private demand for dollar-denominated assets, and then the various sources of supply of dollar-denominated liabilities.

DOLLAR DEMAND

As a first step, rough estimates have been made of the rest of the world's *uncovered* portfolio of dollar-denominated assets. This gives a figure of around $800 billion at end-1984 (table 3.5 and TN12). Two conceptual points:

• The world's banking system does not itself take a significant uncovered position in any currency. When a bank accepts a deposit, it owes that amount in that currency whatever happens to exchange rates. It is true that, when exchange rates were "fixed," banks sometimes took open positions, at least for short periods, and got away with it. Indeed it took the failures of the Herstatt and Franklin banks in 1974 to bring this basic truth home to bankers and bank supervisors; hopefully, it has not been forgotten.

• No doubt some part of the dollar portfolio shown in table 3.5 is "covered" in one way or another. But it follows from the above that, after reshuffling, the corresponding risk is being held by someone else *outside* the banking system.

A part of the $800 billion represents the working balances of the rest of the world's corporate sector.[30] These balances increase steadily with the growth of world trade and the internationalization of corporate activity.

---

29. For other analyses along these lines see Brender, Gaye, and Kessler (1984), Artus (1984), Shafer and Loopesko (1983), and Golub (1983).

30. Perhaps between one-fifth and one-third of the total. For an estimate of working balances, using a somewhat different approach, see Brender, Gaye, and Kessler (1984).

Companies involved in the business of producing and trading goods and services do not normally "speculate"; they will try to avoid a serious mismatch between the currency composition of their current and future assets and liabilities, and generally confine themselves to arbitrage to improve cash flow and reduce borrowing costs.[31] With the rapid rise in exports to the US market since 1982, dollar working balances may have risen quite rapidly. But looking ahead, there is little reason to suppose that this source of private demand for dollars could finance more than a small fraction of increase in the US current account deficits of the magnitude shown in the baseline.

The remainder of the $800 billion is held, directly or indirectly, by the rest of the world's household sector. This brings us to a key point that emerges from the previous analysis. If dollar working balances are on a steady, moderately rising trend, and central banks are no longer prepared to absorb an excess supply of dollars, *any significant acceleration in the supply of dollars has to be matched by increased demand from the world's household sector.*

Table 3.5, line 2, shows the private nonbank dollar portfolio as a ratio of ROECD GNP measured in dollars, at current prices and exchange rates.[32] This ratio, which had been rising by around 0.5 percentage points a year in the second half of the 1970s, jumped by 10 percentage points from 1980 to 1984, suggesting a very sharp acceleration in the private demand for dollars. This is deceptive, however, because two-thirds of the rise was simply the result of the appreciation of the dollar against other currencies. Measured at constant 1975 exchange rates, the ratio still rose, but much more slowly, and more in line with the earlier trend. This valuation component of the apparent increase in the demand for dollars needs to be interpreted with caution. Insofar as foreigners have seen the dollar share in their portfolios rise simply because of a rise in the dollar, there is little reason to suppose that this "demand" for dollars would continue if the dollar was going down.

---

31. Corporate treasurers are, however, human. When the dollar is rising, they are no doubt somewhat less conscientious about converting incoming dollar receipts, and vice versa. Thus, at the margin, working balances will be influenced by exchange rate expectations and, since the sums involved are large, this may give additional momentum to already established trends in the exchange market.

32. It would have been more appropriate to relate the dollar portfolio to the rest of the world's GNP, but this was not done because of the shakiness of the data. Using global GNP figures, excluding the Sino-Soviet bloc, the ratio would be 20 percent to 25 percent lower, but the trend through time would probably be much the same.

TABLE 3.5   **Rest of world's nonbank private dollar portfolio, 1975–90**

	1975	*1978*	*1980*	*1983*	*1984*	*1990*
Dollar portfolio, estimated						
(billion dollars)	130	280	400	750	800	2,100
Dollar portfolio, percentage						
of ROECD GNP						
At current prices and						
exchange rates	5	7	8	16	18	30
At current prices and 1975						
exchange rates	5	8	8	11	11	18

Note: The 1990 figures are based on a simulation of D&D model in the hypothetical baseline case in which the dollar stays at its 1984:4–1985:1 level, on the assumption that, apart from the US current account deficit, the supply of dollar-denominated liabilities from other sources is negligible. For other assumptions, see TN2. For methodology and sources for 1975–84 figures, see TN17.

On the contrary, once foreigners thought that the dollar was into a downswing they could be expected to try to reduce their dollar portfolio to a more normal historical level (box 3.1).

DOLLAR SUPPLY

To meet the rest of the world's private demand for dollars, there are three main sources of supply of dollar-denominated liabilities:

• US current account deficits[33]

• financing of current account deficits by the private sector of countries in the ''dollarized'' world, i.e. those parts of the world where people find it necessary to denominate their foreign liabilities in dollars because of the limited acceptability of their own currencies (and where many people are happy to hold dollar-denominated assets for the same reason)

---

33. But only as long as foreigners are prepared to accept dollar-denominated claims on the United States (chapter 4).

BOX 3.1   **Currency exposure and financial intermediaries**

Investment funds and, more generally, investment bankers, trust banks and mutual credit institutions, include in their portfolios varying amounts of stocks, bonds, and short-term financial assets denominated in foreign currencies. They do so, however, *on behalf* of their clients who carry the exchange risk (together with all other risks). Experienced investors know this and know that, although their holdings in investment funds may be denominated in their own currencies, both capital and income depend on what happens to exchange rates. With deregulation and the recent avalanche of new financial instruments, however, it seems possible that some people have been tempted by high yields into incurring exchange risk against the dollar without really realizing it. This could, for example, be the case in Japan where, for virtually the first time, the household sector now has the possibility of diversifying its substantial financial holdings.

Insurance companies and pension funds may also, within the limits of government regulations, take up open positions in foreign currency. In their case, liabilities in domestic currencies stretch over a long period and their aim is to buy long-term assets, offering the greatest security and the highest rates of return over their lifetime. They are not, therefore, particularly concerned about exchange rate risk insofar as they expect it to balance out over 10 to 15 years and normally do not switch their portfolios. They do, however, adjust their portfolios on the margin, and can have second thoughts when the going gets rough.

Under present regulations, Japanese life insurance companies are allowed to hold 10 percent of their portfolio in foreign assets, provided that they do not increase their foreign assets by more than 20 percent of the increase in their total assets in any one month, with no provision for carryover. During a transitional phase, this has created a steady demand for foreign assets more or less regardless of exchange rate considerations. In principle, these are firmly held, although it is understood that Japanese holdings of Australian assets were significantly reduced after the Australian dollar dropped sharply in early 1985.

- borrowing in dollars by the public sector outside the United States whether or not the country concerned is in current account deficit.[34]

Over the 1970s and up to 1983, there was no net supply of dollars from US current account deficits. By far the most important factor behind the increase in the world's private dollar portfolio during this period was the unusual pattern of current account surpluses and deficits in the "dollarized" world. Large OPEC surpluses created a strong demand for dollars; large nonoil developing-country deficits generated a large supply. In addition, and for partly related reasons, the supply from foreign public-sector borrowing in dollars was also increasing.

The present position is, however, very different:

- Since the debt crisis, the current account deficits of the nonoil developing countries have been reduced by $70 billion; at the same time there has been an even sharper shift by OPEC from surplus to deficit. From 1984 it seems likely that—within the margin of uncertainty created by the world current account discrepancy—supply and demand for dollars from these two sources had dropped sharply and may be roughly in balance.

- From 1983 onward, the counterpart of the large and growing US current account deficit has been growing surpluses in the nondollarized—or much less dollarized—world, i.e. in Japan and those European countries where people's normal preference is to hold their assets in their own currencies.[35]

- Public sector borrowing in dollars outside the United States has dropped as budget deficits have been reduced.

Putting these elements together, it seems likely that, from now on, the supply-demand balance for dollars will be dominated, on the supply side, by the US current account deficit. What then would have to happen on the demand side in the hypothetical baseline case? The ratio of the foreign private dollar portfolio to ROECD GNP would have to rise by a further 12 percentage

---

34. This is, for example, common in many of the smaller OECD countries. It provides a supply of dollar-denominated assets to *private* holders, even though, if the country is not running a current account deficit, it does not lead to a *net* increase in the supply of dollars outside the United States.

35. It is also probable that these surpluses, notably in Europe, are larger than suggested by the official figures because of underreporting of current (mainly investment) income (TN12).

points, to as much as 30 percent in 1990 (table 3.5).[36] The most impressive thing about this projection is perhaps not this ratio, or even the absolute level of a $2 trillion foreign dollar portfolio, but the fact that this very large increase would have to take place even though the dollar was no longer rising.

Another way of looking at the plausiblity of the baseline is to estimate the share of the foreign household sector's total *new* savings needed to finance US current account deficits if capital inflows were to continue on the scale needed to sustain the dollar at its present level (table 3.6). The first point is that, although savings in the ROECD area—net additions to household financial wealth—rose by around 20 percent from 1982 to 1984 as measured in their own currencies, they did not increase at all when measured in dollars at current exchange rates. In other words, the share of these savings needed to finance the US current account deficit was rising sharply, not only because this deficit was rising, but also because it took more foreign currency to finance a dollar's worth of deficit as the dollar rose.

The second point is that already by 1984 the share of the rest of the world's household savings needed to finance the US current account deficit appears to have risen to as much as 22 percent. This is surprising because a country's household savings are normally devoted to financing its own house building, productive investment, and, since the early 1970s, large government budget deficits. It was only because there was an unprecedented surplus of private savings in the rest of the world in 1984 that such a large share could be devoted to financing the savings deficiency created by the US budget deficit (chapter 1).[37] The unsustainability of this situation—absent an economic

---

36. This may be an unduly favorable projection from the point of view of financing US current account deficits since there could well be some continuing net supply of dollar-denominated liabilities outside the United States.

37. A number of analysts have compared US current account deficits with *gross* savings in the rest of the world, i.e. before deducting domestic investment. This suggests that such deficits could or should be financed by reducing investment in the rest of the world. In this connection, Morgan Guaranty (1985) commented: "Much of the world outside the United States is now saving more than it invests at home, the excess being channelled to the United States. . . . While human and capital resources in Europe, Latin America and other developing countries stand idle, US investment opportunities are a net plus for all concerned." This begs the question of the extent to which resources have been standing idle in the rest of the world precisely because of the divergence in macroeconomic policies between the United States and its major allies, which has pushed up real interest rates and produced the lopsided recovery discussed in chapters 1 and 2.

TABLE 3.6 **US current account deficit and financial savings in rest of world, 1982–90** (billion dollars)

	1982	1983	1984	1990
1. US current account deficit	11	41	102	320
2. ROECD financial savings[a]	360	360	360	540
3. ROW financial savings[b]	470	470	470	700
4. Line 1 as percentage of line 3	2	9	22	46

Note: The 1990 figures are based on a simulation of the D&D model in the hypothetical baseline case in which the dollar stays at its 1984:4–1985:1 level. For other assumptions, see TN2. For definition and sources for ROECD financial savings, see TN17.

a. Financial balance of household sector at current prices converted into dollars at current exchange rates. Projection to 1990 assumes unchanged ratio of the household financial balance to GNP of 8 percent, using baseline growth and inflation assumptions (TN2).

b. ROECD savings increased by a factor of 1.3 to allow for financial savings in non-OECD countries.

collapse in the rest of the world—is vividly illustrated by the fact that in the hypothetical baseline case the share of foreign savings needed to sustain the dollar at its early 1985 level would have to rise to a quite improbable 46 percent by 1990.

To sum up:

• If the dollar stayed strong, the external debt indicators for the United States, as conventionally measured, would signal the danger of sovereign risk before the end of the decade.

• Because the United States borrows largely in its own currency, however, the limits on its external indebtedness will be determined more by the exchange rate risk than by illiquidity or sovereign risk. And foreigners already hold an uncovered dollar portfolio of around $800 billion.

• The large rise in the dollar share of foreign portfolios reflects to an important extent simply the rise in the dollar; there is little reason to suppose that this apparent increase in the demand for dollars would be maintained once the dollar was not expected to rise further, or, a fortiori, once it began to go down.

• Because of the dominant size of the US economy, in relation to others, the share of foreign savings that would be needed to generate capital inflows on the scale necessary to sustain the dollar at its early 1985 level would have to rise to a quite improbable level by 1990.

Putting these elements together, it would appear unlikely that capital inflows could continue on the scale necessary to sustain the dollar at its present level for more than a year or two at most. At some point—which may already have been reached—the dollar's decline will begin in earnest, setting in motion a complex set of interreactions in the world's financial and real markets to which we now turn.

4 What Happens When the Dollar Goes Down?

The stability of our capital and money markets is now dependent as never before on the willingness of foreigners to continue to place growing amounts of money in our markets.[1]

When a change comes—and it will—it will be a very sharp change, and sharp changes can be very brutal in their effect.[2]

Let us recapitulate the argument to this point. The industrial countries are locked into a set of incompatible fiscal and monetary policies. As a result, the US economy has become excessively and dangerously dependent on inflows of foreign savings, inconsistent with its longer run position in the world economy. What happens over the next few years thus depends critically on foreigners' willingness to invest their savings in the United States.[3] Unless and until a movement out of the dollar begins in earnest, the prospect is for a "soggy scenario" with slow growth—but no recession—in both the United States and the rest of the world.

---

1. Volcker (1985b, p. 7).

2. Mrs. Thatcher, speaking about the dollar just before a visit to Washington. Reported in the *Financial Times*, 18 February 1985, p. 1.

3. For expositional purposes an ex ante decline in capital inflows is described in what follows as a "decline in foreigners' willingness to invest in the United States." As discussed in the previous chapter, it could just as well take the form of a decline in the willingness of US banks and other entities to run down their foreign assets. This, however, would imply a reduced willingness of foreigners to run down their *liabilities* in dollars and thus would reflect exactly the same motives as a reduced foreign willingness to acquire dollar assets.

But what will happen when the decline in the dollar gathers momentum? A "super-soft-landing" scenario, in which the dollar declines no faster than could be covered by a reasonable interest-rate differential, is shown to be highly implausible. Analysis of the intrinsic instability of exchange rate expectations suggests, on the contrary, that at some point a "crunch" in US financial markets is inevitable, with strong upward pressure on interest rates and downward pressure on the dollar.

This leads to an analysis of the likely timing, speed, and magnitude of the dollar's decline that suggests that it could well fall by as much as 40 percent. The final section presents two quantified scenarios for the US economy over the next five years: an improbable soft-landing scenario and an unpleasant hard-landing scenario.

The Dollar and the US Current Balance

A lower dollar will, in time, help to reduce the US current account deficit. But perhaps the most striking single empirical result of this study is that, *even if the dollar dropped by as much as 27 percent from the baseline level*[4] *over the next three years, the 1989 current account deficit would still be above the $100 billion mark of 1984, and would then start rising again* (figure 4.1). The reason for this surprising and disquieting result is that the benefits from a lower dollar take time to come through (box 4.1) and tend to get swamped by the adverse "gap" factors discussed in chapter 3 (table 3.3).

The problem—which does not seem to be widely understood—is that, unless the dollar declines sufficiently far to start *reducing* the deficit, the gap factors go on getting worse. Once the decline starts to reduce the deficit, however, the exchange rate becomes an increasingly powerful instrument in restoring equilibrium. It is like pushing an automobile up and over a hill. Once the brakes are off, it takes a great deal of effort to stop it from rolling backwards and get it moving uphill. Once it is moving, things get easier. And once it is over the top—i.e. the current balance moves into surplus— gravity starts working the other way. This comes out vividly from the shape of the curves in figure 4.1. As can be seen, while the dollar would have to

---

4. Or by a further 18 percent from its level on October 31, 1985.

FIGURE 4.1   **Time profile of US current balance under different assumptions about dollar, 1984–92**

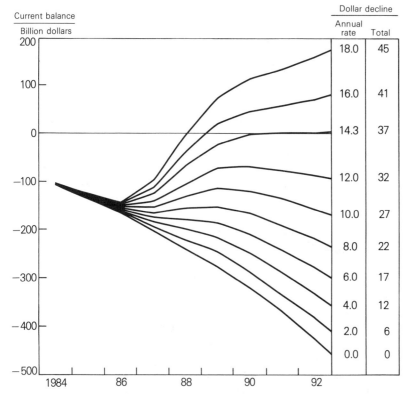

Note: Simulation of D&D model using baseline growth and inflation assumptions. Dollar declines at constant rate from 1985:3 to 1989:1 from its 1984:4–1985:1 baseline. On October 31, 1985, the dollar was 11.4 percent below this baseline. Dollar measured by IMF index; see TN8.

decline from the baseline by 12 percent a year over three years[5] to halve the deficit by 1989, an annual rate only 2 percentage points higher would eliminate it by the same date, and another 2 percentage points would move it into substantial and increasing surplus.

5. In the simulations shown in figure 4.1, the dollar's decline is spread over 14 quarters because it is assumed that on *average* the dollar will not go down very much faster than it came up (see below). Equally, however, the decline is unlikely to be smooth, as evident in what happened between February and November 1985.

BOX 4.1   **Why the current balance responds only slowly to a lower dollar**

When the dollar falls, US exporters can reduce their selling prices or increase their profit margins in foreign markets, or both; foreign exporters will have to raise their selling prices and/or reduce their profit margins in the US market. Over time, the volume of US exports will rise and the volume of US imports will fall as consumers in both markets respond to the fact that US products have become cheaper relative to foreign products. Further gains will be realized over a longer period of time, as US exporters, responding to the change in relative profitability, devote more effort to their foreign markets and foreign exporters less to their US market. The way these effects are quantified in the D&D model appears in line 1 of table 4.1.

But a decline in export prices relative to import prices—a deterioration in terms of trade—in itself *lowers* the dollar value of the trade balance (line 2). Thus, in dollar terms, the improvement really begins to be felt only in the second year (line 3). This is the J-curve effect. Over time, moreover, other consequences of a decline in the dollar at home and abroad will reduce the gains somewhat. By adding to inflation in the United States and reducing inflation abroad, some of the price advantage gained by US producers is eroded (line 4a). By adding to output and demand in the United States, and reducing them abroad, US imports are increased and US exports are reduced (line 4b).

The net gain, after allowing for these feedbacks, is $32 billion for a 10 percent decline (line 5). This is consistent with the widely used rule of thumb that a 1 percent drop in the dollar should improve the trade and current balance by around $3 billion.

The validity of the analysis and policy recommendations in the remainder of this study clearly hinge on the properties of the D&D model with respect to a decline in the dollar. The results depend both on the technical properties of the model and on the exogenous assumptions made about growth, inflation, and interest rates, etc. The model is described in detail in TN1, and the sensitivity of the results to different assumptions is discussed in TN3.

T A B L E 4.1   **Response of current balance to 10 percent decline in dollar**
(billion dollars)

	1985	1986	1987	1988
	Cumulative deviations from baseline			
1. Positive impact on trade volumes	+ 19	+ 40	+ 54	+ 58
2. Worsened terms of trade	− 11	− 12	− 13	− 14
3. Total, excluding feedbacks	+ 8	+ 28	+ 41	+ 44
4. Negative feedbacks from				
a. Inflation	0	− 1	− 3	− 4
b. Demand	− 5	− 8	− 9	− 8
5. Total, including feedbacks	+ 3	+ 19	+ 29	+ 32
Memorandum items				
6. Adverse factors in baseline[a]	− 44	− 88	− 121	− 155

Note: Simulation of D&D model. Assumptions: dollar dropped by 10 percent on January 1, 1985. Baseline-growth and inflation rates, modified from line 4 onwards by demand and price-level feedbacks. Balance on goods and nonfactor services only.
a. Cumulative from 1984 (derived from table 3.3).

The nontechnical reader will be mainly interested in the general plausibility of the results. Basically, all that the simulations in figure 4.1 show is that, to get the current balance back from its 1985 position of a deficit of over $100 billion to its 1981 position of a small surplus, some or all of the factors that caused the deficit since then would have to be reversed. They also suggest that the dollar would have to decline to a level around or below its 1980 trough. This is perhaps surprising because the dollar was generally thought to be below its longer term "equilibrium" value in 1980.[6] There are three reasons for this:

• Although it is assumed in the baseline that from now on the United States grows somewhat more slowly than the rest of the world, it is not assumed that the rest of the world makes up for the ground lost *relative* to the United States in 1983–84.

• Although it is assumed that US exports to Latin American countries recover quite strongly as the debt crisis eases, it is also assumed, following Cline (1984, pp. 178–80), that there has been a once-and-for-all drop in the debtor countries' average propensity to import.

---

6. By 8 percent, according to Williamson (1985, figure A-7).

• Most important, however, is the damage done by the cumulative deficit incurred before the current account comes back into balance. From 1980 to 1990, this would involve a permanent loss of interest earnings of roughly $50 billion. Were it not for this, the decline in the dollar needed to bring the current account back into balance would still leave it 4 percent above the 1980:3 trough, instead of 3 percent below.

The Dollar and the US Investment-Savings Balance

As foreigners' willingness to invest their savings in the United States diminishes, and the dollar goes down, this will, in time, reduce the current account deficit. But this is only half the story. Once the supply of foreign savings begins to dry up, something has to happen to reduce the US economy's *need* for such savings.

This more complicated story involves three key magnitudes (figure 4.2):

• the amount of savings foreigners wish to invest in the United States at current interest rates and the current and expected future level of the dollar (top circle)

• the amount of foreign savings the US economy *needs* to supplement its domestic savings to finance US investment at the current level of economic activity and interest rates (bottom right circle)

• the amount of goods and services foreigners want to buy from the United States, and US residents want to buy from abroad, at the current level of the dollar and economic activity in the United States and abroad (bottom left circle).

After the event, these three magnitudes *will* equal each other. The crucial question is what changes in interest rates, exchange rates, and economic activity bring this about?

In principle, it is fairly straightforward. Suppose that foreigners' willingness to invest in the United States declines. They will want to buy fewer US securities or sell existing holdings, which will push the price of US securities down, and US interest rates up. They will also buy fewer dollars and convert the proceeds of selling US securities into their own currencies. This will push down the dollar. Higher interest rates should act to reduce US investment or increase US savings, thus reducing the need to supplement domestic savings with foreign savings. At the same time, the lower value of the dollar should, by making imports more expensive to Americans and exports cheaper to foreigners, reduce excess US current spending abroad and hence the need to borrow from foreigners.

In practice, however, correcting a major external disequilibrium is not nearly so simple. Significant changes in interest rates or the exchange rate affect economic activity. And changes in economic activity affect investment, savings, and imports—with further feedbacks on interest and exchange rates. Moreover, the speed with which the many actors in the story—foreign savers, domestic savers and investors, importers, and exporters—react to changes in the exchange rate, interest rates, economic activity, and inflation varies greatly. One or another of the corrective market mechanisms can thus easily go too fast or too slowly. If so, automatic stabilizers will develop, helping to control the adjustment process. In some cases, however, these automatic stabilizers may be weak or perverse.

The six key adjustment mechanisms, with their related automatic stabilizers, are shown by arrows in figure 4.2 and described in box 4.2. The key point is that the corrective market mechanisms operating to reduce the "real" components of the present disequilibrium—the excess of imports over exports and the excess of domestic investment over domestic savings—work only slowly.

The reasons for the slow response of the external deficit to a decline in the exchange rate have been discussed above. Correction of the internal savings deficiency can also—given the size of the existing disequilibrium— only be slow and painful. There is little reason to expect that, even with higher interest rates, it could be corrected by any significant rise in private savings (box 2.2). Higher interest rates should, however, discourage private investment, but in practice this adjustment mechanism does not work smoothly. Short-run investment decisions depend far more on the expected pace of economic growth than on interest rates. When expectations are bullish, higher interest rates may not be much of a deterrent. But once expectations turn bearish, with high interest rates, investment could fall *more* than needed to maintain the investment-savings balance (box 1.3).

Cutting the budget deficit would be the right way to improve the domestic investment-savings balance (chapter 5). Even with fair political winds, however, it takes time to cut the budget deficit. And if the budget deficit cannot be cut quickly enough, this means that—under a floating exchange

---

BOX 4.2   **The six key market mechanisms and their automatic stabilizers**

Corrective Market Mechanism ($\longrightarrow$)	*Automatic Stabilizer* ($-\ -\ \rightarrow$)
C1 Reduced foreign willingness to invest savings in America pushes down the dollar.	S1 A lower dollar—beyond some point—increases foreigners' willingness to invest in America.
C2 Reduced foreign willingness to invest savings in America raises US interest rates.	S2 Higher US interest rates attract more foreign savings.
C3 A lower dollar reduces the excess of imports over exports.	S3 A smaller excess of imports over exports reduces downward pressure on the dollar.
C4 Higher interest rates reduce the excess of investment over domestic savings.	S4 Lower investment relative to domestic savings lowers interest rates.
C5 Lower investment relative to domestic savings depresses economic activity.	S5 Weaker economic activity raises the budget deficit and lowers domestic savings relative to investment.
C6 Weaker economic activity reduces imports and hence the need for foreign savings.	S6 A smaller excess of imports over exports strengthens economic activity.

---

rate regime—the forces for adjustment working through market mechanisms will fall mainly on the two key financial prices involved, interest rates and especially the exchange rate. This raises in a rather acute form the question of how effectively the "automatic stabilizers" in the domestic financial and foreign exchange markets can be expected to work in controlling the whole process and preventing the emergence of mismatches between the rate of adjustment in the many markets involved.

As far as interest rates are concerned, the stabilizing mechanism is relatively straightforward. If foreigners' willingness to invest in the United States

FIGURE 4.2 **Reducing US dependence on foreign savings, six key market mechanisms**

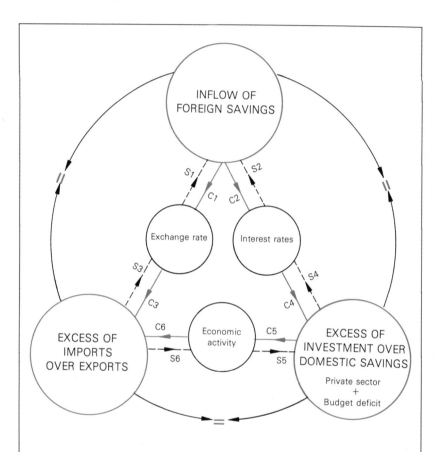

After the event, the import of foreign savings *will* equal the excess of investment over domestic savings, which *will* equal the excess of imports over exports. If foreigners' willingness to invest in America begins to decline, six key market mechanisms (→) work through the exchange rate, interest rates, and the level of economic activity to reduce the excess of investment over domestic savings and of imports over exports so as to bring about this ex post identity. Once at work, they set in motion countervailing stabilizing forces (-→), which help to slow down and control the adjustment process.

BOX 4.3   The implausibility of super-soft-landing scenarios

In a super-soft-landing scenario, two key conditions would have
to be fulfilled simultaneously. The dollar would have to go down
fast enough to prevent US external indebtedness from rising to
an unsustainable level. But it could go down no faster than could
be covered by a differential between a level of US and foreign
interest rates that would be *consistent with a satisfactory growth
and inflation performance in both the United States and the rest
of the world.*

This is implausible because of the quantitative importance of
the adverse ''gap'' factors now at work on the US current balance
(table 3.3). These factors determine the size of the sustained
interest-rate differential needed to offset the exchange rate losses
incurred from the dollar's decline, which must itself be fast
enough to bring the US external debt calculus under control in
time. Assume a 3 percent growth rate in the United States and
ROECD. Assume a 4 percent inflation rate in the United States
and in the countries with the main alternative financial markets.
Assume real short-term interest rates in these countries fall to a
''normal'' 2 percent, with nominal rates at 6 percent. Assume
that US Treasury-bill rates exceed foreign interest rates by the
rate at which the dollar is declining.

Then, using the D&D model, we get:

Annual rate of dollar decline (percentage)	US Treasury-bill rate	Years needed to eliminate current account deficit	Peak level of external indebtedness (trillion dollars)
3	9	22 (21)	5.6 (4.9)
4	10	17 (16)	3.3 (2.6)
5	11	14 (13)	2.3 (1.7)

These scenarios are implausible on two counts. First, it would take 14 to 22 years to bring the current account back into balance, while in the meanwhile US indebtedness would have risen to anything from $2.3 trillion to $5.6 trillion. Second, it is improbable that the US economy could grow at 3 percent over a long period with a real interest rate of as much as 5 percent (3 percent dollar decline case) or 7 percent (5 percent case).

The figures in parentheses show alternative scenarios in which the necessary interest-rate differential is brought about by abnormally low ROECD interest rates (the US Treasury-bill rate stays at 8 percent, and foreign interest rates are less than 8 percent by the rate at which the dollar is declining). The US debt figures are only somewhat less horrific, and in this case it seems improbable that the ROECD area could live with such low or negative real interest rates (minus 1 percent in the 5 percent dollar-decline case) over a long period without suffering a serious outbreak of inflation.

declines sharply, not only will this put upward pressure on US interest rates, but it will also put downward pressure on interest rates in the other major financial centers to which people are trying to move their money. Other things being equal, this widening interest-rate differential will increase the attractiveness of investing in the United States and help to ease the downward pressure on the dollar.

It is the existence of this apparently straightforward stabilizing mechanism that can so easily tempt economists, well trained in the properties of general equilibrium models, to envisage what might be described as a "super-soft-landing" scenario. The key feature in such a scenario is that the dollar would decline no faster than could be covered by a "reasonable" interest-rate differential in favor of the dollar. If so, foreigners would not lose money by keeping it in dollars. If one then makes the further assumption that present interest-rate differentials provide a good measure of how fast the market expects the dollar to decline over the period in question, a super-soft-landing scenario can be constructed as follows (CEA 1984, p. 53):

FIGURE 4.3   **The dollar and the deutsche mark, 1971–86**

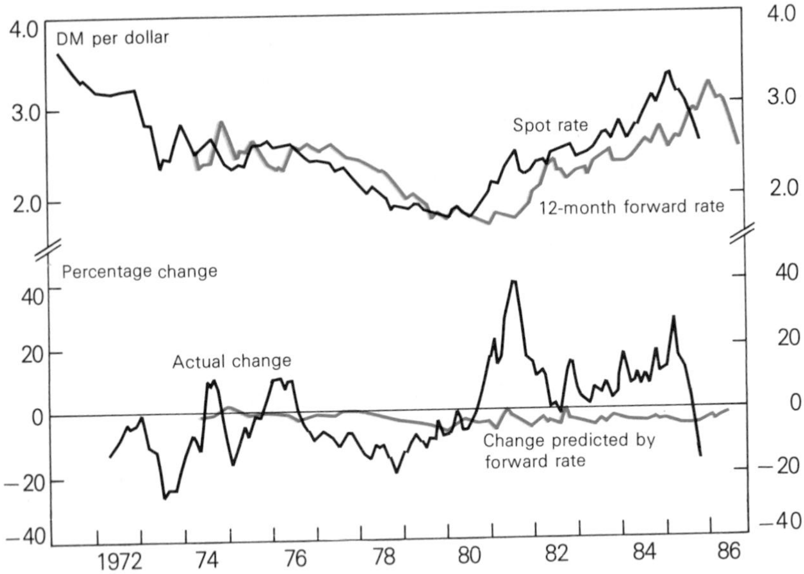

Source: IMF and DRI data bases.

Taking the present 10-year real interest rate differential to be 3.2 points, the implication is that the market expects the dollar to depreciate, in real terms, at an average rate of 3.2 percent over the next 10 years, or 32 percent altogether (ignoring compounding). This . . . would suggest that the market regards the dollar as currently being about 32 percent above its long-run real value.

To judge by past experience, even if there were no unexpected developments, it could be as long as 10 years before the dollar returns to its long-run value.[7]

Some simulations of such a super-soft landing are given in box 4.3. Similar results have been found by Krugman (1985), i.e. he found that in such a scenario it would take 23 years before the US external debt to GNP ratio stabilized, and that by then it would have reached 50 percent! Some academic economists have been inclined to say, so what? Krugman, to his credit,

---

7. For a discussion of the confusion which economists often create by working in terms of *real* rather than nominal interest-rate differentials when discussing exchange rates, see box 1.5.

recognizes that this simply could not happen, and goes on to admit candidly that his paper has "committed what is usually regarded as a cardinal sin in economics. It has argued that a major financial market has simply made a mistake, failing to make proper use of the information available to it." He adds that, "the market has not been behaving as if it makes a rational assessment of long term prospects. What will happen when the market revises its opinion is unlikely to be a sudden access of rational expectations. Rather, the market will simply go make a new set of mistakes. These mistakes could, though they need not be, in the opposite direction, leading to an excessively weak dollar rather than an excessively strong one."

The Instability of Exchange Rate Expectations

EXTRACTS FROM WALL STREET JOURNAL
February 25, 1985 ($1 = 3.44 DM)
Traders say the dollar now could reach astronomical levels at some point this year or in 1986. (p. 33)

March 12, 1985 ($1 = 3.35 DM)
The US dollar plunged yesterday... in what foreign-exchange traders said could be the start of a prolonged downward movement. (p. 35)

This brings us to the stabilizing—or destabilizing—forces at work in the exchange markets. Conventional models often assume that those exposed to an exchange risk in dollars have a fairly clear view about what should be the dollar's "normal" level, and believe that its actual level will not diverge too far or too long from this equilibrium level. If so, a decline in the dollar toward this equilibrium level reduces the perceived risk of holding dollar assets because it has "less far to go." As for the case of widening interest-rate differentials, this should increase the attractiveness of investing in dollars and offset, in part, the pressures generated by the initial decline in foreigners' willingness to do so.

In practice, the assumptions underlying this application of rational expectations are open to many doubts. Consider somebody exposed to an exchange risk between the dollar and the deutsche mark. Since the beginning of 1971, the dollar fell 35 percent over the first 2½ years, oscillated plus and minus 10 percent over the next 2½ years, fell 35 percent over the next four years, rose 99 percent over the five years to late February 1985, and fell 24 percent over the next seven months.

From this experience the markets might well conclude that it is hard to discern any "normal" level for the dollar-DM rate; all that seems clear is that the rate can move a long way for quite a time in one direction before going into reverse. Or, as the market slogan has it: "the trend is your friend."

How far were the markets able to predict these fluctuations? Figure 4.3 shows the actual deutsche mark-dollar spot rate in each month compared with the rate at which dollars could be bought or sold for deutsche marks in the forward market for delivery in that month 12 months previously. Two things stand out. First, as almost all analysis has shown, the predictive value of the forward rate is poor.[8] Indeed, only once, for about 3 months in early 1974, did it predict—wrongly—that the dollar was going to rise over the coming 12 months. Second, it is striking that virtually whenever the spot rate rose, the forward rate 12 months hence rose, and vice versa.[9]

Especially interesting in the context of this study is what happened at turning points. Beginning in mid-1975 the forward rate was (wrongly) signaling a decline in the dollar but, when the decline eventually began in mid-1976, *it was on average five times greater than the "predicted" decline* (compare solid and dotted lines in the bottom panel). The next turning point was even more fascinating. The spot rate and the forward rate predicted 12 months earlier roughly coincided for a short period in 1979–80 as the decline in the dollar leveled off. But then the dollar rose so fast, 40 percent in the 12 months to August 1981, that almost overnight the forward market (wrongly) "predicted" that it would decline—and continued to do so for nearly five years.

Not only is the predictive power of forward rates poor, but it is also doubtful whether they give much of a guide to what the markets actually expect to happen to the spot rate—although this is still hotly disputed among economists (box 4.4). It is therefore interesting to look at the results of a survey in which, since 1981, the *Economist* has been asking a panel of 13 leading international banks for their exchange rate forecasts. The median forecast for the next 12 months is compared with the actual outcome in figure

---

8. See, for example, Frankel (1980), Bilson (1984), Fama (1984), Hodrick and Srivastava (1984), and Bean (1985).

9. In other words, the line for the forward rate in the top panel follows closely the movement of the spot rate 12 months earlier.

BOX 4.4   **What do forward exchange markets tell us?**

What happens to an exchange rate depends to an important but elusive way on what is expected to happen to it. Academic economists have thus always been fascinated by the existence of forward markets in which currencies are being bought or sold for delivery up to 12 months later. Indeed, they have often been tempted to think this provides them with a Rosetta stone—an objective measure of what the markets *expect* exchange rates to be 12 months hence. Market operators know better. The forward discount or premium on a currency is always exactly equal to the interest-rate differential between assets involving similar risks denominated in the two currencies concerned. It has to be so: otherwise somebody could make an assured profit by, for example, buying currency on the spot market with borrowed money, lending the proceeds, and covering himself in the forward market. Since, in contrast to most commodity markets, there are no storage costs or new supplies becoming available later, arbitrage between the spot and forward markets is instantaneous. In practice, operators can choose between entering into a forward contract or borrowing in their home currency to buy spot. As a result, changes in expectations affect the spot rate instantly, without changing the forward discount or premium, unless the interest-rate differential also changes.

Some economists, however, remain undeterred. Believing as they do that markets are efficient and expectations are rational, they solve the problem by turning it upside down: if this is the way forward rates are determined, then it follows that it must be the interest-rate differential that provides an objective measure of what the market expects to happen to the exchange rate. This would have to be the case in their elegant general equilibrium models, but it is not true in the real world. Domestic interest rates are certainly influenced by international capital flows, but they are also determined by a whole series of complex forces at work in domestic financial and real markets. To imagine that the

(Continued overleaf)

BOX 4.4   **Continued**

moment exchange rate expectations change, all these markets will also adjust instantaneously to a new equilibrium position, is just the sort of nonsense to which some of the academic profession has become prone.

Once this is accepted, however, it poses another problem for economists: it means that exchange markets are either not "efficient," or not "rational," or are neither. It took a surprisingly long time to demonstrate empirically that this is indeed the case, but by now the argument has boiled down to whether the main culprit is risk premia or irrational expectations (Froot 1985). We return to this matter in chapter 7 (box 7.7), since it has an important bearing on the controversy about the effectiveness of official intervention in foreign exchange markets.

4.4. The first thing to note is that these forecasts were consistently and significantly more bearish about the dollar than forecasts implicit in the 12-month forward exchange rate. Second, and much more striking, for over three years these 13 leading banks consistently forecast that the dollar would go down over the next 12 months, on average by 10.5 percent, while in fact it consistently went up, on average by 8 percent.[10]

At first sight, the behavior of the exchange markets as illustrated in figure 4.4 is disconcerting, to put it mildly. These are asset markets in which expectations are thought to play a key role. Why, if the most experienced observers in the market were forecasting that the dollar would go down, did it nevertheless go up? The answer is that to an increasing extent *the majority*

---

10. Frankel and Froot (1985) have analyzed these survey data (and data from a similar survey by the American Express) in more detail. They find strong evidence from 1980 onward of what in the jargon is called "unconditional bias"—a nice euphemism for the fact that the forecasts were consistently wrong. From regression analysis in which this unconditional bias is dummied out, they find evidence that exchange rate expectations are inelastic, i.e. that "a current increase in the spot exchange rate itself generates expectations of a future decrease." Putting the unconditional bias in, however, the most important finding, evident in figure 4.4, is that a current increase in the spot rate did not *increase* the expected decrease. In other words, the red arrows are broadly parallel, rather than fanning upwards (extrapolative expectations) or downwards (clearly regressive expectations).

FIGURE 4.4   **Evidence of adaptive (and wrong) expectations in exchange markets, 1981–86** (DM per dollar)

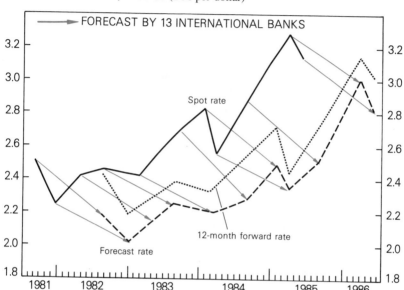

of operators in the exchange markets are concentrating on what is likely to happen in the next few hours or days rather than over the next months or years. Thus:

Market traders and speculators behave in exactly the opposite way to the seminar assumptions. The reality of free money markets is that the overwhelming weight of speculative movement will (rightly from the trader's point of view) be concerned to follow an immediate trend, not to oppose it. Nobody will sell the dollar on Monday in the opinion that it will be lower next year if he thinks he can sell at a higher price in the next hour, next day, next week or next month. Any experienced currency trader will tell you that speculators who take a long-term view usually end up in bankruptcy well before their "long-term view" has been proved true or false.[11]

_____

11. Lord Lever (1985).

In other words, while during this period the markets' longer term view was that the dollar would go down, they thought it was quite possible that in the short run it could go up. And, when it did go up they kept on revising their view of the "longer term" or putting further off into the future the time when it might come to pass. This comes out graphically in figure 4.4: *each time the dollar had gone up since the previous survey, the forecast for 12 months hence was raised by roughly the same amount, and vice versa.*[12] This evidence for the prevalence of adaptive expectations[13] suggests that once an exchange rate begins to move, *this in itself changes expectations about its future level.* It also suggests that there is little reason to expect the dollar's decline to level off as it reaches some average of its previous peaks and troughs.

At this point, let us recall the analysis of the key factors behind the 1980–84 rise in the dollar in chapter 1, and consider what happens when they go into reverse:

● First, once the dollar begins to go down and people's willingness to increase their exposure in dollars dries up, the full force of the very large current account deficit will make itself felt in the foreign exchange markets. Because, whatever happens, this deficit can be reduced only slowly, it will continue to generate an excess supply of dollars at an annual rate of over $100 billion for some time to come.

● Second, changes in relative inflation performance appear to have a strong impact on exchange rate expectations. But once the dollar's decline gathers momentum, US relative inflation performance will be adversely affected by what might be called a *double* double whammy:[14] actual US inflation will

12. Using the *Economist* data, Frankel and Froot (1985, table 5b) found that when the spot rate changed, the respondents revised their three-month forecast, for example, by 96 percent of the change, with a standard error of 2 percent.

13. The term "adaptive expectations" is used rather loosely in this study to describe behavior strongly influenced by what has happened in the recent past as opposed to longer term considerations. It encompasses both "extrapolative" expectations (bandwagons) where the recent *change* in the exchange rate is expected to continue, and behavior of the kind shown in figure 4.4, where expectations "adapted" in the sense that, while the markets clearly thought that the dollar was above its longer run "norm," they kept either revising this norm upwards or putting off further into the future the point at which they thought it would be reached.

14. C. Fred Bergsten has used the term "double whammy" to describe how, when a currency that was appreciating begins to depreciate, the impact on the price level shifts from negative to positive.

go from below to above its domestically generated inflation, while actual inflation in the ROECD area will go from above to below its domestically generated rate. Thus, for example, in the scenarios of the dollar's decline discussed below, the actual inflation differential in favor of the United States goes from *plus* 3 percentage points in 1984 to *minus* 2.7 to 3.5 percentage points in 1988.[15]

• Third, important elements in the "safe-haven" factor behind the rise in the dollar were a consequence of the policies and economic developments that led to the present disequilibrium. As these policies have to be changed, and as economic trends change, the *relative* performance of the US economy will deteriorate, and the image of an American renaissance will tarnish.

To sum up: with flexible rates, the behavior of exchange markets has become increasingly destabilizing because so many market operators have a very short-term time horizon compared with the relatively long lags before the "fundamentals" make themselves felt. At the same time, the present disequilibrium is quantitatively three times larger, as a percentage of GNP, than at the last time of strong downward pressures on the dollar in 1977–79. Thus the potential for the dollar to overshoot downward is far greater than at any time since the inception of the flexible rate system.

This brings us back to the one apparently powerful stabilizing mechanism, a widening interest-rate differential. How much this would serve to increase the attractiveness of putting money into the United States under these conditions is, however, open to doubt. Consider again our hypothetical investor considering a switch from deutsche marks into dollars. If he studies the record since fixed parities were abandoned, he would find a nearly 90 percent chance that the dollar-DM rate could move *in one month* by an amount which—if it were downwards—would wipe out all the benefits to be gained from a 5 percent annual interest differential, and *a 50 percent chance that it could move enough to wipe out a 20 percent interest differential* (table 4.2). Even if he has strong nerves and is ready to lock up his money for a year, there is still a 40 percent chance of a change in the exchange rate of more than 10 percent.

---

15. If one believed the theoretical models relating changes in inflationary and exchange rate expectations of the kind discussed in chapter 1, this adverse shift of nearly 6 percentage points could be expected to lead to a downward revision of expectations about the future level of the dollar by a factor five or more times greater, i.e. by 30 percent or more.

T A B L E 4.2   **Frequency distribution of changes in dollar-deutsche mark cross-rate, 1973–84**

	Change over 1 month	Change over 3 months	Change over 12 months
Percentage occurrence of change at annual rate of			
Over 5 percent	88 (44)	84 (42)	80 (40)
Over 10 percent	75 (36)	69 (33)	42 (17)
Over 20 percent	50 (21)	44 (18)	7 (1)
Over 40 percent	22 (6)	10 (1)	0 (0)

Note: Based on monthly averages. Figures in parentheses give the frequency of *declines* in the dollar at the postulated rate.
Source: IMF data base.

True, these probabilities are about evenly split between the chance of a rise or a fall in the dollar (figures in parentheses). Indeed, it is the prospect of making a profit on the exchange rate on top of a higher interest rate differential that is so tempting. But once the dollar's decline gathers momentum, and begins to look like a one-way bet, the figures in table 4.2 show clearly why an astronomical interest differential would be needed to compensate for the risk of a loss on the exchange rate. This is vividly demonstrated by episodes of sharply rising interest rates and rapidly declining currencies in other countries, and in the United States in 1977–79 (box 5.1).

There is a paradox here. People talk about foreigners "getting out of the dollar," but the rest of the world *cannot* reduce its claims on the United States; it will have to go on *increasing* them unless and until the US current account deficit is eliminated. This is not because the US authorities could be expected to impose exchange controls; it is simply a consequence of market-clearing logic of a floating exchange rate system. If individual foreigners decided to run down their holdings of dollar-denominated assets, they would be free to sell the proceeds on the foreign exchange market. In a floating exchange rate system, some private buyer has to be found. The market will clear. The question is at what level of US interest rates, and at what level of the dollar?

The strength of the potential downward pressure on the dollar, and upward pressure on US interest rates, becomes only too apparent once it is realized that, because the current account deficit is so large, substantial further deficits

TABLE 4.3   **Exchange rate losses in different scenarios**

Scenario	Foreign dollar portfolio (billion dollars)			Cumulative exchange rate losses[a]	
	Estimated	Projected		Billion dollars	Percentage of portfolio
	End-1984[b]	End-1988	End-1990		
Hard-landing	800	1,180	1,050	430	38
Soft-landing	800	1,390	1,590	370	25
Cooperative	800	1,260	1,290	280	22

Note: Based on simulations of D&D model. For description of scenarios, see text and TN2.
a. On the assumption that the "home currencies" of foreign holders are proportionate to their respective MERM weights in the effective exchange rate index for the US dollar. The percentage loss on the successive additions to the dollar portfolio after the dollar starts going down are less than on the initial stock because they are acquired at a lower level of the dollar.
b. For sources and methods, see TN17.

are bound to be incurred—and hence will have to be financed—even after corrective forces have come into play. There is, indeed, perhaps no better way of illustrating the fragility of the situation now facing the United States than to point out that even in the hard-landing scenario discussed below, involving rapid external adjustment, *foreigners would have to go on increasing their uncovered financial claims on the United States by around $380 billion while the dollar was declining by over 40 percent* (table 4.3 and figure 4.5).

In fact, it is worse than this. Foreigners are already exposed to an exchange rate risk on a dollar-denominated portfolio estimated very roughly at $800 billion at end-1984 (chapter 3). Thus, whatever happens, a lot of people are going to lose a lot of money. Illustrative figures for these losses, measured in terms of a weighted basket of foreign currencies, are shown in table 4.3 for the three scenarios analyzed in the remainder of this study. Several points should be made:

• The losses will be very large, ranging in the different scenarios from just under $300 billion to over $400 billion.

• Losses will be proportionately greater to investors whose obvious alternative investment would be in, say, deutsche marks (table 6.4).

• Foreign holders of dollar-denominated assets would lose least under a cooperative scenario in which policy changes by both the United States and its major allies helped to limit the decline in the dollar (chapter 7).

True, for many people these foreign exchange losses will be the mirror image of gains made while the dollar was going up, and in the meanwhile they will have benefited from higher US interest rates. But for most people this will not be much consolation since, being human, they quickly became accustomed to the idea that they had been made richer by high US interest rates and the dollar's rise. So why not cash in these gains by selling off their dollar holdings before the dollar's decline begins to exceed the interest-rate differential?

It may seem implausible that, despite the inevitability of enormous exchange rate losses, several hundred billions of dollar-denominated assets are going to be added to portfolios even while the dollar is dropping 10 percent or more a year. Surely, nobody could be that stupid. The record suggests that indeed they can: that at almost every point some people will be prepared to bet that the dollar has, at least temporarily, gone down too fast or too far—and lose. This has been vividly illustrated by recent events. Between late February and early October 1985 the dollar dropped 16 percent (IMF index),[16] but despite this, capital continued to flow into the United States on a scale sufficient to finance a current account deficit running at an annual rate of over $120 billion.

At some point, to avoid what begins to look like almost certain losses on the exchange rate, foreigners may begin to insist on denominating new claims on the United States in currencies other than the dollar—and also try to switch the currency denomination of their existing claims away from the dollar. If so, the United States would have to take on liabilities denominated in foreign currencies when they were appreciating against the dollar. In a floating rate system this means that private US citizens would thus have to take over the exchange risk from foreigners—even though the foreign private sector would still have to go on increasing its claims on the United States.

This would only cease to be true if the Federal Reserve or other central banks, or both, began to intervene heavily in the exchange markets to buy up dollars the private sector wanted to unload. Until very recently they said they had no such intentions, but this may change.[17]

---

16. At an annual rate of around 27 percent, i.e. enough to wipe out the benefits of a 27 percent interest-rate differential.

17. After September 22, 1985, there was intervention in the opposite direction, i.e. designed to mop up some of the excessive capital *inflow*. How effective this may prove to be as long as the underlying forces behind these inflows remain unchanged is discussed in chapter 7.

One final point. It is sometimes suggested that people will never try to get out of the dollar on a large scale because there is nowhere else to put their money. Memories are short: as recently as 1978–80 conventional wisdom had it that diversification out of the dollar was inevitable because the world was moving toward a multicurrency system.[18] It is not difficult to guess where people will try to move their money. Both Japan and Germany, the second and third largest western economies, have lower rates of inflation than the United States, have rising current account surpluses, not deficits, and have been steadily reducing—and in Germany's case eliminating—their structural budget deficits. Moreover, as the dollar goes down and US inflation accelerates, other countries' "fundamentals" will look better relative to those of the United States. To repeat what was said in chapter 1, exchange markets are subject to fashion, and fashions change.

Against this, it can be argued that financial markets outside the United States are too small and thin to absorb large capital inflows. This is to miss the point: there cannot and will not be large-scale capital inflows, net, into other countries unless and until the US current account moves into surplus. But people's *attempts* to move into other countries' currencies will have a strong influence on exchange rates and interest rates precisely because of the lack of depth of their financial markets.

The upshot of this analysis is as follows. Because of the size of the existing disequilibrium in the "real" US economy—the excess of investment over savings and of imports over exports—and because this disequilibrium can only be reduced slowly, the brunt of a sharp decline in foreigners' willingness to invest in the United States will fall heavily on the financial and exchange markets. It will show up in divergent movements in interest rates and, more particularly, in a sharp decline in the dollar—since, under the present regime, exchange rates ultimately take the strain. Thus, because the correction of the "real" disequilibrium will lag behind these reactions in the financial markets, there is bound to come a time, as the dollar's decline gathers momentum, when foreigners' willingness to invest their savings in the United States dries up faster than the US economy's need for them. This may not happen until the dollar has gone quite a long way down. But when it does, a "crunch" will develop in the financial markets and the US economy will be headed for trouble.

---

18. Indeed, considerable efforts were devoted to trying to create a "substitution account" in the International Monetary Fund to deal with this eventuality—efforts that were subsequently overtaken by events as the pendulum of the flexible rate system swung back toward the dollar.

A Soft or Hard Landing?

The scenarios of the future set out in the remainder of this chapter are full of numbers and dates. Their purpose is to provide some idea of the magnitude of the forces that will come into operation as the dollar goes down, their time sequence, and their interrelations. The author attaches no great confidence to either the timing or the exact figures shown, especially since there is no satisfactory way to quantify the key relationships at work in the financial markets. These scenarios nevertheless provide a better basis for analyzing the policy issues facing the industrial world than others available which either assume that the dollar stays where it is,[19] or declines only very slowly.[20]

WHEN, HOW FAST, HOW FAR?

> As for timing, it is an art. That says nothing—and everything.
> Manias, Panics, and Crashes—Kindleberger (1978, p. 18)

Economic analysis cannot establish precise outer limits for US external creditworthiness (chapter 3). Moreover, the experience of other countries that got into this situation suggests that while the underlying economic forces at work are inexorable, the trigger setting off a major reversal in exchange rate expectations has often turned out to be some unforeseen sequence of economic or noneconomic events. It could be economic in nature, such as an unexpectedly sharp slowdown in the US economy, or a series of major financial failures. Or it could just as well be a noneconomic event—the departure of Paul Volcker from the Fed, a foreign policy misadventure, illness, or assassination.

The important point is that the longer the dollar stays too high, the more unmanageable and costly its decline becomes. This is illustrated in table 4.4. The first column shows what would happen if the dollar declined from the third quarter of 1985 (over 14 quarters) by an amount sufficient to eliminate the US current account deficit in five years. The second column shows that, if a similar decline started a year later, the current account deficit would rise

19. This is the "technical" assumption made in the forecasts published semiannually in the *OECD Economic Outlook*.

20. As assumed by the staff of the IMF (box 7.2).

TABLE 4.4   **What happens if the decline in the dollar is delayed?**

Dollar starts to decline in	1985:4	1986:4	1987:4	1988:4
Current account deficit in that year (billion dollars)	123	168	209	246
Decline in dollar[a] needed to eliminate current account deficit over five years (percentage)	43.4	45.2	46.7	48.1
Peak level of net external debt (billion dollars)	578	835	1,133	1,480
"Equilibrium" level of dollar[b] (1980:3 = 100)	89.7	86.8	84.5	82.2
Decline in "equilibrium" level of dollar from previous year (percentage)				
Nominal	n.a.	−3.2	−2.7	−2.6
Real[c]	n.a.	−2.4	−2.3	−2.2

Note: Derived from simulations of the D&D model. The assumptions about growth and inflation are the same as those made in the soft-landing scenario (TN2). The dollar declines over 14 quarters by enough to bring the current account into balance over five years.

a. From the baseline (average in six months to March 1985). On October 31, 1985, the dollar was 11.4 percent below this baseline.

b. Level of the dollar consistent with a zero current balance on the postulated growth and inflation assumptions.

c. Deflated by price deflators for US and ROECD domestic demand, adjusted as described in TN1, paragraph 6.

another $45 billion before beginning to shrink and, more ominously, that net external debt would rise to a peak $250 billion higher, before leveling off. With a delay of two years, net debt would surpass the trillion-dollar mark before leveling off. Equally, the amount of the decline in the dollar needed to bring the current account into equilibrium (five years after it began) would rise steadily toward the 50 percent mark (second line), and this "equilibrium" level of the dollar would itself decline by around 2.5 percent a year (bottom line). This is because with each year of a large current account deficit, and hence rising external debt, interest payments on this debt rise and have to be defrayed by higher exports or lower imports.

Thus, the longer the dollar's decline is delayed, the greater the risk that it will overshoot because of the rapid growth of US external indebtedness in the meanwhile, and the higher the costs to the United States, in terms of both inflation and real resources. In what follows, it is assumed that the dollar's long-awaited decline is now under way. This assumption could turn out to be wrong, but it has the advantage of providing the basis for analyzing the policy issues under the least unfavorable circumstances.

Many possible scenarios could be envisaged. In what follows, the guiding principle has been to assume that, in very broad terms, history will repeat itself:

• First, as analyzed above, correction of the internal and external imbalances in the US economy will involve a complex set of interreactions in financial and "real" markets which, because of the lags involved, will take time. Looking at the historical record since the move to flexible exchange rates, the first three half-cycles of improvement and deterioration in the US current balance averaged three years (figure 4.5). The present half-cycle has, however, lasted for nearly five years, and, given its greater magnitude, it seems reasonable to assume that the next half-cycle might take as long, i.e. that the corrective forces will not have run their course until around 1990.

• Second, it is assumed that even in a "hard landing" the dollar will not go down very much faster than it came up. Thus, in the following scenarios, the dollar's decline is spread over a period of 3½ years (compared with 4½ years of rise from 1980:3 to 1985:1). For convenience, the dollar's decline is spread linearly over this period, although in practice it is much more likely to take place in a series of lurches, as evident in events since February 1985.

Working with these parameters, the key question is what happens to foreigners' ex ante willingness to put more savings into the United States in relation to the US economy's need for them:

• In a *soft-landing* scenario it is assumed that the supply and demand for savings move roughly in line with one another. Capital inflows decline slowly from 3 percent of GNP in 1985 to 1½ percent in 1990 ($90 billion at 1990 prices). The budget deficit is cut enough to make up for this (table 5.1). And, with a reasonable balance between overall savings and investment, the economy grows in line with the medium-term projection made by the Congressional Budget Office (CBO), averaging 3.4 percent 1986–90.[21] The

---

21. CBO (1985a, table I-10). The CBO's medium-term projection is based on the assumption that over the seven years following the 1980–82 recession, the average growth rate would be the same as the average growth rate of the seven years following recessions since World War II. The unemployment rate is assumed by the CBO to stabilize close to the 6 percent level thought to be consistent with noninflationary growth.

implications for the dollar and US external indebtedness, discussed below, suggest that this is an implausible scenario.

• In a *hard-landing* scenario, foreigners' ex ante willingness to put more savings into the United States dries up more rapidly than the US economy's need for them. The dollar overshoots, and by 1990 there is a net *outflow* of capital equivalent to 1½ percent of GNP. The ex ante shortfall of savings can only be eliminated, ex post, by a recession, assumed to be about half-way between the severity of the 1974–75 and 1980–82 downturns.

• In both these scenarios it is assumed that the other OECD countries stick to their present policies: they simply allow the positive and negative effects of the US external adjustment to feed back on them. In the *cooperative scenario*, however, in which policies in both the United States and the ROECD area countries are successfully directed to preventing the dollar from overshooting, and maintaining a reasonable growth rate in the OECD area as a whole, the dollar goes down by enough—but no more than enough—to bring the US current account into approximate balance by 1990.

Before considering these scenarios in more detail, there is the question of whether history, on this occasion, might not repeat itself. There is no precedent, under flexible exchange rates, for the world's major vehicle currency to be so out of line for so long. The dollar's decline could therefore be much sharper than anything seen before. In that case all the issues discussed in the remainder of this study would emerge both more quickly and more brutally than assumed here. A world financial crisis and world depression would be an extreme case, rather than the hard landing analyzed here, which adds up to a relatively straightforward, if unpleasant, world recession.

There are, on the other hand, a number of reasons for believing that the dollar will not fall into a black hole overnight. It will take time for the underlying divergence in investment-savings balances to start shifting back again. There is a certain inertia in all economic events so that, absent some major noneconomic event, admiration for the "American renaissance"—and pessimism about the prospects of other countries—will change relatively slowly and progressively. The dollar, moreover, is such an important price in the world economy that there will be an instinctive feeling that it cannot—or will not—be allowed to fall too fast. For these various reasons, any particularly sharp dollar decline will tend to be moderated by the many short-term operators in the market speculating on the possibility that it has

BOX 4.5   **What would be the optimum rate of decline in the dollar?**

A case can be made that the dollar should drop overnight to its "equilibrium" level. If—but only if—the markets then decided that no further decline was likely, there would be no upward pressure on US interest rates. Since the current account would respond quite slowly, there would be time to cut the budget deficit pari passu. Further structural damage to the US economy would be minimized, and protectionist pressures should subside.

In the real world, this looks like a pipe dream, since neither the US or the ROECD economies would be able to absorb such a sudden shock. The US economy would have to absorb the full inflationary impact of up to 6 percentage points on the price level in little more than a year. Actual inflation would rise into double digits, and it would be hard to prevent an acceleration in domestically generated inflation. The rest of the world would have to absorb a major deflationary impact. Export profit margins in the US market would have to be slashed, and there would be a negative wealth effect as dollar holders all over the world found themselves suddenly much poorer. Given the lags involved, there would not be enough time for a shift to more expansionary policies to make itself felt in time to offset these negative factors. Under these conditions it would be unrealistic to assume that the dollar would stabilize at its longer run equilibrium level—it would almost certainly overshoot.

What then, would be the optimum rate of the dollar's decline? In general terms, the answer is at the fastest rate compatible with its *not* overshooting. This means, in particular, giving the United States enough time to absorb the inflationary shock, and the rest of the world enough time to absorb the deflationary shock. While there are many uncertainties in this equation, the average rate of decline incorporated in the cooperative scenario analyzed here might, in the author's view, be close to optimum. This decline could well be front-loaded, in order to get the necessary adjustments underway. It should be realized, however, that the real problems will only arise after the dollar has gone most of the way down, and the full effects begin to make themselves felt.

FIGURE 4.5   **Decline in dollar and US current balance in different scenarios, 1970–90**

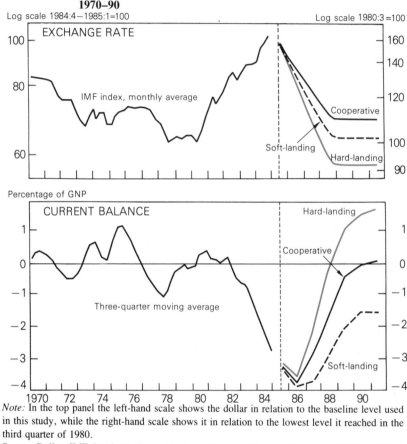

Note: In the top panel the left-hand scale shows the dollar in relation to the baseline level used in this study, while the right-hand scale shows it in relation to the lowest level it reached in the third quarter of 1980.

Source: Dollar, IMF data base. Current balance, *Survey of Current Business;* 1985:4 to 1990:4 are simulations of D&D model.

temporarily gone down too fast or too far. (The optimum rate for the dollar's decline is discussed in box 4.5.)

On the assumptions described above about how the US and ROECD economies behave, the D&D model can be used to estimate at what rate, and to what level, the dollar would have to decline to bring the current account balance in line with the three different assumptions made about the inflow or outflow of foreign savings in 1990. The results are shown in figure 4.5 and table 4.5.[22]

---

22. Table A in TN2 gives the main numerical assumptions and results for the scenarios, many of which are given only in graphical form in the text.

TABLE 4.5 **Decline in dollar in different scenarios, 1985–90**

	Percentage change[a]				
	Total		Annual rate[c]	Other currencies against dollar[d]	1989 level[c] (1980:3 = 100)
Scenario	Nominal	Real[b]			
Hard-landing	−42.5	−35.7	−14.7	+74	91.5
Soft-landing	−35.5	−29.7	−11.8	+55	101.9
Cooperative	−29.3	−24.6	−9.6	+41	111.8

Note: Simulations of D&D model. IMF MERM-weighted dollar index (box 1.4).
a. Assuming a linear decline from 1985:3 to 1989:1, with the decline starting from the baseline used in this study (average of the six months to March 1985). On October 31, 1985, the dollar was 11.4 percent below this baseline.

b. Deflated by price deflators for US and ROECD domestic demand, adjusted as described in TN1, paragraph 6.

c. Nominal.

d. Reciprocal of the change in the IMF dollar index, i.e., a weighted average of the rise in the currencies in this index against the dollar. For a discussion of how individual currencies might move, see chapter 6.

The most striking result is that the dollar declines a long way in all three scenarios. Thus, despite the very different assumptions on which they are based, the drop from the baseline ranges from 29 percent in the cooperative scenario to over 42 percent in the hard-landing scenario (20 percent to 35 percent from the end-October 1985 level). This is another graphic illustration that the dollar has to go down a long way simply in order to prevent things from getting worse because of the magnitude of the initial disequilibrium. For the same reason, once it is assumed that capital inflows cannot go on increasing indefinitely, it turns out, perhaps somewhat surprisingly, that the "required" decline in the dollar is only moderately sensitive to the assumption made about the level of capital flows in 1990.[23]

---

23. If, for example, in the hard-landing scenario it were assumed that the capital inflow in 1990 was zero instead of minus 1.5 percent of GNP, the required decline in the dollar would be only 6 percentage points less.

THE SOFT-LANDING SCENARIO

In both the soft-landing and hard-landing scenarios, the domestically generated rate of inflation is the same as the one assumed by the CBO in its medium-term projection (4.2 percent). The CBO's projection is, however, internally inconsistent, since it assumes lower capital inflows without making any allowance for the decline in the dollar that would be needed to bring the current account deficit down in line with these reduced inflows (TN19). But as we have just seen, a very substantial decline in the dollar would be needed even in the soft-landing scenario, and this would push up the inflation rate.

Growth, inflation, and domestic spending in this scenario are shown in figure 4.6. Perhaps the most striking result is that, even on assumptions that are distinctly favorable to the United States, there would be a dramatic change in the relation between the performance and the wellbeing of the US economy. Since resources have to be shifted into exporting more and making do with fewer imports, domestic spending rises less fast than GNP (top panel). And since the dollar declines sharply, actual inflation rises above the domestically generated rate, to around 6 percent in 1987 and 1988 (second panel). The performance of the economy, as measured by the growth of GNP and the domestically generated rate of inflation, drops below the very good 1984 outcome, but remains 1 point above the historical average (bottom panel). Despite this, the wellbeing indicator drops very sharply because of the significant swing from a positive (black shading) to a negative (red shading) contribution from external factors.[24] In 1987 and 1988, because inflation accelerates by about 3 percentage points, and the growth of domestic spending slows down by more than 6 percentage points, the wellbeing indicator falls nearly 2 percentage points below its historical norm. This is still somewhat better than in the high inflation and recession years of 1981 and 1982, but it is a dramatic change from the outcome in 1984 when the wellbeing indicator was 7 percentage points above this norm.

The second key feature of this scenario is that, despite this considerable external adjustment with its attendant costs, *US net external debt goes on rising into the future, reaching nearly $800 billion in 1990 and one trillion dollars in 1992* (figure 4.8, top panel). This is so because it is assumed that the United States continues to import foreign savings to the tune of 1½

---

24. By construction, the black and red areas in the bottom panel equal the sum of the black and red areas in the first and second panels.

FIGURE 4.6   **Soft-landing scenario**

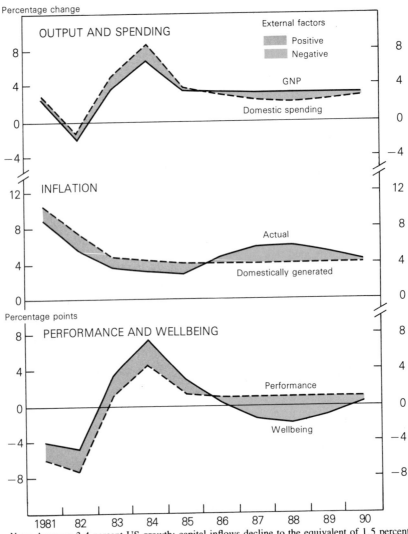

Note: Assumes 3.4 percent US growth; capital inflows decline to the equivalent of 1.5 percent of GNP in 1990. For description of performance and wellbeing indicators, see box 2.3.

Source: OECD data base and simulation of D&D model.

FIGURE 4.7   **Hard-landing scenario**

Percentage change

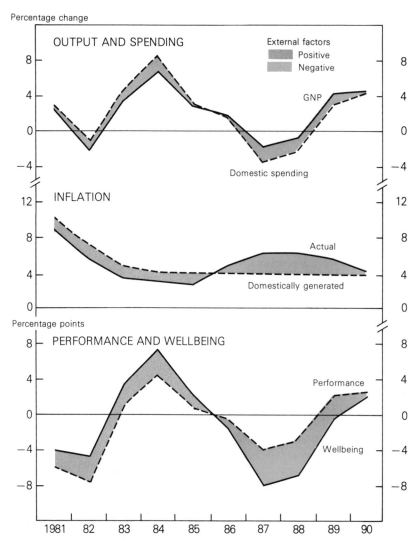

Note: Recession in US and ROECD; US capital balance shifts to outflows equivalent to 1.5 percent of GNP. For description of performance and wellbeing indicators, see box 2.3.

Source: OECD data base and simulation of D&D model.

percent of GNP in 1990 and thereafter. The rapid rise in the external debt to GNP ratio slows down, but nevertheless it continues to rise at around 0.75 percentage points of GNP more or less indefinitely.

These results cast considerable doubt on the plausibility of this scenario. On the one hand, it seems doubtful whether the United States could achieve an average growth rate of over 3 percent for five years if inflation accelerated this much. On the other, this scenario implies that, even with inflation accelerating, foreigners would invest another $800 billion dollars in the United States by 1990, even though the dollar would have fallen by 36 percent in the meanwhile. This seems decidedly improbable.

THE HARD-LANDING SCENARIO

The hard-landing scenario assumes that a "crunch" in the financial and exchange markets is inevitable as people try to avoid the exchange rate losses involved in so sharp a decline in the dollar. This and the inevitable policy response push the US economy into a recession.

It would not, of course, be unusual to have a recession after four years of cyclical upswing. Indeed, the CBO has provided an alternative low-growth projection, with a recession broadly similar to that incorporated in the hard-landing scenario (CBO, 1985a, table I-12). But the analogy stops there. While the CBO recession is essentially domestically generated, as all US recessions have been since the war, the recession in the hard-landing scenario envisaged here is driven by a rapid decline in foreigners' willingness to invest in the United States; it therefore has two quite atypical features: accelerating inflation and upward pressure on interest rates.

According to the D&D model, inflation would double between 1985 and 1987, rising further to around 6.5 percent in 1988. What would actually happen may not, however, be very well tracked by the D&D model. Initially, foreign exporters may not raise their prices as the dollar falls, but instead cut their profit margins.[25] On the other hand, the analysis in chapter 2 of the extent to which prices and profit margins have been shaved by the exceptionally high level of the dollar suggests that the D&D model may underestimate the price increases that could come through once the decline in the dollar goes beyond a certain point.

---

25. It is thus not surprising that the drop in the dollar from February to October 1985 appeared to have little impact on the rate of inflation.

FIGURE 4.8   **US net external debt in different scenarios, 1983–92**
(end-year figures)

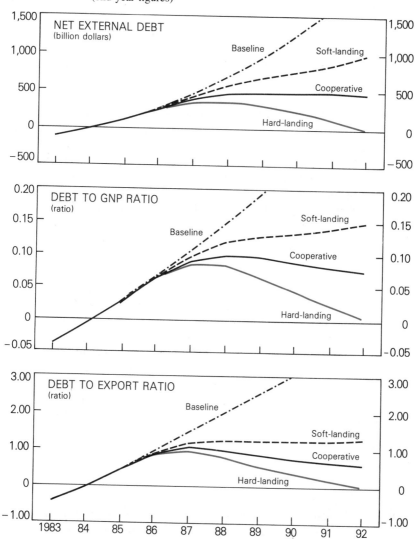

Source: Survey of Current Business and simulations of D&D model.

B O X 4.6   **What happens to the "equilibrium" exchange rate?**

According to my colleague John Williamson's latest estimate, the dollar was 37 percent above its "fundamental equilibrium exchange rate" (FEER) in 1984:4, i.e. it would have to fall by 27 percent in real terms to reach this level, on his assumption that an appropriate target for the US current account is a small deficit (1985, pp. 82–83). According to the D&D model, on baseline growth and inflation assumptions, the dollar would have to come down by 31 percent in real terms from 1984:4 (when it was 3 percent below the baseline used in this study) to reduce the current deficit to this level by 1990.

Williamson, however, does not take into account the additional debt that the United States will incur before the current deficit is eliminated. Allowing for this would bring his results close to those produced by the D&D model, since, as can be seen from table 4.4, each additional $100 billion of debt lowers the real "equilibrium" dollar rate by about 1 percent.

Thus, the "equilibrium" rate for a currency is not carved in stone, but can change over time as the result of many factors, including its creditor or debtor position and any sustained change in its growth rate relative to other countries. This is why in the soft-landing scenario, with debt building up fast, a decline in the dollar which brings it down close to Williamson's FEER still leaves a US current account deficit of 1.5 percent of GNP. In the cooperative scenario, on the other hand, a dollar rate above his FEER suffices to eliminate the current account deficit by 1990 because of the benefits from a period of years when the rest of the world grows faster than the US economy.

It is much more difficult to predict the likely course of interest rates. A useful starting point is the analysis in chapter 2 of how capital *inflows* in the 1983–84 recovery helped keep interest rates down. Without these capital inflows interest rates would—other things being equal—have to have been at least 5 percentage points higher in order to keep investment in line with the reduced supply of savings available to finance it (box 2.1). This gives an idea of the strength of the upward pressure on interest rates once people start trying to get out of dollars. Other things, however, will not necessarily be equal. The more that the economy had slowed down before the crunch came, the more weaker credit demand would offset the upward pressure. On the other hand, accelerating inflation from the dollar's decline would add to it by raising inflationary—and hence interest-rate—expectations.

The key point is that interest rates would have to rise *however much was necessary to bring about an ex post balance between investment and available savings*. As discussed above, even a very sharp rise in interest rates would do little to stem foreigners' desire to get out of dollars once a bandwagon got underway. It follows that what actually happened to interest rates would depend essentially on the strength of investment demand at the time, and what subsequently happened to monetary and fiscal policy.[26] The reasons for believing that a recession would be unavoidable are:

• If the economy were not already in a recession, interest rates would have to rise by enough to choke off investment demand by enough to generate one.

• With inflation accelerating and the dollar falling sharply there would be little scope to ease monetary policy. Under these conditions, moreover, it could well become necessary to make significant cuts in the budget deficit even though the economy was weak (chapter 5).

In this scenario the adjustment necessary to bring the US current balance back into a sustainable position is brought about both by a shift in relative prices via the exchange rate and by a period of significantly slower US growth relative to the rest of the world. These two adjustment mechanisms have very different costs in terms of inflation, employment, and real income (box 4.7). These costs are inevitably high. Thus in the hard-landing scenario, because of what would be, for the United States, a historically unique combination of a recession accompanied by a sharp decline in the dollar, the

---

26. In the D&D model, interest rates enter only as a determinant of US interest payments abroad. For this purpose, it is assumed that the economy is on its baseline path when the dollar goes down, i.e. that investment demand is quite strong. It is assumed that, under these conditions, the Treasury-bill rate would be 13 percent and 11 percent, respectively, in the first and second years after the decline begins, i.e. 4 to 5 percentage points higher than the CBO's assumption in its low-growth scenario.

BOX 4.7   **The external Phillips curve and expenditure switching**

From the point of view of income and employment, it is
unambiguously best for a country to correct an external disequilibrium by what is called, in the jargon, expenditure switching,
i.e. maintaining a high and rising level of output but switching
it from domestic consumption to net exports via a change in
relative prices, in this case a decline in the dollar.

Unfortunately, however, this can only be done at a fairly high
cost in terms of increased inflation. In the D&D model, a drop
of 10 percent in the dollar adds 0.8 percent to demand and 1.5
percent to the price level over two years. Thus the slope of this
"external" Phillips curve (Bergsten 1976, p. 156) is six to eight
times less favorable than the more traditional US Phillips curve,
estimates of which typically lie between 0.15 and 0.25.

For this reason, most countries have found that the only way
to correct a large external disequilibrium is to combine expenditure
switching with expenditure *reduction*. As can be seen from the
second line of table A in TN3, a 1 percent lower growth rate
over two years should improve the US current account by around
$30 billion, i.e. by roughly the same amount as a 7½ percent
drop in the dollar with, if anything, a small negative effect on
the price level. But the costs are high in terms of unemployment
which would, in this case, be about 1.2 percentage points higher
at the end of the three years.

---

wellbeing indicator for the US economy *would fall to minus 7 percent in two
consecutive years—its lowest level since the Great Depression.* Unemployment
would rise to over 10 percent in 1988, and still be 1 percentage point above
the 1984 level in 1990.

This is a measure of the heavy macroeconomic costs of allowing an
external disequilibrium to become so large. There will also be major
microeconomic costs as the structural distortions in the US economy created
by the overvalued dollar are reversed (chapter 2). The all-important counterpart
to these costs would show up in the United States' external financial balance
sheet. The rise in net external indebtedness would be halted by 1988 at $350

billion, and by 1993 the United States would have regained its status as a creditor nation (figure 4.8).

It will be obvious by this point, however, that the hard-landing scenario would also have unpleasant consequences for the other industrial countries and, especially, the heavily indebted developing countries. These are discussed in chapter 6. Before turning to them, however, the next chapter looks at the policy options facing the United States, in particular, whether a change in US policies could, in itself, stave off a hard landing.

5 Policy Options Facing the United States

You and I as individuals can, by borrowing, live beyond our means, but only for a limited period of time. Why should we think that collectively, as a nation, we are not bound by that same limitation?[1]

We are in a real sense living on borrowed money and time.[2]

If I were going there, I wouldn't start from here.[3]

The policy dilemma facing the United States can be simply stated. America has become excessively dependent on large inflows of foreign savings, which will at some point dry up. Cutting the budget deficit is the only certain way to increase US savings to make up for a reduced supply of foreign savings. But nobody knows when or how fast the inflow will ebb. This chapter first addresses two interrelated questions. Could prompt action to reduce the budget deficit stave off a hard landing? If not, could prompt action to cut the budget deficit, coupled with an easier monetary policy, do the trick? A negative conclusion is reached to both.

The next section provides estimates that in the hard-landing scenario the structural budget deficit would have to be cut from its currently projected level by 5 to 6 percentage points of GNP by 1990 to prevent continuing crowding out even after the dollar's decline has leveled off. The more quickly

---

1. Ronald Reagan, first inaugural speech, 20 January 1981.

2. Volcker (1985b, p. 7).

3. Old Irish joke.

the deficit is cut, the less dangerous will be the crunch in the financial markets. The conclusion reached, however, is that the fortunes of the US economy over the next few years have become hostage to the whims of its foreign creditors, and to economic developments and policies in its major allies.

There Is No Way of Getting the Fiscal Sums Right

What few seem to realize, when talking about the budget deficit, is that at some point, when the dollar's decline has gathered momentum, people's *ex ante* willingness to increase their exposure in dollars is going to fall to zero— and, indeed, turn negative. At that point, crowding out in US financial markets will become inevitable *unless, by then, the structural budget deficit had been reduced to close to zero.*[4] But that point may well be only a year or two away, and obviously the budget deficit cannot be reduced that quickly. In other words, there is now no way in which the United States could get its fiscal sums right because they have become so heavily dependent on what has become the most fickle of economic variables: exchange rate expectations. As Paul Volcker put it, ". . . so long as demands on our capital markets exceed our capacity to save, the stability of our own financial markets is, in effect, hostage to a large continuing inflow of foreign capital."[5]

So when the movement out of the dollar gathers real momentum, there will be a "crunch" in US financial markets, whatever is done about the budget deficit. And, with the dollar dropping fast and inflation picking up, the stage will be set for what, in other countries, has been called a "stabilization crisis." At that point, what happens to the confidence of investors in the domestic financial and foreign exchange markets will be crucial. Judging by the experience of other countries, there will be a clear risk of a self-feeding spiral of eroding confidence between the two markets:

• In the domestic financial markets, the combination of upward pressures on interest rates and accelerating inflation will be taken as evidence that all the

4. Ex post, the US current account will still, of course, be in deficit. This will further increase the pressure that people's ex ante unwillingness to increase their exposure in dollars will put on interest rates and the exchange rate (chapter 4).

5. Volcker (1985a, p. 17).

long-felt fears about the inevitable consequences of excessive budget deficits were coming true with a vengeance: this would add to upward pressure on interest rates.

• In the foreign exchange market, the combination of a strongly positive interest-rate differential and a falling dollar will be taken as evidence that the long-held view that the size of the US external current deficit was unsustainable was also coming true: this would add to the downward pressure on the dollar.

• These psychological reactions in the two markets will feed on each other. The fall in the dollar will unsettle the domestic financial markets. Accelerating inflation and falling bond prices will unnerve foreign investors. Strengthening downward pressure on the dollar will put further upward pressure on interest rates, pushing bond prices down further. And so on.

At this point, strong pressures would begin to build up on the administration and Congress to do something about the budget deficit. Here again, however, experience from other countries is painfully relevant. There is a great deal of difference between the confidence-building impact of action to cut an excessive budget deficit *before* the markets lose confidence, and the impact of the same measures after the markets have begun to ''speak'' (box 5.1).

Easier Monetary Policy?

What about monetary policy? If the United States were a closed economy, the prescription might be relatively straightforward. Many economists—with the exception of convinced monetarists—would argue that if firm action is taken to reduce the budget deficit, monetary policy should and could be eased so as to offset the short-term depressive effect of reduced public expenditure or higher taxes. Thus, for example:

It is vital that the monetary authorities be prepared to change their own policies so as to offset the depressive effect of the fiscal restraint and maintain recovery along the agreed-upon path. They should not establish rigid targets for either interest rates or the money supply, emphasizing instead goals for real output and employment growth consistent with a nonacceleration of inflation.[6]

---

6. Rivlin (1984, p. 42).

BOX 5.1   **Two stabilization crises**

The UK stabilization crisis of 1975–76 stemmed from very high structural budget deficits, which started during the oil crisis, but continued into the 1976 recovery when the total public-sector deficit reached 5 percent of GNP. With high interest rates, a large inflow of private capital, peaking at 3 percent of GNP in late 1974, helped finance the current account deficit. But the markets became increasingly aware that the government had lost control over wages and prices, as inflation rose to over 25 percent. Capital inflows fell off through 1975 and turned into massive outflows in 1976, despite a very sharp rise in interest rates (by 5 percentage points from trough to peak). And, although inflation was rapidly declining and the current account was improving— and despite massive intervention backed by a $5 billion credit line from the Bank for International Settlements—the pound fell by 34 percent against the dollar over 20 months. What is striking in the US context is that during 1976 three major packages of fiscal restraint were announced (in February, July, and December) amounting—on paper—to as much as 4 percent of GNP. While, at least until the IMF was called in, these did little to restore confidence, they paved the way for the subsequent growth recession.

Closer to home, events in the United States in 1978–79 have a similar ring. The background was the same: an initially expansionary fiscal policy, a deteriorating current account, and an inflation performance deteriorating relative to other countries. The first in a long series of anti-inflationary programs came in May 1978, including smaller pay increases for federal workers and a $5 billion reduction in planned tax cuts. Another package in October 1978 included a pledge to reduce the share of federal spending in GNP from 23 percent to 21 percent in FY 1980, and a 7 percent voluntary limit on wage increases. On November 1, 1978, a $30 billion line of foreign credits was mobilized to help support the dollar. In September 1979, the President announced a National Accord to ''deal effectively with inflation.'' On October

5, 1979, the discount rate was raised—for the tenth time since January 1978—to 12 percent, and the Federal Reserve Board announced a major change in the conduct of monetary policy.

Despite the fact that the current balance had been improving for over a year, none of this did much to stem the loss of confidence in the dollar which fell by 35 percent against the DM in the four years to December 1979, even though the federal funds rate rose dramatically from 5 percent to 15 percent in the two years to the first quarter of 1980. The shift to fiscal restraint, and more particularly the change in monetary policies, did, however, pave the way for the 1980–82 recession, and by the fall of 1980 the dollar had started its long ascent.

But this prescription fails to take sufficient account of the fact that the United States is an open economy, with a greatly overvalued currency, and massive current account deficits that will have to be financed one way or another for some time to come.

In such circumstances, the Fed is facing a Catch-22 situation. An easing of monetary policy and lower interest rates can help to set off the necessary downward adjustment of the dollar; and, with the economy slowing down and inflation well under control, the Fed has been moving in this direction since the autumn of 1984. The agreement reached by the finance ministers and central bank governors of the Group of Five countries in September 1985 that "an appreciation of nondollar currencies" should be an explicit policy objective, coupled with the threat of coordinated intervention in the exchange markets to prod the dollar down, has put additional downward pressure on the dollar.

Under prevailing conditions, this makes good sense. But looking ahead it is important to realize that a time will come when the Fed will have to tighten up again to prevent the dollar's decline from getting out of control.[7] Once the dollar starts going down in earnest, inflation will pick up, and, rightly or wrongly, the financial markets have been conditioned to believe that money supply and inflation are closely related. Evidence that the Fed

---

7. And—if the experience of other countries is any guide—that the Fed will then be accused of having eased up too much.

was prepared to accommodate rising inflation by printing more money would give a further boost to inflationary expectations. Since there would also be upward pressure on interest rates, it would also be seen as evidence that, when the choice between cutting the budget deficit or monetizing it could no longer be avoided, the pressures on the Fed to resort to the printing press were becoming overwhelming.

Similarly acute psychological problems would surface in the foreign exchange market. Exchange rate expectations appear to be sensitive to changes in inflation and inflationary expectations (chapter 1). Moreover, attempts by the Fed to mitigate the upward pressure on interest rates from foreigners' attempts to get their money out of dollars would blunt the automatic stabilizing mechanism—a widening interest-rate differential—that might otherwise help to slow down the dollar's decline. More generally, foreigners would interpret signs that the Fed was prepared to tolerate a faster rate of monetary expansion as evidence that the United States was also going to monetize its *external* deficit, with ominous consequences for inflation, not only in the United States, but in the world economy.

Summing up at this point:

• Once the decline in the dollar gathers real momentum and the inflow of foreign savings dries up, there may be little option but to cut the budget deficit even if, as seems probable, the US economy is already weakening because of normal cyclical forces and crowding out from the over-strong dollar.

• However determined the efforts made to reduce the deficit, interest rates will stay high for some time, because, with a declining dollar, foreigners' willingness to supply savings to the United States will be declining faster than its need for them.

• Under these conditions, the Fed would have little or no scope to fend off recession by stepping up the money supply because this would aggravate both inflationary expectations at a time when inflation was accelerating, and negative exchange rate expectations at a time when the dollar was falling.

The upshot is that if the US economy is not already in recession by that time, the necessary policy response to a major reversal of the external position will make a recession inevitable.

This conclusion would be contested by many US economists. True, the recession should be relatively short-lived as net exports pick up in response to the lower dollar (unless there were a financial crisis). But the fact is that the economy will almost certainly *have* to be depressed for a while to correct such a large external disequilibrium, both to contain the inflationary pressures coming from the fall in the dollar, and to free up resources for exports and import substitution. This will probably prove to be as true for the United States as it has been for, for example, France, Mexico, or Brazil.[8]

What Should Be Done About the Budget Deficit

The fact that there is no way of getting the fiscal sums right does not mean that what is done about the budget deficit does not matter—quite the contrary. First, the severity of the crunch in US financial markets will depend on the size of the deficit at that time and, more particularly, on expectations about its future course. Second, even after the dollar goes down to or below its "equilibrium" level, and foreigners stop trying to get out of the dollar, crowding out in US financial markets will continue unless, by then, the budget deficit has been reduced enough to bring savings into line with investment in the US economy at whatever level of capital inflows or outflows then proves sustainable.

The orders of magnitude of this medium-term budget calculus can be illustrated using the alternative assumptions about the supply of foreign savings made in the scenarios developed in the last chapter. Past behavior of the US private sector's investment-savings balance suggests that, with unemployment at 6 percent, the private sector plus state and local governments should have surplus savings equivalent to around 0.5 percent of GNP (TN18). In other words, with zero capital inflows, overall balance between US investment and savings could be maintained with a structural federal deficit of 0.5 percent of GNP. From there, it is possible to estimate what level of the structural federal budget deficit in 1990 would be consistent with the assumed capital flow in the different scenarios (table 5.1).[9]

---

8. The partial exceptions have been highly competitive countries such as Japan or South Korea which can shift sales quickly from domestic to foreign markets.

9. It should be emphasized that what is relevant here is the *structural* budget deficit. With a given level of capital inflow, an increase in the deficit resulting from a weakening of the economy will not worsen the *overall* investment-savings balance because it will normally be matched, or more than matched, by a rise in the private sector's surplus savings (chapter 1 and TN6).

BOX 5.2   An internal or an external debt constraint?

It is fascinating to see how most of the budget debate has been
about the potential damage to the economy from large-scale
Federal borrowing in domestic financial markets, i.e. in terms of
the US government's growing indebtedness to its own citizens.
Early on, the principal concern was about crowding out private
investment. Since this did not happen—because of massive capital
inflows—attention shifted to longer term concerns, in particular,
to the projected rise in the ratio of federal debt held by the public
to GNP from 30 percent in 1984 to 50 percent in 1990 (figure
6.5). Thus, the Congressional Budget Office Director, in testimony
to Congress, while emphasizing that every bit of deficit reduction
helps, suggested that a prudent aim would be to stabilize the
public debt to GNP ratio in 1988 (Penner 1985), which would
require reducing the budget deficit to 3 percent of GNP in that
year.
    The story looks quite different, however, if the focus is shifted
to the rate at which the United States, as a nation, is going into
debt to the citizens of other countries. This has not escaped the
attention of US observers, but, at least until recently, the concern
was only about the longer run consequences: "Borrowing from
abroad is borrowing from the future for current consumption,
since these debts to foreigners will have to be repaid with interest
out of future national production" (Rivlin 1984, p. 7).
    But foreign borrowing on a large scale involves dangers with
a much shorter time horizon (chapter 3). The 1988 objective
proposed by the CBO Director, while it would stabilize the
domestic public debt to GNP ratio, would *not* stop the US *external*
debt to GNP ratio from rising. This emerges from the CBO's
own analysis of the US investment-savings balance, in which, in
a rather revealing way, capital inflows are projected as a residual
(TN19). Thus, a structural budget deficit of 3 percent of GNP in
1988 would imply the need for an inflow of foreign savings of
2.5 percent of GNP, and that would imply both a very large
continuing current account deficit, and that the US external debt
to GNP ratio would rise for a very long time into the future.

TABLE 5.1   **US structural budget position[a] projected by CBO and as required in different scenarios, 1988 and 1990**
(percentage of GNP)

	1988	1990
CBO projections[b]		
Baseline	−4.3	−4.8
Under August 1985		
Congressional Budget Resolution	−2.3	−1.8
As required to achieve overall investment-savings balance in D&D scenarios[c]		
Baseline	−5.6	−6.2
Soft-landing	−3.6	−2.0
Cooperative	−2.3	−0.5
Hard-landing	−1.1	+1.0

Source: CBO (1985b, table I-14) and simulations of the D&D model.
a. Cyclically adjusted federal budget position based on 6 percent unemployment rate trend GNP (TN6).
b. Fiscal years, unified budget basis.
c. Calendar years, NIPA basis.

The Congressional Budget Office (CBO) has estimated that, without action to cut it, the structural deficit would rise to 4.8 percent of GNP by 1990. In the soft-landing scenario it would have to be cut to 2 percent to maintain overall balance between savings and investment. According to the CBO, this would be achieved if the Congressional Budget Resolution adopted in August 1985 were fully implemented (1985b). But, as we have seen, the assumption in this scenario of continued large-scale capital inflows to 1990 and beyond seems implausible (chapter 4 and box 5.2). On the assumption made in the hard-landing scenario that the capital inflow would turn to a capital outflow by 1990, *continuing crowding out could only be avoided if the structural deficit were cut by 5.5 percent of GNP or more by 1990.* Seen in this light, much of the current debate about cutting the budget deficit sounds like Alice in Wonderland.

What then *should* be done about the budget deficit? The first answer is simple, if unhelpful. The right time for a sharp cut was during the first 18 months of the recovery. But there is no point crying over spilled milk.

Now, there is no simple answer. On one hand, large and rising structural federal deficits are the major reason why the economy became excessively dependent on foreign savings; this, in turn, has created the conditions for an externally generated recession. On the other hand, cutting the deficit would, other things being equal, tend to push the economy into recession. And a recession could well trigger off a flight from the dollar.

A GRADUAL APPROACH?

Given these conflicting considerations, a case can be made for a relatively gradual approach to cutting the deficit. It is suggested that the goal should be a "credible" program of major budget cuts spread over, say, five years. Such a program, it is argued, should have an "announcement" effect in the financial markets, shortening the lag before the stimulus from lower interest rates and a lower dollar offset the negative impact on income flows from cutting the deficit.[10]

There are, however, serious difficulties with this approach. President Reagan's attitude to the budget deficit remains ambiguous. He still seems to believe that "the single best deficit program is an all-out push for economic growth."[11] He and influential members of his party remain adamantly opposed to tax increases which would have to form part of a credible program (chapter 7):

I have my veto pen drawn and ready for any tax increase that Congress might even think of putting up. And I have only one thing to say to the tax increasers: 'Go ahead, make my day.'[12]

Moreover, the President's proposals for tax reform, however worthy in themselves, have at best distracted attention from the more pressing issue of cutting the deficit, and could, at worst, end up as a tax cut in disguise.

---

10. This was perhaps most strongly pressed by Martin S. Feldstein while he was Chairman of the Council of Economic Advisers (1983b, p. 12). "Note that what matters most is not the current budget deficit but the expectation of future budget deficits. If Congress acts this fall to reduce the prospective budget deficit, the long-term interest rate and the exchange value of the dollar will both decline immediately." This was also the logic behind Feldstein's idea for a "standby tax" to come into effect if the deficit did not come down quickly enough, which was included in the 1984 Budget proposals, but never seriously considered by Congress.

11. Radio Address to the Nation from Camp David, Md., 9 February 1985.

12. Remarks of the President to the American Business Conference, 13 March 1985, page 1.

Beyond this, it would appear that the US political system, with its division of power, lack of party discipline, frequent elections, and vulnerability to special interests, is less well suited than most to taking "credible" fiscal action which is only to come into effect some years hence. In fiscal matters, the administration proposes, but Congress disposes. The fiscal decisions of the first Reagan administration shifted the structural fiscal position from rough balance to a deficit equivalent to nearly 5 percent of GNP over a period of five years. The consequence may well be that US public finances are getting out of control in the same basic *political* sense as happened in many other countries in the 1970s. And the experience of these countries shows that even when governments became convinced of the need to make major cuts in the budget deficit, and had clear parliamentary majorities, they greatly underestimated the intrinsic political difficulties involved.[13] That this could be equally true for the United States is suggested by opinion surveys showing large majorities in favor of cutting the budget deficit, but against every way it might be done.[14]

This may be considered an unduly pessimistic assessment. The CBO estimates that the Congressional Budget Resolution adopted in August 1985 would, if fully implemented, involve a substantial reduction in the budget deficit by 1988 (CBO 1985b). There has, however, been much scepticism about both the figures in this resolution[15] and the likelihood of its implementation. At the time of writing, Congress is considering legislation which would "force" the budget into balance by 1991. Symptomatically, these cuts would be "back loaded," with the main effort put off until after the

---

13. Perhaps most graphically illustrated by the difficulty Mrs. Thatcher has had in getting UK public expenditure under control. Other examples are provided by events over the last few years in Belgium, the Netherlands, and Denmark.

14. According to a Washington Post-ABC news poll taken in January 1985, 94 percent of respondents were against cutting Social Security benefits, 79 percent against an increase in taxes, 62 percent against cutting spending for social programs, and 51 percent against cutting military spending. *Washington Post*, 20 January 1985, p. A14. In a Louis Harris survey taken a year earlier, in which 71 percent considered that big deficits were "very serious," the results were broadly similar, except that 62 percent were in favor of a substantial increase in taxes on corporations. *Business Week*, 30 January 1985, p. 8.

15. Capra and Sinai (1985) suggest that the resolution incorporates net reductions in the deficit of only about $20 billion for FY 1986 and around $70 billion by FY 1988. This would leave a deficit in the range of 3 percent to 4 percent of GNP in 1988.

1986 elections. Moreover, as noted by the *New York Times*, the 96th Congress repealed a law passed by the 95th Congress requiring a balanced budget by 1981—not a very encouraging precedent.[16]

It thus seems only too likely that these will turn out to be yet more episodes in an unending sequence of lengthy discussions on successive fiscal packages that on paper add up to sizable cuts over a period of years.[17] But these are from a "baseline" that just keeps growing each time the CBO does the sums.[18] As Budget Director David Stockman put it shortly before resigning:

As the fiscal crisis has worsened and the political conflict intensified, we have increasingly resorted to squaring the circle with accounting gimmicks, evasions, half-truths and downright dishonesty in our budget numbers, debate and advocacy.[19]

This is definitely *not* the way to inspire confidence in financial markets. And the longer this phony war on the deficit continues, the more skeptical the markets will become, and the more immediate and massive will be the action needed to restore confidence once it begins to evaporate.

THE CASE FOR CUTTING THE DEFICIT AS QUICKLY AS POSSIBLE

Acceptance of the serious risk of a hard landing casts a very different light on US policy options. The key issue then centers on what course of action could most help to increase the manageability of the situation once a bandwagon develops in the foreign exchange markets. How could it help to favor the operation of stabilizers discussed in chapter 4? How would it affect the maneuvering room of the authorities—particularly the Fed—to take discretionary action to keep the decline in the dollar from getting out of hand (table 5.2)?

---

16. "The Balanced Baloney Act of 1985," *New York Times*, 4 October 1985, p. A-30.

17. It was encouraging, however, that by the fall of 1985 the link between the trade deficit and the budget deficit had become better understood in political circles. This meant that the rising concern about the trade deficit, and the protectionist pressures generated by it, helped to keep alive the issue of making further efforts to cut the budget deficit.

18. For example, after three years of budget proposals and budget resolutions apparently involving significant "cuts," the administration's 1986 budget projections in February 1985 showed a 1988 deficit $27 billion *higher* than it had projected for that year three years earlier.

19. In an off-the-record speech to the New York Stock Exchange, 5 June 1985.

TABLE 5.2   **Risks involved in gradual versus rapid reduction in budget deficit**

Risk of	Gradual	Rapid
A. Slowdown because of negative effects on income flows	Less	More
B. Strong upward pressure on interest rates	More	Less
C. Strong downward pressure on dollar		
Short run	Already discounted?	Could be positive
Later	Less	More
After bandwagon starts	More	Less
D. Risk of fiscal stabilizers becoming neutralized	More	Less
E. Constraints on the Federal Reserve Board's room for maneuver	More	Less
F. Risk of financial crisis (developing countries and US financial institutions)		
From A above	Less	More
From B above	More	Less
From C above	Ambiguous[a]	Ambiguous[a]
From E above	More	Less

a. In principle, the faster and further the dollar falls the better for developing-country debtor countries and for US banks with loans to exposed sectors of the US economy (for example, agriculture). Against this, the faster the dollar falls the greater, beyond a certain point, are the risks of a recession in the United States and the world economy more generally.

Seen in this light, the case for cutting the budget deficit as quickly as possible is as follows:

• First, US interest rates would be lower for any given decline in the ex ante inflow of foreign savings. This, in itself, would reduce the risk of a financial crisis through renewed financial pressures on the developing-country debtors and on exposed US financial institutions. The Fed would thus have more room either—according to the circumstances—to ease policy to counter recessionary tendencies and reduce the risk of a financial crisis, or to tighten up to prevent a bandwagon from developing against the dollar.

• Second, the level to which the *actual* budget deficit would rise would be less for any given weakening in US growth; and the less frightening the deficit figures, the less the adverse impact on confidence in financial markets, leaving more scope to allow the automatic stabilizers to cushion a recession.

The first consideration could be crucially important. The Fed has rightly shown its concern about the fragility of both the international banking system following the debt crisis, and the US domestic financial system following problems at Continental Illinois and the Ohio and Maryland savings and loan associations, and the financial pressures in the agricultural and energy sectors. A hard landing would put the Fed in an extremely difficult situation. Easing up could jeopardize the gains from the painful battle to control inflation; not easing up could run the risk of a major financial crisis with incalculable consequences. Moreover, even if the period of intense downward pressure on the dollar were successfully negotiated, the Fed would still face the same dilemma unless and until the budget deficit had been brought down to levels consistent with a much lower inflow—or quite possibly an outflow—of capital.

The importance of the second consideration is illustrated by the fact that, in the hard-landing scenario, the budget deficit could rise, without action to cut it, to as much as $425 billion or nearly 9 percent of GNP by 1990 (TN20). Such a widening of the cyclical element in the budget deficit should not normally cause concern, since it simply reflects the operation of the automatic stabilizers helping to dampen cyclical fluctuations. But, under conditions of accelerating inflation and a falling dollar, the psychological impact on market sentiment of deficits of this size could be devastating. As in other countries, a situation could arise in which budget cuts seemed essential to offset a *cyclical* rise in the deficit, thus, in effect, neutralizing the automatic stabilizers.[20] Equally, the larger the actual deficit became, the more the markets would be frightened by it, and thus the less the scope to mitigate the recession by easing monetary policy.

The impact of a determined attack on the budget deficit on the dollar itself is, at first sight, more ambiguous. It can be argued that since US interest rates should be lower, deficit-cutting action would hasten the move out of the dollar. But it can also be argued that foreigners' confidence in the US economy would be strengthened by decisive action to deal with the budget

---

20. The classic case was the 1981 Budget in the United Kingdom (which, for this reason, was strongly criticized in a letter signed by 364 British economists). During the 1981–82 recession, many other examples occurred in Europe of governments feeling that there was no option but to "chase the budget deficit downhill" in this way.

deficit—the one thing that more or less everybody has agreed is wrong. "A cut in the federal deficit would strengthen the dollar because investors would have increased confidence in the long-term health of the American economy."[21]

What is the right answer? Exchange markets are fickle. In the short run, unexpectedly strong action to cut the deficit could strengthen the dollar. But the key factor behind its strength in 1983–84 was the divergence between rising structural budget deficits in the United States and reduced structural budget deficits in many other countries in the world (chapter 1).[22] Once the positive effects on confidence wore off, and as interest-rate differentials narrowed or disappeared, the stage would be set for a bandwagon against the dollar. It would be *then* that concrete evidence that "what is wrong is being fixed" would help most to make the dollar's decline more manageable.

Summing up: in the short term, a determined effort to cut the budget deficit might strengthen the dollar; in the slightly longer term, it would probably weaken the dollar by lowering interest rates; but beyond this point, once a bandwagon gets underway, it would be crucially important in helping to prevent the dollar from going down too fast and too far.

Some important conclusions can be drawn from this and the preceding chapters. In 1983–84 strong action to reduce the US budget deficit, together with an appropriate response by the Federal Reserve, would have put the US recovery on a sustainable course. This window of opportunity has long since closed. The budget deficit should nevertheless be reduced as quickly as possible. But it is unrealistic to believe that the negative impact on demand could be fully offset by an easier monetary policy. Indeed, at some point, monetary policy will almost certainly have to be tightened to prevent the dollar from overshooting. In other words, the United States is no longer fully in control of its economic fortunes over the next few years; these now depend, as never before, on the whims of its foreign creditors and, more fundamentally, on economic developments in—and the policies followed by—its major allies. To these we now turn.

---

21. Leland S. Prussia, Chairman, Bank of America, quoted in *Business Week*, 8 October 1984, p. 167.

22. When the new US Secretary of the Treasury, James A. Baker III (1985), said: "I've never heard of an economy that got its fiscal affairs in order and had its currency weaken," he appears to have overlooked that this is exactly what has happened to Japan and Germany, to name only two of many recent examples.

6 Policy Options Facing Europe and Japan

Our key trading partners, directly or indirectly, have been relying on our markets to support their growth, and even so, most of them remain mired in historically high levels of unemployment.[1]

If the other major OECD countries stick to their present policies, a hard landing for the US economy will have unpleasant consequences for them and, especially, for the developing countries. Unemployment in Europe could rise to over 14 percent and the developing countries would be hit by a repeat of the 1981–83 debt crisis. An analysis of the constraints on a shift to more expansionary policies—inflation, large budget deficits, wage and other rigidities, etc.—suggests that they can easily be exaggerated. Europe could and should "grow out" of its real wage problem, and Japan needs to make more use of its surplus private savings at home.

The Hard-Landing Scenario

Through 1984 and into 1985, there were widespread hopes that the recovery in the rest of the OECD area, stimulated by a strong boost from external demand, would progressively gather momentum. Indeed, the basic premise of the policies being followed was that with renewed confidence bred by low inflation and reduced budget deficits, and with improving profitability, there would be a "self-levitating" recovery spurred by a strong rise in private investment.

---

1. Volcker, (1985d, p. 9).

161

162   DEFICITS AND THE DOLLAR

TABLE 6.1   **Hard-landing scenario in rest of OECD area, 1985–90**
(percentage change from previous year)

	1985	1986	1987	1988	1989	1990
Net exports[a]	0.2	−0.1	−1.3	−1.1	−0.6	−0.2
Domestic demand	2.8	2.7	1.9	2.2	2.5	2.8
GNP	3.2	2.6	0.6	1.1	1.9	2.7
Price level	5.8	4.5	3.3	3.1	3.7	4.6

Note: Simulation, using the D&D model, of the impact on the ROECD area of the hard-landing scenario for the dollar described in chapter 4. For details, see TN2.
a. Change from previous year as percentage of GNP.

By late 1985, it was clear that these were vain hopes. The best of the world recovery was already over. The growth of world trade slowed down sharply from 9 percent in 1984 to 3 percent in the first half of 1985 in volume terms. The first effects were, as usual, felt in Japan[2] and the export-oriented economies of Southeast Asia; by the fall of 1985, they were also creating renewed concern about the prospects for the heavily indebted countries in Latin America. With a somewhat longer lag, the effects of the slowdown in world trade were beginning to make themselves felt in Europe. Thus, as 1985 drew to a close, the export boom was fading for the ROECD area as a whole, and the negative impact of restrictive fiscal policies and high interest rates was reasserting itself.

IMPACT ON EUROPE AND JAPAN

What then would happen if the hard-landing scenario for the US economy materializes? The strong stimulus from export demand would not only evaporate, but would, in time, go sharply into reverse. This would be a dramatic reversal of what happened from 1980 to 1984 (figure 6.1). It is likely, moreover, that most of the negative counterpart of the improvement in the US current balance would fall on the other OECD countries, since the developing countries—with upward pressure on US interest rates and an

2. The latest OECD forecast for Japan showed GNP growth slowing down from 5.8 percent in 1984 to under 4 percent in 1986 (*Economic Surveys* of Japan, August 1985).

FIGURE 6.1   **Domestic demand and GNP: Japan, Europe, and United States, 1980–84** (indices 1980 = 100)

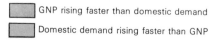
GNP rising faster than domestic demand

Domestic demand rising faster than GNP

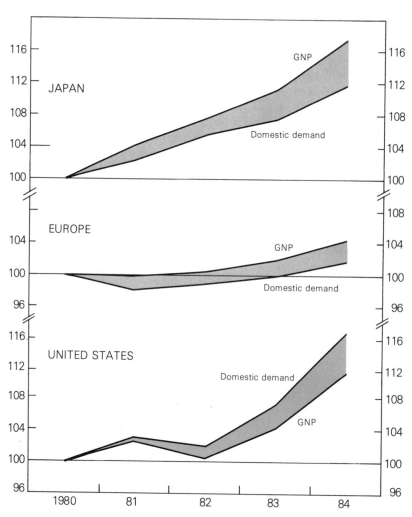

Source: OECD data base.

incipient world recession—would be in no position to finance larger current account deficits (see below). The result would be that in the hard-landing scenario the net exports of other OECD countries would fall by the equivalent of 3 percent of ROECD GNP over the three years 1987–89 (table 6.1). Other things being equal, moreover, this would have strong multiplier effects on domestic incomes and investment which could more than double the negative impact on GNP.

There would, however, be important positive effects from the decline in the dollar on inflation and interest rates. According to the D&D model, lower import prices, together with the feedback on wages and other prices, would, by 1990, have reduced the ROECD price level by around 6 percentage points from what it would otherwise have been. As for interest rates, once sentiment swings sharply against the dollar, they should become fully "decoupled" from US rates, so that even with unchanged monetary policies they could well drop by 2 or more percentage points to more historically normal levels in real terms.[3] In themselves, lower inflation and interest rates should stimulate domestic demand and help to offset the negative impact of declining net exports, and the D&D model makes an allowance for this (TN1, paragraph 14). How much they would do so is, however, open to some doubt under a scenario in which business confidence would be adversely affected by recession and financial strains in the United States and renewed difficulties in the indebted developing countries.

Putting these various elements together, and assuming that countries stick basically to their present restrictive fiscal policies, the hard-landing outcome for the ROECD area might be something like that summarized in table 6.1. There would be a severe growth recession in 1987–88; by 1990, GNP would be around 6 percent below the level assumed in the baseline, and unemployment would have risen sharply. Against this, inflation would drop to under 3.5 percent in 1987–89; indeed, it could well be lower than this since the D&D model makes no allowance for the effect of slow growth on world commodity prices or on domestically generated inflation.

The impact would, however, be quite sharply differentiated between countries, depending on how much their currencies appreciated against the dollar, and the closeness of their trade links with the United States.

---

3. It should be noted, however, that in the hard-landing scenario some countries could get caught in a "liquidity trap" (as in the 1930s) since inflation might temporarily become negative while interest rates would remain, of necessity, positive.

Somewhat surprisingly, regression analysis of the period since exchange rates began to float shows that although movements in the dollar itself have been difficult to explain, movements in other currencies *relative* to the dollar have been reasonably consistent (TN21). These movements can be divided into two components:

• First, when the dollar has been moving against *all* currencies, the other currencies that have tended to move most in the opposite direction have been those of countries whose financial markets provide the most attractive alternatives to the dollar, and have relatively small bilateral trade with the United States (table 6.2, first column). The Swiss franc has been the extreme case, followed by the deutsche mark. Because of their close links with the deutsche mark, the French franc and the currencies of countries in the "DM bloc"—Austria, Belgium, and the Netherlands—also moved much more than the average of other currencies when the dollar rose or fell. At the other extreme, the Canadian dollar and the Finnish mark showed no systematic tendency to move against the dollar when the latter was moving against all other currencies. The currencies in the middle are generally floating independently.[4]

• Second, there has been a trend factor with individual currencies appreciating or depreciating over time against the dollar because of differences in inflation rates and other factors affecting the country's competitivity and the structure of its balance of payments (table 6.2, second column). The Japanese yen, for example, shows a positive trend against the dollar of nearly 4 percent a year over 1970–84, reflecting no doubt both Japan's competitive strength and its excellent inflation performance since the mid-1970s. Italy, on the other hand, shows an equally strong negative trend, no doubt mainly reflecting its high inflation rate.

In assessing the impact of exchange rate changes in the different scenarios, both of these components are relevant, although in somewhat different ways. As just noted, the *trend* factor largely reflects changes in nominal rates needed to offset different inflation rates and other longer run factors affecting competitivity. It is thus the *relative* factor which largely determines the impact of a movement in the dollar on a country's competitive position and its *real* effective exchange rate. Projections of how this factor might affect

---

4. Or, in the case of the lira, has wide margins against the deutsche mark in the European Monetary System.

TABLE 6.2   **Behavior of MERM currencies vis-à-vis dollar, 1970–84**

Relative change when dollar moves vis-à-vis all currencies[a]	Annual time trend against dollar
More than 1.5	*Strong appreciation (>3.5 percent)*
Swiss franc	Swiss franc
	Japanese yen
1.3 to 1.5	
Deutsche mark	*Appreciation (1 to 3.5 percent)*
Belgian franc	Deutsche mark
French franc	Austrian schilling
Netherlands guilder	Netherlands guilder
Danish kroner	Swedish kroner
Austrian schilling	
	No strong trend (+1 to −1 percent)
1 to 1.3	Norwegian kroner
Japanese yen	Belgian franc
Norwegian kroner	
Italian lira	*Depreciation (1 to 3.5 percent)*
Swedish kroner	Danish kroner
Pound sterling	Australian dollar
	Canadian dollar
Less than 1	French franc
Australian dollar	Finnish mark
Spanish peseta	Pound sterling
Close to zero	*Strong depreciation (>3.5 percent)*
Finnish mark	Spanish peseta
Canadian dollar	Italian lira
	Irish pound

Note: For methodology and sources, see TN21.
a. A coefficient of 1.5 implies that if the weighted average of all the MERM currencies (using US MERM weights) appreciates by 10 percent against the dollar, the currency in question typically appreciates by 15 percent.

the currencies of the major countries in the three scenarios are shown in table 6.3.[5] The first column shows the appreciation against the dollar in each

5. Using the equation in TN21 for the Canadian dollar would have produced little change against the US dollar, and hence a strong depreciation in the Canadian dollar's MERM-weighted

TABLE 6.3   "Relative" adjustment of exchange rates in different scenarios
(percentage appreciation)

	Cooperative		Soft-landing		Hard-landing	
	Dollar[a]	Effective[b]	Dollar[a]	Effective[b]	Dollar[a]	Effective[b]
Deutsche mark	63	18	85	23	118	30
French franc	60	17	80	21	111	28
Yen	43	16	57	21	77	27
Pound sterling	41	3	54	4	73	5
Italian lira	44	2	58	3	79	3
ECU	57	n.a.	77	n.a.	107	n.a.
All MERM						
currencies	n.a.	41[c]	n.a.	55[c]	n.a.	74[c]

Note: Simulation of D&D model. Percentage appreciation from the base period (average over the six months to March 1984) assuming that the total dollar decline in each scenario took place overnight. For dollar cross-rates in the base period, see table 6.4. For methodology, see TN21.
a. Dollar cross-rate.
b. MERM-weighted nominal effective index, each currency.
c. Reciprocal of decline in MERM-weighted nominal effective dollar index.

scenario. The second shows what happens to the country's effective (trade-weighted) exchange rate; this depends on how all the other currencies move against the dollar and the relative importance of the dollar and the other currencies in the trade relations of the country concerned. Thus, for example, although the yen appreciates much less against the dollar than the deutsche mark, Japan's effective rate appreciates by nearly as much because dollar markets are more important to it. The effective rates for the United Kingdom and Italy, on the other hand, appreciate very little because of the importance of their markets in European countries whose currencies appreciate more than theirs against the dollar.

These projections suggest that the competitive position of Germany, Japan, and France (and the smaller countries in the DM bloc) would be most

index. This seems implausible since Canada is running a substantial current account surplus, and according to an extension of Williamson's (1985) analysis the Canadian dollar is not currently overvalued. Thus, in the projections in tables 6.3 and 6.4, it is assumed that there is no change in the nominal effective (MERM-weighted) exchange rate of the Canadian dollar over the projection period (see TN21, paragraph 8).

adversely affected, with their effective rates appreciating by 27 percent to 30 percent in the hard-landing scenario. By the same token, however, these countries would also benefit most in terms of reduced inflation, since this is also a rough measure of how much their real exchange rates might appreciate.[6] There are two qualifications, however:

• With the liberalization of Japanese financial markets and the emergent dynamism of Southeast Asia, the relative appreciation of the yen could well be stronger than suggested by the 1970–84 regression results.

• Because of overdue realignments within the European Monetary System (chapter 7), the French franc would almost certainly not appreciate as much as shown in table 6.3.

These projections show what might be expected to happen if the dollar declined in one fell swoop. This is unlikely, and in the scenarios the decline is spread over the period to early 1989 (chapter 4). Over this time horizon, the trend factors discussed above would become increasingly important, not so much because of their impact on competitivity and real exchange rates, which should be modest, but because of their strong impact on *nominal* dollar cross-rates, and hence on the exchange rate gains and losses involved in holding different currencies.

Projections of dollar cross rates in the three scenarios in the first quarter of 1989, resulting from the combined operation of the relative and trend factors over this period, are shown in table 6.4. Both the DM-dollar and yen-dollar rates appreciate very strongly—in the hard-landing scenario by 100 percent or more, to levels 30 percent and nearly 40 percent, respectively, above their previous peaks in the late 1970s. In contrast, the dollar rates for the Italian lira, French franc, and UK pound appreciate much less and remain well below their previous peaks, largely reflecting an implicit assumption that inflation continues to be higher than in their major competitors.

A number of conclusions can be drawn from the analysis of the differential impact of the hard-landing scenario on other OECD countries:

• Inflation gains would be particularly marked for Japan, Germany, and countries with currencies closely linked to the deutsche mark, but much smaller for the United Kingdom, Italy, and Canada (and other countries with

---

6. The inflation gains would be most closely related to the currency composition of *imports*, and especially the importance of oil imports. Japan, in particular, would score on both counts.

TABLE 6.4   **Projected 1989 dollar cross-rates in different scenarios**
(national unit per dollar)

	Peak since 1970	Baseline 1984:4 + 1985:1	1989 projections[a]		
			Cooperative	Soft-landing	Hard-landing
Deutsche mark	1.73	3.16	1.78	1.57	1.33
Yen	176	252	158	144	128
French franc	4.02	9.67	6.57	5.82	4.98
Pound sterling[b]	2.60	1.16	1.44	1.58	1.77
Italian lira	582	1,956	1,713	1,557	1,379
ECU	0.69	1.39	0.89	0.79	0.67
SDR	0.76	1.02	0.81	0.76	0.70

Note: Simulation of D&D model. For methodology, see TN21. Historical data from IMF data base.
a. First quarter 1989.
b. Dollars per pound.

a low "relative" exchange rate coefficient, table 6.2). All countries would, however, benefit from a drop in the home-currency price of oil.

• The negative impact on GNP growth would be much greater in Japan than in Europe. Rough calculations suggest that by 1990 Japanese GNP might be 7 percent to 8 percent below what it would otherwise have been, against 4 percent to 5 percent for OECD Europe (TN22).

• The impact on unemployment, however, would be more serious in Europe than in Japan, both because of the much higher starting level and differences in labor market behavior; in Europe the unemployment rate could rise to over 14 percent (from 11 percent in 1984), compared to around 4 percent in Japan.

• Exchange rate losses would be particularly heavy for dollar asset holders whose "bread currency" was the Swiss franc,[7] deutsche mark, or yen.

---

7. Using this method of projection, the dollar-Swiss franc rate appreciates extremely strongly because of a high relative coefficient *and* a strongly positive trend factor, to SF 0.93 to the dollar in the hard-landing scenario! This seems implausible. The relative attraction of the Swiss franc has probably diminished since the 1970s because of the spread of Europessimism and the emergence of alternative tax havens outside Europe. Equally, it seems unlikely that the Swiss economy could absorb another such substantial appreciation in its real exchange rate.

IMPACT ON THE DEVELOPING COUNTRIES

For the developing countries the hard-landing scenario would involve an unpleasant replay of the 1981–83 debt crisis.[8] As then, the purchasing power of their export earnings would be severely hit by slow OECD growth, deteriorating terms of trade, and high US interest rates. There would, however, be one major difference: the dollar would be falling, not rising. This would do little to alleviate the squeeze on the purchasing power of their export earnings, but would improve their debtor status and reduce the real resource cost of debt servicing.

In the hard-landing scenario, OECD growth might fall to around zero in 1987–88 (figure 6.2). By 1988 the volume of developing-country exports to the OECD area could be 15 percent below the baseline, and their terms of trade might have deteriorated by 15 percent to 25 percent from their mid-1984 peak (box 6.1). Between 1986 and 1988, the purchasing power of developing-country exports might drop by around 10 percent (it dropped 11 percent between 1980 and 1982)—and more if there were a break in oil prices. In addition a temporary surge in US interest rates, and hence in the London Interbank Offer Rate (LIBOR), might have reduced the foreign currency available for imports by a further 2 percent to 3 percent.

Unless they could obtain additional finance, the developing countries would be forced, once again, to cut back their imports. Last time, after the import boom of the late 1970s, they were able to cut import volume by 8 percent between 1981 and 1983 and still achieve an annual growth rate of around 1.5 percent. This amount of belt-tightening would obviously be more difficult a second time around.

A great deal would depend on how the banks and the International Monetary Fund responded to the prospect of a repeat performance of 1981–83. There would be heavy pressure to provide more finance, especially as the origin of

---

8. The author's colleague William R. Cline has been one of the principal protagonists of the view that the developing-country debt problem is one of illiquidity, not insolvency, and so far events have proved him right (Cline 1984). For this reason, in the baseline case, in which the assumptions are in most respects similar to those made in his projections, we have followed him and put developing-country growth at 4.5 percent. In his study, however, Cline "implicitly assumes that the problem of the US budget deficit will be reduced to manageable proportions, and that the United States will not be forced into a sharp recession either because of high interest rates or as a means of reducing its large external current account deficits" (ibid., p. 160). These assumptions would not hold in the hard-landing scenario.

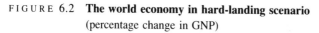

FIGURE 6.2 **The world economy in hard-landing scenario**
(percentage change in GNP)

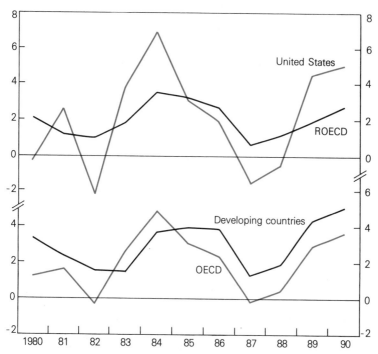

Source: OECD data base and simulation of D&D model.

the new problems would clearly lie in the North. Against this, it might not be easy to mobilize more "involuntary" lending by the banks because of heightened concern about social and political stability in the debtor countries and strains in the financial system generated by a hard landing in the United States. As compared with the 1981–83 debt crisis:

• The initial level of debt-export and debt-GNP ratios would be around 40 percent higher than in 1980 (figure 3.4). In addition, large amounts of rescheduled and other debt would be coming up for repayment in 1986 and 1987.

• These debt indicators would be just as adversely affected by the declining export volumes as they were in 1980–82.

B O X 6.1   **Nonoil commodity prices in different scenarios**

On the demand side, the prices of nonoil commodities are much more sensitive to variations in the OECD growth rate than prices for manufactured products. Thus, the purchasing power of commodities in terms of manufactures normally increases quite sharply in cyclical upswings, and vice versa (figure 6.3). Two additional features are relevant:

• The strong positive response of commodity prices to OECD growth has weakened since the early 1970s, especially for metals and minerals. This doubtless reflects more efficient use of basic materials, substitution of synthetic materials, and slower OECD growth. It is estimated that an OECD growth rate of 4 percent may now be needed to hold commodities constant in real terms (*OECD Economic Outlook,* no. 37, June 1985, p. 35)

• Atypically, commodity prices *fell* by over 10 percent in real terms from mid-1984 to mid-1985 during a recovery phase. Among the explanatory factors are: better harvest prospects for many agricultural products; increased capacity in extractive industries; distress selling by heavily indebted producing countries; high real interest rates; and the concentration of the recovery in the United States, which imports fewer primary commodities.

From the above, it seems that in the hard-landing scenario the terms of trade between commodities and manufactures could easily fall below the 1982 trough, i.e. by 20 percent to 25 percent from the mid-1984 peak, or 10 percent to 15 percent from their mid-1985 level. Since nonoil commodities now account only for 40 percent of nonoil exports from developing countries, this would depress their overall terms of trade by, say, 8 percent to 10 percent. A significantly worse outcome could not be ruled out, given the increasing signs of weakness in world commodity markets.

In the cooperative scenario, with OECD growth averaging nearly 4 percent, it would be reasonable to expect purchasing power of commodities in terms of manufactures to recover to, or above, the mid-1984 peak, an improvement of 10 percent or more from the mid-1985 level.

FIGURE 6.3   **Nonoil commodity terms of trade, 1970–85**
(indices 1975 = 100)

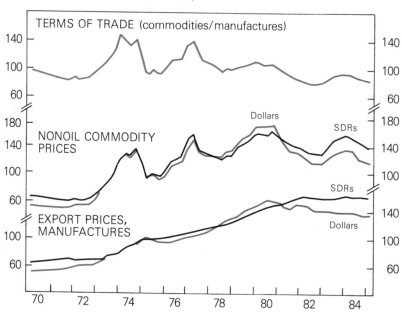

Source: OECD Economic Outlook, no. 37, June 1985, and OECD Secretariat.

• On the other hand, the dollar's decline would, in itself, substantially increase the dollar value of the debtors' export earnings relative to their dollar-denominated debt, and hence help to *improve* their debt calculus (box 6.2). Indeed, on the assumption that imports were cut back in line with lower export earnings, their debt to export ratios would actually *decline* (box 7.1).

It seems fruitless to speculate further on what the actual outcome might be for the developing countries in the hard-landing scenario. For the purpose of assessing the feedbacks on OECD countries, it has been assumed that they would not be able to obtain significant additional finance, but that nevertheless the setback to their growth would be no worse than in 1982–83 (figure 6.2). The much wider economic, social, and political implications of such an outcome lie outside the scope of this study.

B O X 6.2   **World trade prices and the dollar**

When the dollar rises, world trade prices *measured in dollars* fall, and vice versa. Thus, since 1980, trade prices measured in dollars have risen less or fallen more than the same prices measured in terms of a basket of currencies (figure 6.3). For a small country this would be a one-for-one relationship; an appreciation of its currency has no impact on world trade prices, and thus world trade prices measured in its currency fall by the full amount of the appreciation. But this is not so for the United States because of its size in the world economy. When the dollar rises, US dollar-export prices are not reduced by the full amount of the appreciation because US exporters are to some extent price setters in world markets. And, by the same token, other countries' exporters are able to raise their own prices—measured in their own currencies—somewhat, because of less price competition from US suppliers.

As a rough rule of thumb, a 10 percent rise in the dollar thus tends to be associated with an 8 percent drop in world trade prices measured in dollars, and vice versa (Cline 1984, pp. 160–61). This does not apply to trade in oil, where prices are fixed in dollars (except to the extent that OPEC's pricing policy is influenced by movements in the dollar). In the scenarios the direct consequences of a substantial decline in the dollar are that:
• For all countries, both import and export prices measured in dollars would rise sharply.
• US terms of trade would deteriorate, and ROECD terms of trade would improve.
• The terms of trade of oil-exporting countries would deteriorate, and those of oil-importing countries would improve.
• Apart from the above, there would be little systematic change in the terms of trade of the developing countries.
• But developing-country export earnings, measured in dollars, would rise relative to their dollar-denominated debt (box 7.1 and TN23).

To this point, it has been assumed that, even as the US economy went into recession, the other major OECD countries would stick to their present policies. This is unrealistic. Strong pressures would build for a shift to less restrictive policies. As of late 1985, however, the governments of the key countries involved were extremely reluctant to consider such a shift; the "statements of policy intentions" by Japan, Germany, and the United Kingdom at the Group of Five meeting in New York in September 1985 were essentially a reiteration of their present policies (chapter 7). They are committed to steady-as-you-go monetary and fiscal policies based on medium-term considerations. In their view, a significant shift to more expansionary policies would involve serious risks and be subject to important constraints. The remainder of this chapter is devoted to an assessment of these risks and constraints.

The Inflation Constraint

After the inflationary excesses of the 1970s, governments are understandably concerned about the risk that more expansionary policies would rekindle inflation. Yet the situation in this respect now varies enormously between countries. It is often overlooked that inflation in Germany and Japan, which account for nearly 40 percent of ROECD GNP, is now below the level of the "golden" 1960s, and in Japan is less than half what it was then (table 6.5).

These low rates of inflation, moreover, were achieved despite the price-raising impact of the decline in their currencies against the dollar. True, this was dampened by the weakness of world commodity prices, itself partly a consequence of the strong dollar; but it was nevertheless significant, especially via the price of imported oil on which both countries are heavily dependent.[9] Indeed, it may well be that by 1984 the *domestically generated* rate of inflation was under 1 percent in both countries; unit labor costs in manufacturing, for example, *fell* by 2 percent in Germany and more than 6 percent in Japan between 1982 and 1984.[10]

---

9. Between 1980:3 and 1985:1, for example, the dollar-price of oil fell by 13 percent, but in yen it rose by 7 percent and in DM by 60 percent.

10. *OECD Economic Outlook*, no. 37, June 1985, table 20.

TABLE 6.5   **Inflation in ROECD countries, 1961–84**
(annual percentage change in consumer prices)

	Weight in ROECD GNP 1982	Average 1961–70	First oil crisis peak[a]	Post-oil crisis trough[b]	Second oil crisis peak[c]	End-1984[d]
Germany	14.6	2.6	6.9	2.7	5.4	2.0
Japan	23.5	5.8	24.4	3.8	8.0	2.6
United Kingdom	10.7	4.1	24.3	8.3	17.9	4.9
France	11.9	4.2	13.6	9.1	13.8	6.9
Others						
High inflation[e]	18.4	4.6	16.6	14.0	21.5	16.1
Low inflation[f]	20.8	3.3	11.3	6.3	9.7	4.5
"DM bloc"[g]	9.7	3.5	10.1	3.3	5.9	4.5
Total ROECD	100.0	4.1	14.8	6.7	11.6	6.2
Memorandum items						
Total ROECD with						
MERM weights	n.a.	3.6	13.0	7.0	10.0	4.5
United States	n.a.	2.8	10.9	5.8	13.5	3.9

Source: OECD data base.
a. 1974 (1975 for United Kingdom).
b. 1978 (1976 for United States).
c. 1980 (1981 for low inflation group).
d. Twelve months to December or latest available figure.
e. Over 6 percent in 12 months to end-1984: Finland, Greece, Iceland, Ireland, Italy, New Zealand, Portugal, Spain, Sweden, and Turkey.
f. DM bloc plus Australia, Canada, Denmark, and Norway.
g. Austria, Belgium, the Netherlands, and Switzerland.

From this starting point, it seems quite probable that, in the hard-landing scenario, inflation in Germany and Japan could actually become negative for a time as a result of strong effective appreciation of their currencies, weak commodity prices, and increasing slack in their economies. There would also be strong currency appreciation and downward pressure on inflation in the other countries of the "DM bloc," where inflation is in the 3 percent to 5 percent range, which account for another 10 percent of ROECD GNP.

But what would happen if sufficient action were taken to raise the growth rate, as canvassed in chapter 7? Once unemployment began to fall, would domestically generated inflation pick up sharply? Unfortunately, three recent studies of this question are inconclusive, to say the least (TN25). There are two reasons for this:

• Since 1973, *variations* in inflation have been dominated by fluctuations in world commodity prices, particularly oil prices (table 6.5). At the same time, however, these fluctuations in commodity prices have been roughly correlated with rising and falling demand pressures in the OECD area, and hence with changes in unemployment. Because of this joint correlation, it is perhaps not surprising that while some analysts claim that the 1981–84 decline in inflation can be explained largely in terms of rising unemployment, others have suggested that it can be explained entirely by the decline in commodity prices.[11]

• Since 1973 there have also been major fluctuations in real exchange rates, and empirical work shows that these have had a powerful and quite rapid impact on prices and wages. Given this it has become more difficult to separate out and measure with any precision the impact on prices of changing domestic demand pressures and unemployment.

Despite these difficulties and uncertainties, two conclusions can be drawn from the present state of knowledge that are highly relevant in the present context. First, it is becoming increasingly clear that an individual country's rate of inflation depends more than is yet fully realized on commodity prices, *and hence on demand pressures and unemployment in the OECD area as a whole.* This supports the suggestion made at the end of chapter 1 that, if all OECD countries had followed the United States and shifted to strongly expansionary fiscal policies in 1981, there could well have been a new outbreak of world inflation. But it also follows that the governments of other OECD countries were, in 1985, probably significantly overestimating the inflationary risks involved if they took expansionary action at a time when US growth is slowing down. As long as the *aggregate* OECD growth rate did not exceed 3 percent to 4 percent there would be little risk of a strong rise in commodity prices, especially given the enormous overhang of unused capacity in the world oil market and, to a lesser extent, in many other commodity markets.

The second conclusion is that for an individual country, with flexible exchange rates, the inflationary consequences of a given course of action

---

11. This is the view taken by Beckerman (1985, 1986), who points out that imports of commodities are equivalent to around 8 percent of GNP, and, since there was a swing from rising to falling commodity prices of 50 percent to 60 percent between 1978 and 1982, this could, in simple arithmetic terms, account for a 5 percentage point drop in inflation even without allowing for a price-wage feedback.

depend more, over a period of one to three years, on what happens to the exchange rate than on what happens to domestic demand pressures and unemployment. Attention has already been drawn to the importance of this for Japan, Germany, and the DM bloc. For these countries, expansionary action which coincided with a decline in the dollar—and, indeed, helped to promote such a decline—could, given the orders of magnitude involved, well turn out to be *anti*-inflationary.

The position is different for many of the other OECD countries. One group of countries, which includes Italy and accounts for around 18 percent of ROECD GNP, still has an average inflation rate over three times higher than in the 1960s. Since most of them are also subject to a fiscal constraint (see below), they have little or no scope for expansionary action. This leaves the United Kingdom and France, where inflation is still higher than in the 1960s and where an appreciation of the real exchange rate would seem undesirable, given the weakness of their current balance of payments. In both countries, however, unemployment has been on a steadily rising trend and, especially in the United Kingdom, has already reached intolerably high levels (figure 2.5). For both countries, therefore, a key question is whether action to halt and reverse the rise in unemployment would lead to a significant acceleration in domestically generated inflation.

This leads us to the often confusing debate about the NAIRU (nonaccelerating inflation rate of unemployment). Some have argued that since actual unemployment in most European countries is above the NAIRU, according to their estimates, lower unemployment would not lead to higher inflation (Layard et al. 1984). Against this, others have argued that if actual unemployment is above the NAIRU, then inflation should be decelerating, but is not.[12] It has not, however, been accelerating either. One answer to this riddle could be that, by a fluke, actual unemployment was exactly equal to the NAIRU, and that the latter was rising at exactly the same rate as the former. A more plausible conclusion is that at least in some countries the domestically generated rate of inflation has not much to do with the level of unemployment at all, but mainly reflects a stubborn price-wage spiral with a life of its own.

For such countries, the real problem may lie elsewhere. Persistence in restrictive demand-management policies in the face of strong "inertial" inflation (and price shocks from commodity prices or the exchange rate)

---

12. For example, the *Economist* in commenting on Layard et al. (1984), 19 May 1984, p. 79.

could well, over time, *increase* the inflation proneness of these economies, or, to use that dubious concept, the NAIRU. Inadequate investment increases the mismatch between labor and capital and raises the level of unemployment at which demand pressures could emerge in goods markets; slow growth increases the degree of real wage moderation needed to restore profitability; high and rising unemployment undermines the work ethic. It could well be such factors that explain the disquieting tendency for estimates of the NAIRU to be raised more or less pari passu with the rise in actual unemployment:

Although unemployment rates are generally projected to level off or increase somewhat . . . , inflation is expected to remain relatively stable implying little difference between the actual and natural rates. There are few changes in structural factors . . . that would explain such a dramatic rise in the natural rate. . . . [Because of] the analytic fuzziness of the NAIRU concept when applied to economies out of long-run equilibrium, the policy relevance of the NAIRU may not be great.[13]

We return to this issue of the broader trade-offs involved in a shift to more expansionary policies in Europe below.

This brings us to what is regarded by many of the governments concerned as the crucial issue. They are committed to the "three Cs": consistency, credibility, and continuity of medium-term monetary and fiscal policies that will not "accommodate" inflation. They are therefore very much concerned lest the *psychological* consequences of a shift to more expansionary policies could lead quite quickly to rising inflationary expectations and accelerating inflation.

There are two sides to this question. On one hand, empirical analysis tends to find little measurable impact of "announcement" effects of a shift to nonaccommodating monetary and fiscal policies on the actual process of wage and price determination.[14] Such analysis tends, moreover, to indicate the prevalence of adaptive rather than rational expectations in goods and labor markets.[15] On the other hand, there is much evidence to suggest that the "credibility"—or otherwise—of a country's monetary and fiscal policy can have a powerful influence on its *financial* markets and, especially, on

---

13. Coe and Gagliardi (1985, pp. 11, 29).

14. For example, Perry (1983).

15. Coe and Gagliardi (1985, pp. 15–18).

the foreign exchange markets. This led Andrea Boltho to suggest that Europe may be caught in an "expectations trap":

Expansionary policies could well lead to runs on currencies and/or higher interest rates, as the financial sector, imbued with monetary orthodoxy, expects inflation to accelerate. Yet restrictive policies could affect the much more Keynesian expectations of the industrial sector. [The government] frames its [policy] stance in the light of its perception of the short-run reactions of the private financial sector to policy changes, while the private industrial sector bases its longer-run spending decisions on what it perceives the stance of macroeconomic policies to be.[16]

Or, as James Tobin (1983) put it: "Policies capable of achieving prosperity and growth may not be those in which business leaders and financiers have confidence; those which do inspire their confidence may not work."

This emphasis on the dichotomy between expectations and behavior in financial markets and "real" markets provides a valuable insight into the central dilemma facing Europe. One of its most important aspects is the effect of large budget deficits on the confidence and behavior of the financial markets, to which we now turn.

The Fiscal Constraint

As we have seen, for countries accounting for nearly 50 percent of ROECD GNP, the inflation risk involved in a shift to more expansionary policies appears to be small, and, in the event of a sharp decline in the dollar, nonexistent. For the governments of these countries, the main constraint is seen to come from the high level of budget deficits and high or rapidly rising levels of public debt. To them, the operative arm of the "expectations trap" is their belief that while larger budget deficits might stimulate the real economy, the adverse impact on confidence in the financial markets could push up interest rates so much as to fully offset the positive stimulus to demand. The outcome would at best be only a temporary fillip to demand at the cost of an additional rise in public debt and the burden of servicing it.

In assessing such a fiscal constraint it is essential to distinguish clearly between:

---

16. In Emerson (1984, pp. 26–27).

• the impact of the current and expected budget deficits on *flows* of savings and investment in the economy, and

• the impact of past, present, and expected future deficits on the *stock* of public debt and the costs involved in servicing it.

The impact of budget deficits on flows of private savings and investment since 1980 was discussed in chapters 1 and 2. The conclusion was that there is little reason to believe that private demand in the ROECD area has been crowded out by unduly large budget deficits. Surplus savings in the private sector remained at abnormally high levels, while structural budget deficits were being reduced. Quite a number of countries—especially Japan—were in consequence generating excess savings being sucked into the United States. It is, indeed, a basic thesis of the analysis underlying this study that for such countries a less restrictive fiscal policy might well have *improved* the domestic investment-savings balance, via stronger domestic demand, by reducing the relative attractiveness of investing savings in the United States (box 1.3).

Against this, it can be argued that the financial markets would not have seen it this way because of the longer run consequences of larger budget deficits. ROECD budget deficits, which had been negligible in aggregate until the first oil shock, have averaged 3.7 percent of GNP since then. In consequence, the public debt to GNP ratio which had gradually fallen to 12 percent in 1974 had shot up to 35 percent by 1984.[17]

The question of the impact of public debt on interest rates is one of the most controversial and difficult in economics. In theory it is quite straightforward: the larger the stock of government debt and the larger the current additions to it, the stronger will be the downward pressure on the prices of government securities, and hence upward pressure on interest rates. In practice, however, the story is much more complicated.

• There have been very large differences in debt levels between countries and in the same country at different times. In the United States, for example, the debt-GNP ratio for the federal government fell from over 50 percent to under 30 percent between the late 1950s and the early 1980s, but real interest rates were much higher in the latter period than the former. In the United Kingdom, the debt-GNP ratio—which had been over 150 percent for 37

---

17. Unless otherwise noted, the figures given here are for the *net* debt of *general* government, i.e. including state and local governments, and the assets of social security agencies (TN25).

years prior to 1955[18]—was around 50 percent in the early 1980s, but real interest rates were generally higher than in Belgium where it was 100 percent. Thus: "there appears to be no generally optimal ratio of gross government debt to GDP—in proximate terms, any fixed debt-GDP ratio might, within wide bounds, be said to be a 'steady state' (i.e. sustainable) position . . ." (Muller and Price 1984b, p. 5).

• In the short run, moreover, most research shows that there is usually a *negative* correlation between budget deficits (and hence additions to public debt) and interest rates.

• Both logic and empirical work suggest that factors other than the stock of debt will have a more powerful influence on interest rates—notably monetary policy, current budget deficits in relation to the flow of savings, international capital flows, and cyclical fluctuations in credit demand.

Given these complexities it was perhaps not altogether surprising that the US Treasury (1984), in a much criticized report, was able to conclude that "the idea that budget deficits cause interest rates to rise . . . is not at all certain."[19] It is comforting, therefore, that work being done at the OECD, designed to separate out the influence of the different relevant variables, tends to confirm the common sense view that budget deficits and government debt "measured on an averaged and forward looking basis affect interest rates positively," both in the United States and a cross-section of 15 other OECD economies (Muller and Price 1984b, p. 2). In view of the complexities involved, however, it would be fair to say that there remains a rather wide margin of uncertainty about the quantitative importance of the debt term and the time horizon over which it operates, especially because of the difficulties of capturing the influence of capital flows under flexible exchange rates.

The methodology used in the following analysis is described in more detail in TN25.[20] The main points are:

• Concern in the financial markets will be greater the higher the present level of public debt in relation to GNP, and the larger the current additions being made to it. In the case of the latter, it is the "primary" deficit, i.e. the deficit excluding net interest payments, which is most relevant to the

---

18. *OECD Economic Outlook*, no. 37, June 1985, chart A.

19. Donald T. Regan, Foreword to a report by the US Treasury (1984).

20. The author is indebted to Paul Armington for help in developing this analysis.

longer run debt calculus (TN25, paragraph 9). Moreover, it is the average
level of this deficit over the course of the business cycle, not the actual level
in any one year, that determines the growth rate of public debt over the
medium term.

• The way in which the deficit and debt variables will interact in the future
depends in a rather complex way on the future growth rate of the economy
and the rate of interest. Faster growth lessens the burden of servicing the
debt; higher interest rates increase the size of the current deficit and the costs
of servicing accumulated debt in the future.

The way in which these factors interrelate is shown in figure 6.4, which
plots 1984 net debt to GNP ratios and "mid-cycle" primary structural deficits
for 17 OECD countries, together with three diagonal "iso-danger" lines.
These have been constructed in such a way that countries whose 1984 deficits
and levels of debt put them on one of these lines—or equidistant from one
of these lines—are at the same risk that over a given number of years in the
future their debt to GNP ratio would rise to a given level.[21] The middle line
is for a "normal" world in which, over the longer run, the interest rate
equals the growth rate (both measured in either nominal or real terms). The
lower line is for the "abnormal" world of the early 1980s, when interest
rates exceeded the growth rate by around 3 percentage points on average in
the OECD area. The upper line is for the "abnormal" world of the 1960s,
when the growth rate exceeded interest rates by around 2 percentage points.
Two things stand out from figure 6.4:

• First, the position varies enormously from country to country. There are
three countries where the deficit-debt situation would look bad in more or
less any kind of world: Belgium, Italy, and Greece. At the other extreme,
the present position looks extremely comfortable in Norway (largely because
of revenues from North Sea oil).

• Second, it makes a great difference what kind of world the future has in
store. If we are condemned to go on living in a world of high interest rates
and low growth rates, countries such as Spain and Canada were already in

---

21. As drawn, the lines reflect a situation in which if the 1984 primary mid-cycle deficit were
to continue indefinitely, the debt-GNP ratio would rise to 1.0 in 20 years. This choice of criteria
is clearly arbitrary, but using different criteria would not greatly change the *relative* position of
different countries. The "danger" is the same for two countries the same perpendicular distance
from an iso-danger line.

"danger" on these criteria in 1984, and the United States, Japan, and Sweden would not be far from it. If, on the other hand, one assumes that, over time, a more normal relationship between growth rates and interest rates should emerge, their situation looks a lot better. These large differences arise from the compounding effects, over a number of years, of relatively small differences in growth and interest rates on the public sector's debt calculus; it is not easy for the layman to grasp, but has become familiar to the financial markets.

In the context of this study the main questions relate to the fiscal position of Germany, Japan, the United Kingdom, and the United States[22] (figure 6.5). There has clearly been a remarkable improvement in the fiscal position of Japan, Germany, and the United Kingdom since 1978–80; by 1985 the position looked quite comfortable, even using a more severe criterion for the United Kingdom (TN25, paragraphs 15–16). The contrast with the United States is striking. There, the deficit-debt situation, which was very comfortable in 1981, has been deteriorating rapidly, and the Congressional Budget Office projections (based on its baseline estimates of the current services deficit) show it getting close to the "danger" zone by 1990 even in a normal world.

It should be stressed that the purpose of the iso-danger lines shown in figures 6.4 and 6.5 is only to illustrate the *relative* risks facing different countries. It is not being suggested that a country on an iso-danger line is, for example, currently likely to experience 100 percent crowding out. All that can be said is that if it continued to run its present primary deficit indefinitely, then under the postulated growth and interest rate assumptions, its debt to GNP ratio would reach 100 percent twenty years hence (a level already reached by Belgium). In most cases, even if the primary deficit were to widen in the short run, there would still be time left to bring the longer term fiscal situation under control. "Even if deficits exceeded their sustainable levels, it would obviously not imply bankruptcy—only that fiscal policy would have to change at some time in the future." (Layard et al. 1984, p. 27)

---

22. The degree of financial decentralization in the public sector varies greatly among countries. For reasons of international comparability, all levels of government are covered in data used to construct figure 6.4. In figure 6.5, US data are for the federal government only, because state and local governments have great financial autonomy and borrow in their own right. This is also true, but to a lesser extent, in Germany and Japan.

FIGURE 6.4   **Public deficit and debt calculus for OECD countries, 1984**

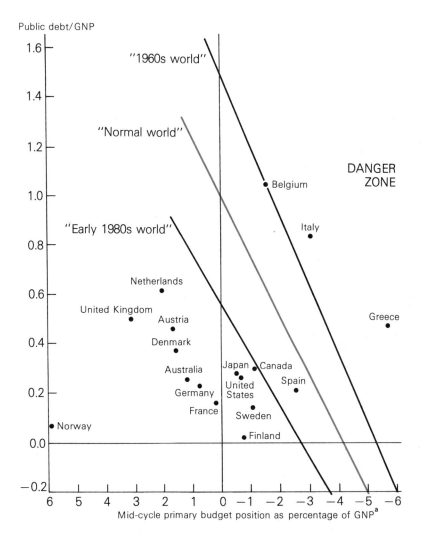

Note: Diagonal lines are "iso-danger" lines, TN25. Net public debt, general government.
Source: Muller and Price (1984a), updated by OECD Secretariat.
a. The structural budget position calculated at the *cyclically average* level of unemployment, less interest payments.

More important, in the present context, is the sensitivity of this calculus to whether the real interest rate exceeds, equals, or is lower than the growth rate. In a "normal" world, with the two rates equal, the debt to GNP ratio will remain stable as long as the primary budget position is in balance. But if the interest rate exceeds the growth rate, a country has to run a primary *surplus* in order to maintain a stable debt to GNP ratio, and the higher the debt to GNP ratio, the larger the necessary surplus. If, however, the growth rate exceeds the interest rate, the reverse is true.

In normal circumstances, this creates an unpleasant dilemma for the authorities. Fiscal expansion could raise the growth rate and hence improve the deficit-debt calculus, but this would be offset if it also raised the real interest rate. The present position facing ROECD countries is, however, abnormal in the sense that the high level of real interest rates is linked to an important extent to the strength of the dollar (chapter 2). *Once the dollar weakens, and ROECD interest rates decline, this could in itself make an important contribution to improving the fiscal calculus.* First, lower interest rates would help to reduce actual budget deficits. Equally important, lower interest rates and a higher growth rate would improve the whole longer term deficit-debt calculus.[23] Some illustrative calculations are given in TN25 and can be summarized as follows:

• In the hypothetical baseline, with the dollar remaining strong (and, by implication, large US structural budget deficits), real interest rates might remain at around 5 percent, i.e. 2 percentage points higher than the assumed growth rate. Germany, Japan, and the United Kingdom might be able to hold their debt-GNP ratios roughly constant, since, according to OECD projections, they are running primary surpluses in 1985 of just about the critical size.

---

23. A decline in the dollar will lead to a more immediate benefit to the public debt calculus for those countries whose governments have borrowed substantial amounts abroad in dollars, both lowering debt-GNP ratios and reducing debt service. In the case of Denmark, for example, public debt denominated in dollars was equivalent to as much as 13 percent of GNP at end-1984 (Denmark Ministry of Finance 1985, tables 2 and 3). Thus, for example, the drop in the dollar against the kroner from December 1984 to October 1985 should, in itself, have reduced the debt-GNP ratio by about 2 percentage points. Other countries with a large external public debt are (figures in parentheses are central government debt held abroad as percentage of GNP): New Zealand (19 percent, 1982), Sweden (10 percent, 1981), Austria (10 percent, 1982), and Belgium (6 percent, 1980) (Chouraqui and Price 1984, table C.3). See also TN25.

FIGURE 6.5 **Public deficit and debt calculus, four OECD countries,
1970–90[a]**

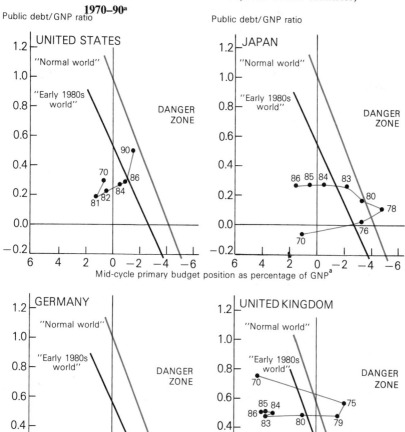

Note: Diagonal lines are "iso-danger" lines, TN25. Net public debt. Federal government for
the United States, central government for others.

Source: Muller and Price (1984a), updated by OECD Secretariat. 1990 for US, CBO (1985a).

a. The structural budget position calculated at the *cyclically average* level of unemployment,
less interest payments.

● In the hard-landing scenario, however, a further rise in debt to GNP ratios would be inevitable. Interest rates would be down, but so would growth; more important, actual deficits would widen sharply, pushed up by the automatic stabilizers as growth slowed down.

● In the cooperative scenario set out in chapter 7 the story would be quite different. ROECD interest rates should come down 2 to 3 percentage points, and growth would average 1 percent or more than in the baseline. Thus, for a temporary period over the remainder of the 1980s, ROECD growth might exceed the real interest rate by, say, 2 percentage points. Under these conditions, countries could run deficits instead of surpluses and still hold their debt to GNP ratios constant. Rough calculations in TN25 suggest, for example, that Germany, the United Kingdom, and Japan could accept an *ex post* deterioration in their fiscal position, compared with that projected by the OECD for 1986, equivalent to around 1.0, 1.5, and 2.0 percent of GNP, respectively, and still be as well off in terms of their debt to GNP ratio as in the baseline case—and much better off than in the hard-landing scenario.

In the cooperative scenario, moreover, the automatic stabilizers would also help to improve the fiscal calculus. According to OECD calculations, for each percentage point that ROECD GNP is higher than it would otherwise be, the budget deficit is reduced by the equivalent of about 0.4 percent of GNP.[24] This means, for example, that if action were taken which increased the budget deficit, *ex ante,* by 1 percent of GNP, and if the fiscal multiplier was, say, 1.5,[25] the *actual* budget deficit would, with a lag, only increase by about 0.4 percent of GNP. This, for example, is roughly what happened in the ROECD area in 1978–80 (figure 1.2). Thus, in order to estimate the amount of expansionary action that Germany, Japan, and the United Kingdom could take in the cooperative scenario without raising their debt to GNP ratios, the numbers given above should be multiplied two to three times.

To sum up: there does not appear to be a constraint on a shift to more expansionary policies in much of the ROECD area arising from the size of budget deficits in relation to current *flows* of private savings and investment. The extent to which there may be a constraint because of the level of the

---

24. Muller and Price (1984a, table A2.6). The coefficients estimated for Japan, Germany, and the United Kingdom are 0.3, 0.4, and 0.6 percent of GNP, respectively.

25. For *joint* ROECD action, the multiplier could well be higher than this (TN16, paragraphs 5 and 6).

stock of public debt in relation to GNP is complex and controversial. To the extent that there is such a constraint, it would appear to vary greatly from country to country: Japan, Germany, and the United Kingdom are in a relatively comfortable position. The deficit-debt calculus would be improved for all ROECD countries when, as the dollar declines, their interest rates become decoupled from US rates. It would be further much improved in the cooperative scenario because of higher growth rates and the operation of automatic stabilizers. The arithmetic suggests that in this scenario, Germany, Japan, and the United Kingdom could take expansionary fiscal action equal to several percentage points of GNP while at the same time stabilizing their debt to GNP ratios at roughly the present level.

Europe: Capital Shortage, Real Wages, and Other Rigidities

There is a widely held view that the scope for faster growth in Europe is limited because of problems on the supply side, at both the macroeconomic and microeconomic level.

At the macroeconomic level, Edmond Malinvaud (1982, pp. 1–2) described the problem, with his usual diffidence, as follows:

It might be that, even confronted by sufficient demand for their product, some firms will not recruit the full labor force that they could employ . . . because this would not be profitable enough. Narrowly understood, such a logical possibility does not seem to correspond to a frequent situation: where demand and productive capacities exist one seldom observes that production does not follow. But this is just a short run observation . . . The relation between profitability and unemployment is not instantaneous but involves the process of capital formation . . . Too low profitability might explain why . . . not only does productive capacity seem to increase too slowly, but it also seems to be too capital intensive . . .

Almost every aspect of this thesis that Europe is suffering from ''classical'' rather than ''Keynesian'' unemployment remains controversial, both within the economics profession and at the political level. Nevertheless, the basic story has, by now, been fairly clearly established. From the early 1970s to around 1980, real wages in Europe rose faster than labor productivity. Both the pretax share of profits in value added and the rate of return on capital

FIGURE 6.6   **Cyclically adjusted pretax profits and rates of return in manufacturing, 1970–84**

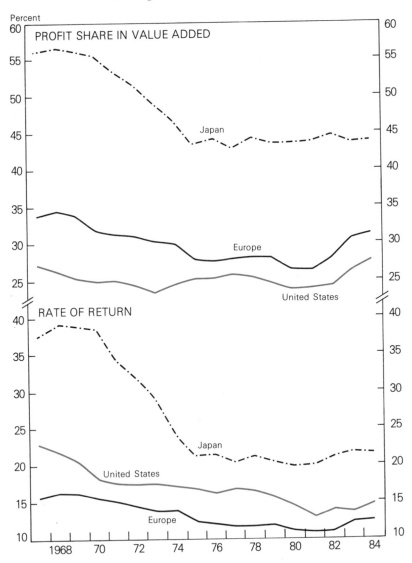

Note: For sources and methodology, see TN26.

TABLE 6.6   **Factor prices and factor substitution: Europe versus the United States, 1973–83** (average annual percentage change, 1975 prices)

	European Community	United States
1. GDP	1.6	2.0
2. Employment[a]	−0.3	1.4
3. Labor productivity (1 − 2)	1.9	0.6
4. Real labor cost per employee[b]	2.1	0.5
5. Capital stock[c]	2.7	1.7
6. Capital per employee[c] (5 − 2)	3.0	0.3
7. Capital productivity[c] (1 − 5)	−1.1	0.3
8. Gross rate of return on capital[c,d]	−1.8	0.4

Source: Mortensen (1984), tables 18 and 19.
a. Man-years for the EC, full year equivalent for the United States.
b. Compensation of employees, including an inputed labor income to self-employed, deflated by the GNP deflator.
c. Based on estimates of the capital stock and the gross rate of return for the whole economy, made by Mortensen, as described in his paper. As he stresses, there are great difficulties involved in making these estimates, and a considerable margin of error surrounding the results.
d. Annual average percentage change.

declined (figure 6.6), and the share of private investment in GNP fell (figure 6.7).[26] Evidence for the substitution of capital for labor comes particularly from a comparison with the United States: the stock of capital rose faster in Europe than in the United States, and the productivity of capital declined; labor productivity rose faster in Europe than in the United States, and employment declined in Europe but rose strongly in the United States (table 6.6).

A major factor raising labor costs in Europe was increasing social security contributions paid by employers and other nonwage labor costs such as longer paid holidays. At the same time, the "tax wedge" between the cost of

---

26. The same was true for Japan, but for largely different reasons. See below and TN27, paragraph 2.

employing labor and the net take-home pay of workers was increased by higher employee social security contributions and rising effective rates of income tax. The Commission of the European Communities (1984, p. 26) has estimated that this tax wedge rose from 41 percent to 54 percent in Europe from 1971 to 1984. This compares with an estimated 41 percent in the United States in 1981, which had dropped to 34 percent by 1983 following the 1981 tax cuts. On the other side of the coin, taxes on capital, and especially on new investment, were being reduced in many European countries during this period (figure 3.1), thus accentuating the rise in the price of labor relative to capital.

In the author's view, the evidence is sufficiently convincing that Europe is suffering from a "real wage" problem, even though there remain many unresolved issues about its origins, magnitude, and theoretical underpinnings (TN27). The emphasis here will therefore be on the policy implications. There are two:

• If investment has been too low and Europe has a "capital shortage," does this mean that faster growth would quickly run into capacity constraints and would soon be aborted by accelerating inflation?

• If real wages are too high, does this mean that, even if capacity were available, employers would not take on more labor because it would not be profitable to do so?

The first issue is of more immediate concern since, as Malinvaud noted, in the short run, "where demand and productive capacities exist one seldom observes that production does not follow."

There is strong evidence of a growing mismatch between labor supply and the stock of capital in Europe. In April 1985, capacity utilization in industry in the European Community was 81 percent, when economy-wide unemployment was around 11 percent; at a similar level of capacity utilization in 1979, unemployment was 5.5 percent, and in 1974 it was only just over 3 percent.[27] The implications of these capacity figures need, however, to be interpreted with caution. In much of the economy outside industry, increasing output is largely a matter of taking on more workers rather than increasing

27. Commission of the European Communities (1984, graph 10), and *European Economy*, supplement B, no. 5, May 1985. For a similar analysis of the rise in unemployment associated with a given degree of slack in the economy (as measured by deviations of GNP from its phased trend) see *OECD Economic Outlook*, no. 37, June 1985, chart J.

the capital stock. Moreover, the capital stock required mainly takes the form of construction, and construction remains one of the most depressed sectors with a large margin of spare capacity.

There is, however, a more fundamental question. If Europe needs to increase physical capacity in order to reduce unemployment, the only way to achieve this may be to allow demand to rise fast enough to put real pressure on existing capacity. Industrial investment has picked up strongly, especially in machinery and equipment, and this has been welcomed. But survey results show that this is largely the wrong kind of investment—75 percent of it is for rationalization and replacement rather than for increasing capacity.[28] Diehard protagonists of the real wage thesis will claim that this is because wages are too high. A more commonsense view is that, with capacity utilization still 5 percentage points below its 1973 peak, and the prospect of only a modest growth of domestic demand more or less indefinitely into the future, there is not a sufficient incentive to take the risk of increasing capacity. "The experience of the 1980s in Europe strongly confirms that if firms do not see improved sales prospects, they will not increase capacity in response only to an improvement in factor prices." (Blanchard et al. 1985, p. 33)

But would putting more pressure on capacity utilization lead quickly to accelerating inflation? This is much less obvious than is often assumed. European inflation in the 1960s originated in very tight labor markets, not in product markets. Inflation in the 1970s originated in the world's energy and commodity markets, which are flexprice markets. Cases of a serious inflationary problem *originating* in noncommodity product markets, via a sharp markup of profit margins, are comparatively rare. The paradox, moreover, is that a major aim of present policies is, precisely, to raise profit margins.

This brings us to the real wage problem. Unfortunately, the commonly accepted terminology could hardly be more confusing. To an economist the term "real wages" is a convenient shorthand for the relationship between wages and prices. But the layman can hardly be blamed for thinking that the problem so described relates to wages, not prices; yet, rather than say wages need to be lower relative to prices, it is just as true to say that prices need to be higher relative to wages—and much more helpful than either to talk explicitly in terms of the need to increase profit margins.

---

28. *European Economy*, supplement B, no. 1, January 1985, p. 2.

The logic which—consciously or unconsciously—lies behind the strategy Europe has been following to raise profit margins is as follows. Holding demand in check has created excess supply in the labor market. Initially, it also created excess supply in product markets, leaving the outcome for the relation between prices and wages—and hence profit margins—ambiguous. But over time, with capacity held down by low investment and accelerated scrapping, while the labor force continues to grow, the balance of market power will be shifted from wage bargainers to price-setters.

There are two things to be said about this strategy. The first is that over time, and however painfully, it has begun to work. The rise in real wages has slowed down and now lags behind the growth of labor productivity (box 6.3). The pretax share of profits in value added in industry has risen—as strongly if not more strongly than in the United States on a cyclically adjusted basis (figure 6.6). The rate of return on capital has also picked up, although, because of the decline in the productivity of capital, it remains below the level of the early 1970s.

Second, a good case can be made that in 1979–80 this was the only feasible strategy. The second oil crisis created a new cost-raising shock on the supply side, and the overriding priority had to be to prevent this from leading to a further ratcheting up of inflationary expectations, and a further erosion of profit margins. Circumstances have changed, however, and there are several reasons for suggesting that this strategy should now be reconsidered.

First, most studies show that there is a significant "Keynesian" element in European unemployment.[29] As the OECD Secretariat put it (1985, p. 36):

There seems to be general agreement that the rapid growth in real labour costs in many European countries contributed significantly to the growth of European unemployment from 5.6 million in 1973 to 10.3 million in 1979. Since then . . . unemployent has risen by more than 80 percent but . . . real labour cost growth has decelerated sharply. Even allowing for the fact that the adjustment lags are long and rather uncertain, this is prima facie evidence that other factors than just the growth of real labour costs alone have accounted for the rise in European unemployment . . . In particular, the decision . . . to adopt a non-accommodating macro-economic policy stance meant that . . . a rise in unemployment was an unavoidable consequence.

---

29. Andersen's (1984, table 3) results, for example, show the weak growth of GNP accounting for more of the rise in unemployment from 1974 to 1983 than real labor costs in all five

Second, while most of the numerous studies of the subject suggest that lower real wages should—in themselves and over time—lead to higher employment,[30] they also show that because they also have a negative impact on demand, the joint outcome for employment is likely to be small or negative (TN27, paragraph 6). That this is not just a theoretical construct is clear from recent events in Europe. Employment continued to decline until the second half of 1984, and after nearly three years of recovery it is still expected to be 2½ percent below its prerecession (1980) peak in 1985.

This experience has led to calls for a "two-handed" approach to the European employment problem, combining further efforts to improve profitability with more accommodating fiscal and monetary policies. This was the essence of the approach proposed by the European Commission in its 1984–85 Annual Report. It is interesting to see that a similar line was taken in *Employment and Growth in Europe: A Two-Handed Approach* (Blanchard et al. 1985), whose authors included Herbert Giersch, perhaps the earliest and most forceful advocate of the real wage thesis.

A major difficulty with these proposals, however, is that they call for a further reduction in the price of labor relative to capital without being very clear how this is to be brought about. The suggestion being made here is, therefore, somewhat more radical. It is that the boost given to demand should be sufficiently strong to create some excess demand in product markets, enabling prices to be raised relative to wages, and at the same time providing a strong incentive to shift from capital-deepening to capital-widening investment.

This suggestion is predicated in part on the fact that Europe's external environment has changed since 1979–80, and will change more dramatically when the dollar goes down. For those countries whose real exchange rates are likely to appreciate quite strongly (table 6.3), this will provide a negative— i.e. cost-reducing—supply-side shock. Put another way, the improvement in

---

European countries covered: Belgium, Denmark, Germany, the Netherlands, and the United Kingdom. Layard and Nickell (1985, tables 6 and 8) attribute 60 percent to 70 percent of the rise in UK unemployment from 1975–79 to 1980–83 to demand factors.

30. Hamermesh (1985), after reviewing more than 20 econometric studies, put the long-run wage elasticity of employment at between -0.2 and -0.5. The UK Treasury (1985) put it at between -0.5 and -1, but its simulations implicitly also involved a policy stimulus to demand (NIESR 1985).

BOX 6.3   The United Kingdom: odd man out

The United Kingdom appears to be suffering from a particularly severe and persistent real wage problem. Profits and rates of return have recovered since 1981 from the very low level to which they had fallen (figure 3.1). In contrast to the rest of Europe, however, this reflects abnormally strong labor productivity gains in 1982–83, rather than a slowdown in the growth of real wages, which on the contrary has accelerated despite an unemployment rate of over 13 percent. This is suggestive evidence that the capital stock has been adjusted to overly high real wages, rather than the other way around, leading to a sharp increase in "classical" unemployment (TN27, paragraph 3). In addition, the pound is overvalued, and its necessary downward adjustment will further reduce the scope for real wage increases.

	Real product wage[a]	GDP per person employed	Real unit labor costs[b]
EC 10			
1973–81	2.3	1.9	0.4
1982–84	0.9	1.8	−0.9
United Kingdom			
1973–81	0.9	1.0	−0.1
1982–84	1.9	2.9	−1.0

Sources: Commission of the European Communities (1984), tables 3.8, 3.9, and 3.10
a. Compensation of employees deflated by GDP deflator.
b. Real product wage divided by GDP per person employed.

Thus, excessive real wages, rather than inflation per se, appear to be the main reason for the United Kingdom's serious economic difficulties, and there is little or no evidence that present policies will lead to any significant improvement. Contrary to trends elsewhere, wages have recently been rising faster than predicted on the basis of past relationships (*OECD Economic Outlook*, no. 37, June 1985, p. 45).

There are two alternative options. A "radical conservative" option would involve a much stronger attack on the labor market "rigidities" which prevent unemployment from putting enough downward pressure on real wages. A "center-left" option would involve some form of incomes policy. Neither would be likely to be politically feasible—or could succeed—without a shift to more expansionary demand management policies.

the terms of trade will enable a part of the growth in real wages to be met without putting pressure on profit margins. To say that "a dollar depreciation could easily wipe out the gains made in Europe on the real wage front in the last few years" (Blanchard et al. 1985, p. 27) is to miss the point. True, *export* prices will have to be reduced; this makes it all the more important that domestic demand be sufficiently buoyant to enable *domestic* prices to be raised relative to costs. Trying to solve a real wage problem through an undervalued exchange rate is a zero-sum game at the international level; specifically, trying to solve Europe's real wage problem at the cost of the continuing decimation of US industry would be in neither party's longer run interests.[31]

To be sure, trying to "grow out" of the real wage problem involves risks. But these must be weighed against the risks involved in a continuation of the present situation—with too many people out of work, too little investment, and too much of what investment there is labor-saving instead of job-creating. The risk of a rapid acceleration of inflation has already been discussed; it varies considerably among countries, but—given the amount of slack in the labor market—can easily be exaggerated. In the present context, the more relevant risk is that, because of "real wage resistance," efforts to improve profit margins by raising prices will be negated by higher wage claims.

There are two counter arguments. First, the productivity gains associated with faster growth would provide more scope to raise profit margins for any

---

31. It is thus hard to follow Giersch (1984), who argued that the dollar might stay strong for another five years, that this would be good for Europe, and, by implication, that the US economy is sufficiently dynamic to absorb the consequences. (German thinking on this point is influenced by the fact that concern about structural problems in the German economy first surfaced in the late 1970s, at a time when the dollar was *undervalued*.)

198   DEFICITS AND THE DOLLAR

given growth of real wages.[32] Second, there is accumulating evidence of wage moderation in Europe, i.e. actual wages have been rising less fast than predicted on the basis of past relationships (with the notable exception of the United Kingdom—box 6.3).[33] How lasting a change this may prove to be is an unanswered question. That it is not just a statistical artifact is evident in the efforts made in quite a number of countries—for example, Belgium, Denmark, France, Italy, the Netherlands, and Switzerland—to reduce the formal or informal indexing of wages to prices.

Turning briefly to the problem of rigidities at the microeconomic level, the real problems lie in the labor market. In part, they are a consequence of the welfare state—one man's "rigidities" are another man's job security or unemployment benefit. In part they stem from the strength of the union movement and its stress on "fair wages" and the protection of existing jobs. These features of European labor markets already existed in the 1960s when Europe achieved a high growth rate. But when growth slowed down in the 1970s, and necessary structural change involved more job losses and less job creation, they came to the forefront as obstacles to structural adaptation. They also help to explain why the massive rise in unemployment did not put more downward pressure on the real wages of those lucky enough to have jobs (Lindbeck and Snower 1985).

There can be little doubt that—however socially desirable in other respects—Europe went too far down this road. Many countries are now trying to reform welfare provisions and labor market regulations to reduce their adverse impact on incentives and labor market flexibility. But, in itself, this will do little to increase employment. Faster growth, on the other hand, would both reduce the social costs involved and make these changes more politically palatable. As the authors of *The Two-Handed Approach* put it: "Rigidities of all sorts are . . . important. Austerity and high unemployment may wear out some of them, but they hardly seem to be the best tools for the job." (Blanchard et al., p. 29).

---

32. It should be stressed that what is being suggested here is not the same as the idea of trying to grow out of an *inflation* problem, which was tried at various times in the 1960s, and generally failed because of excess demand in the labor market. The idea here is to grow out of a *real wage* problem, by creating conditions under which price-setters can restore profit margins to adequate levels, at a time when there is substantial excess supply in the labor market.

33. *OECD Economic Outlook,* no. 37, June 1985, pp. 40 and 45.

Japan: the Investment-Savings Balance

Japan's structural problems are of a very different nature. With the labor market organized quite differently, real wages adjusted smoothly to the second oil crisis, and both inflation and unemployment are low by international standards. The key structural problem, in the context of the present study, is the chronic excess savings in the private sector. Correcting the US external imbalance will require both a reduction in the shortfall of savings in the United States, *and* a rise in investment relative to savings in Japan, given the importance of the trade relations between the two countries. As George Shultz put it: "Japan must deal with its savings-investment balance if its chronic imbalance in trade is to be corrected."[34]

Several recent studies have analyzed the relation between Japan's investment-savings balance and its large current account surplus in some detail.[35] The basic story is relatively straightforward. Following the first oil shock, the Japanese economy changed gears: the growth rate, which averaged 10 percent in 1960–73, fell to 3.9 percent in 1973–84. Less investment was needed to support this much lower growth rate, and the share of private investment in GNP fell by 11 percentage points, from 32 percent to 21 percent (figure 6.7). Initially, there was also a sharp decline in corporate savings (gross) by about 5 percentage points, but they then leveled out at around 15½ percent of GNP. Household saving rose sharply in the mid-1970s, but then dropped back to around 12½ percent of GNP in 1982–84, about one percentage point higher than in 1970–72. The net outcome was the emergence of substantial surplus private savings, equivalent to 7 percent of GNP in 1978, and still over 5 percent of GNP in 1984 despite a cyclical upswing that gave Japan its strongest GNP growth since the first oil crisis (figure 6.7).

Until 1978, the growth of surplus savings in the private sector was largely matched by a massive deterioration in the structural budget position. Since then, however, the structural budget deficit has been steadily reduced, and excess savings have spilled abroad with the current account surplus rising to an estimated 3 percent of GNP in 1985.

---

34. Shultz (1985, p. 15).

35. Including Bergsten and Cline (1985); the *OECD Economic Survey* of Japan, part II, August 1985; a report by a private advisory group to the Director General, Industrial Policy Bureau, Ministry of International Trade and Industry (MITI 1985); and Yoshitomi (1985b).

A number of factors, in addition to slower growth, lay behind the sharp drop in the propensity to invest:

• Public investment has been held in check as part of the program of fiscal retrenchment; it was still below the 1979 level in 1984 (at 1975 prices).

• Residential construction fell by as much as 20 percent between 1978 and 1984, the main factors being the high price of urban land,[36] high real interest rates, and the slow growth of after-tax personal incomes.

• In the corporate sector there has been a significant rise in the user cost of capital since the 1970s because of higher tax rates, lower tax-free reserve provisions, reduced reliance on borrowed funds and, in particular, lower inflation (Noguchi 1985). Most studies suggest that the real burden of company taxation is high by international standards (Japan Economic Institute 1984, MITI 1985). At the same time, the corporate sector's financing needs have been reduced by a fall in the relative price of many investment goods. Investment has been heavily concentrated in the electrical machinery sector, and much of it has been export-oriented.[37]

These trends have accentuated the contrast between Japan's modern high-tech industrial sector and the backwardness of much of the rest of its economic and social infrastructure. Living space per capita in Japan is 21, 37, 37, and 57 percent less than in France, Germany, the United Kingdom, and the United States, respectively. Over 50 percent of housing is without flush toilets, compared with 21 percent in France, and less than 3 percent in Germany, the United Kingdom, and the United States. There are only 8 kilometers of highway per automobile, compared with 15, 26, 32, and 43 kilometers, respectively, in the United Kingdom, France, Germany, and the United States (MITI 1985, table 2-5).

---

36. The price of urban land rose 22 percent relative to nominal disposable income between 1978 and 1983 (MITI 1985, figure 2-7).

37. Capacity is estimated to have doubled in the electrical machinery sector between 1980 and 1985, against little or no increase in the rest of manufacturing industry. Estimates by the Japan Development Bank suggest that about three-quarters of the rise in investment in 1984 stemmed, directly or indirectly, from the influence of exports (OECD Economic Survey of Japan, part 2, August 1985, pp. 10, 12).

FIGURE 6.7   **Investment-savings balances in Europe and Japan, 1970–84**

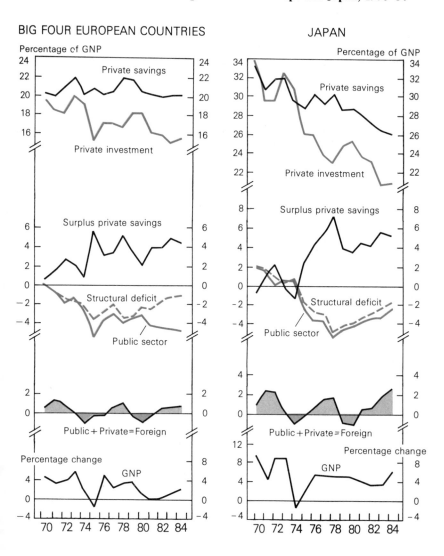

Note: For sources and definitions, see TN4.

On the savings side, the main reasons for the high household savings rate (18 percent of disposable income, against 5 percent in the United States) are the need to provide for retirement, the high cost of housing, and heavy educational expenses. The Japanese population, now comparatively young, will age rapidly over the next few decades. The resulting decline in personal savings and rise in public expenditure on pensions, medical insurance, etc., is a matter of concern in Japan, and is often cited as one of the reasons for the need for fiscal retrenchment. This problem, however, still lies some way in the future. Present projections show that the share of the population over 65 in 1995 would (at 13.6 percent) still be below the figure already reached in 1981 in Sweden, Germany, and the United Kingdom. It is only after the year 2000 that the share of population of working age will start dropping quite sharply below its 1980 level.[38]

The policy implications seem clear enough. As put by MITI's study group on macroeconomic policy:

Japan is far behind the United States and other countries in terms of social overhead capital stock. Yet its savings are not used effectively within the country, but are flowing out overseas. If the situation is left as it is, no progress will be made in the accumulation of such physical capital . . . for housing and social overhead, and for the plant and equipment which should be the foundation for long-term economic growth. Japan would therefore see an aging population supported by a poor capital stock. In other words, the current massive outflow of capital is preventing the realization of the medium and longer-term goal of maximizing the welfare of the people.[39]

Having considered both the constraints on, and need for, faster growth of domestic demand in both Europe and Japan, we turn to what should be done about it.

---

38. *OECD Economic Survey* of Japan, August 1985, table A6, and MITI (1985, p. 79).

39. MITI (1985, p. 105).

7   The Right Answer

*The combined economies of Japan and Europe, working in a
coordinated way, could become a second locomotive pulling the
world economy . . .*[1]

*If other countries are to take advantage of the easing of interest
rates . . . from a cut in the U.S. fiscal deficit, they will have to
adhere to sound financial policies and press on with structural
adjustment rather than resort to deliberate demand stimulus.*[2]

The right answer to the present disequilibrium in the world economy is to
correct its basic cause: the divergent trend in investment demand relative to
domestic savings in the United States and the rest of the world. This can
and should be achieved by a major change in the mix of fiscal and monetary
policy by the United States and its major allies. The objectives of such a
cooperative program of action should be to:

• eliminate the US current account deficit and concomitant deficiency of
domestic savings by 1990

• achieve a growth rate in the rest of the OECD area sufficient to set off a
significant rise of the share of investment in GNP and, especially in Europe,
to start reducing unemployment

---

1. Ex-Chancellor Helmut Schmidt, "The Trade War Threat," *The Washington Post Magazine*,
16 June 1985, p. 35.

2. Jacques de Larosière, Managing Director of the IMF (address to the Forum Creditanstalt,
Vienna, 22 May 1985).

203

- maintain a growth rate of 3 percent to 4 percent in the OECD area as a whole so as to enable developing countries to resolve their debt problems and resume an investment and export-led development process

- reverse the rising tide of protectionism in the United States, and create conditions under which a major improvement in the US trade balance can be achieved without provoking protectionist reactions in its trading partners

- bring down the dollar by enough to achieve these objectives—but no more

- bring down real interest rates into line with potential growth rates.

This chapter sets out the main features of such a cooperative scenario. A simulation of the D&D model shows considerable benefits from cooperation for all concerned. Subsequent sections discuss the various elements in an international policy package designed to reap these benefits and achieve the objectives set out above. Particular emphasis is put on how to break out of the various forms of expectations trap facing countries both nationally and internationally.

The Cooperative Scenario

The cooperative scenario generates a whole series of positive feedbacks yielding significant benefits to all concerned. These can be illustrated by a simulation of the D&D model. The key assumptions built into this simulation are that:

- The US structural budget deficit is reduced to around zero by 1990.

- The rest of the OECD area takes expansionary monetary and fiscal action sufficient to offset the decline in its net exports and achieve a period of "catch-up" growth of 4.5 percent in 1987–89.

- The dollar is brought down and stabilized at a level consistent with rough balance in the US current account by 1990.[3]

_____

3. There is nothing magic about a zero current balance. It is put forward here as a target for 1990 simply on the grounds that, with the United States going heavily into debt in 1985–88, a period in which it ceases to go further into debt will be necessary to reassure the exchange markets, and create the necessary conditions for stabilizing the dollar at a sensible level without overshooting. It was argued in chapter 3 that, looking to the 1990s, the United States is likely, on average, to run current account surpluses.

Neither the specific timing nor precise numbers given below should be taken too seriously: as with the other scenarios, the simulation is intended simply to bring out the orders of magnitude involved and the international feedbacks.

For the *United States,* the costs of rectifying the present disequilibrium are reduced in terms of both inflation and growth. Inflation is less because the dollar declines by under 30 percent instead of over 40 percent (table 4.5). Export demand is stronger, despite the smaller drop in the dollar, because of faster growth in the rest of the world. And a less dramatic decline in the dollar would put less upward pressure on US interest rates. Together, these help to offset the negative impact on demand from the reduction in the budget deficit.

How exactly the positive and negative influences on demand would balance out cannot be determined using the D&D model. But it seems reasonable to assume that the US economy would experience only a modest slowdown in 1986–87 followed by a sharp pickup, so that growth over the five years to 1990 might average close to 3 percent. In this case, the gains to the United States in the cooperative scenario, compared to the hard-landing scenario, would be, by 1990, a 2.5 percent lower price level, 5 percent more GNP, and 2 percentage points less unemployment.[4]

Eliminating the current account deficit would still, of course, involve significant costs in terms of both inflation and domestic spending. But on average, the wellbeing index over the four years 1986–89 would be less than 2 percentage points below the 1960–82 norm compared with 4 points in the hard-landing scenario (figure 7.1).

For the *other OECD countries,* the most important gains come from their own faster growth. By 1990, their GNP would be 7 percent higher than in the baseline and as much as 13 percent higher than in the hard-landing scenario. This, combined with lower interest rates, should give a strong boost to private investment. Unemployment in Europe might be brought down from 11 percent to 8 percent to 9 percent, still uncomfortably high, but much better than the 14 percent or more in the hard-landing scenario.

---

4. There is an arbitrary element in this split between the inflation and the growth gains for the United States. Alternative scenarios could be constructed, yielding the same current account outcome, with faster growth and a larger decline in the dollar, and hence more inflation; or vice versa. The important point is that whatever the exact split, the gains are quantitatively important.

FIGURE 7.1 **Cooperative scenario, United States**

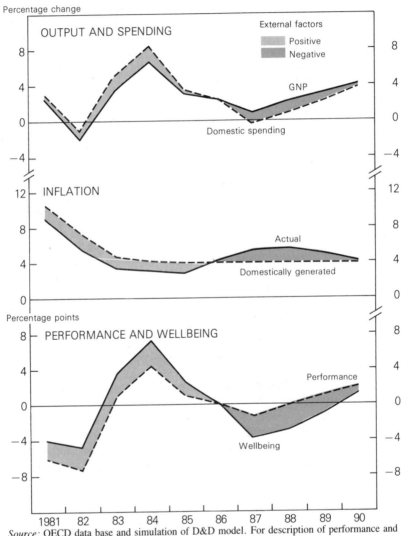

Source: OECD data base and simulation of D&D model. For description of performance and wellbeing indicators, see box 2.3.

FIGURE 7.2   **Cooperative scenario, rest of OECD area**

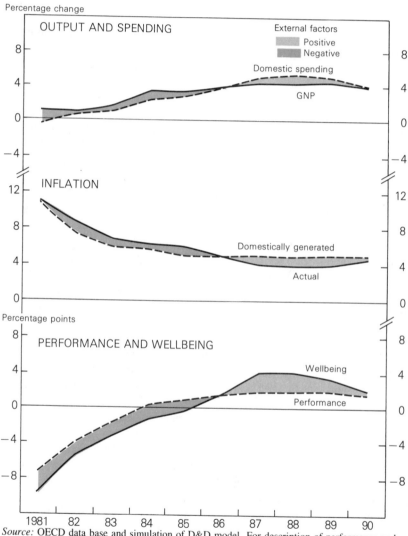

Source: OECD data base and simulation of D&D model. For description of performance and wellbeing indicators, see box 2.3.

This scenario yields other important gains for the ROECD countries. They would be spared the considerable costs and structural distortions involved in a downward overshooting of the dollar and an overadjustment of the US current account. The inflation gains from currency appreciation would be somewhat less, but, by the same token, so would the squeeze on export profit margins. The ROECD area would also benefit from the stronger growth of the developing countries (see below). Taking these factors together, the direct negative impact from lower net exports might be on the order of 2 percent of GNP, compared to over 3 percent in the hard-landing scenario. Finally, perhaps the most striking feature of this scenario is that the ROECD area would enjoy several more years of steadily improving economic wellbeing in terms of both lower inflation and a faster rise in domestic spending (figure 7.2). This, in itself, should greatly help to dissipate "Europessimism."

The cooperative scenario would also bring major gains for the *developing countries*. The average growth rate in the OECD area as a whole in 1986–90 (3.7 percent) would be comfortably above the critical level required for a satisfactory resolution of the debt crisis. By 1990, the volume of developing-country exports to the OECD area would be as much as 30 percent higher than in the hard-landing scenario (TN23). Equally important, with sustained growth in the industrial countries, commodity prices should progressively strengthen in Special Drawing Right (SDR) terms; indeed this would be desirable to encourage investment and adequate future supplies. The developing countries' terms of trade should at least move back to their mid-1984 peak (box 6.1), and the purchasing power of their export earnings might be 40 percent higher than in the hard-landing scenario. In addition, debtor countries would benefit from a less sharp and prolonged rise in US interest rates.

There would also be a dramatic improvement in the developing countries' debt calculus. Although the dollar declines somewhat less than in the hard-landing scenario, this is swamped by the benefits from the higher volume of exports and better prices (box 7.1).[5] Thus, with sustained growth in the OECD area and a return to normal levels for the dollar and interest rates, the debt to export ratio for the seven major developing-country debtors would be halved between 1984 and 1990, to well below its 1977 level. In other

---

5. In contrast to figure 3.4, the figures in box 7.1 are for the ratio of *net* debt, i.e. gross financial debt less official reserves, to exports.

words, by 1990 the accumulated damage done to the creditworthiness of the developing countries since the mid-1970s would have been reversed—essentially by a reversal of the factors that caused it.

The benefits to the developing countries would, however, depend heavily on their policy response. Despite serious inflationary problems in a number of important developing countries, there are grounds for some optimism on this score. Over the past decade, there has been a fairly general shift in the developing world toward more market-oriented policies with more emphasis on competitive exchange rates, positive real interest rates, realistic food and energy prices, proper incentives for productive investment, and fewer inhibitions about foreign capital. If this continues, then under favorable external conditions prospects would be good that many developing countries could progressively achieve the kind of investment and export-led growth enjoyed by the more successful among them in the 1970s. In this case, they should be able to attract more external finance, and enjoy some modest net inflow of real resources from the industrial world instead of, as at present, a net outflow (table 1.1). Thus, in the cooperative scenario, growth in the developing countries picks up progressively (averaging 5.1 percent in 1985–90), and it is further assumed that they would be able to finance somewhat larger current account deficits (an increase equivalent to around one-fifth of the reduction in the US current account deficit).

To sum up: the cooperative scenario gives promise of a world in which, by 1990: the US internal and external deficits have been eliminated; the dollar has been brought down and stabilized at a sensible level; the rest of the OECD area has enjoyed a period of fast growth and falling unemployment; and the Third World has resumed a satisfactory rate of economic development.

This may sound too good to be true. And indeed, it would require a major change in policies and attitudes toward economic cooperation that may not be forthcoming. But before dismissing it out of hand, it should be borne in mind that the underlying conditions for a period of sustained growth in the world economy are better today than at any time since the 1960s. There is little or no risk of a new explosion in energy prices for at least the remainder of the decade. Inflation has been brought down to manageable levels in a large part of the industrial world. Lessons have been learned from past mistakes: there is stronger political support for bringing public expenditure under control and reforming the excesses of the welfare state; wage claims have become more realistic; and the declining trend in profitability, which set in the late 1960s, has been reversed.

BOX 7.1   **Developing-country debt calculus in different scenarios**

A model based on Cline (1984) has been used to project net debt to export ratios for two groups of developing countries in the different scenarios (TN23). The main results are shown opposite. In these projections, a break in oil prices is assumed in the hard-landing scenario, to $24 a barrel in 1985 and $20 in 1986–90.

In the baseline, debt to export ratios decline even without a decline in the dollar. This reflects sustained OECD growth and the fact that many important debtors are now running trade surpluses.

• In the hard-landing and cooperative scenarios, there are very substantial benefits from the dollar's decline which raises export prices measured in dollars relative to dollar-denominated debt (box 6.2). In absolute terms, these gains are greater the higher the debt to export ratio; they are lower in the cooperative scenario because the dollar declines less.

• In the hard-landing scenario, these benefits are more than offset for the seven major debtors by the impact of slower OECD growth, and lower oil and commodity prices on export earnings, and by higher interest rates. This is not the case for the broad category of indebted developing countries, mainly because as a group they are less affected by lower oil prices. These results depend critically, however, on the assumption that debtor countries cannot obtain additional finance and are forced to cut back imports in line with lower export earnings (TN23).

• In the cooperative scenario, the benefits from higher export earnings because of faster OECD growth and better terms of trade are taken in the form of faster growth and higher imports in the debtor countries, rather than less borrowing; indeed, it is assumed that they are able and willing to finance somewhat larger current account deficits. Their debt to export ratios nevertheless decline well below 1977 levels because of the drop in the dollar and the strong rise in their export earnings.

Seven major developing-country borrowers

		Net debt to export ratio	
1977	. .	1.48	. .
1983	. .	2.37	. .
1984	. .	2.11	. .
	Baseline	*Hard landing*	*Cooperative*
1990	1.45	1.57	1.07

Difference from baseline in 1990 due to		
OECD growth	.43	−.06
Dollar	−.63	−.33
LIBOR	.08	.00
Oil price	.24	n.a.

Indebted developing countries

		Net debt to export ratio	
1977	. .	0.94	. .
1983	. .	1.35	. .
1984	. .	1.27	. .
	Baseline	*Hard landing*	*Cooperative*
1990	1.18	1.18	0.78

Difference from baseline in 1990 due to		
OECD growth	.38	−.13
Dollar	−.49	−.26
LIBOR	.03	.00
Oil price	.08	n.a.

Source: IMF, *World Economic Outlook* and simulations of D&D model. For details, see TN23.

Chickens and Eggs

They say, we don't like your deficit. We say, "neither do we."
Where do you go from there?[6]

The central feature of this cooperative scenario is a close but complex interdependence between policy action and the response to policy action, both nationally and internationally. Nationally, a satisfactory outcome for the United States requires both a sharp cut in the budget deficit *and* a substantial decline in the dollar. Either without the other would severely depress the economy: if the deficit was cut but the dollar remained strong, domestic output would be crowded out by the exchange rate; if the deficit was not cut but the inflow of foreign savings dried up, investment demand would be crowded out by rising interest rates. Equally, a satisfactory outcome for the ROECD area requires fiscal stimulus *and* a strong appreciation of their currencies against the dollar. Without a decline in the dollar, fiscal expansion could lead to higher inflation and interest rates; without fiscal expansion a decline in the dollar could lead to a severe recession.

Internationally, the key point is that a prompt but manageable decline in the dollar can only be brought about by both a shift to fiscal restraint in the United States *and* a shift to fiscal stimulus in the rest of the OECD area. By itself, significant fiscal restraint in the United States could simply lead to a worldwide slowdown: in the absence of any upward shift in investment demand relative to savings in the rest of the world, the dollar could well remain strong and the damage to the structure of the US economy and the fabric of the world trading system would go on building up. In the end, the dollar bubble would no doubt burst; but a decline in the dollar triggered by loss of confidence in the US economy would be far more difficult to control than one prompted by strengthening confidence and faster growth in the rest of the world. Equally, however, a substantial fiscal stimulus in the ROECD area without a corresponding cut in the US budget deficit would, in time, lead to worldwide crowding out.

So far, officialdom has concentrated almost exclusively on the need to cut the US budget deficit. But there is a chicken-and-egg problem not properly

---

6. Unnamed US official attending the London summit meeting, quoted in *New York Times*, 9 June 1984.

understood on either side of the Atlantic or Pacific. Thus, even such an experienced and internationally minded observer as Masaru Yoshitomi has argued that, "international policy coordination requires that Japan's fiscal policy should be expansionary in order to reduce its large [external] surplus, *if* and *only if* US fiscal policy becomes less expansionary and the Japanese economy is hit very adversely."[7] Equally, until the early months of 1985, the political focus on the US side was almost exclusively on the need to cut the deficit, although more recently there has been growing recognition of the importance to the United States of a concomitant shift to more expansionary policies in the ROECD area.

Yet what emerges clearly from all the preceding analysis is that:

• A less restrictive fiscal stance in the rest of the OECD area is a *necessary condition* for a manageable decline in the dollar.

• Such a decline in the dollar should be of the highest priority for both the United States *and* Japan and Europe; the longer it stays at its present level the greater the damage to the US economy and the world trading system, and the greater the risk that the dollar's decline, when it comes, will be uncontrollable and lead to downward overshooting.

• Waiting for the United States to first take decisive action to cut its budget deficit could be like waiting for Godot. The political realities are such that decisive action quite probably will only be taken when the dollar's decline gathers momentum and crowding out begins to be felt in earnest in US financial markets.

• There are, moreover, no longer grounds for ROECD countries to wait for fiscal action by the United States before shifting to a more expansionary policy stance. In Europe, the rise in unemployment has hardly been halted, let alone reversed. In Japan, the economy is slowing down as the stimulus from the United States fades; continuing massive capital outflows show that little progress has been made in absorbing enough domestic savings at home; and rising US protectionist pressures pose an ever-increasing threat.

In other words, the need for faster growth in the ROECD should be moved to the top of the international agenda.

---

7. Yoshitomi (1985b, p. 22). Emphasis in the original.

Faster Growth in Europe and Japan

What we really need is their recovery to bring their money up in value comparable to ours.[8]

Herr Stoltenberg insisted that he had come under no pressure . . . to indulge in "artificial" stimulation of the West German economy, to help make up for the present slowdown in U.S. growth.[9]

Can I ask you what you mean by reflation? If it means what I think it means, the answer is no . . . printing money is ruled out completely.[10]

As the US economy slowed down from mid-1984 onwards, the idea that the ROECD area should aim for faster growth picked up scattered support. In its 1984 Annual Report (1984, p. 5), the Commission of the European Communities argued that, "Europe and Japan should be prepared to support the buoyancy of world trade with adequate domestic demand in a phase of sharp slowdown in the United States." It suggested that Europe should aim for a temporary period of "cyclical catch-up" growth of 3.5 percent to 4 percent, and proposed a wide-ranging set of measures to achieve this, including "a pause in the reduction of deficits where these have been brought soundly under control to permit reduced tax burdens" (p. 37).

By early 1985, this theme could also be heard on the US side of the Atlantic, notably in speeches by Paul A. Volcker (1985c) and George P. Shultz (1985). In Japan, elements within the Liberal Democratic Party began to advocate a less restrictive fiscal policy. And in its mid-1985 *Economic Outlook,* the OECD Secretariat argued, after much beating around the bush, that "in countries where inflation and budget deficits have been brought under control, yet growth is too slow and unemployment too high, attention

---

8. Ronald Reagan, The *Washington Post,* 2 February 1985, p. A-13.

9. Remarks by the West German finance minister on returning from the Group of Five meeting in New York on 22 September, 1985, reported in the *Financial Times*, two days later, p. 4.

10. Margaret Thatcher, interview given to the *Wall Street Journal,* 2 May 1985, p. 34.

could usefully be paid to . . . appropriately designed tax cuts. . .''[11] By September, the same theme was being sounded by the Bank of England which suggested that ''relief to the U.S. external position from faster growth in Europe and Japan may call for coordination of measures to open markets and ease macroeconomic policies in those countries in which cost pressures pose no serious problems.''[12]

These suggestions, however, fell on deaf ears as far as the respective governments were concerned. True, press reports suggest that US pressure on Japan and Germany for more expansionary policies increased during the run-up to the Group of Five meeting in New York on September 22, 1985. But if so, little was achieved. The ''statements of policy intentions'' made by each participant after the meeting were very largely a restatement of existing policies.[13] And in this they received support from the International Monetary Fund which argued in April that ''recent trends give no grounds for a change in fiscal and monetary policy in the European countries and Japan'' (1985, p. 8) and apparently took much the same line in the documentation submitted to its Annual Meeting in Seoul in October (see box 7.2).

The remainder of this chapter is nevertheless devoted to making the case that, if the governments better understood the international ramifications of their fiscal and monetary policies, the policy action needed to achieve an outcome along the general lines of this cooperative scenario would be seen as both feasible and highly desirable.

BREAKING OUT OF THE EXPECTATIONS TRAP: THE INTERNATIONAL DIMENSION

In the cooperative scenario, Europe and Japan would need to aim for a two-to-three-year period of catch-up growth of 4 percent to 4½ percent and 5½

11. *OECD Economic Outlook,* no. 37, June 1985, p. xvii. Six months earlier, the *International Herald Tribune* had commented editorially: ''The OECD economists hint only subliminally at this, in tones less audible than a bat's squeak.'' (21 December 1984, p. 6)

12. *Bank of England Quarterly Bulletin,* vol. 25, no. 3 (September 1985), p. 345.

13. It was noteworthy, in particular, that Germany did not agree to advance the tax cut planned for 1988, as urged by many in Germany; and that Japan reiterated its intention to reduce the central government deficit—although local governments ''may be favorably allowed to make additional investment in this FY 1985.'' (Group of Five 1985)

BOX 7.2   **The International Monetary Fund's medium-term scenarios**

The International Monetary Fund, in a laudable effort to direct governments' attention to the interaction of national policies over the medium term, has for some time produced scenarios of possible developments over the next five years. There were, however, some odd features of the scenarios published in the *World Economic Outlook,* April 1985 (pp. 4–14, 72–96).

In the baseline scenario, assuming "most likely policies," the growth rates used are virtually identical to those in the baseline case discussed in chapter 3. But, according to the IMF estimates, if the dollar were to stay at its present level, the US current account deficit would deteriorate almost as much as shown in table 3.2. So the IMF assumes, "for convenience," that the dollar depreciates by 5 percent a year against all industrial currencies except the Canadian dollar, starting in 1987. Oddly enough, the same assumption is made in the "better policies" scenario, i.e. there is no suggestion that better policies should be aimed at producing faster correction of the overvaluation of the dollar.

Even more surprising, although these scenarios contain a very detailed quantitative analysis of possible trends in the external debt of the developing countries, there is no discussion at all of what would happen to US external debt on these assumptions. But as we have seen (box 4.3), with a 5 percent annual decline in the dollar, it would take 14 years to eliminate the US current deficit, and in the meanwhile US external debt would have risen to $2.3 trillion—in fact more, since in this simulation the decline begins in 1985, not 1987. That the world's foremost international monetary organization should feign to ignore what is clearly the most disturbing current trend in the world economy is a sad commentary on its deference to its largest shareholder.

There is another odd feature of these scenarios. The Fund has been courageous in criticizing US fiscal policy and thus under "better policies" the US budget deficit is cut by another 1.5

percent of GNP. There is also a "substantial" cut in the Canadian deficit, and other industrial countries are urged to stick to their present (restrictive) fiscal stance. Despite this, however, industrial countries' growth rises from 3.1 percent to 3.5 percent, because of lower real interest rates and "successful structural policies" in Europe. It is disconcerting that the Fund should suggest that extra fiscal restraint, equivalent to 0.6 percent of OECD GNP, should lead to nearly half a percent *faster* growth—especially since it has published no empirical analysis to justify this assumption that the industrial countries are suffering from more than 100 percent crowding out. One is left uneasily wondering whether "better" policies lead to better results in these scenarios to some extent at least simply because they are the policies currently advocated by the finance ministers and central banks of the Fund's largest member countries.

percent, respectively. By 1990, ROECD GNP would be 7 percent above the level projected on the basis of present policies.[14] To achieve this goal despite declining net exports, domestic demand in 1990 would need to be 9 percent above the baseline projection.

As in the United States in 1982–83, both monetary and fiscal policy would have an important role to play. In an initial phase, ROECD monetary policy should not be eased, in order to help promote a decline in the dollar, as discussed further below. But once the dollar's decline gathered momentum, ROECD central banks should follow the Federal Reserve's pragmatic example and be prepared to raise their monetary targets by enough and for long enough to bring about a sharp decline in interest rates. Lower inflation because of currency appreciation would allow scope for both short- and long-term interest rates to drop significantly while still remaining positive in real terms, especially in Germany and Japan. At the same time, the monetary authorities should emphasize that while they would raise targets for monetary expansion in line with faster real growth, they would not do so to accommodate any reacceleration in inflation.

---

14. The average ROECD growth rate over the five years 1986–90 would be 4.3 percent, 0.9 percentage points higher than in 1976–80, but 1.4 percentage points lower than in 1969–73.

A sizable, albeit temporary, fiscal stimulus would also be needed. Exactly how large it would need to be is not easy to judge. First, allowance should be made for the fact that present forecasts for domestic demand are based on a further shift to fiscal *restraint*, notably in Japan, equivalent to 1.0 percent of ROECD GNP in 1985 and 1986.[15] Second, and more important, the multiplier effects of fiscal action would be higher than suggested by conventional estimates, precisely because of the international context in which it was being taken:

• Interest rates would sharply drop because of the reflux of funds from the United States and the temporary shift to an easier monetary policy. The response of investment demand to a fiscal stimulus should thus be much stronger than would otherwise be the case.

• The multiplier effects of fiscal action are significantly stronger when several countries act together than if they act alone (TN16).

Taking these factors together, the cumulative change needed in the fiscal stance *from present policies* might be on the order of 3 percent of GNP, raising—temporarily—the ROECD structural budget deficit by 2 percent of GNP from the 1984 position by 1988. The increase in actual budget deficits would, of course, be very much smaller because of the operation of the automatic stabilizers.[16]

The governments of the countries concerned are convinced that a shift of this magnitude would be very dangerous, leading mainly to higher inflation and interest rates rather than to increased demand and output. But, whatever the strength of such arguments as applied to the past and to each country in isolation, they will, to an important extent, cease to be valid once the dollar's decline gathers momentum.

For as long as the dollar was strong, the impact of the highly unbalanced US fiscal-monetary policy mix gave other OECD countries an external demand stimulus, but at the same time held up both interest rates and—

15. *OECD Economic Outlook*, no. 37, June 1985, table 3.

16. See chapter 6. Simulations of *joint* fiscal action by the European Commission showed that "in the medium-term, fiscal action becomes self-supporting," i.e. after two to three years there was little or no increase in ex post budget deficits (Commission of the European Communities 1984, p. 185).

FIGURE 7.3   **Cooperative scenario, United States, OECD, and rest of OECD
area, 1981–90**

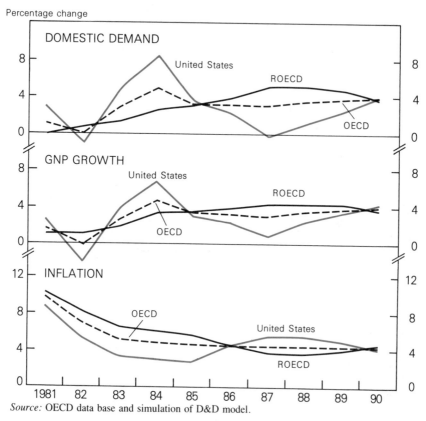

Percentage change

Source: OECD data base and simulation of D&D model.

through currency depreciation—inflation. Once a sharp shift out of the dollar
begins, the sign on all three of these terms will be reversed; there will be
downward pressure on interest rates in the rest of the OECD area, and
currency appreciation will *reduce* inflation; but, by the same token there will,
after a lag, also be a *negative* external impact on demand. In other words, a
new situation will develop that will both increase the need for more
expansionary policies, and make it more likely that they will boost domestic
demand and employment rather than inflation and interest rates. As Paul
Volcker put it, with his usual tact:

I am a central banker. I can well appreciate and sympathize with the priority that those [other industrial] countries have attached to budgetary restraint and particularly to the need to restore a sense of price stability in their own economies. They have had a large measure of success in those efforts in the face of depreciation of their currencies vis-à-vis the dollar, which has made the process more difficult. The pull of capital into the United States, and the reduced outflow from the United States, has also had effects on their own financial markets and interest rates, and thus on the possibilities for "home grown" expansion. But as those adverse factors diminish in force, or even begin to be reversed, opportunities surely exist for fostering more expansion at home, in their own interest as well as that of a better balanced world economy.[17]

Put more bluntly, the paradox is that Reaganomics, by provoking such a strong and unsustainable rise in the dollar, has created the potential for a "Reagan miracle" in Europe and Japan of the kind enjoyed by the United States in 1983–84. They could take a strong dose of fiscal expansion, and set off a strong rise in domestic demand, while inflation would be held down because their currencies would be appreciating, and budget deficits would not push up interest rates because their savings would be flowing back from the United States (figure 7.3).[18]

The scope for applying the Reagan recipe varies considerably, however, among countries (chapter 6). It would be greatest for countries with currencies that would attract investors trying to move out of the dollar. Among the major countries this points clearly to Germany and Japan. Most other OECD countries are less favorably placed. For each of them, in isolation, the expectations trap seems only too real: the benefits of expansionary action could well be nullified by adverse reactions in the financial and foreign exchange markets.

This "prisoner's dilemma" is perhaps where the conflict between nationally determined macropolicies and the collective interest arises most acutely in a flexible exchange rate system. Both history and empirical analysis show that expansionary action taken in isolation leads quite quickly to currency depreciation and accelerating inflation for most OECD countries other than

---

17. Volcker (July 1985d, pp. 23–24).

18. Investors' ex ante desire to shift into ROECD currencies would push interest rates down, even though there would still be, ex post, a capital inflow into the United States for as long as the current account was still in deficit.

the United States. The unhappy experience of the French socialist government in 1981–82 is repeatedly cited as "proving" that Keynesian expansionary policies no longer work (but see box 7.3).

The historical record also shows, however, that when domestic demand in the ROECD area *as a whole* rose faster than in the United States, the dollar was *weak*, not strong; the ROECD currencies in general *appreciated* against the dollar (chapter 1). Thus the only way to break out of the prisoner's dilemma is through a coordinated shift in monetary and fiscal policies. The lead would have to come from the countries with the greatest credibility in the markets; once they had taken the initiative, scope would open up for others to follow suit, though on a more modest scale. And with countries acting together, "each country will experience a given expansion of output at a lower net budgetary cost and a lower balance of payments cost than if it had acted on its own." (Layard et al. 1984, p. 33)

In principle, the risks would be less for the countries with currencies linked to the deutsche mark within the European Monetary System (EMS). Unfortunately, however, the weaker EMS currencies have been shielded by the strength of the dollar, and the needed realignments within the EMS needed to offset different inflation rates and other factors were not made for over two years.[19] As a result they have become large enough to be difficult to accomplish smoothly without upsetting the markets. Moreover, the projections for individual currencies given in chapter 6 suggest that, even in the cooperative scenario, significant changes in the cross rates within the EMS would be likely by 1990, including a depreciation of the French franc and a further depreciation of the lira against the deutsche mark. Once a large-scale move out of the dollar into the deutsche mark begins, pressures on the weaker currencies in the EMS could force the countries concerned into restrictive monetary and fiscal policies. To avoid this danger, prompt and skillful realignments within the EMS would be a necessary feature of the cooperative scenario.

The United Kingdom is in a somewhat special position, and probably has more to gain than most from a cooperative approach. Faster growth is badly needed, both to bring down unemployment and make it easier to solve the real wage problem (box 6.3), and there has been a major improvement in the fiscal position (figure 6.5). But domestically generated inflation is stuck

---

19. There were seven realignments between the inception of the EMS in March 1979 and March 1983, but none from then until July 1985 when the lira was devalued by 7.8 percent.

BOX 7.3   **The French débâcle of 1981–82**

There were two main planks in the program of the new French government elected in May–June 1981. The first was a wide range of "socialist" measures, including the nationalization of five major industrial groups and 36 banks; a wealth tax; higher minimum wages and social benefits; a shorter statutory working week; and a fifth week of paid annual leave.

The second plank was to give a fiscal stimulus to domestic demand to help bring down unemployment. The structural budget position deteriorated by 1 percent of GNP in 1982, reversing the restrictive stance of the previous government which had improved it by 2.5 percent of GNP in 1979–80. Domestic demand, which had dropped 0.9 percent in 1981, responded strongly, rising by 4.1 percent in 1982. But this could not have come at a worse time, since the rest of the world was in recession—in 1982, domestic demand fell by 0.3 percent in the OECD area, excluding France, and by 2.2 percent in Germany, its largest trading partner. Moreover, under the "strong franc" policy of the previous government, France's competitive position had deteriorated by over 10 percent between the first halves of 1979 and 1981 (as measured by relative unit labor costs in manufacturing).

The inevitable result was that as much as half of the rise in domestic demand spilled abroad, GNP rose by only 2.0 percent, the rise in unemployment slowed down but was not reversed, and the current balance deteriorated by $7 billion. With investors leery of the government's socialist orientation, there were strong pressures on the franc, which had to be devalued three times within the EMS, in October 1981, June 1982, and March 1983. Price control was used to try to contain the inflationary impact; combined with higher social changes, this led to a sharp profit squeeze, and private investment fell by 12 percent in 1983. By this time, the government had reversed its course and was following policies broadly similar to those elsewhere.

Many conclusions can and have been drawn from this experience, most of which lie outside the scope of this study. The one conclusion that *cannot* be drawn—although this may come as a surprise to readers of the *Wall Street Journal*—is that Keynesian fiscal policy no longer has a strong influence on domestic demand. The important conclusion that can be drawn is that, in an increasingly interdependent world with highly mobile capital, the scope for a medium-sized country to buck the prevailing trend elsewhere in either its demand management policies, or its domestic social policies, is—for better or worse—quite limited.

Sources: OECD Economic Survey of France, January 1982, March 1983 and July 1984, and *OECD Economic Outlook,* various issues.

at a higher level than in major competitor countries, and the independently floating pound has proved uncomfortably vulnerable to shifts in confidence. Once the dollar's decline gathers momentum, the government could face an unpleasant dilemma. If it was perceived to be sticking to its present policies, the pound could appreciate quite strongly—as indeed it already has—which would clearly be undesirable given the weakness of the United Kingdom's competitive position. If, on the other hand, the government appeared to be making its long-predicted "U-turn," downward pressure on the pound and upward pressure on interest rates could be strong enough to prevent even a continuation of the present modest rate of growth.[20]

This dilemma could be resolved if a shift to a more expansionary fiscal policy, instead of looking like an admission of defeat, could be presented as part of an internationally coordinated response to a slowdown in the US economy, in which the United Kingdom was following, on a smaller scale, the lead set by better placed countries such as Germany and Japan. If, moreover, sterling was brought into the exchange rate mechanism of the European Monetary System at a sensible level, the risk that the UK economy could be knocked off course by renewed attacks on the pound would be greatly reduced.

---

20. This risk would be all the greater if there were to be a break in world oil prices, as is particularly likely in the hard-landing scenario.

BREAKING OUT OF THE EXPECTATIONS TRAP:
THE DOMESTIC DIMENSION

To this point the emphasis has been on the importance of the international linkages that have created the potential for a "Reagan miracle" in Europe and Japan. But such a strategy could succeed only if Europe and Japan did not make the same monumental mistake as the Reagan administration. What is needed is a substantial but *temporary* fiscal stimulus. Once the share of private investment in GNP began to rise to more normal and satisfactory levels, prompt action would be needed to make room for it by cutting back the public sector's demands on domestic savings. This is what the United States should have done in 1983–84. So far, the United States has been able to get away with it because of the indulgence of foreign investors; it would be a mistake for other countries to think they could do the same.

The issues at stake here are more political than economic. By now, the economics have become relatively straightforward. The hope that present policies would set off a sustained investment-led recovery sufficient to reverse the rise in unemployment has proved unfounded, despite the strong external stimulus from the United States. Against this, recent history shows that, despite all the arguments to the contrary, Keynesian fiscal policies still work, in both directions. It has become clear that Europe's *only* hope of significantly reversing the rise in unemployment is by a temporary shift from restrictive to expansionary fiscal policies. Equally, this is the *only* way Japan can set in motion the basic macroeconomic adjustments—involving a shift in both the investment-savings balance and relative prices—needed to halt the rising tide of protectionism against Japan.

The present leaders of Japan, Germany, and the United Kingdom have ruled out fiscal policy for short-term demand management. This rejection probably stems mainly from a gut feeling that it was acceptance in the 1960s and 1970s of the Keynesian idea that budget deficits are not always bad that explains the failure to mobilize the political support needed to keep the rise in public expenditure within the limits that people were willing to pay for. There is a lot in this view, even though other factors were at work. Indeed, the present disillusionment with Keynesian economics among policymakers probably owes far more to the *political* lessons they draw from the past than to the sophisticated arguments of the rational expectations school of economists. In Europe there is by now agreement over a wide range of the political spectrum that the rise in public expenditure has been excessive and that this is at least partly responsible for Europe's current difficulties. In Japan there is understandable concern that it might be tempted to follow down the same road. Hence the emphasis on fiscal discipline.

These interrelated economic and political considerations lie at the heart of the dilemma facing political leadership in Europe and Japan. The external stimulus is fading and, with important elections in the next two or three years, time is running out. If governments continue with a wait-and-see attitude, the analysis in this study suggests strongly that political pressures for a change in present policies will become irresistible as external circumstances change. But the more grudgingly this change is made, the less credible—and the less effective—it would be. And the greater the risk that countries in the weaker position would move first.

It would nevertheless require very skillful political leadership to make a major change of course without losing face vis-à-vis the financial markets and the electorate, especially since the governments concerned have invested so much political capital in the rightness of their present policies. One way around this problem, as discussed above, would be to present this change of course—correctly—as a necessary and desirable collective response to a changing external environment. But this would still leave open the central domestic issue: such a change of course would only be justified, and would only work, if governments could convince themselves—and the markets—of their *political* ability to keep the lid on public expenditure and to reverse the fiscal stimulus as and when this became necessary. Here they would have two important advantages over the Reagan administration. First, they should understand from the outset what they were doing, which unfortunately the Reagan administration did not. Second, with their more cohesive parliamentary political systems, they are generally better placed to make credible fiscal policy commitments for the duration of their electoral mandate than the US government (chapter 5).

THE NATURE OF THE FISCAL STIMULUS

These economic and political considerations have an important bearing on the nature of the fiscal stimulus that should be given. For *Europe*, especially, the emphasis should be on tax cuts rather than expenditure increases. Europe's general strategy should be to cut taxes now, while at the same time putting in place programs to cut expenditures and restore the appropriate structural budget balance over a period of years. The US example suggests that, in political terms, this tactic of trying to control public expenditure by first cutting taxes can be quite effective—as long as it is not taken too far.

On the expenditure side:

• Once the decision has been made to go for faster growth, plans should be made in advance to phase out programs justified mainly or solely by slow growth and high unemployment, for example, subsidies to lame-duck industries and the panoply of labor market programs that have served mainly as palliatives for high unemployment. In some cases, a trigger mechanism might be appropriate to tie such phasing out automatically to the achievement of faster growth and higher employment.[21]

• Beyond this, further adjustments may still be needed to bring the future evolution of social benefits into line with the countries' ability to pay for them, although these also should only be phased in as and when the growth of domestic demand picks up.

• In a number of countries, on the other hand, a good case can be made for some increase in public infrastructure investment, which has borne too much of the brunt of budgetary restraint.[22]

On the tax side, Europe is in something of a dilemma. It would be tempting to follow the US example of 1981 and make tax changes designed to produce a significant increase in after-tax rates of return on new investment. As long as the dollar remained strong, this could make sense as a temporary measure because it would help to insulate domestic investment from high US real interest rates, and help promote a reflow of capital from the United States. But from the domestic point of view, it would be inconsistent with Europe's

---

21. In Germany, for example, subsidies to the economy, which declined slightly in the early 1980s, rose by 19 percent in the two years to 1984, to DM 72.5 billion (*Financial Times*, 10 October 1985, p. 2). The Kiel Institut für Weltwirtschaft puts the 1984 figure at DM 121.5 billion (7 percent of GNP) after adding in many items not included in the official subsidy report, and has proposed a program combining a major cut in subsidies with a much larger tax cut than presently envisaged by the government, which would do no more than compensate fiscal drag since 1982 (*OECD Economic Survey* of Germany, June 1985, p. 7).

22. Between 1979 and 1984, the ratio of public investment to GNP in the six largest ROECD countries fell from 4 percent to 3.5 percent (*OECD Economic Outlook*, no. 37, June 1985, table 4).

need to lower the price of labor relative to capital (chapter 6),[23] and, internationally, would heat up the "savings war" (box 7.4). Thus, as proposed by the Commission of the European Communities in November 1984:

• Tax cuts should be directed primarily to reducing the wedge between the cost of labor to employers and the after-tax incomes of employees resulting from both income taxes and, especially, high social security charges (chapter 6).

• These cuts should be substantial and permanent. If there is a need to make up for lost revenue as recovery gathers momentum, the yield from indirect taxation should be increased (possibly by raising taxes on oil consumption as the dollar's decline cuts the domestic currency price of oil).

The EC Commission suggested that the ratio of direct taxes and social security contributions to GNP should be cut by 4 percentage points between 1984 and 1987, partly offset by a 1 percentage point increase in the ratio for indirect taxation. These could well be roughly the right orders of magnitude, although the increase in indirect taxation should be phased in later.

For *Japan,* the relevant considerations are somewhat different. It is not the present level of public expenditure that is so much of immediate concern. It is rather the expected scissors movement, as the rapid aging of the population gathers momentum in the late 1990s, between rising demands on public expenditure and declining private savings.[24] During a transitional phase, and as long as surplus savings are significant, Japan can and should run larger budget deficits. With the yen appreciating, there would be no risk

---

23. A case can be made, however, for a *combination* of temporary incentives to new investment *and* marginal wage subsidies (or tax relief) for employers taking on additional labor (Blanchard et al. 1985). If designed to be neutral with respect to relative factor prices, it would, with a preannounced cutoff date, have the advantage of providing a quick-acting boost to demand and employment.

24. Important measures to reduce the future cost of existing pension schemes were enacted in April 1985, and at the same time the rate of contribution was increased from 10.6 percent to 12.4 percent, effective 1 October 1985. It would have been more sensible to put off the increase in contributions until later. As it is, the present surplus on pension funds is likely to rise by 0.4 percent of GNP in FY 1986, dampening domestic demand, and shifting the investment-savings balance in the wrong direction from the point of view of the necessary external adjustment (*OECD Economic Survey* of Japan, August 1985, pp. 48–50, 91–97).

BOX 7.4   **Avoiding a savings war**

With capital increasingly mobile, capital flows are more and more sensitive to differences in tax regimes and changes in them. In present circumstances, with the United States sucking in savings from the rest of the world on so large a scale, there is the potential for a "savings war," as countries deliberately (or inadvertently) manipulate their tax regimes to attract savings from each other.

So far, the most vivid example was the US decision in July 1984 to abolish the 30 percent witholding tax on nonresident holders of US bonds. This was perceived as a deliberate attempt to attract capital by other countries, and Germany, France, and Japan decided to follow suit. In the event, foreign purchases of US Treasury and corporate debt rose by $18 billion between 1983 and 1984—although it is an open question how much of this inflow would have taken place anyhow in some other form. There can be little doubt that the main winners from this competition between national tax authorities were the world's tax evaders.

There are also signs that other countries may be tempted to copy some of the features of the Economic Recovery and Tax Act that helped to attract savings into the United States (chapter 2). Dr. Johannes Witteveen (1984) has proposed a temporary regime of accelerated depreciation for the Netherlands, and the Keidanren and the Ministry of International Trade and Industry have argued for an investment tax credit in Japan.

This raises an important issue that does not seem to be well understood. If the US tax measures had raised both investment *and* savings, as intended, other countries would have had no cause for complaint—indeed they would be well advised to follow suit. But savings appear to be unresponsive to tax incentives and higher interest rates, both in the United States and in other countries (box 2.2). Thus, at the world level, tax changes designed to encourage investment may become a zero-sum game. World interest rates get pushed up, without any significant increase in world savings or investment. The losers are countries that cannot

---

compete in this contest for world savings because they lack international creditworthiness, especially the developing countries.

Thus the need is growing for much closer consultation among the major industrial countries on the international ramifications of changes in their tax systems likely to affect capital flows, which are still considered very largely only on their domestic merits. As of now, there is no adequate institutional framework for such consultations, which involve highly complex matters. Three general principles could provide a starting point:

- Tax evasion does not normally provide a good basis for the efficient allocation of the world's scarce savings.

- Countries should aim as far as possible at tax neutrality between capital and labor and between different uses of capital.

- The major countries should consult with other countries before making large changes in their tax regimes, which, whenever possible, should be phased in over a number of years.

---

of accelerating inflation, and Japan is one of the countries whose public-debt calculus stands to benefit most from faster growth and lower interest rates (TN25).

The main domestic consideration is how best to use the present surplus of domestic savings to prepare for the aging of the population. It makes sense to export part of these savings to build up income-earning assets abroad, but there are limits to the size of the current account surpluses that can be run without provoking destructive trade tensions. At the same time the development of Japan's economic and social infrastructure—transport, social amenities, and especially, housing—has lagged behind its rapid industrial development (chapter 6). Given the aging problem, therefore, maximum use should be made of the present surplus of domestic savings to finance improvements in this infrastructure, including housing, health care, and leisure and recreation facilities, for the older population.

B O X 7.5   **The tax treatment of interest payments and receipts**

The US tax system is unusually generous to household borrowers. The United States, among 16 industrial countries surveyed by the IMF, is the only one which neither taxes imputed rent from owner-occupied housing nor limits the amount of mortgage interest that can be deducted from taxable income (Tanzi 1984). Interest payments on all other consumer loans are also deductible without limit (only the Netherlands, Switzerland and the Scandinavian countries have a similar provision). In 1983, interest deductions in individual income tax returns amounted to $132.5 billion, 4 percent of GNP (*Washington Post*, 5 June 1985, p. F4).

This feature of the US tax system has often been criticized by other countries because, by reducing the after-tax cost of borrowing, it pushes up US interest rates and, indirectly, rates in the rest of the world. The administration's proposals for tax reform would introduce limits on interest deductibility, but it appears that the effect would be relatively small (ibid.). It may thus be politically unrealistic to expect major changes in the United States, in which case, however undesirable on other grounds, other countries may have to adapt their tax systems accordingly. This applies particularly to Japan, where the tax system strongly favors investment in financial assets as against housing or consumption. The limit on the deductibility of mortgage interest is very low while interest income is free of tax on savings of up to $55,000 per household, on bank deposits, postal savings deposits, and certain government bonds, with no limit on the number of savings accounts a taxpayer may have.

This provides another example of how differences in tax systems may have international ramifications (box 7.4). As the IMF study put it: "While tax regimes of major industrial countries vary widely . . . some subsidy to consumption . . . is prevalent—policies of the United States being among the most liberal and those of Japan being among the least liberal. These and related tax policies may have significant effects . . . on exchange rates and international capital movements." (Tanzi 1984, p. 39)

On the tax side, Japan differs from most other OECD countries in that the effective marginal tax rate on profits has been rising. Since Japan, unlike Europe, is not suffering from a real wage problem, a good case can be made that it should follow the US example with tax changes designed to increase the after-tax return on new investment, via, for example, investment tax credits or accelerated depreciation.

Objections to this proposal have been voiced outside Japan on the grounds that increased investment would strengthen Japanese competitivity and further exacerbate trade tensions. This misses the point. The Japanese trade problem is essentially of macroeconomic origin: the overhang of domestic savings keeps depressing the exchange rate, so that with wrong price signals too much investment is devoted to exports and too little to meeting domestic needs. It is in Japan's interest—and, for that matter, the interests of other countries with deficient savings—to solve this problem as far as possible by encouraging investment rather than discouraging private savings. And a rise in investment relative to domestic savings is, in reality, the *only* way of bringing about the substantial and lasting appreciation of the yen needed to ensure that Japan invests and consumes more of the fruits of its remarkable productivity at home, rather than exporting it in the form of unemployment to its less efficient trading partners.

This said, it would be a good idea to tailor tax cuts and other incentives to encourage the kinds of investment needed to meet Japan's longer term domestic needs. In the field of company taxation, this could be done, for example, by granting more favorable investment tax credits or depreciation schedules for domestically oriented investment. Outside the corporate sector, there is considerable scope for fiscal incentives and other action[25] to encourage home ownership, as well as the provision of social and cultural amenities by the private sector, or jointly by the private and public sector at the local level, along US lines, so as to avoid as far as possible the dangers involved in the more centralized and bureaucratic approach followed in Europe. In this context the tax treatment of interest payments and receipts (and charitable contributions) needs to be reconsidered (box 7.5).

---

25. In particular, the extensive regulations governing construction could be revised, and the tax system changed so that land-holding is more heavily taxed, and the preferential tax treatment at present given to lightly used agricultural land in surburban and even urban areas removed (*OECD Economic Survey* of Japan, August 1985, p. 53).

While desirable, these tax changes would not provide enough stimulus to the economy in the short run, since Japan will be hit particularly hard by the necessary correction of the dollar and the US current balance (chapter 6 and TN22). This will require some combination of increased public investment and cuts in income tax. The effective rate of income tax has risen sharply over the last decade, and the last major cut was as far back as FY 1974. Over the longer run it will be necessary to widen the tax base, possibly by introducing a value-added tax, but this should be postponed until the necessary shift in the investment-savings balance is well under way.

Eliminating the US Savings Deficiency

In the cooperative scenario, the aim would be to bring the US current balance into approximate equilibrium by 1990. This would mean that the structural budget deficit would have to be cut to around zero to achieve an overall balance between investment and savings, compared with the Congressional Budget Office projection of 4.8 percent on the basis of current legislation (table 5.1). These cuts should be "front loaded" in order to minimize the risk of a stabilization crisis (chapter 5).

The basic fiscal problem facing the United States is that the existing tax base is too narrow to support the level to which federal expenditure has risen and is likely to continue. This assessment assumes that large cuts in defense expenditure are unlikely (whether they would be desirable lies outside the scope of this study). It is also assumes that the Reagan administration's strenuous efforts to cut nondefense expenditure have by now established fairly clearly the political limits to further moves in this direction.

This problem is not new. Other countries which, like the United States, rely heavily on direct taxation, have found that as public expenditure rose over the last two decades, marginal tax rates rose to punitive levels, and had to widen their tax base by raising or introducing new indirect taxes.[26] In retrospect, indeed, this was probably too easy a way to increase revenue and one reason for the failure to curb the rise of public expenditure soon enough.

---

26. In 1981, the share of personal income tax in total revenue was 38 percent in the United States, against 28 percent in the European Community (unweighted average) and 25 percent in Japan. Other countries with a high share were New Zealand, Denmark, Australia, Finland, and Sweden (OECD 1983b).

There is obviously a moral here for the United States, but something will nevertheless have to be done to broaden the tax base. One possibility might have been to do this by eliminating the many loopholes in the direct tax system. This, however, may now have been preempted by President Reagan's proposals for tax reform which involve trading off a widening of the direct tax base against lower tax rates. Whatever the final outcome of these proposals, it seems likely that—in addition to distracting attention from the budget deficit—the end result could well be a situation in which it will have become politically difficult to cut the deficit by any significant increase in the yield from direct taxation.

Proposals have been made to increase the tax base by introducing some form of federal tax on consumption, for example, a value-added tax. This is not the place to discuss the pros and cons of these proposals. But, apart from the administrative costs involved, the main objection could be that this could prove too easy a way to raise too much revenue.

To the non-US observer, the most obvious alternative would be to raise taxes on oil consumption, and especially on gasoline. Many Americans would object on the grounds that the automobile plays such an important role in their way of life, and that higher prices would have painful distributional effects both between regions and income groups. Against this, it would seem that driving habits adjusted to higher gasoline prices after the two oil crises of the 1970s without too much difficulty. Moreover, the technology and manufacturing capacity now exists so that mileage could be maintained through a shift to more fuel-efficient automobiles.

This is obviously not a panacea. Many other things will have to be done to solve the fiscal problem, especially with regard to the longer run evolution of social security and public health programs (Petersen 1986). But a hefty rise in the gasoline tax, phased in in stages over the five years to 1990, could provide a good part of the additional revenue needed (box 7.6), while providing time to adapt the automobile stock and driving habits. Moreover, if legislated in advance, with an element of front loading, it would be the kind of clear-cut measure most likely to convince the financial markets that real action was being taken to deal with the deficit problem on a permanent basis.[27]

---

27. Legislation would be needed to enable the proceeds to be used to reduce the deficit. In political terms, this should be relatively easy to obtain compared with most other deficit-cutting options.

BOX 7.6   Gasoline taxes

The after-tax retail price of gasoline in the United States in 1984 was significantly lower than in other OECD countries at current exchange rates. Measured at exchange rates reflecting the domestic purchasing power of each currency, it cost only one-third to one-half as much. Taxes accounted for much of the difference; they averaged over 50 percent of the retail price in most other OECD countries, against 24 percent in the United States:

Gasoline retail prices in selected countries
(1984 average, dollars per US gallon)

	At current exchange rates	At purchasing power parity[a]	Share of taxes (percentage)
United States	1.22	1.22	24
Germany	1.86	2.28	49
United Kingdom	2.04	2.80	55
France	2.23	2.90	43
Japan	2.39	2.72	36
Italy	2.78	4.00	66

Source: International Energy Agency (1984).
a. First column converted at 1984 purchasing power parities taken from Hill (1984, table 3).

US gasoline prices fell relative to the general price level by more than 25 percent between their 1981 peak and 1984, and demand has already shifted back to larger cars. The Transportation Department has agreed to a request from manufacturers to ease the regulations limiting the average gasoline consumption of their product line (*New York Times*, 19 July 1985, p. A-12).

Each cent per gallon of additional tax would raise approximately $1 billion. A tax increase sufficient to restore the 1981 real price level would yield $40 billion. An increase that brought the share of taxes in the US price to the average of other OECD countries would yield some $65 billion. Bringing the US price up to the German price in terms of purchasing power parity would raise more than $100 billion.

> The longer term case for maintaining or raising the real price of oil to US consumers is compelling, in both the national and international interest. There is disquieting evidence that the world oil market is locked into a medium-term cycle of glut and shortage. The present glut will probably last into the early 1990s. But the record now shows clearly that while the short-run elasticities are low, over the medium run, both demand and supply are quite responsive to price changes. Thus, a continuation of the present trend of falling oil prices in real terms would almost certainly set the stage for a new price explosion in the 1990s, with the same heavy costs for the world economy as in 1974–75 and 1981–82.

Monetary Cooperation and Exchange Market Intervention

> *Intervention in foreign exchange markets would be an exercise in futility that would probably enrich currency speculators at the expense of American taxpayers.*[28]

> *Ministers and Governors were of the view that recent shifts in fundamental economic conditions . . . have not been reflected fully in exchange markets . . . some further orderly appreciation of the main non-dollar currencies is desirable. They stand ready to cooperate more closely to encourage this when to do so would be helpful.*[29]

The role of monetary cooperation and exchange market intervention in the cooperative scenario is relatively straightforward, albeit controversial.

---

28. President Reagan, *Economic Report of the President,* February 1984, p. 5.

29. Group of Five (1985, paragraphs 5 and 18).

In a first phase, the aim would be to prod the dollar down. The United States should follow a somewhat easier monetary policy, and the other major OECD countries somewhat tighter monetary policies, than would be appropriate on purely domestic grounds. Exchange market intervention would be useful, and in this phase it would be the willingness of the United States to participate on a substantial scale that would have the largest psychological impact. It would also be a wise precaution for the United States to build up a "war chest" of foreign currencies for future use against the day when intervention may be needed to slow the dollar's decline.[30]

In a second phase, the aim would be to slow the dollar's decline and stabilize it at a level compatible with the longer run evolution of the US current and capital account. This would require a tighter US monetary policy and easier ROECD monetary policies than would be appropriate on purely domestic grounds. Large-scale intervention—or at least the threat of it—would also be needed to prevent the dollar from overshooting downwards because of the size of the present disequilibrium and the lags involved in correcting it. In this phase, the willingness of the other OECD countries to participate in coordinated intervention on a very substantial scale would be particularly important, although the United States would also have to accept a fair share of the exchange risks involved.

A first step was taken in the right direction at the meeting of the Group of Five in New York on September 22, 1985, as discussed further below. In assessing the significance of this meeting, however, it is important to realize how far the idea of using monetary policy, backed by exchange market intervention, to achieve a given outcome for the exchange rate, runs counter to today's conventional wisdom—notably in the United States, but also to varying degrees in other countries.

THE ECONOMIC ARGUMENTS

Oversimplifying, the case against can be summarized as follows. Monetary policy has a central role to play in achieving the domestic objective of growth without inflation. If all countries follow monetary policies appropriate to

---

30. Robert V. Roosa, for example, has proposed that the Treasury should authorize the Federal Reserve to expand US holdings of foreign currencies to $50 billion, which could be used, together with drawings of $25 billion or more from existing swap lines, to staunch a run on the dollar should this develop (Roosa 1985, p. 7).

achieving these objectives then, over time, exchange rates will adjust accordingly. To deviate from the monetary policy appropriate to achieving these domestic objectives for exchange rate reasons could jeopardize their achievement, and, by doing so, could in the end lead to more exchange rate instability rather than less.

This was the position argued strongly by the US Treasury while Beryl W. Sprinkel was Under Secretary for Monetary Affairs, as exemplified in a Treasury report published in March 1985. "Domestic monetary policies would . . . once again be subject to an external exchange rate target, with less flexibility to pursue low inflation and economic growth objectives" (US Treasury 1985, p. 16). A stronger form of the argument is that: "It is highly questionable whether official judgement can determine an exchange rate that is more appropriate than the market rate" (ibid. p. 13). But while this latter argument is still often used as a debating point, the real issue—after the aberrant behavior of exchange rates in recent years—has tended to narrow down to the question of whether the costs of trying to achieve greater stability would outweigh the benefits.

The case against intervention in the exchange market follows by logical extension. It is argued that sterilized intervention, i.e. intervention that has no effect on domestic monetary conditions, will not have much impact on the exchange rate; while unsterilized intervention, which involves deviating from domestic monetary objectives, is open to the objections just discussed.

The fallacy in these arguments lies in the sharpness of the dichotomy made between an "external" exchange rate objective and "domestic" inflation and growth objectives. The rise in the dollar over the past five years has powerfully aided US inflation objectives, but is now severely hampering its growth objectives. When the dollar goes down, the reverse will be true. Over the whole cycle little will have been gained in terms of either inflation or growth—but substantial economic and social costs will have been incurred, and protectionism and subsidization ratcheted up, through an unnecessary cycle of deindustrialization and reindustrialization.[31]

Thus, in terms of achieving the key domestic objectives of low inflation and growth, keeping the exchange rate within a sensible range is as important as, for example, keeping the growth of the money supply within a sensible

---

31. It can be argued that, in welfare terms, the macroeconomic growth and inflation outcome could be positive or negative depending on the relative weight given to the two objectives and the time horizon considered (Sachs 1985). This ignores, however, the microeconomic costs which are substantial and to some extent irreversible (chapter 2).

range. Indeed, recent experience with floating exchange rates has shown that the exchange rate has become just as powerful a channel of transmission from monetary policy to the level of domestic output and prices as the traditional channels of liquidity, wealth, and interest rates.

The trouble is that, like all of us, government officials have a slow learning function. Using monetary or other policies to defend an exchange rate which is *not* sensible—i.e. is inconsistent with the medium term evolution of a country's competitive strength and sustainable capital flows—*will* lead to either inflation, or slow growth, and in the end quite possibly to both. This was the lesson painfully learned a generation ago in the 1960s with the ''fixed'' rate system. But it does not apply to cooperative action to correct the present misalignment, which is much greater than the one just before the Bretton Woods system broke down.

The same problem of a slow learning function is evident in current attitudes toward intervention. Conventional wisdom has it that: ''the role of exchange market intervention can only be a limited one, as intervention will normally only be useful when complementing and supporting other appropriate policies'' (Group of Ten 1985b, paragraph 4v). The proposition that intervention can have only a limited role if other policies are *not* appropriate would be widely accepted. But it does not follow that it can play only a limited role when other policies *are* appropriate. Experience with the Bretton Woods system and the EMS shows that, if other policies are appropriate, then intervention can play a powerful role—as long as it is being used to defend a sensible rate (box 7.7).

A number of other lessons can be drawn from postwar monetary experience:

- Monetary policy and exchange market intervention have a more powerful impact on exchange rates when used in tandem (Jurgensen 1983, paragraph 46).

- Monetary action and exchange market intervention coordinated between the monetary authorities on both sides of the exchange rate will have a greater impact, and will involve smaller deviations from domestic monetary objectives than will individual action (Jurgensen 1983, paragraph 60).

- It is fallacious to describe intervention as ''spending'' money; all it involves is a reshuffling of the currency composition of official assets and liabilities. In present circumstances, with the dollar so clearly overvalued, intervention should yield exchange rate profits to the participating monetary authorities.

B O X 7.7   Intervention and the efficiency of exchange markets

There is a vast technical literature on this subject, much of which does not deal with the basic political issues involved. In general, however, accumulating evidence for the importance of adaptive expectations in the exchange markets, and hence of the potential for bandwagons to develop (chapter 4), has strengthened the case for more management of the floating rate system. Specifically, the extensive empirical work done for the study on exchange market intervention commissioned by the Versailles summit, as well as more recent work (box 4.4), leads to rejection of the "joint hypothesis" that all relevant information is utilized by exchange market participants, and that assets denominated in different currencies are perfectly substitutable in private portfolios.

The subsequent report to the Williamsburg summit pointed out: "If markets . . . fail to assign appropriate weight to information on macroeconomic variables in determining exchange rates, action to influence the exchange rate, including intervention could be an effective component of macroeconomic policies. In this case intervention would have its impact through . . . its influence on expectations about underlying economic conditions and policies. Alternatively, if . . . unexploited profits are evidence of time-varying risk premia . . . official operations in the exchange market, by changing the currency composition of private port-folios, would alter risk exposure . . . and thus have a lasting effect on exchange rates." (Jurgensen 1983, paragraph 66)

• The argument that intervention would need to be on an astronomically large scale because the daily turnover on the US foreign exchange market alone has reached an estimated $150 billion to $200 billion is dubious. Much of this is what has been described as "self-balancing froth";[32] what matters is the *net* balance of supply and demand for dollars which is only a fraction

---

32. Lever (1985).

of total turnover, and which can itself be strongly influenced by official
intervention.

• In present circumstances there is a good case for a policy of "leaning with
the wind," i.e. intervention to accentuate a downward movement of the
dollar originating in the market, as advocated by C. Fred Bergsten (1984),
rather than the more traditional policy of only leaning against the wind when
the dollar is rising. This could well help to get the necessary adjustment
underway, although—absent the much wider approach to the problem
advocated here—the "wind" could quickly turn into a gale.

THE POLITICAL DIMENSION

The central issues involved here are not technical, however, but political in
the broadest sense. The postwar record shows clearly that *the extent to which
it is necessary to deviate from domestic monetary objectives and to intervene
in the exchange market to achieve a given impact on the exchange rate
depends, above all, on the market's perception of the degree of the
government's political commitment to achieving a given outcome for its
exchange rate.*

This is vividly demonstrated by the experience of the European Monetary
System since 1979. The political commitment to cooperate together to
maintain a reasonable measure of exchange rate stability within the EMS
takes several forms. The first is to intervene in the markets to keep cross
rates within narrow margins over the relatively short run. This is backed up
by arrangements for automatic, large, short-term credits to finance these
interventions. But a second and much more important commitment was made
credible vis-à-vis the foreign exchange markets only by acts, not words. This
is the commitment that, once these pegged cross rates have to be altered—
as will be inevitable from time to time—the changes will be mutually
negotiated and limited to the amounts needed to avoid unnecessary or
undesirable changes in real exchange rates.

The EMS has gone through sticky patches and will no doubt go through
more, so it has taken time to convince the exchange markets of the reality
of this second commitment. But what is interesting is that as governments
have demonstrated in practice their willingness and ability to live up to it, it
has proved possible to maintain a significant degree of stability in real

exchange rates between the members of the system, without massive intervention, through relatively modest departures from domestic monetary objectives. And this has been achieved despite major economic and political shocks, including a tripling of the price of oil, a world recession, a more than 50 percent depreciation of the ECU against the dollar, and the accession to power of a socialist government with communist participation in France.

Again, what should be emphasized about this experience is the primacy of the political over the technical aspects. Within a week after the French Socialist government was elected, Chancellor Helmut Schmidt made a highly publicized visit to Paris to pledge his government's support for French efforts to remain within the EMS. Equally, when it became known in the spring of 1983 that a faction within the French government was arguing in favor of leaving the EMS, President François Mitterrand moved decisively to reaffirm the French commitment to stay in. True, this required him to shift French economic policy more into line with the more conservative policies of the German government. But that would have been inevitable anyway, even if the French had left the EMS—indeed, in that case, the policy change would almost certainly have had in the end to be sharper and more disruptive.

This contrasts with the experience of the United Kingdom, which elected to stay outside the exchange rate mechanism of the EMS. Not only did the United Kingdom experience far wider swings in its real exchange rate, but it was also forced into major departures from its domestic monetary objectives each time pressures developed on the pound because of the ambiguity surrounding its exchange rate objectives.

It is, however, the contrast with the United States which could not be more stark. Indeed, as far as the dollar is concerned, the world is caught in another form of the expectations trap. Throughout the postwar period, US attitudes and policies toward the balance of payments have been characterized by "benign neglect." There were, of course, exceptions. In particular, during the second half of the Carter administration, a policy of active cooperation began to emerge with the Bundesbank and, to a lesser extent, the Bank of Japan, designed to achieve a more stable relationship between the three major currencies. But these efforts tended to be discredited by other economic and political circumstances at the time, and were repudiated by the Reagan administration in May 1981.[33]

---

33. Sprinkel (1981, pp. 17–21).

Since then, the markets have seen—until very recently—the US administration accept with indifference, if not pride, an unprecedented rise in the dollar with a very damaging impact on the exposed sector of the economy. Up to September 1985, US participation in the infrequent attempts to slow or reverse the dollar's rise through coordinated intervention was so halfhearted as to raise some suspicion that the US Treasury was deliberately trying to prove the rightness of its views about the ineffectiveness of intervention. Perhaps the *summum* of benign neglect was reached on February 21, 1985, when just as the central banks were planning a major coordinated intervention to halt a speculative run in the exchange markets, President Reagan made some offhand and disparaging remarks against ''toying around'' with the value of the dollar.

It is much to be hoped that the position taken by the United States at the meeting of the finance ministers and central bank governors of the Group of Five in New York on September 22, 1985, marked an important step in the right direction. For the first time, under the Reagan administration, the US Treasury committed itself publicly to the view that a decline in the dollar should be an explicit aim of policy. For the first time the Group of Five explicitly recognized that bringing the dollar down depended not only on US fiscal and monetary policies, but also on the macroeconomic policies of the other major industrial countries.

This was enough to have a significant ''announcement'' effect in the exchange markets, and the dollar fell sharply. There are, moreover, grounds for hoping that this will continue since, combined with the weaker performance of the US economy, it could prove sufficient to reverse the ''bandwagon''[34] in favor of the dollar that appeared to have developed in 1984 and early 1985 (chapter 2).

It remains to be seen, however, whether this turns out to be a major turning point. In the short run, much will depend on how much of a change there has been in US attitudes to exchange market intervention, which will not become clear for some time. Neither is it clear whether there was any significant move to a closer coordination of monetary policies, although subsequent actions by the Bank of Japan went in the right direction. Thus, while it appeared to be accepted that the Fed should continue with a relatively easy policy, there was no explicit recognition that the other countries should

---

34. Or, using a different terminology, remove the ''speculative bubble'' that some analysts believe they have detected in the dollar's rise, for example Krugman (1985).

be prepared to tighten up, at least temporarily, in order to avoid a repetition of what happened earlier in 1985, when the decline in US interest rates was to a considerable extent matched by declines elsewhere, still leaving positive interest rate differentials in favor of the dollar.[35]

The most worrying aspect of the New York meeting was, however, that the cart was put before the horse. The most important single element in a cooperative scenario must be major changes in fiscal policies on both sides. But at New York, the United States had nothing new to say about reducing the budget deficit, and the other participants essentially reaffirmed their intention to pursue their present restrictive fiscal policies. Since it is these divergent policies that are largely responsible for the strength of the dollar, there is a risk that the monetary authorities concerned will use up valuable ammunition in a vain cause. In doing so they would also be losing "credibility"—which will be sorely needed when the time comes to try to prevent the dollar from going down too far.

To sum up: the record shows that governments can have a strong influence on the exchange rate—as long as they do not abuse it. But for the United States to acquire this influence, after years of benign neglect, would require not only a change in present attitudes, which may be under way, but also a demonstration to the markets over an extended period of time that it is prepared to *act* accordingly. It would also require much closer macropolicy cooperation between the United States and its major allies.

Cooperative Scenario: The Policy Package

The thesis of this chapter is that the cooperative scenario would not only involve substantial benefits for all concerned but would also be feasible in terms of the policy actions required. It would, nevertheless, be far from easy to pull off, essentially because of the difficulty of breaking out of several forms of an expectations trap. It would, in particular, require two major departures from current conventional wisdom:

---

35. Thus, Karl Otto Pöhl, President of the Deutsche Bundesbank, was quoted as saying, after the Group of Five meeting: "Of course we have not committed ourselves to raise our interest rate level and thus narrow the gap with US rates and achieve a correction of the dollar through this means. Nobody would have demanded this nor would I have agreed." (*Financial Times*, 15 November 1985, p. 19)

BOX 7.8   A replay of the first Bonn summit?

The last major attempt to coordinate macroeconomic policies internationally was made at the first Bonn summit, in July 1978. In the event this turned out to be a last Pyrrhic victory for international Keynesian demand management, since within two or three years it became widely accepted that it had been a bad mistake, especially in Germany and Japan, largely because it was followed by a new outbreak of inflation.

Whether or not this assessment is correct will remain controversial, mainly because the subsequent course of events was dominated by the second oil crisis, which began just over a year later. Some elements of the program set out in this chapter are similar to the decisions taken at the first Bonn summit—notably the shift to more expansionary fiscal policies in Japan and Europe. It should therefore be stressed that the situation in 1985 differed in many important respects from 1978–79:

• The dollar is greatly overvalued, whereas in 1978–79 it was undervalued. The necessary exchange rate adjustment will thus help to dampen inflation in Europe whereas last time it added to it.

• Domestically generated inflation is under better control, especially in Japan and Germany (and unemployment is higher, especially in Europe).

• Nonoil commodity prices are weak, and there is virtually no danger of another oil price explosion, at least until the 1990s.

• Real wage pressures have moderated and profit margins have improved, especially in Europe.

• The ROECD fiscal position is significantly better than it was in 1978–79, especially in Germany, Japan, and the United Kingdom (figure 6.5).

• The world economy has become more vulnerable to a slowdown in the industrial world because of the still fragile position of the indebted developing countries and the increasing pressures on OPEC.

• The governments of the other major OECD countries would have to become convinced that a temporary fiscal stimulus, rather than being dangerous and self-defeating, would, in the present international context, be highly beneficial.

• The US administration would have to demonstrate that it had become genuinely converted to the idea that an active and cooperative policy toward the dollar was not only desirable but would work.

• And in both cases, the conversion from present attitudes would have to be sufficiently convincing to convince the markets as well.

If, but only if, these conditions were fulfilled, the various policy actions needed to achieve the cooperative scenario could be put together in a mutually self-reinforcing international policy package:

• The shift to more expansionary policies in the other OECD countries could be presented as part of an agreed collective response to the changing international environment, to maintain the momentum of the recovery in the world economy as a whole, stem the outflow of domestic savings to the United States, and bring down the dollar to a sensible level in an orderly manner.

• The US administration could point out to Congress that this action by other countries, which would have important benefits for the United States, would at the same time increase the urgency of making deep cuts in the budget deficit.

• Governments of other OECD countries could point out that since the United States was taking the most important step, and had agreed to work with them to bring down the dollar, a situation would be created in which a fiscal stimulus would both become more necessary and would have the desired positive effect on output and employment rather than the much feared negative effects on inflation and interest rates.

• Agreement by the countries best placed to give this fiscal stimulus, Germany and Japan, to take the lead, would progressively create scope for other OECD countries to follow suit.

• The emphasis would be on tax cuts, wherever possible, with a supply side connotation relevant to the circumstances of the country concerned. But in order to make it clear that the mistake made by the United States in 1981 was not being repeated, plans would be laid down in advance to phase in reductions in public expenditure—especially in Europe—or tax increases—notably in Japan—as and when rising private investment required a reduction in the public sector's absorption of domestic savings.

• The US monetary authorities would be able to point out to the financial markets that this policy package would substantially reduce the risk of a serious financial crisis. Significant action to cut the budget deficit would greatly reduce the likelihood of a sharp spike in US interest rates as the dollar goes down; a lower dollar would ease the financial pressures on developing-country debtors and the exposed sectors of the US economy.

• Finally, the industrial countries could point out to the developing countries that they were doing their best to create a world environment favorable to development by maintaining growth, bringing down the dollar, and normalizing real interest rates. It would be up to the developing countries to take full advantage of this by pursuing appropriate anti-inflationary and market-oriented policies.

If the scenario described in this chapter seems implausible, it is essentially because the governments of the OECD countries are still strenuously fighting the battles of the 1970s instead of facing up to the challenge and opportunities of the 1980s (box 7.8). If they continue to do so, a major crisis will become inevitable.

8 Crisis Management

A slowdown in the U.S. economy—especially if it is accompanied by a major weakening of the dollar . . .will cut through some of the more extreme forms of laisser-faire rhetoric which have vitiated serious discussion of international policy co-ordination.[1]

This chapter discusses what can be expected to happen if the changes in attitudes and policies discussed in the previous chapter are not forthcoming in time. It suggests that if, as events unfold, the action taken is too little, too late, and quite possibly misguided, a crisis will become inevitable. It goes on to suggest ways in which constructive use might be made of this crisis to promote desirable changes in the exchange rate regime, monetary policies, the summit process, and the broader institutional framework for economic cooperation between the United States and other major economic powers.

Too Little, Too Late—and Misguided?

Absent some untoward event, the crisis may develop quite slowly; inertia is inherent in all well-established economic and political trends. In the United States, enthusiasm for cutting the budget deficit may wane with the weaker trend in the economy and as the 1986 elections approach—quite apart from the distractions of tax reform. It may well not be until after the dollar has been declining for some time that a bandwagon develops strong enough to

---

1. *Financial Times* editorial, 15 April 1985, p. 14.

generate pressures in US financial markets sufficiently severe to overcome President Reagan's opposition to tax increases.

The other OECD countries are also likely to respond only slowly to the changing situation. Indeed, in the first phase of the dollar's decline, they may feel rather satisfied with the course of events. Their interest rates will be coming down and so, as their currencies appreciate, will inflation. Given all that had gone before, they would no doubt be tempted to say ''I told you so'' to the United States, and feel justified in their determination to stick to their present policies. True, their exports to the United States have already slowed down, but as long as the dollar remains at or near its current level their exporters will continue to enjoy a strong competitive edge in the US market. Given the long lags involved, it would only be a year or two after the dollar had gone down quite a long way that the negative impact on world demand would be fully felt.

Thus, we could well see a ''soggy'' scenario, with continued relatively slow growth in the United States, while the recovery in the rest of the world gradually loses momentum. In other words, just as the ''pull'' of the US economy on world savings began to ease, the ''push'' factors from poor performance and investment opportunities in the rest of the world might be on the rise again. If so, the dollar could remain in a state of suspended animation for some time to come. Because of long recognition lags before the need to change policies becomes sufficiently apparent, and because of the further lags before it has its desired effects, the shift to a less restrictive policy in the ROECD area could well be too little and too late (and then quite possibly too much and too inflationary). In the meantime, the longer the crisis is delayed and the greater the disequilibrium becomes, the greater the likelihood of misguided action that would only make matters worse.

The most serious danger is that protectionist pressures in the United States become irresistible. Protectionist bills have been piling up in Congress and, despite valiant resistance by the administration, the dam could break, especially if the run-up to the 1986 mid-term elections coincided with an unexpected slowdown in the economy.

Perhaps the most seductive proposal is for a heavy import surcharge, the proceeds of which would be used to reduce the budget deficit. In practice, this would almost certainly backfire. It would be taken by the markets as evidence that the administration was losing its nerve; the threat of retaliation by other countries would raise the specter of a 1930s-type trade war; the financial markets would not be impressed since, as the surcharge would have to be removed as the dollar came down, the budget deficit would be bound to increase again at precisely the moment when it most needed to be reduced. Nevertheless, it seems quite possible that misguided protective action will be taken, in one form or another, if the present situation continues much longer. As Bergsten (1985) has suggested, it could be this rather than some event in the financial sphere that could trigger what he has called "the second debt crisis."

Making Constructive Use of a Crisis

If, as events unfold, the action taken is too little, too late, and quite possibly misguided, then we are indeed headed for a crisis. This need not necessarily be a pessimistic conclusion. History shows that genuine reform—or simply change—in the untidy and amorphous entity constituting "the international monetary system" has often only taken place as the result of a crisis and has then sometimes happened quite quickly. So, to be realistic, perhaps the most important issue is how constructive use might be made of a crisis.

In this context, a first question is who is likely to lose their nerve first, the United States or its allies? A year or so after the turn comes, the situation will become distinctly unpleasant for the US authorities. Inflation will be accelerating, interest rates will be high, the economy will be weak, and stories about the falling dollar will, after they have gone on for some time, be very damaging to the image of the United States "standing tall." The record shows clearly that it is under these conditions, when the US external economic position is weak (the 1960s, 1977–79) that the United States turns away from benign neglect and becomes more enthusiastic about the international coordination of monetary and fiscal policies and deliberate attempts to manage the exchange rate system.

Postwar history, however, also teaches another lesson. If the situation deteriorates far enough, then, because of the weight of the United States and the dollar in the world economy, it may be the other countries that lose their nerve first. In an uncoordinated and unconditional way, they may start intervening in the exchange markets on a significant scale to slow down the appreciation of their currencies against the dollar. For the same reasons, and partly as the direct result of such intervention, their monetary authorities may begin to tolerate excessive rates of monetary expansion. In other words, it could be the central banks of the other OECD countries that end up printing the money needed to finance the US budget and balance of payments deficits.

In fact, perhaps the safest bet is that there will be massive official intervention in the exchange markets from both sides before the end of the day, despite present views that this would be a mistake. Indeed, the uncomfortable fact is that periods of US balance of payments weakness (under fixed rates) or a falling dollar (under flexible rates) have almost always been associated with excessive rates of monetary expansion in the world, and to a subsequent burst of world inflation.[2]

What must be hoped is that at some point in this game of chicken a window of opportunity opens up during which the United States becomes sufficiently worried about the situation to be fully convinced of the need for cooperation, and is prepared to pay the price, while the other major OECD countries are still sufficiently unworried about the situation to be able to respond constructively and collectively to US requests for help.

Assuming that such a window does open up, the initial focus would no doubt be on trying to deal with the immediate situation. Essentially this would involve putting into effect as much as possible of the cooperative policy package discussed in chapter 7 as soon as possible. It is probable that by this point the question of intervention in the exchange markets to stem the dollar's decline would have already have come very much to the fore, and that the United States would be asking for help. The main question would then be whether a sufficiently close linkage could be established between agreement on arrangements for large-scale coordinated intervention to support the dollar with firm commitments from both sides to take the fiscal and monetary policy actions needed to make such intervention effective.

The more interesting question is how such responses to the immediate situation might, de facto, pave the way to longer lasting changes in attitudes toward—and the institutional arrangements for—management of the world economy. The remainder of this chapter therefore discusses how, under the pressure of events, some greater order might emerge from the present disorder, no doubt in a messy and unplanned way.

The author is well aware that most of the ideas considered below appear to be pretty unrealistic—as of now. The deputies of the Group of Ten have just completed a two year study of the international monetary system (G-10 1985a). Many proposals for improvement were considered, and some received

---

2. McKinnon (1984, chapter 4).

minority support. But the conclusion reached by the finance ministers and governors of the Group of Ten at their meeting in Tokyo on June 21, 1985, was that "the basic structure of the present system . . . remains valid and requires no major institutional change." (G-10 1985b, paragraph 2). Despite this apparent complacency in official quarters there are widespread signs of increasing dissatisfaction with the way the system is working in both business and political circles, including most recently in the United States. Indeed, even the G-10 deputies noted that countries with adequate access to external financing, i.e. the United States and other larger countries, "appear to have been able on occasions to sustain policy courses not fully compatible with the goals of international adjustment and financial stability" (paragraph 36).

The presumption underlying what follows is that if and when something like the hard-landing scenario analyzed in this study materializes, dissatisfaction with the way the system has been working could crystallize quite quickly, and could lead to significant changes in the major countries' perception of the economic and political issues involved.

In this optique, there is an element of inevitability about the oncoming crisis. By the early 1980s, the major countries had become convinced that if each country got its own "fundamentals" right then, with floating exchange rates, the world economy would look after itself. There is, of course, a very important element of truth in this stress on the need for sound national economic policies. And it may to some extent be a historical accident that the philosophy that each country should do its own thing was carried so far as to create such a massive disequilibrium in the world economy.

But something was bound to go wrong. National monetary and fiscal policies must not only be sound in themselves, they must also be internationally consistent. The idea that efforts to achieve this were not only unnecessary but could even be counterproductive, was based on an unwarranted degree of confidence in the self-stabilizing properties of financial markets and an unqualified acceptance of academic models in which, with floating exchange rates and instantaneous adjustment in all markets, the impact on other countries of changes in prices and demand in one country is fully neutralized.[3] The chickens are slowly coming home to roost, and:

There are tentative signs of a sea-change in governments' thinking on economic matters . . . the concept of international coordination of monetary, exchange rate

---

3. Marris (1984, pp. 7–9, 18–23).

and even fiscal policies is re-emerging from the obloquy and ridicule to which, for five years or more it has been fashionably consigned.[4]

This has not yet gone far. But if and when the hard-landing scenario materializes, the realities of the degree to which the US economy—and US policymaking—have become interdependent with the rest of the world will be brought home to US political leadership and the general public in a particularly vivid and unpleasant manner. This could have far-reaching consequences. The central issues involved in improving the functioning of the international monetary system are political, not technical. And the central political issue is that the United States has not yet understood the extent to which, in an increasingly interdependent world economy, its own national interest requires it to give more weight to international considerations in the formulation of its monetary and fiscal policies. If this were to change, so also might much of today's conventional wisdom about the matters discussed below.

The Exchange Rate Regime

"I get a little bit impatient with this generalized Jabberwocky. It won't do." Leaning back, she said with a smile, "I trust I made myself clear."[5]

From the point of view of the longer run evolution of the system, the single most important question is whether it proves possible to prevent a serious downward overshooting of the dollar. If this happened, it would greatly reinforce the exchange market's perception that since the move to floating rates we have become locked into a cycle of major swings in the dollar of increasing amplitude and duration. The markets would become even more

---

4. *Financial Times*, 15 April 1985, p. 14.

5. Margaret Thatcher referring to a tripartite approach to establishing a fixed relationship between the ECU, the dollar, and the yen. Interview in the *Wall Street Journal*, 2 May 1985, p. 34.

firmly convinced that "the trend is your friend" and even more inclined to concentrate on making short-term profits and to discount fundamentals such as current account positions and inflation differentials. With further large and prolonged swings in real exchange rates generating painful cycles of "dein-dustrialization" and "reindustrialization," pressures on the world's trading system, up to now reasonably well contained, could build up to a breakdown comparable to the 1930s.

Both the United States and its major allies have a strong national interest in trying to prevent the dollar from going down too far. For the United States, it would involve serious inflationary dangers and, more generally, would have a very negative impact on its economic and political image in the world, as happened in 1977–79. For Europe, nothing could set back its efforts to overcome its structural problems more than a new period of overvalued currencies as in the latter part of the 1970s. And for Japan, with its excessive dependence on exports and high export profit margins, the shock could be even greater.

As events unfold, one idea that may well emerge is that a "floor" should be put under the dollar. If so, a number of lessons might be drawn from past experience. It would be a mistake to start trying to put a floor under the dollar too soon: nothing could be more damaging to the authorities' credibility than a series of failed rearguard actions.[6] While intervention to slow down the decline could play a role, the authorities should not give the impression that they are trying to stabilize the rate at a specific level until it is quite clear that it has fallen far enough. Once this point is reached, however, they should be prepared to challenge the markets in a big way in an attempt to establish a "floor" rate. If, moreover, this only proved possible after the dollar had overshot somewhat, a major effort should be made to move it back up again before this rate became validated by adaptive expectations in the exchange markets, and before the undesirable effects on the "real" economy—prices, output, employment—began to make themselves felt (box 8.1).

There is little point in speculating further on exactly how events might work out. But there is the fascinating possibility that, in responding to the crisis, the two key and closely interrelated ingredients of a new regime for the major currencies might emerge, de facto, in a pragmatic way:

---

6. As, for example, in 1971–73.

BOX 8.1   **Monetary authorities and adaptive expectations**

From the author's experience at the OECD, monetary authorities also suffer from adaptive expectations in a floating rate system. As time elapses, and a rate remains reasonably stable, they manage to convince themselves that this is an appropriate rate even though 6 or 12 months earlier they would have regarded it as quite inappropriate. One reason for this is that the real economic costs of misaligned rates take a long time to emerge—and show up mainly in areas outside monetary authorities' direct responsiblities (i.e. employment or trade policy). This helps to explain the paralysis in official attitudes to the dollar: a preference for the status quo over the difficulties and dangers once the dollar's decline gets underway in earnest. It was neatly summed up by Otmar Emminger, paraphrasing St. Augustine: "O Lord, give us a lower dollar, but not too soon or too abruptly." (1985b, p. 16).

• agreement between the governments concerned on the desirability of keeping the dollar rate against the deutschemark and the yen within a certain range, *and*

• a demonstration to the markets that they were both able and willing to do so.

This might just be a flash in the pan, with the participants reverting to benign neglect as the crisis receded. But it could lead to some formalization of a new regime, either quite quickly, or progressively over time.

There is a very tricky trade-off involved here. In one sense, the exchange rate regime is, as such, of secondary importance: what matters is whether governments are prepared to follow monetary and fiscal policies consistent with the exchange rate objectives implied in the chosen regime. But there is also an important circularity involved, because the more that governments are prepared to give a quantified indication of their exchange rate objectives to the markets, the easier they will be to achieve (chapter 7).

In practice, supposing events evolve as envisaged, it seems likely that the most that the central banks concerned would try for would be a "managed float,'' i.e. they would try to agree on appropriate target ranges for the dollar, but would give no public indication of what they were (box 8.2). The advantage of this approach is that it is economical on "credibility": the authorities would commit themselves to no more than they found that, ex post, they could achieve. But, by the same token, this might not be good enough. The exchange markets would be left in the dark. More fundamentally, it is doubtful whether a secret understanding between the central banks would prove a strong enough fulcrum to mobilize the *political* support needed to achieve the required degree of consistency in the overall macroeconomic policies of the countries concerned.

These doubts have led to proposals for a "target zone" approach, under which the governments concerned would publically announce, "a range beyond which the authorities are unhappy to see the rate move, despite *not* being prepared to precommit themselves to prevent such movements."[7] It is argued that this would both serve as an anchor for expectations in the exchange markets and impose an element of discipline on the conduct of national monetary and fiscal policies. It is perhaps no surprise that the majority of the G-10 deputies regarded this proposal at best as "impractical."[8] These officials are only too aware that over the past few years every available means of putting international pressure on the United States to change its fiscal policy—from public statements to private one-on-one discussions between heads of state—has been used to the full with no apparent effect. What reason is there to suppose that the existence of a target zone with "soft shoulders" would have changed the mind of President Reagan or Congress?

Let us, however, try to peer forward into a "post-crisis" world. Suppose that the consensus favored a managed float, but that gradually the markets began to get the upper hand again. Remembering how damaging this had been in the past, the question could then arise as to whether it might not be sensible to make a "jump" to a more formal regime in order to cash in on its stabilizing impact on exchange rate expectations. The establishment of the EMS in March 1979—after quite a long period of trial and error—

---

7. Williamson (1985, p. 64).

8. G-10 (1985a, paragraph 32). It should be noted, however, that a minority wanted further study of this proposal, and that the developing countries have come out in favor of it (G-24 1985, paragraph 5).

BOX 8.2   **Exchange rate regimes**

There are three main alternatives to a floating exchange rate regime:

Managed floating. A number of smaller countries have a managed float, i.e. their currency is not publicly pegged to any other currency, but they are prepared to intervene heavily or to take monetary measures to maintain their effective trade-weighted exchange rate at a sensible level. Some attempt was made to manage the dollar/deutschemark rate between 1978 and 1980. One verdict reached was that ". . . U.S. efforts to provide more effective and forceful intervention support for the dollar did, at least in the first instance, help to demonstrate to the market . . . that the U.S. government was concerned about the large and rapid decline in the dollar and was prepared to do something about it. But when intervention actions were not soon followed up with consistent and effective actions to deal with the underlying causes of the dollar's weakness, any positive short-term impact of the intervention faded." (Greene 1984, p. 40)

Target zones. This approach, closely associated with the name of John Williamson, was supported by some G-10 Deputies in their latest report: they described it as a system in which, " . . . the authorities concerned would define wide margins around an adjustable set of exchange rates devised to be consistent with a sustainable balance of payments. Target zones would be phased in progressively. They could, however, trigger consultations that would induce, step by step, more direct links between domestic policies and exchange rate considerations. This would not necessarily involve rigid commitments to intervene in exchange markets." (G-10 1985a, paragraph 31). Williamson has suggested that, at least initially, the margins might be as wide as plus or minus 10 percent.

Adjustable pegs. This is the regime within the EMS. Central rates are established, with fixed margins at which the central banks are obliged to intervene (plus or minus 2.25 percent, but

6 percent for the lira). Central rates can only be changed by mutual agreement. The main problem is that governments are often reluctant to agree in time on necessary changes in central rates, as happened under the Bretton Woods system. A related question concerns the width of the margins, since this regime is likely to operate much more smoothly if the changes made in central rates at any one time are equal to or smaller than the width of the band between the margins.

Williamson and others have suggested that in either target zone or adjustable peg regimes the central rates might be adjusted automatically for differences in the rate of inflation in different countries. Many would probably object, at least for as long as inflation remains a serious problem, because this would take some of the pressure off high-inflation countries to do better.

provides an interesting precedent. It was greeted with much skepticism, but in the event has worked better than expected by most experienced observers at the time.

It is one thing to suggest that such a "jump" may be a necessary step on the way to finding a workable compromise between the excessive rigidity and excessive flexibility of the major currencies that have bedeviled the world economy for a century or more. It is quite another to suggest that the necessary conditions for making such a step are likely to be fulfilled in the not too distant future. This will depend in the first instance on how thoroughly the major countries—especially, but not only, the United States—are converted to a more cooperative ethos by the forthcoming crisis. But, over time, it will also depend on how far it proves possible to *institutionalize* such a change in attitudes. Experience suggests that this is not so much a matter of writing new rules; in the monetary field these have been honored as much in the breach as in the observance. It is just as much a matter of trying to build a change of attitudes into a strengthened institutional framework—as was done just after World War II—so as to ensure that the necessary degree of *political* support for collective and longer run national interests, as opposed to short-term domestic political considerations, can be mobilized.

Monetary Cooperation

In a hard-landing scenario, the Federal Reserve and the other central banks would be thrust into the limelight. By the end of the road, much would have changed. Domestically, the long trail of reluctantly undertaken bailout operations could well have swung the pendulum back toward more regulation, especially in the United States. Internationally, the major central banks would find that they had, de facto, not only become involved in a much closer coordination of their monetary policies, but that they had also acquired the primary responsibility for operating a swap network which might by then have reached $100 billion or $150 billion.

All this would no doubt be messy, with a lot of ad hocery. But there are a number of reasons for being moderately optimistic:

• Over the last three years, the monetary authorities, commercial banks, and international organizations have acquired considerable experience in trying to stave off financial crises and, so far at least, have proved quite good at it.

• There has been a significant evolution in thinking about the implementation of monetary policy. While the emphasis on maintaining a firm anti-inflationary stance has been reinforced over the past few years, there has been a general tendency to downplay strict adherence to predetermined targets for the growth of the monetary aggregates as the sole or best means to this end. In particular, the Fed has been able to cash in on its determination to tough it out against inflation in 1981–82 to give itself more room to maneuver in response to unexpected developments in the economy and the demand for money.

• All the OECD central banks *other* than that of the United States have for some time allowed exchange rate considerations to play a significant role in the implementation of monetary policy. This has in fact been true for the Bundesbank over much of the postwar period, and has by now become something of a fine art among the participants in the EMS. Until recently, it was much less true in Japan where a relatively "dirigiste" monetary policy was geared primarily to domestic objectives. But this has changed with the liberalization of the Japanese financial system and the acuity of the trade tensions generated by the persistent undervaluation of the yen. In the United Kingdom, lip service is still paid to the central role of monetary policy in achieving the objectives of the Medium-Term Financial Strategy, but events have shown that, in practice, exchange rate considerations now also play a major role.

There is thus really only one missing piece left in the puzzle: explicit recognition that the monetary authorities of the United States should also accept that the need to achieve and maintain a sensible level for the dollar should play an important role in the implementation of US monetary policy. In fact, it seems probable that the Fed is at least half converted to this idea already. But as long as it is not supported by the Treasury, and ultimately by the President, it cannot go far in this direction. If, however, this were to change under the pressure of events, the main operational features of a new regime of monetary cooperation between the major central banks can already be discerned:[9]

• First, they would try to ensure that taken together they maintained an appropriate anti-inflationary policy stance.

• Second, they would stand ready to deviate in opposite directions from their medium-term domestic monetary objectives if the exchange rate between their currencies was moving out of line with the "fundamentals."

How this might work out in practice is, of course, far from clear. But it is at least possible that, in a crisis, the governments concerned might be induced—and could see its being to their political advantage—to signal such a new approach through institutional innovation. This could take many forms. Probably the most important question would be whether it led in one way or another to the emergence of a de facto triumvirate of the Federal Reserve Board, the Bundesbank, and the Bank of Japan, with responsibility for the day-to-day management of the dollar-deutsche mark-yen nexus.[10]
This might be narrowly conceived, or might form part of a broader framework linking a larger number of central banks in an embryonic "federal reserve system." In the narrower context, the institutional arrangements might, for example, include some or all of the following:

---

9. This approach has long been advocated by McKinnon (1984), although the importance of what he has been saying has been obscured by his predilection for strict monetary rules, his down playing of fiscal policy, and doubts about some technical aspects of his analysis.

10. De facto, the Bundesbank plays a preponderant role in determining the response of the EMS to external monetary developments (Micossi and Padoa-Schioppa 1984). As a practical matter, therefore, it could probably adequately represent the interests of the EMS on its own, at least in an initial phase, although this would be hotly contested by the other members.

- provisions for regular meetings at the highest level and prior consultation on major policy changes

- representation of each bank in an observer status on the decision-making body of each of the other participants[11]

- authority to extend large credits to each other to finance exchange market intervention, subject, as discussed below, to some review procedure[12]

- liaison with other participants in the European Monetary System.

There would be a host of political and institutional difficulties to resolve. The treasuries of the principal participants would not like the idea at all; there would be an outcry from countries being left out; and there would be fierce institutional rivalries, with the IMF, the BIS, and the Commission of the European Communities each trying to torpedo the idea or turn it to their advantage. These are precisely the kind of things that normally stymie significant institutional reform. Equally, history suggests that they are the kind of things that can be resolved quite quickly when the stakes are high enough.

It would be a mistake, however, to imagine that once the major countries had become convinced of the need for the kind of monetary cooperation described above, the whole matter of exchange rates could be left to the central bankers. Indeed, this syndrome was partly responsible for the breakdown of the Bretton Woods system. As long as the monetary authorities were able to defend fixed rates—which they generally did with much zeal and ingenuity—nobody bothered too much; but, by the time they were no longer able to do so, the underlying disequilibria had become so large that it was too late to do much about it. The issues involved in achieving greater exchange rate stability extend far beyond the competence of central banks. It follows that any institutional innovation in the monetary sphere would have to be paralleled by changes in the broader institutional framework for economic cooperation between the major countries; and that, being more political, these would be more difficult to bring about.

---

11. This was proposed as long ago as 1969 by Charles Kindleberger, but with voting rights (1969, pp. 6–7).

12. In the case of the United States, this could involve transferring more of the responsibility for intervention from the Treasury to the Fed.

Summits

When the first meeting of the heads of state of the major countries to discuss economic issues took place, in November 1975, it appeared to be a sensible and logical step.[13] The postwar political consensus in favor of economic cooperation had weakened as the remarkable recovery rolled on through the 1960s and memories of the 1930s began to fade. It had become evident that, with steadily growing economic interdependence, many of the most important issues increasingly cut across the departmental responsibilities of the different agencies dealing, for example, with money, finance, trade, employment, agriculture, and energy.[14] Perhaps most important, as economic performance deteriorated in the 1970s, the issues involved in economic cooperation acquired a much higher domestic political profile. It thus seemed increasingly clear that the key economic issues could and should be resolved only at the highest political level.

Eleven years later there is widespread disillusionment with summit meetings, even—or especially—among those most closely involved. This should, however, be seen in perspective. For the last several years, the majority of the heads of state participating in these meetings have been convinced that there was no *need* to coordinate their monetary and fiscal policies; on the contrary, the emphasis has been on the vague concept of "convergence of economic performance in the direction of sustainable non-inflationary growth" [G-10 1985b, paragraph 4(i)]. Thus, the fact that recent summits have produced little more than statements in favor of motherhood cannot necessarily be held against the process as such. Nevertheless, the evolution of summits into massive media events increasingly directed to serving the domestic political interests of the host government and the other participants, has, by now, seriously impaired their usefulness as a forum for the coordination of macroeconomic policies at the highest political level.

Here again, a crisis might be useful. It was, after all, the dramatic demonstration of serious *collective* economic dangers in the aftermath of the first oil crisis that led to the creation of summits in the first place. If, for

---

13. See Putnam and Bayne (1984) for an excellent analysis of summitry and the evaluation by Solomon in De Menil and Solomon (1983).

14. Indeed, as was perhaps only to be expected, it often proved easier to reach agreement among representatives of the same agencies from different countries than among those of different agencies from the same country.

example, the imminence of a hard landing led to a decision to hold an "emergency" summit, various opportunities for institutional innovation might open up:

• It could be billed as a working session devoted exclusively to economic matters.

• It need not be held under the rotating host-country formula. One possibility, for example, might be to hold it at the headquarters of the IMF or the OECD. This could provide a major boost to the prestige and public profile of the international organizations—which they badly need. It could limit photo opportunities and underline the focus on the problems of the world economy. And supposing that the many institutional and political difficulties could be overcome, it might create a useful precedent for holding limited group meetings at a high level within the existing institutional framework for multilateral economic cooperation.

• Under the pressure of events it might be possible to update the participation to bring it more closely in line with economic and political realities. One or two developing countries might be invited; one or two of the present participants might not.

• The Managing Director of the IMF, and the heads of the other international organizations most closely involved, could be invited to participate directly in the discussions. Representatives of the world's private business and banking community might be invited to put their views to the heads of state in some appropriate way.

• Finally, and most important, it might be agreed that meetings in the new format should be held regularly, perhaps twice a year, while retaining the existing annual format as a more political and media-oriented event dealing with foreign policy and defense issues.

Changes in the summit process could have other institutional ramifications. Without going into detail, the central question would be how far the changes made helped to bring the realities of international economic interdependence more fully into the domestic political processes of economic decision making. Take, for example, the new "monetary triumvirate" discussed above. Supposing that this were created by a decision of an "emergency" summit, it would be only natural to request it to report regularly to the heads of state. The "managing board" of the new body could therefore be required to report to the summit on the use made of its mutual credit arrangements and, in particular, to draw attention to changes in *other* policies needed if the participants are to honor their exchange rate commitments.[15] This might be done directly, or via some new body bringing in finance and trade ministries, or via the IMF or the Group of Ten. Following the precedent of the Fed's open market committee, the proceedings and recommendations of the managing board might, after a delay, be made public.

Some Longer Run Institutional Issues

To this point, the emphasis has been on the opportunities that a crisis might provide to strengthen the institutional framework for cooperation in an ad hoc way. But there is a flip side to the coin. The instinctive response of governments to new problems has not been to strengthen or reform the existing institutional framework, but rather to add on new bits and pieces. The result is that the existing framework is in a mess (box 8.3).

It is to be hoped, therefore, that in responding to the crisis at least some thought will be given to tidying up this mess and paving the way to longer term institutional reform. Whenever possible, innovations should be grafted onto the existing framework, while at the same time this framework should be progressively reformed to bring it more into line with today's economic and political realities. Only a few of the general issues will be touched on here.

A weakness of the summit process is that it has downgraded one essential ingredient of effective international cooperation—the direct injection of a *non*-national element into the deliberations of national governments, so as to provide an independent assessment of the collective interest and critique of national policies. This loss of an international "conscience" happened to some extent inadvertently as a result of the decision to hold summit meetings outside the existing institutional framework. It has been compounded by the regrettable fact that the capacity—or at least the willingness—of the international organizations to provide this kind of objective analysis and advice appears to have been impaired by the political and ideological pressures to which they have been subjected (box 7.2). As a result, both at summit

---

15. It might make sense to take advantage of the prestige and experience that Paul Volcker has already acquired in international monetary matters, and the key role he is likely to play if the hard-landing scenario materializes while he is still in office.

264 DEFICITS AND THE DOLLAR

BOX 8.3 **The institutional framework for policy coordination**

During the 1960's, the most effective forum for policy coordination among the major countries was Working Party 3 of the OECD's Economic Policy Committee. It operates essentially through peer group pressure; membership includes the summit countries, the Netherlands, Sweden, and Switzerland, with participation from the IMF, the BIS, and the European Commission. Its influence waned after the move to floating rates and the establishment of the EMS.

When the new exchange rate arrangements were ratified in 1975, emphasis was put on "strengthened surveillance" by the IMF in its bilateral relations with member countries. But, at least as far as the major countries are concerned, this has remained largely a dead letter. In the late 1970s, the focus shifted to the summit mechanism and to "secret" meetings of the finance ministers and central bank governors of the Group of Five to which, since the Versailles summit of 1982, the Managing Director of the IMF is usually invited for part of the agenda. The much publicized meeting in New York on September 22, 1985, could well be the forerunner of an enhanced role for the Group of Five.

From the onset of the debt crisis, attention shifted sharply away from the affairs of the major countries, and the IMF, finance ministries, and central and commercial banks became deeply involved in the economic fortunes of the many debtor countries. The BIS continued to play a discreet role as a convenient club for central bankers, and the Group of Ten emerged briefly from obscurity with the enlargement of the General Arrangements to Borrow and a report on the functioning of the international monetary system.

In the trade field the GATT was unable to prevent a steady erosion of the world trading system, and there has been increasing emphasis on bilateral relations and meetings of trade ministers in various groupings outside the established framework. Efforts to bring finance and trade ministers together to face up to the serious problems created by misaligned exchange rates have been largely unsuccessful.

Summarizing briefly, the main weaknesses in the present set-up are:

- There is too much overlap in work on the coordination of monetary and fiscal policies of the major countries between the summit, the Group of Five, the IMF, the OECD, the European Communities, and the BIS. National officials find themselves attending innumerable meetings to discuss essentially the same questions in a different political and bureaucratic context, often without ever getting to the real point.
- There is too much compartmentalization in the work done by different international bodies on issues which cut across departmental responsibilities for monetary and fiscal policy, trade policy, industry and agricultural policy, tax policy, financial regulation, etc.
- The proliferation of different groupings at the political level—the Group of Five, of Seven, of Ten, of Twelve, of Twenty-Four, of Seventy-Seven—is extremely cumbersome, if to some extent inevitable.

meetings and during their preparation there has been an inherent tendency to duck the really central and difficult economic issues. Each country is aware that its own policies are not perfect, and, for political reasons, they all want to be nice to each other. This natural tendency is particularly evident when one of the partners, the United States, is so disproportionately powerful.

Various things might be done to try to improve matters. The pretense that summits are intended to be no more than informal fireside chats could be dropped. Institutional linkage with the existing international bodies should be strengthened, both in the preparation of the meetings, and in following up the decisions taken. The "new format" summit suggested above might need a permanent secretariat. One possibility might be a "joint secretariat" composed of officials from national capitals and the relevant international organizations.[16] This could also be a useful first step toward breaking down

---

16. The Group of Ten, with a joint secretariat drawn from the IMF, the OECD, and the BIS, provides a precedent.

the excessive compartmentalization of interests in the fields of finance, trade, and other policies (box 8.3). Over time, however, real progress in this direction would require significant rationalization and reform of the existing international organizations. Equally important, more needs to be done to lessen the political pressures on these organizations from their largest members and strengthen their independence and objectivity. More input might also be sought from the private sector, parts of which have become extremely knowledgeable about the issues involved in intergovernmental economic cooperation and have a strong self-interest in its success.

To conclude, the agenda for any change in present international arrangements—be it by informal agreement or institutional reform—will remain blocked for so long as nothing goes seriously wrong. But under the pressure of unpleasant events this could change quite quickly. One of the great strengths of the United States is its capacity to respond to new problems; it is a "fix it" country. With US leadership, much could be done to improve the management of the world economy that now seems out of the question. The ideas canvassed above are not meant as a blueprint for reform. They are put forward simply in the hope of stimulating some more imaginative thinking in official and private circles.[17]

---

17. The report on "The Functioning of the International Monetary System" by the G-10 deputies was published in June 1985. It was not an epoch-making document. To the aficionado of this kind of officialese there is perhaps somewhat more implicit self-criticism, and more emphasis on the "consistency and mutual compatibility of national policies" (paragraph 50), than in most pronouncements on this subject over the last few years. The deputies even suggested that effective surveillance "may require . . . consideration of the introduction of new arrangements." (G-10 1985a, paragraph 49). True, they could not agree what these should be. But then there is nothing like a crisis to concentrate the mind!

Technical Notes

TN1 The D&D model

Description of the model

1. The D&D model is designed to simulate the US current account on alternative exchange rate and growth assumptions. Unlike the major multi-country models (i.e., those developed by the Federal Reserve, OECD, and the Economic Planning Agency of Japan), the D&D model does not incorporate the complex interactions of exchange rates and interest rates; these financial variables are set exogenously.

2. The model treats the rest of the world (ROW) as two aggregates: the rest of the OECD (ROECD) area, and the developing countries. Foreign trade price and income elasticities, and feedbacks from trade prices and volumes on domestic prices and output, are modeled for the United States and the ROECD area, but not for the developing countries. The US trade balance with the developing countries is assumed to remain constant in real terms from 1985 onwards (except in the cooperative scenario). Changes in the dollar vis-à-vis the currencies of the developing countries and the associated price and volume changes are not incorporated.

3. GNP growth rates for the United States are set exogenously. For the rest of the world (ROW) they can either be set exogenously, or derived from the model on the basis of assumed feedbacks. In the latter case, ROECD growth diverges from the initially assumed rate because of the multiplier effects of a shift in net exports. The adjustment to developing-country growth is more mechanical: it is assumed that for each percentage point that OECD growth rises above 3 percent, developing-country growth increases above its trend (4½ percent) by a like amount; and when OECD growth falls below 3 percent, developing-country growth is correspondingly reduced.

4. US merchandise trade volumes are forecast from previous year volumes, adjusted on the basis of price and income effects. The income elasticities are 1.5 for merchandise exports and 1.8 for nonoil imports; these are applied to current annual growth rates. ROW growth is a GNP-weighted average of growth rates in the ROECD area (0.67) and developing countries (0.33).

5. Volumes are assumed to adjust to relative price changes in the current year and two previous years. Relative price changes are expressed in terms

269

of the ratio of import prices to the domestic price level. The price elasticity for US exports is -1.2, and that for US nonoil imports is -1.3. The timing of the response to relative price changes is assumed identical for exports and imports: 40 percent of the volume adjustment occurs in the first year, 40 percent in the second, and 20 percent in the third.

6. All projections are in terms of current prices. In the absence of exchange rate changes, inflation is assumed to be 4.2 percent in the United States and 5 percent in the ROECD area. However, for reasons discussed in TN10, it is assumed that the price level and cost level directly relevant to assessing changes in US competitive strength in world markets (and hence used to drive the price elasticities and derive real exchange rate movements) rise at 0.85 times the overall ROECD inflation rate, or 4.25 percent at constant exchange rates.

7. Exchange rate changes exert both direct and indirect influence on relative prices. The direct effect is captured by the pass-through coefficients, assumed to be 0.3 on both sides for the export price adjustment, in the *home* currency, to an exchange rate change. In terms of price competition, this means that if the dollar declines by 10 percent, the price of US exports in foreign markets is lowered by 7 percent, and the price of imports in US markets rises by 7 percent.

8. Relative prices are also influenced by the impact of exchange rate changes on the domestic price level. Import prices change, and in addition these changes induce changes in the prices of domestic products competing with imports; and these changes in prices induce changes in wages which feed back onto prices. The model approximates these effects through the use of price level feedback coefficients. For the United States, a 10 percent depreciation is assumed to lead to a 1 percent rise in domestic prices in the first year, and a further 0.5 percent rise in the next year. For the ROECD area, depreciation vis-à-vis the dollar inflates the price level by 0.6 percent in the first year, and a further 0.4 percent in the second. Actual rates of inflation diverge from the "domestically generated" rate by the amount of the feedback, and are reflected in home-currency export prices.

9. Because the model projects export and import volumes from previous year levels, the trade position in the base year (1984) is important. It seems likely that some part of the deterioration in 1984 was due to factors that may have been reversed in 1985. Accordingly, two special adjustments have been

made. The first is a downward adjustment of projected import volumes, removing the suspected effect of an exceptionally large inventory buildup in 1984 which may have boosted US imports by about $10 billion. The second adjustment, of $5 billion, reflects the assumed partial reversal of the adverse impact of the Latin American debt crisis on US exports in 1983–84. Both these adjustments ("add factors") are favorable to the US trade balance in 1985 and thereafter.

10. Oil imports are projected as the difference between domestic consumption and domestic production. The latter is assumed fixed at 1984 levels. The elasticity of oil consumption with respect to US income is 0.8; no price elasticity has been included. The price of oil is held constant in nominal dollar terms at the mid-1985 level through 1986, and in real terms thereafter.

11. Nonfactor services are assumed to grow at the same rate as merchandise exports and nonoil imports. The application of identical income and price elasticities to goods and services is an oversimplification, but it is in keeping with the aggregative nature of the model and is unlikely to greatly affect the results. Military transactions are excluded from the service accounts and are assumed to balance. Private and official transfers are held constant in real terms.

12. Direct investment capital flows and investment income payments and receipts have been introduced into the model as exogenous variables (see TN2, paragraphs 11–13).

13. Two simplifying assumptions have been made concerning interest flows. First, it is assumed that the interest rate on the financing for current deficits, from 1985 onward, is equal to the Treasury-bill rate. Second, there is no reshuffling of the existing portfolio of US financial assets and liabilities (which gave rise to net interest receipts of $5.6 billion in 1984), or reshuffling is neutral in terms of its impact on net interest flows. With these assumptions, year-to-year changes in net interest flows are determined exclusively by the accumulation of financial debt and the Treasury-bill rate in the projection period.

14. The model also allows for the effects of a change in US net exports on the level of output (and hence imports) in other countries, and vice versa. Results from simulations with the OECD Interlink model suggest that the multiplier effects of a change in net exports are of broadly similar magnitudes in the United States and the ROECD area; a rise in net exports equivalent to

1 percent of GNP boosts income by 2 percent in the first year, and by 2.5 percent in the following year. In the scenarios analyzed in this study, however, the cause of the reduction in ROECD net exports is a sharp decline in the dollar. As discussed in the text, this is likely to be associated with a decline in ROECD interest rates which would help to offset the negative impact of the decline in net exports. Assuming that on unchanged policies, interest rates would fall back to the 1978 level (a drop of about 2.5 points), and applying a typical monetary multiplier (see TN16), the combined effect yields a negative foreign trade multiplier used here for the ROECD area of 1.9 and 1.8 in the first and second years.

15. In the absence of offsetting policy action, an increase in US net exports would simultaneously boost US GNP and lower ROECD GNP. The presence or absence of offsetting policy action is postulated in different variants of the model; GNP growth can be predetermined (as in the baseline), or allowed to reflect the multiplier effects of a net export shift. Thus, when neither US nor ROECD growth is fixed, the model solves simultaneously for both growth rates and the net export shift. When only US growth is fixed, it solves for ROECD growth and the net export shift.

16. The net investment position is calculated by adding the current balance in each year to the investment position in the preceding year, starting with the recorded figures for end-1984 (table 3.4). In practice, there are good grounds to believe the US net investment position at end-1984 was both understated and overstated. It was understated for two reasons. First, direct investment is carried at book value, and, since US direct investment abroad still exceeds foreign direct investment in the United States (by $73 billion at end-1984), the positive balance in favor of the United States would be larger if valued at current market prices. Second, the US gold stock was valued at the official price of $42.22 an ounce ($11 billion at end-1984). Since official gold holdings have become "frozen" to a large extent, it is hard to know at what price they should be valued (at the current market price, the end-1984 US gold stock was worth $84 billion). On the other hand, the US net investment position is overstated because it is generally thought that a significant fraction of the very large "errors and omissions" item in the US balance of payments ($140 billion 1979–84) was in fact unrecorded capital inflows (TN12). In the view of analysts at the Department of Commerce, this may mean that the United States had already become a net debtor before the end of 1984 (*Survey of Current Business*, vol. 65, no. 6, June 1985, p.

28). Given the many uncertainties, however, it seems best to assume that the positive and negative factors roughly canceled out at the end of 1984.

17. Changes in the US net investment position reflect changes in the value of existing assets and liabilities as well as changes in them during the period in question. These result primarily from changes in market values and exchange rates. They are likely to be small relative to the size of the current account deficits studied here, and have been ignored in the projections (such adjustments cumulated to minus $33 billion for 1970–83, reflecting changes in financial asset prices, with a small negative contribution from exchange rate losses in recent years).

18. Many analysts believe that the recorded figures overstate the size of the US current account deficit and hence the deterioration of the US net investment position associated with it. The main justification for this assumption is that, at the world level, recorded current expenditures exceed receipts by around $100 billion, and it seems logical to assume that the United States accounts for some part of this "world current account discrepancy." Such an adjustment (typically on the order of $20 billion) has, however, not been made here for reasons discussed in TN12.

19. Putting these elements together, the two key assumptions are that the positive and negative errors in the published estimates of the US net investment position at end-1984 roughly offset each other, and that changes in it will equal the recorded US current balance as projected using the model.

20. *Sources:* Base year, *Survey of Current Business, OECD Economic Outlook,* and other official sources.

Choice of coefficients

21. The coefficients used in the model (table E) have been chosen on the basis of a literature review and fall near the middle of the range of published estimates. A comprehensive survey of the literature can be found in Goldstein and Khan (1983). Unfortunately, the range of price and income elasticities in published studies appears to be very wide indeed, and problems of comparability make simple averaging impractical. In choosing from among the range of values for price and income elasticities, somewhat more weight has been given to recent estimates, including those contained in the major multicountry models. Additional adjustments have been made as a result of

the "backcasting" exercise (described below), in which the model was used to "predict" the evolution of the nonoil trade balance in 1981–84.

22. Literature review and experimentation with the model have underscored the importance of ensuring consistency between the index used to measure the exchange rate, the pass-through factors, and the price elasticities; it is the combination of all three that determines a model's overall response to a change in the dollar. Thus, in fitted models using the Federal Reserve Board's dollar index, which tends to move more than other indices (see TN8), either pass-throughs or elasticities are likely to be lower than in models using a different dollar index. Equally, there is a similar tendency for models with high pass-throughs to use lower elasticities, and vice versa. This is evident, to take only one example, in a comparison of the coefficients estimated by Hooper (1976) and Feldman (1982) (although these two studies cover different periods). This phenomenon makes it difficult, in particular, to assess published estimates of price elasticities, since the corresponding estimate of the price pass-through is often not specified (nor, in some cases, the exchange rate index to which they apply).

23. The combined effect of the price elasticity and the pass-through factor is seen not only in the size of volume changes, but in the shape of the J-curve. Thus, the coefficients of this model produce the results shown in table A for a 10 percent dollar depreciation:

TABLE A   **Impact on trade values of a 10 percent depreciation[a]**
(percentage change from previous year)

	Year 1	Year 2	Year 3
Exports	+6.6	+3.5	+1.8
Nonoil imports	+3.3	−3.9	−1.9

a. Based on a 10 percent average depreciation, using price elasticities and pass-throughs from the model, and ignoring inflation feedbacks.

In the first year, about half the benefit on the export side is offset by a rise in the value of imports as higher dollar prices more than offset lower volumes.

24. The price elasticities (1.2 and 1.3 for exports and nonoil imports, respectively) appear to be near the middle of the range of published estimates. Stern reports a "best estimate" of 1.41 for total US exports, and 1.66 for

total imports (1976, tables 1 and 2), but estimates have been lower in some more recent studies, and the inclusion of nonfactor services probably justifies lower elasticities than those estimated for broad categories of US merchandise trade. The pass-through coefficients used in the model are similar to those estimated in several other studies (Spitäler 1980, Hooper 1976, and Yoshitomi 1984), but the range of available estimates is uncomfortably large. This may be due to the different time periods covered, and the likelihood that pass-throughs vary over the course of the business cycle.

25. The range of estimates for income elasticities is also large. However, the evidence now seems to suggest a smaller gap between US import and export elasticities than that identified in early studies (Houthakker and Magee 1969).

26. Sensitivity tests were performed to assess the implications of alternative assumptions about price and income elasticities.

TABLE B   **Sensitivity of results to elasticity assumptions**

	Depreciation required[a] to eliminate deficit by 1990
Baseline	38.3
"Pessimistic" income elasticities[b]	41.7
"Optimistic" income elasticities[c]	34.7
"Pessimistic" price elasticities[d]	43.4
"Optimistic" price elasticities[e]	34.7

a. Depreciation beginning in fourth quarter 1985 and continuing to first quarter 1989. Baseline growth, inflation, and interest rate assumptions.
b. Ten percent higher income elasticity for imports, and 10 percent lower income elasticity for exports, relative to baseline.
c. Ten percent lower income elasticity for imports, and 10 percent higher income elasticity for exports, relative to baseline.
d. Twenty percent lower price elasticities for both imports and exports, relative to baseline.
e. Twenty percent higher price elasticities for both imports and exports, relative to baseline.

The results show how much depreciation would be required to eliminate the current deficit with different sets of elasticities (table B). The results suggest that the magnitude of implied present dollar overvaluation is not very sensitive to the elasticities used, and hence tends to confirm the importance of "gap factors" as determinants of the "equilibrium" exchange rate.

27. The impact of exchange rate changes on the US price level is a subject of continuing controversy. A recent paper by Wing Woo (1984) finds no statistical association between import prices and the US consumption deflator, excluding food and fuel. However, a reformulation by Sachs (1985) reaches different conclusions. See also Goldstein and Khan (1983, table 8) for a comparison of several studies. A more recent survey by Pigott, Rutledge, and Willet (1984) gives estimates that a 10 percent dollar depreciation could boost the US price level by between 1.5 percent and 3.5 percent. As in the case of price elasticities, comparison of different studies is rendered difficult by the use of different exchange rate indices (Solomon 1985c). Allowing for this, the exchange rate price level feedback of 1.5 percent over two years used in the D&D model appears to lie in the middle of the range used in other studies.

28. For the rest of the OECD area, the relevant exchange rate is not the effective exchange rate as in the case of the United States but rather the dollar exchange rate. Relevant factors in the choice of the coefficients were that ROECD GNP is about 50 percent larger than US GNP but that, on the other hand, commodity prices denominated in dollars are likely to rise as the dollar goes down and the feedback from import prices to domestic costs and prices may be stronger than in the United States because of more de facto and de jure wage indexation. The coefficient used of 1.0 over two years appears to be at the low end of the range used in other models.

Backcasting, 1980–84

29. To assess the properties of the model, a backcasting exercise was performed (tables C and D). Using 1980 trade values as a base, the model was used to project the 1981–84 balance on goods and nonfactor services (excluding oil), based on actual exchange rate movements, inflation rates, and growth rates. Two special adjustments were made. First, actual changes in export volumes to developing countries during 1981–84 were compared to the changes in total export volume predicted by the model. The comparison revealed an "unexplained" surge in US exports to developing countries in 1981, followed by a sharp reduction in 1982–83 as the debt crisis unfolded. Actual changes in export volume to developing countries have been incorporated into the backcasting. Second, the actual export price change in 1981 (8.5 percent) has been substituted for the one that would have predicted (5.0

percent) on the basis of US inflation and dollar appreciation. The large price increase in 1981 appears to be related to the unusually strong demand for US exports in developing countries.

30. The model gives a reasonably good prediction for the period as a whole, partly because of errors in opposite directions. The largest error is an underprediction of import volume increase—especially in 1984. As noted previously, this may be due to a cyclical effect not captured by the model: an unusually large inventory buildup. On the other hand, the model overpredicts the decline in export volumes—again, chiefly because of an error in 1984, when actual export volumes grew by over 4 percent despite a strengthening dollar. Dollar prices of exports are also underpredicted, compounding the shortfall of predicted exports of goods and nonfactor services in 1984.

TABLE C   **Balance on goods and nonfactor services**[a] **(excluding oil), 1980–81** (actual values; *predicted values*)

	1980	1981	1982	1983	1984
	Billion dollars				
Exports	262	279	253	243	262
		273	*256*	*241*	*245*
Nonoil imports	202	221	221	246	312
		218	*220*	*253*	*297*
Balance	60	58	32	−3	−51
		58	*37*	*−12*	*−52*
	Percentage change				
Export volume	7.0	−1.6	−10.2	−5.7	4.3
		−2.8	*−8.8*	*−7.5*	*0.8*
Import volume	−0.1	6.8	1.8	11.9	27.4
		7.3	*2.2*	*13.5*	*17.4*
Export prices[b]	11.0	8.5	1.0	1.5	3.4
		8.5	*1.8*	*1.7*	*0.8*
Import prices[b]	13.0	2.7	−1.9	−0.8	−0.3
		0.7	*−1.2*	*1.5*	*−0.2*

Source: Simulation of D&D model and *Survey of Current Business.*
a. Excluding military transactions.
b. Implicit price deflators.

TABLE D   **Cumulative changes, 1980–84** (percentage change)

	Predicted	Actual
Export volume	− 17.3	− 13.1
Export prices	+ 9.5[a]	+ 15.0
Import volume	+ 46.0[b]	+ 55.2
Import prices	+ 0.8	− 0.3

Source: Simulation of D&D model and *Survey of Current Business.*
a. + 13.3 percent with special adjustment for 1981.
b. + 52.1 percent with special adjustment for 1984 inventory buildup.

31. Other simulations were performed in which exchange rates remained at 1980 levels, and growth rates in the United States and the rest of the world were such as to nullify the effect of different income elasticities. Results of these simulations were used to construct table 1.2.

Model specifications

32. The nominal effective exchange rate affects the US price level as follows:

(1) $UPI_t = UPI_{t-1} * 1.042 * [1 + ([(ER_t / ER_{t-1}) - 1] * -0.1)$
$+ ([(ER_{t-1} / ER_{t-2}) - 1] * - 0.05)],$

where UPI_t is the US price index in year t, 1.042 is the domestic inflation factor, and ER_t is the nominal effective exchange rate index (defined with foreign currency in the numerator so that a decline means dollar depreciation). Asterisks denote multiplication.

33. The foreign price index (FPI_t) is derived in the same way, but with the exchange rate terms inverted:

(2) $FPI_t = FPI_{t-1} * 1.05 * [1 + ([(ER_{t-1} / ER_t) - 1] * -0.06)$
$+ ([(ER_{t-2} / ER_{t-1}) - 1] * -0.04)].$

34. US and foreign inflation rates are given by:

(3) $UIN_t = (UPI_t / UPI_{t-1}) - 1$, and

(4) $FIN_t = (FPI_t / FPI_{t-1}) - 1.$

35. Inflation of ROECD tradeables ($FINT_t$), is lower than that for the overall price level (see TN10, paragraph 2):

(5) $FINT_t = 0.85 * FIN_t$.

The price index for ROECD tradeables ($FPIT_t$), constructed in chain fashion from (5), is used to calculate relative price changes in (11) below, and the real exchange rate index (RER_t):

(6) $RER_t = ER_t * (UPI_t / FPIT_t)$.

36. US export prices in dollar terms (PX_t) are determined by US inflation and the US export price coefficient (ZU):

(7) $PX_t = PX_{t-1} * (1 + UIN_t) * [1 + (-ZU * [(ER_t / ER_{t-1}) - 1])]$.

37. Equation (8) gives the foreign currency price of US exports (FPX_t):

(8) $FPX_t = PX_t * ER_t$.

38. US import prices in foreign currency (FPM_t) are determined by foreign inflation and the foreign export price coefficient (ZF):

(9) $FPM_t = FPM_{t-1} * (1 + FIN_t) * [1 + (-ZF * [(ER_{t-1} / ER_t) - 1])]$.

39. And dollar prices of US imports (PM_t) are given by:

(10) $PM_t = FPM_t / ER_t$.

40. Merchandise export volumes (VX_t) respond to the foreign growth rate (GFO_t) and to changes in foreign currency prices of exports relative to the foreign price level. The income response is instantaneous, whereas the price response is distributed over three years:

$$
\begin{aligned}
(11) \quad VX_t = VX_{t-1} * (1 + &[EXY * GFO_t]) \\
* (1 + [EXP * 0.4 * &([(ER_t * PX_t * FPIT_{t-1}) \\
&/(ER_{t-1} * PX_{t-1} * FPIT_t)] - 1)]) \\
* (1 + [EXP * 0.4 * &([(ER_{t-1} * PX_{t-1} * FPIT_{t-2}) \\
&/(ER_{t-2} * PX_{t-2} * FPIT_{t-1})] - 1)]) \\
* (1 + [EXP * 0.2 * &([(ER_{t-2} * PX_{t-2} * FPIT_{t-3}) \\
&/(ER_{t-3} * PX_{t-3} * FPIT_{t-2})] - 1)]).
\end{aligned}
$$

EXY is the elasticity of exports with respect to foreign growth (GFO_t), defined as a weighted average of growth in the rest of the OECD area and in developing countries. EXP is the export price elasticity.

41. Similarly, nonoil merchandise import volumes are determined as follows:

$$(12) \quad VM_t = VM_{t-1} * (1 + [EMY * GUS_t])$$
$$* (1 + [EMP * 0.4 * ([(ER_{t-1} * FPM_t * UPI_{t-1})$$
$$/(ER_t * FPM_{t-1} * UPI_t)] - 1)])$$
$$* (1 + [EMP * 0.4 * ([(ER_{t-2} * FPM_{t-1} * UPI_{t-2})$$
$$/(ER_{t-1} * FPM_{t-2} * UPI_{t-1})] - 1)])$$
$$* (1 + [EMP * 0.2 * ([(ER_{t-3} * FPM_{t-2} * UPI_{t-3})$$
$$/(ER_{t-2} * FPM_{t-3} * UPI_{t-2})] - 1)]).$$

EMY is the elasticity of import volume with respect to US income (GUS_t), and EMP is the price elasticity.

42. In value terms, merchandise exports ($XTOT_t$) and nonoil imports ($MNOL_t$) are given by:

$$(13) \quad XTOT_t = PX_t * VX_t, \text{ and}$$

$$(14) \quad MNOL_t = VM_t * PM_t.$$

43. Oil imports are determined separately. The quantity of oil demanded ($DOIL_t$) is a function of US income:

$$(15) \quad DOIL_t = DOIL_{t-1} * (1 + [0.8 * GUS_t]).$$

With domestic production of oil (DOP) held constant, oil imports ($MOIL_t$) are given by:

$$(16) \quad MOIL_t = POIL_t * (DOIL_t - DOP).$$

The price of oil ($POIL_t$) is held constant in nominal dollar terms through 1986; thereafter it rises with US inflation.

44. Exports and imports of nonfactor services ($XNFS_t$ and $MNFS_t$) grow in direct proportion to merchandise exports and nonoil imports:

$$(17) \quad XNFS_t = (XNFS_{t-1} / XTOT_{t-1}) * XTOT_t, \text{ and}$$

$$(18) \quad MNFS_t = (MNFS_{t-1} / MNOL_{t-1}) * MNOL_t.$$

TABLE E **Elasticities used in projections**

Notation	Assumed value	Description
EXY	1.5	Elasticity of US export volumes with respect to foreign income
EMY	1.8	Elasticity of US nonoil import volumes with respect to US income
EXP	−1.2	Elasticity of US export volumes with respect to relative price changes
EMP	−1.3	Elasticity of US nonoil import volumes with respect to relative price changes
ZU	+0.3	US export pass-through coefficient: elasticity of US export prices in dollars with respect to dollar depreciation
ZF	+0.3	Foreign export pass-through coefficient: elasticity of foreign export prices in foreign currencies with respect to foreign currency depreciation

45. As noted above, the model permits growth rates to be affected by the multiplier effects of a shift in US net exports. Equation (19) establishes this relationship for the rest of the OECD area:

$$(19) \quad AGRD_t = GRD_t - 1.9 * [(RNX_t - RNX_{t-1})/RFGNP_{t-1}]$$
$$+ 0.1 * [(RNX_{t-1} - RNX_{t-2})/RFGNP_{t-2}].$$

$AGRD_t$ is the ROECD growth rate incorporating the multiplier effects of a shift in US net exports; GRD_t is the growth rate in the absence of such effects; RNX_t is US net exports in constant prices; and $RFGNP_t$ is ROECD GNP in constant prices. In the first year, a positive shift in US net exports equivalent to 1 percent of ROECD GNP causes a growth reduction of 1.9 percent; this is only slightly offset in the second year.

46. Similarly, US growth can be allowed to reflect the trade multiplier:

$$(20) \quad AGUS_t = GUS_t + 2.0 * [(RNX_t - RNX_{t-1})/RUGNP_{t-1}]$$
$$+ 0.5 * [(RNX_{t-1} - RNX_{t-2})/RUGNP_{t-2}].$$

$AGUS_t$ is the US growth rate incorporating the multiplier effects; GUS_t is the growth rate in the absence of such effects; and $RUGNP_t$ is US GNP in constant prices. A positive shift in US net exports equivalent to 1 percent of US GNP boosts growth by 2 percent in the first year, and a further 0.5 percent in the second.

47. Feedbacks to developing-country growth are based on equation (21):

(21) $AGLDC_t = GLDC_t + (GOECD_t - 0.03)$.

$AGLDC_t$ is the adjusted developing-country growth rate; $GLDC_t$ is the growth rate in the absence of feedback from the OECD; and $GOECD_t$ is the OECD growth rate—a weighted average of growth in the United States and ROECD area (based on shares in OECD GNP at 1982 exchange rates; the weights are 0.4 and 0.6, respectively). Deviations of OECD growth from 3 percent cause developing-country growth rates to deviate from their trend.

48. By substituting the adjusted growth equations (19) to (21), or any combination thereof, into an equation for real net exports, the model can be made to solve simultaneously for growth rates and the associated net export shift.

TN2   *Assumptions used in scenarios and summary of the results*

1. Table A summarizes the assumptions built into the three scenarios and the main results.

T A B L E A   **Scenarios: assumptions and outcomes**

	1986	1987	1988	1989	1990
US current account (billion dollars)					
Baseline	−171	−205	−235	−275	−320
Soft	−161	−169	−144	−107	−87
Hard	−154	−94	−16	53	85
Cooperative	−149	−125	−75	−20	0
Nominal dollar depreciation (percentage change)					
Baseline	−0.7	0.0	0.0	0.0	0.0
Soft	−9.9	−12.6	−12.6	−6.5	0.0
Hard	−12.1	−15.7	−15.7	−8.2	0.0
Cooperative	−8.0	−10.1	−10.1	−5.2	0.0

TABLE A   *Continued*

	1986	1987	1988	1989	1990
Real dollar depreciation (percentage change)					
Baseline	−1.3	0.0	0.0	0.0	0.0
Soft	−9.1	−10.1	−9.9	−4.6	0.5
Hard	−11.1	−12.6	−12.3	−5.7	0.7
Cooperative	−7.5	−8.1	−7.9	−3.6	0.4
US Treasury-bill rate (percent)					
Baseline	8.7	8.2	8.2	8.2	8.2
Soft	10.0	10.5	10.0	9.0	8.0
Hard	13.0	11.0	9.0	7.0	6.5
Cooperative	9.5	9.0	8.0	6.5	6.5
Change in US price level (percentage change)					
Baseline	3.8	4.2	4.2	4.2	4.2
Soft	4.8	6.0	6.2	5.5	4.5
Hard	5.0	6.5	6.6	5.9	4.6
Cooperative	4.6	5.7	5.8	5.3	4.5
Change in ROECD price level (percentage change)					
Baseline	5.3	5.0	5.0	5.0	5.0
Soft	4.6	3.6	3.5	4.0	4.7
Hard	4.5	3.3	3.1	3.7	4.6
Cooperative	4.8	3.9	3.8	4.2	4.8
US growth rate (percentage change)					
Baseline	3.0	3.0	3.0	3.0	3.0
Soft	3.2	3.3	3.4	3.4	3.4
Hard	2.0	−1.5	−0.5	4.5	5.0
Cooperative	2.5	1.0	2.5	3.5	4.5
ROECD growth rate (percentage change)					
Baseline	3.0	3.0	3.0	3.0	3.0
Soft	3.0	2.2	1.7	2.0	2.6
Hard	2.6	0.6	1.1	1.9	2.7
Cooperative	4.0	4.5	4.5	4.5	4.0
LDC growth rate (percentage change)					
Baseline	4.5	4.5	4.5	4.5	4.5
Soft	4.6	4.1	3.9	4.1	4.4
Hard	3.9	1.3	1.9	4.4	5.1
Cooperative	4.8	4.7	5.5	6.0	6.0
US export prices (percentage change)					
Baseline	4.0	4.2	4.2	4.2	4.2
Soft	7.9	10.0	10.2	7.6	4.5
Hard	8.9	11.5	11.7	8.5	4.6
Cooperative	7.1	8.9	9.0	6.9	4.5
US import prices (nonoil, percentage change)					
Baseline	5.0	4.2	4.3	4.3	4.3
Soft	11.5	12.9	12.7	8.3	4.0
Hard	13.2	15.1	14.9	9.3	3.9
Cooperative	10.2	11.1	11.0	7.4	4.1

TABLE A *Continued*

	1986	1987	1988	1989	1990
US export volume (percentage change)					
Baseline	2.4	4.8	5.6	5.3	5.3
Soft	5.1	10.0	12.0	10.4	7.6
Hard	5.0	8.4	12.5	12.2	8.7
Cooperative	5.7	11.4	14.1	12.7	9.2
US import volume (nonoil, percentage change)					
Baseline	7.9	5.9	5.1	5.3	5.3
Soft	5.2	−0.1	−2.4	−0.4	3.3
Hard	2.2	−13.5	−6.7	−0.1	5.4
Cooperative	4.6	−2.7	−2.3	1.1	5.8
Net indebtedness (trillion dollars)					
Baseline	0.26	0.47	0.71	0.99	1.31
Soft	0.26	0.43	0.58	0.68	0.77
Hard	0.25	0.34	0.36	0.31	0.22
Cooperative	0.24	0.37	0.45	0.47	0.47
Direct investment income (billion dollars)					
Baseline	12.9	14.0	15.1	16.4	17.8
Soft	15.4	20.2	25.9	30.1	32.2
Hard	16.1	22.1	29.5	34.7	37.0
Cooperative	15.2	20.0	25.8	30.4	33.1
Transfers (billion dollars)					
Baseline	10.9	11.4	11.8	12.3	12.8
Soft	11.0	11.7	12.4	13.1	13.7
Hard	11.0	11.7	12.5	13.3	13.9
Cooperative	11.0	11.6	12.3	12.9	13.5
US wellbeing index (percentage points)					
Baseline	1.7	1.0	0.9	0.9	0.9
Soft	0.5	−1.4	−1.9	−1.0	0.5
Hard	−1.2	−7.7	−6.7	−0.3	2.1
Cooperative	−0.1	−3.7	−2.6	−0.7	1.7
US performance index (percentage points)					
Baseline	0.8	0.8	0.8	0.8	0.8
Soft	1.0	1.1	1.2	1.2	1.2
Hard	−0.2	−3.7	−2.7	2.3	2.8
Cooperative	0.3	−1.2	0.3	1.3	2.3
ROECD wellbeing index (percentage points)					
Baseline	−0.2	0.4	0.4	0.4	0.4
Soft	0.8	1.6	1.5	1.1	0.7
Hard	0.8	1.2	1.6	1.4	0.7
Cooperative	1.7	3.9	4.1	3.3	1.9
ROECD performance index (percentage points)					
Baseline	0.5	0.5	0.5	0.5	0.5
Soft	0.5	−0.3	−0.8	−0.5	0.1
Hard	0.1	−1.9	−1.4	−0.6	0.2
Cooperative	1.5	2.0	2.0	2.0	1.5

GNP

2. The growth rate of GNP in 1985 was put at 3.0 percent for the United States and the ROECD area, and 3.8 percent in the developing countries (for the United States this may turn out to be too high). In the baseline case US and ROECD growth rates for 1986–90 are both set exogenously at 3.0 percent, and the developing-country growth rate at 4.5 percent, giving an ROW growth of 3.5 percent.

3. For the United States, the baseline growth rate assumed is lower than the CBO's baseline of 3.4 percent and the administration's projection of 4 percent.

4. For Europe, the European Commission's medium-term projection is for a GNP growth rate averaging 2.8 percent for 1985–88 (1984, pp. 69–71). This assumes some further increase in net exports (mainly in 1985). Adjusted for this, the projected growth of domestic demand was around 2.5 percent, against 1.8 percent in 1984. For Japan, the Economic Planning Agency used a 4 percent growth rate for domestic demand as a working assumption in *Prospects and Guidelines for the Economic Society* (August 1983). It is thus assumed that on unchanged policies, and absent a decline in net exports, GNP growth in 1986–90 might average between 2 percent and 2.5 percent, 4 percent and 4.5 percent, and 3 percent, respectively, for Europe, Japan, and the other OECD countries, giving a weighted average of 3 percent for the ROECD area as a whole.

5. For the developing countries the baseline growth rate is the same as that used by Cline (1984).

6. In the three other scenarios the US growth rate has also been set exogenously. In the soft-landing scenario the CBO's baseline growth rate has been used (CBO 1985b, table I-2). In the hard-landing scenario a recession is assumed of a magnitude about halfway between those of 1974–75 and 1980–82, followed by a sharp pickup driven by net exports. In the cooperative scenario, with significantly stronger growth in the rest of the world, there is a more mild slowdown about halfway between the soft and the hard landing.

7. In the soft- and hard-landing scenarios, ROECD growth is set, ex ante, at 3.0 percent as in the baseline, but is negatively affected, ex post, by the decline in net exports resulting from currency appreciation. In the cooperative scenario, however, ROECD growth is set exogenously at a rate sufficiently

high to both offset the negative impact from declining net exports and achieve a period of "catch-up" growth so as to reduce unemployment. In the soft- and hard-landing scenarios, the entire counterpart of the improvement in the US current balance falls on the ROECD area; in the cooperative scenario the developing countries are assumed to be able to take up 20 percent of it because of their much better financial position (chapter 7).

8. In all three scenarios the developing-country growth rate rises above, or falls below, the 4.5 percent assumed in the baseline, by the amount that total OECD growth exceeds or falls short of 3 percent.

Inflation

9. As measured by the price deflator for domestic demand, actual inflation in 1985 is put at 2.9 percent in the United States and 5.8 percent in the ROECD area. For 1986–90 the domestically generated rate of inflation (TN11) is set exogenously at 4.2 pecent for the United States and 5.0 percent in the ROECD area. The actual rate of inflation is derived in the model from the domestically generated rate via the exchange rate price level feedback coefficients. The model does not attempt to capture the effect of domestic demand pressures on the rate of inflation. The justification for this simplifi- cation is that the focus of this study is on the impact of a large change in the dollar exchange rate and, as discussed in box 4.7, the slope of the "external" Phillips curve is many times steeper than the domestic trade-off between growth and inflation.

Interest rates

10. For the reasons discussed in chapter 1, these are set exogenously. In the baseline, the Treasury-bill rate is 8.2 percent, or close to that assumed by the CBO. In the soft-landing scenario, with a rather strong decline in the dollar, the T-bill rate rises to 10.5 percent in 1987, and, because of the continuing need to attract capital inflows, is still 8 percent at the end of the decade. In the hard landing, with a steeper drop in the dollar, the T-bill rate rises to 13 percent in 1986, but by the end of the decade has dropped back to a more normal 6.5 percent (2.3 percent real). In the cooperative scenario, with close cooperation between, and intervention by, the major central banks, and a smaller drop in the dollar, the T-bill rate only rises to 9.5 percent in 1986 and then comes down fairly quickly to 6.5 percent.

Direct investment

11. During most of the postwar period, the United States has been a net exporter of direct investment capital. In the 1980s, there have been some net inflows, with lower US outflows reflecting poor business conditions in Europe and the developing countries, and higher foreign inflows attracted by the strong US recovery and the threat of import restrictions. However, even at the high 1984 level (partly explained by a large corporate takeover), the net inflow financed only about 15 percent of the current account deficit.

12. In the baseline, with the rest of the world assumed to grow somewhat faster than the United States and the dollar remaining overvalued, it is assumed that direct investment flows would balance to zero over 1985–90. The same assumption has also been made for the other scenarios, although in both the hard-landing and cooperative scenarios it might be more appropriate to assume a resumption of net outflows.

13. US income from direct investment declined from a peak of $32 billion in 1979, to an unusual $12 billion in 1984. This reflected the reduction in the strong cyclical position of the United States relative to other countries, which raised foreign earnings in the United States and depressed US earnings abroad, and the appreciation of the dollar, which reduced the dollar value of these latter earnings. US net income from direct investment is projected to recover in the baseline because of the assumed reversal of the US/ROW growth gap, and by somewhat more in the scenarios in which the dollar declines.

TN3   Sensitivity analysis of the baseline case

1. Table A shows the sensitivity of the projected outcome for the US current account deficit and net indebtedness to changes in each of the main assumptions built into the baseline case taken individually.

2. The response to a change in the dollar is greater than shown in table 4.1 because there are no feedback effects on US and ROECD growth in the baseline case, and this simulation includes gains to the current account from

a smaller increase in net external indebtedness, and hence lower net interest payments. A 1 percent lower US growth rate (each year) benefits the current balance, after two years, somewhat less than a 10 percent decline in the dollar. Over five years, the gain is substantial but still only reduces the deficit by one-quarter. A 1 percent lower rate of US inflation (each year) has a somewhat less powerful effect. The benefits from a 1 percent lower level of US interest rates are much smaller, but, given the greater variability of interest rates, the potential gains (or losses) are larger than this calculation implies.

3. As might be expected, the results are sensitive to the rate of growth and the rate of inflation in the rest of the OECD area, although somewhat less so than for the corresponding US magnitudes.

T A B L E A   **Sensitivity analysis of D&D model** (billion dollars)

	Current account deficit			Net indebtedness
	1985	*1987*	*1990*	*1990*
Baseline	124	200	320	1,310
		Deviations from the baseline		
The dollar, higher (or lower) by 10 percent	±8	±40	±60	±230
US GNP growth rate, faster (or slower) by 1 percent	±8	±30	±85	±250
US inflation rate, higher (or lower) by 1 percent	0	±15	±50	±120
ROECD GNP growth rate, slower (or faster) by 1 percent	±2	±10	±30	±90
ROECD inflation rate, higher (or lower) by 1 percent	0	±8	±30	±75
US interest rate, higher (or lower) by 1 percent	±1	±5	±15	±40
Oil price, 10 percent lower in 1985 and thereafter	−6	−10	−15	−60

Note: Simulations of D&D model. Changes starting from beginning 1985.

4. Technically, the results shown in this table are additive and thus changes in several assumptions in the appropriate direction could have a large impact on the current balance. Most such combinations would, however, be inherently implausible. Lower US growth and inflation, for example, are likely to be associated with lower, not higher, ROECD growth and inflation; a lower level of the dollar is likely to be associated with higher, not lower, inflation and interest rates in the United States and with lower, not higher, inflation in the rest of the OECD area. Bearing this in mind, it is apparent from table A that no plausible or desirable combination of different assumptions could produce a major improvement in the US current balance that does not include a significant decline in the dollar.

TN4   *Definitions and sources of investment-savings balances*

Definitions

1. For the United States and the ROECD area, the analysis of investment-savings balances throughout this study is based on the national accounting framework.

2. *Private investment* is measured gross (i.e., before depreciation) and includes fixed assets, residential construction, and additions to inventory, but not household purchases of automobiles or other consumer durables. A similar analysis can be carried out using flow-of-funds data, in which the latter two items are treated as investment; but, while the figures are different, the upshot is much the same.

3. *Private savings* are also normally measured gross and include household savings plus undistributed profits plus depreciation, and include any statistical discrepancy. For the United States, for reasons discussed in TN5, the surpluses of state and local governments have been included in private-sector savings.

4. *Public-sector "savings"* are defined as the difference between all kinds of income and both current and capital expenditure. This is an improper use

of the term savings insofar as current income is being used to finance public investment. In the United States, little capital expenditure is financed through the federal budget, but in most other countries, quite a lot is. Since public investment is generally not subject to major cyclical fluctuations, using a proper definition of public savings, while it would change the numbers, would not significantly change the analysis.

5. For the developing countries (figure 1.3), it is not possible to make a meaningful distinction between private- and public-sector investment-savings balances.

Source: United States, *Survey of Current Business,* various issues. Other OECD countries, Muller and Price (1984a), *OECD Economic Outlook,* no. 37, June 1985, and data supplied by the OECD Secretariat. Developing countries, World Bank 1985.

TN5   *US state and local governments*

1. It has sometimes been argued, in particular by supply siders, that concern about large federal budget deficits is exaggerated because state and local governments have been running surpluses equivalent to around 1.5 percent of GNP (Paul Craig Roberts, *Business Week,* 25 June 1984).

2. There are two reasons for being dubious about this argument. Over the longer run, the buildup of these surpluses has been entirely accounted for by the operation of social insurance funds. This buildup has, however, reduced the need for private savings for retirement and has been accompanied by a roughly equivalent decline in the private-sector savings rate (TN18, paragraph 1 and table A).

3. Regarding the small surplus on "other funds" ($9.5 billion in 1983), the evidence suggests that state and local fiscal behavior has become increasingly procyclical, i.e. similar to that of the private sector. During the 1980–82 recession, sharp cuts in expenditure and emergency tax increases prevented any significant deterioration in the overall position of state and local governments, in marked contrast to the federal government (figure 1.1). Equally, however, their position improved less than might have been expected

during the recovery, as expenditure accelerated in 1984 and previous tax increases were rescinded from mid-1984 onwards (*Survey of Current Business,* vol. 65, no. 1, January 1985, pp. 19–22). In other words, if cyclically adjusted figures were available, they would no doubt show that the "structural" surplus of state and local governments rose during the recession and probably through 1983, but began to drop in 1984. The indications are that this is likely to continue through 1985 and 1986 (*Business Week,* 22 October 1984, pp. 62–64). If so, it will *add* to the pressures on the US investment-savings balance coming from the federal government.

TN6   *Structural budget deficits*

1. For the United States, the cyclically adjusted federal budget deficit based on 6 percent unemployment rate trend GNP has been used (de Leeuw 1982, de Leeuw and Holloway 1983, Holloway 1984). For other OECD countries, estimates made by the OECD Secretariat have been used (Muller and Price 1984a, referred to below as MP) and *OECD Economic Outlook,* no. 37, June 1985. While the techniques used are broadly similar, the OECD figures include state and local governments as well as the central government.

2. There are many conceptual and statistical difficulties involved in these calculations, and there is an extensive literature on the subject. The methods used by the OECD are described in some detail in MP. In the context of this study, the most important point is that the estimates are quite sensitive to the estimated growth of potential output. For the five years 1979–83, the OECD's fairly conservative estimates of the annual percentage growth of potential output are: Japan, 4.1; United States, 2.8; Germany, 2.3; United Kingdom, 2.1 (and 3.0 for the seven major OECD countries). A 1 percent higher (lower) growth of potential output would reduce (raise) the estimated structural budget deficit in 1983 in percentage points of GNP by 1.5 for Japan, 2.0 for the United States, 1.8 for Germany, and 3.7 for the United Kingdom (MP, table A2.5).

3. This has important policy implications. A persistent tendency to overestimate growth potential (as was generally the case in the second half of the

1970s) and hence to underestimate the size of the structural component in the budget deficit may lead to overexpansionary fiscal policies and crowding out. Equally, however, underestimating growth potential could introduce a restrictive bias into fiscal policy. There is, moreover, a circularity here. Unduly restrictive fiscal policies, leading to slow growth and discouraging investment, could, in time, lower the potential growth rate, thus increasing the structural budget deficit and suggesting the need for even more restrictive fiscal policies.

4. Estimates of potential output depend, in part, on estimates of structural rates of unemployment. For 1983, OECD estimates put this at around 2.25 percent in Japan, 6 percent in the United States, and 7 percent to 7.5 percent in the four largest European economies.

5. In Europe one criticism often heard about this whole approach is that since there seems to be no prospect of reducing unemployment from present levels more or less indefinitely into the future, today's budget deficits should be regarded as 100 percent "structural." This implicitly assumes that all present unemployment is "classical" rather than "Keynesian," a view not supported by empirical studies, although there are significant differences in the quantitative estimates of the Keynesian element (TN27). It also could involve the circularity mentioned above, whereby persistently high and rising unemployment lowers the potential growth rate and thus raises the structural element in both the budget deficit and unemployment.

6. While these are very important issues for policy, *changes* in structural budget positions are relevant for estimating the short-term impact of fiscal policy on the economy. These changes are largely insensitive to the assumptions made about growth potential and the level of structural unemployment.

7. Year-to-year changes in structural budget positions are significantly affected, however, if an "inflation adjustment" is made to allow for the effect of rising prices in eroding the real value of the public debt held by the public. To the extent that "permanent income" is affected by this decline in real wealth, spending may be reduced and the savings rate may rise. The importance of such "wealth effects" on demand appears to differ a good deal between countries. But they are presumably the reason why the OECD

has found that changes in inflation-adjusted structural budgets are more significantly correlated with demand than unadjusted budget positions—although the latter are also significantly correlated (Chouraqui and Price 1985, note 11). Despite this, unadjusted structural positions seemed a better measure of the impact of fiscal policy on demand for the purposes of this study. Wealth effects are much less well established than income effects, and changes in inflation may affect demand in other ways. It thus seems better to concentrate on the demand impact of fiscal policy on income flows and treat inflation as a separate factor affecting spending decisions.

TN7   *Regression analysis of the US investment-savings balance*

1. In equation (1), changes in "private surplus savings" were regressed on changes in the cyclical and structural components of the federal budget deficit. The results confirm the existence of a two-way relationship between I-S balances in the private and public sectors: a rise in GNP sufficient to reduce the cyclical component of the budget deficit is associated with reduced private savings; an increase in the structural deficit is initially associated with a rise in private savings but, as the economy is stimulated, the sign is reversed.

2. The coefficient on the cyclical component is significantly greater than 1. Since the sum of the I-S balances of the private and public sector equals the foreign balance, a rise in GNP sufficient to reduce the cyclical component of the budget deficit will, with an unchanged structural deficit, be associated with a deterioration in the current balance.

3. In equation (2) a term was added for the difference between the growth of domestic demand in the United States and the rest of the world. The coefficient on R is negative (and significant), and the coefficient on C falls to around 1. This equation suggests that the very much faster growth of domestic demand in the United States than in the rest of the world in 1983–84 could have been expected to be associated with an increased inflow of

foreign savings equivalent to 1.8 percent of GNP, compared with an actual increase of 2.3 percent.

4. All variables for half-years, 1970–84:

(1) $P_t = -0.15 - 1.36\,C_t - 0.84\,S_t$, and $\bar{R}^2 = 0.85, DW = 1.47$.
     (1.6)   (8.7)   (6.1)

(2) $P_t = -0.13 - 1.01\,C_t - 0.91\,S_t - 0.08\,R_t$. $\bar{R}^2 = 0.88, DW = 2.06$.
     (1.6)   (5.3)   (7.2)   (2.7)

where P = change in private-sector financial balance, including state and locals and statistical discrepancy (percentage of GNP)

C = change in cyclical component of federal budget deficit (percentage of GNP)

S = change in 6 percent unemployment structural budget position (percentage of GNP)

R = change in US domestic demand less change in ROW domestic demand (percentage points, seasonally adjusted half-yearly data at annual rates).

5. Results not reported here show that with a lag of one to three half-years, the coefficient on S becomes positive, i.e., after a time an increase in the structural budget deficit stimulates the economy and reduces surplus private savings (box 1.2).

TN8   The Morgan Guaranty, Federal Reserve Board, and International Monetary Fund indices for the dollar

1. There is no single measure for the external value of the dollar, but rather a series of cross-rates between it and each other currency. To measure the change in "the" dollar as it affects US imports and exports, changes in these exchange rates have to be weighted together according to the importance of the countries concerned as competitors in US domestic and export markets. Unfortunately, there is no unambiguously correct way to calculate such an "effective" or "trade-weighted" index.

2. The simplest method is to assign a weight to each currency proportionate to that country's share in US imports and exports in a given base period. This system of *bilateral* trade weights is used to construct the effective exchange rate index published by the Morgan Guaranty Trust Company (now based on 1980 weights). It is most obviously open to question on the export side. The United States may, for example, have relatively small exports to a country (for example, Japan), which is nevertheless a major competitor for US exporters in *third* markets. Equally, on the import side, a country with no exports to the United States (and therefore a zero weight) could start competing in the US market at a different exchange rate. Carrying this line of reasoning to its logical conclusion, one could argue that *all* countries are potential competitors with US goods in *all* markets, and therefore that their exchange rates should be weighted together according to the relative importance of their total imports and exports in world trade. This system of *world trade* weights is used in the construction of the effective exchange rate index published by the Federal Reserve Board (based on 1972–76 data). These weights, however, tend to give undue importance to countries in Europe, which form a largely integrated market and have close trade relations with each other. The resulting bias is particularly strong for the countries participating in the European Monetary System since their currencies tend to move together against the dollar.

3. Since neither of these approaches appears to be fully satisfactory, the International Monetary Fund has constructed a dollar index, using its Multilateral Exchange Rate Model (MERM). Each currency is weighted in the MERM so that the same percentage change in any currency against the dollar would have the same quantitative impact on the US trade balance in billions of dollars (and similarly for all 17 currencies covered in the model, TN21). There are many conceptual and empirical difficulties involved in estimating these weights; they have not been revised since 1977, and no developing-country currencies are included. Nevertheless, this index should provide a better measure of the impact of changes in "the" dollar on US imports and exports than either of the other two, and has therefore been used throughout this study.

4. There is a relatively consistent and systematic relationship between the behavior of these three indices. The amplitude of movements in bilateral trade-weighted indices tends to be much less than for world trade-weighted

indices, with a MERM-weighted index lying in between. Regression analysis gives the following relationship between the MERM index (M), the Federal Reserve index (FR), and the Morgan Guaranty Trust index (MGT). All variables are expressed in first differences of logarithms. The equations were estimated using quarterly data from 1970:2 to 1984:4:

(1) $FR = 0.0001 + 1.18\,M$, and $\bar{R}^2 = 0.97,\ DW = 1.45.$
        (0.1)   (41.6)

(2) $MGT = -0.0003 + 0.86\,M.$ $\bar{R}^2 = 0.98,\ DW = 1.53.$
          (0.6)   (47.2)

The estimated coefficients indicate that, for a 1 percent change in the MERM index, the Federal Reserve index changes by 1.18 percent, and the Morgan Guaranty index changes by 0.86 percent.

5. These coefficients can be largely explained by the fact that cross-rates tend to move less between countries whose bilateral trade accounts for a large share of their total trade (for example, United States–Canada) than between countries with a relatively smaller bilateral trade (for example, United States–Germany and other European countries). In other words, the volatility of individual cross-rates is positively correlated with the weights in the Fed index and negatively in the Morgan Guaranty index. This can be illustrated by comparing the weight assigned in the various dollar indices to Canada and to Italy (which have about the same level of total trade, but Italy has only a fraction of its trade with the United States):

TABLE A   **Behavior of different dollar indices**

Weighting	Indices	Depreciation[a]	Appreciation[b]	Percentage weight Canada	Italy
World	Federal Reserve	51.7	83.3	9.1	9.0
Multilateral	IMF	24.4	63.1	20.6	7.6
Bilateral	Morgan Guaranty	22.2	51.3	30.3	4.1

a. Percentage decline in dollar from 1970:1 to 1978:4
b. Percentage rise in dollar from 1980:3 to 1985:1

As can be seen from the first two columns, the relationship between the indices was similar during the depreciation of the dollar in the 1970s and its appreciation in the 1980s, with the IMF index closer to that of Morgan than to the Fed index.

TN9   *The two-way relationship between the dollar and the US current account*

1. In the top panel of figure 1.4, the change in US current balance (billion dollars) between years t_n and t_{n+2} is regressed on the percentage change in the nominal effective dollar exchange rate (IMF MERM index) between t_{n-1} and t_{n+1}:

(1) $CA_{t_{n+2}} - CA_{t_n} = -9.44 - 2.18 (XR_{t_{n+1}} - XR_{t_{n-1}})$. $\bar{R}^2 = 0.63$,
          (1.6)   (4.5) $DW = 1.57$.

2. Bottom panel: change in dollar between years t_n and t_{n+2} regressed on change in current balance between years t_{n-2} and t_n:

(2) $XR_{t_{n+2}} - XR_{t_n} = 1.9 + 0.49 (CA_{t_n} - CA_{t_{n-2}})$ $\bar{R}^2 = 0.45, DW = 0.967$.
          (0.7) (2.7)

In this regression, the observations for 1983 and 1984 were dropped. This raised $\bar{R}^2$ from 0.34 to 0.52 and improved the significance of the coefficient for CA, despite the smaller number of observations.

3. It should be stressed that the results of these regressions are used essentially as an expositional device in chapter 1 to illustrate one of the key features of the way the flexible exchange rate system has been working. For this reason no attempt was made to include the other obvious explanatory variables (for example, relative growth and inflation rates, interest rates). They are certainly not good equations to use for predictive purposes—the surprising thing is that the $\bar{R}^2$ are as high as they are.

Source: IMF data base.

TN10   *ROECD interest rates and inflation*

1. In figure 1.5, short-term interest rates are for a 90-day maturity; long-term rates are for long-term government bonds. ROECD aggregates include only Canada, France, Germany, Italy, Japan, and the United Kingdom and are constructed using 1982 GNP weights. It should be noted that such weights understate the importance of the deutsche mark, yen, and Swiss franc in world financial markets. Interest rates on assets denominated in these currencies have generally been below both US and other ROECD rates since the mid-1970s. Such weights therefore understate the positive US interest-rate differential over this period.

2. The ROECD/US relative price index is derived from the respective consumer price indices (ROECD aggregate constructed using 1982 GNP weights). *Source:* OECD data base. (Elsewhere in this study US and ROECD price levels are measured by the implicit price deflator for total domestic demand.) Again, since inflation has been lower than average in several of the countries that have the most important alternative financial markets, and are among the most important US competitors in world trade, these measures tend to systematically overestimate the most relevant inflation differential in favor of the United States (compare the lines for ROECD consumer prices constructed using GNP and MERM weights in table 6.5).

Sources: IMF data base, and Commission of the European Communities (1984).

TN11   *Actual and "domestically generated" rates of inflation*

1. The actual rate of inflation, as defined in this study, is the rise in the prices of the things on which the citizens of a country are actually spending their money; i.e., including imports but excluding exports. This is measured, from national accounts data, by the implicit price deflator for total domestic demand (called the "absorption" price index in academic literature). When a country's terms of trade or exchange rate or both change, there will be systematic differences between the implicit price deflator for GNP (which

includes exports and excludes imports) and the deflator for domestic spending. The consumer price index should move more closely in line with the latter, but the correspondence is fairly loose because the CPI covers only a part of total domestic spending (and because of conceptual and measurement differences).

2. Domestically generated inflation is defined here as the actual rate of inflation which could be expected to occur *in the absence of any change in the exchange rate* (in real terms). It has been estimated for the past using the exchange rate-domestic price level relationships built into the D&D model. For the future, it has been projected on the basis of recent trends. Domestically generated inflation can be expected to be positively related to domestic demand pressures. To simplify matters, however, this latter relationship (the Phillips curve) has not been built into the D&D model because in the scenarios analyzed in this study the role of the exchange rate would, in quantitative terms, be several times more important (box 4.7).

3. Domestically generated inflation is similar to, but not exactly the same as, the more familiar concept of the "core" rate of inflation, which is an estimate of what would be happening to the price level in the absence of any major deviations from the normal behavior of food, agricultural, energy, and other raw material prices and the exchange rate (often based mainly on what is happening to wage costs and productivity). But when the exchange rate declines, not only do import prices rise, but the price of domestically produced competing products tends to rise and a "price-wage multiplier" is set in motion as higher prices and improved profits generate higher wage claims. These induced price and wage increases are quantified in the D&D model and are therefore *not* treated as part of domestically generated inflation as defined in this study even though *ex post,* they are hard to measure and hence are normally included in the core rate as usually measured.

4. Over time the distinction between these induced effects of an external price shock from the exchange rate and domestically generated inflation becomes increasingly blurred. Thus, for example, if the actual rate of inflation rises well above the domestically generated rate this could in time lead to a basic upward shift in inflationary expectations, and could push up domestically generated inflation and thus lead to a larger rise in the actual rate than would be expected simply from the decline in the dollar and the operation of the normal feedback from the exchange rate to domestic costs and prices.

TN12   *The US balance of payments and the world statistical discrepancy*

1. Since 1977, the US balance of payments shows large positive errors and omissions (EO) that could reflect unrecorded current receipts or unrecorded capital inflows or both. Since 1975, the sum total of the world's current payments and receipts shows a large deficit (WCAD). The interpretation of the US EO and of the WCAD is of importance for two sets of figures used in this study. It affects the reliability of the current account figures for the United States and for the rest of the world and has implications for the US net investment position and the way it is projected into the future.

2. Most US observers closely concerned with collection and analysis of US balance of payments data have concluded that the positive balance on US errors and omissions largely reflects unrecorded capital inflows, since its time profile has followed closely that of recorded capital inflows and has been especially high at times when the "safe-haven" factor has seemed important (for example, 1982). This position has been taken most explicitly by Bach (1983) and Kubarych (1984) and has been traced back in the discrepancy between different measures of savings in the national accounts by de Leeuw (1984). If accepted, it implies that the net investment position of the United States is, for this reason, substantially worse than shown in the reported figures, possibly by as much as $125 billion, as suggested by Wallich (1984).

3. This is important because estimates of US interest payments and receipts included in the recorded current balance are not based on any direct information concerning such payments and receipts, but rather by applying a relevant interest rate to the *recorded* amount of each category of US liabilities and assets. In other words, if, as seems very likely, US liabilities are underreported, *it follows that the US net investment income is overstated,* perhaps by $10 billion or more. On this score, therefore, it seems likely that the recorded US current account deficit is *under*estimated. (It also follows that for other countries the negative discrepancy on investment income is greater than shown in table A.)

4. Considerable work has been done by the OECD and the IMF on the WCAD, and the IMF recently appointed a high-level working party to study the matter more thoroughly. Most of this work has concentrated on trying to break the WCAD down by category of transaction and suggests that after

adjustments for differences in timing and valuation, the most important factor appears to be underrecording of receipts from transport and investment income.

TABLE A   **Breakdown of world current account discrepancy, 1983**
(billion dollars)

Trade	+ 25
Transport	− 30
Other nonfactor services	− 5
Investment income	− 48
Official transfers	− 13
Total	− 71

Sources: OECD *Economic Outlook,* no. 37, June 1985, and IMF, *Balance of Payments Statistics,* vol. 35, part 2.

5. There is, however, an important point that deserves more attention than it has received. If the only problem is an underrecording of current receipts, then the counterpart of the WCAD should show up in an equal and opposite amount in the sum of world errors and omissions. But as Oliveiria-Martins and Leroy of the Centre d'Etudes Prospectives et d'Informations Internationales (CEPII) have pointed out in an important study (1984), as much as four-fifths of the WCAD shows up *not* in world errors and omissions but in the world capital account (table B). In other words, there is, somewhere in the world, not only a significant underrecording of current receipts but also a substantial underrecording of capital inflows.

6. The CEPII analysts have also shown that instead of finding many countries with positive EO reflecting the counterpart of underrecorded current receipts, one finds that the relatively small positive world total is the net outcome of very large positive figures for one group of countries, including the United States, Switzerland, and the rest of Northern Europe (group A below), and only a somewhat smaller total of negative figures for another group of countries in Latin America, the Middle East, and Southern Europe (group B below). This distribution is highly suggestive and has led CEPII to conclude that the gross figures for EO reflect to a large extent capital flows from the second group of countries to the first that are not recorded at either end, thus strengthening the view that US EO should be regarded as largely capital inflows.

TABLE B   **Cumulative world discrepancies and errors and omissions,
1969–81** (billion dollars)

World discrepancies		Errors and omissions	
Current account	− 199	Group A	+ 237
Capital account	+ 158	Group B	− 196
Errors and omissions	+ 41	World	+ 41

Source: Oliveira-Martins and Leroy (1984).

7. This brings us back to the relation between the WCAD and the US current account. A number of analysts have taken the position that, since the United States is a large country, it is likely that it accounts for a not insignificant part of the world's unrecorded current account receipts. They argue, therefore, that the recorded US current deficit is probably smaller than it appears, typically by amounts of between $10 billion and $25 billion. This is the position taken by Wallich (1984), the Morgan Guaranty (1985), and Williamson (1985), for example. Apart from investment income, however, the other main component of the WCAD is transportation and travel, where there is a discrepancy of around $30 billion (table A). The United States accounts for less than 15 percent of recorded world exports in this category. It therefore seems unlikely its unrecorded current receipts exceed the $10 billion by which it was suggested above that US net interest receipts are being overestimated. In projecting the US net investment position, it is therefore assumed here that the recorded current account deficit is neither underestimated nor overestimated. A similar position was taken by the CBO (1984a) and Islam (1984) in making such projections.

8. In view of the difficulties and uncertainties involved, no attempt has been made to project the WCAD in the scenarios presented in this study or to try to break it down by region. It follows from the above, however, that if the United States accounts for less of the WCAD than is sometimes suggested, other countries must account for more. It also follows that the WCAD may be quite heavily concentrated on those parts of the world that appear likely to have had large unrecorded capital outflows, i.e., the Middle East, Latin America, and Southern Europe. It further seems possible that both foreign investment income and domestic savings may be quite significantly underestimated for Europe as a whole, as suggested by Brender (1985).

TN13   *Shifts in the flow of real and financial savings under fixed and flexible exchange rates*

1. Under both fixed and flexible rates the common starting point is that, when there is a divergence in national investment and savings rates, capital flows respond more quickly than trade flows.

2. Consider the case of a country whose I-S balance is shifting upward relative to the rest of the world. Under *fixed rates*, private capital inflows increase faster than the current account deteriorates (the "Wallich thesis," see chapter 1). But this excess of financial inflows over the inflow of goods and services—excess "financial savings"—is mopped up by intervention in the foreign exchange market. Under normal circumstances, the authorities try to sterilize this intervention. To the extent they succeed, this reduces the liquidity and interest-rate-lowering impact of the private capital inflow and helps to slow down the upward shift in the I-S balance.

3. At the same time, because the exchange rate is pegged, the corresponding increase in the supply of foreign real resources to the economy is quite modest. Imports rise faster than exports only to the extent that domestic demand—working through income elasticities—rises faster at home than abroad and not because foreign goods become cheaper than domestic goods, as is the case with flexible rates. As a result, pressures build up in the goods and labor markets more rapidly. Under fixed rates, moreover, the inflationary pressures thus generated are not dampened by an appreciation of the currency.

4. This more rapid buildup in demand pressures and inflation prompts policy changes. The monetary authorities intensify their efforts to sterilize capital inflows and, in time, go beyond this and aim explicitly to tighten monetary conditions. Moreover, if there is clear evidence of "overheating," the government's typical response in the 1960s was to tighten up on fiscal policy as well; in other words it tried to reduce the domestic I-S imbalance by reducing the structural budget deficit.

5. Thus, with fixed rates the inflationary and crowding-out effects of an imbalance between national investment and savings are bottled up within the domestic economy to a greater extent than under flexible rates. As a result, the need becomes apparent earlier to make policy changes, on *domestic* grounds, to prevent an upward shift in the I-S balance from going too far.

Unless and until doubts arise as to whether the fixed exchange rate might be changed, foreigners will be happy to go on supplying funds—and earning higher interest rates—because there is no perceived exchange risk. (And even when such doubts arose, governments were, during the 1960s, overly eager to provide official finance to stave off devaluation of a major currency.) Developments in the foreign exchange market only become an important factor when the fixed rate becomes suspect.

6. Under *flexible exchange rates,* it is a different story. With no intervention in the exchange markets, the full impact of the inflow of foreign funds is felt in the domestic financial markets. In other words, the normal corrective mechanism—whereby, in a closed economy, a rise in the domestic I-S balance is slowed down by a rise in interest rates—does not operate. At the same time, however, the exchange rate appreciates. As discussed in chapter 4, the way in which this currency appreciation affects the capital inflows is both the most controversial and important question in the whole story. In theory, a rise in the exchange rate should increase the probability of a future decline and hence increase the exchange rate risk perceived by foreigners. To the extent this is the case, a declining willingness of foreigners to provide funds will increasingly exert upward pressure on interest rates, setting off the domestic corrective mechanism by crowding out private investment.

7. But appreciation can—and often does—set off expectations of further appreciation. If it does, the capital inflow may pick up momentum, prolonging the duration or strengthening the forces making for an upward shift in the I-S balance.

8. At the same time, appreciation of the currency makes foreign goods cheaper, thereby accelerating the inflow of real resources in response to the rise in financial inflows. Pressures, therefore, build up less fast in goods and labor markets. Moreover, any tendency for inflation to accelerate is dampened by the appreciation of the currency. For these reasons, the *need* to take corrective action on domestic grounds becomes apparent more slowly. Indeed, in a case like the current one of a very strong divergence in investment-savings balances, this need may not be perceived until the authorities are forced into action by developments in the foreign exchange market, the most volatile of the many markets involved.

9. The above discussion relates essentially to short-term shifts in I-S balances originating in either the public or private sector of a cyclical or policy-

induced nature. It can be argued, however, that the more rapid adjustment of trade flows to capital movements is a desirable feature of flexible rates in the event of structural shifts in I-S balances resulting from secular changes in countries' propensities to save and invest. Against this, the analysis in chapters 1 and 3 suggests that cyclical and policy-induced fluctuations in I-S balance have been much larger than structural shifts. Given this, and given the tendency of the present regime to overshoot, a good case can be made that the somewhat slower adjustment of trade flows to capital movements in response to structural I-S shifts under a managed float or adjustable peg exchange rate regime would be an advantage—as long as the regime was well managed!

TN14   *Major shocks to the world investment-savings balance, 1970–89*

1. *Figure 1.8, top panel.* Current account balances at current prices as percentage of OECD GNP at current prices. The data used have been "harmonized" to eliminate the world current account discrepancy [Oliveiria-Martins and Leroy (1984) and later data supplied by CEPII]. In contrast to the second panel, "shocks" to the world investment-savings balance are being measured ex post, i.e. after some part of the corrective mechanisms discussed in the text had begun to be felt. Ex ante measures yield somewhat larger figures, around 2 percent of OECD GNP (Llewellyn 1983).

2. *Second panel* data have been taken from Muller and Price (1984a), except that from 1981 the cumulative change in the US structural federal budget deficit in the CBO's baseline case is shown (1985b). Note that the shifts in structural budget positions for both the United States and the ROECD area are shown as a percentage of OECD GNP.

3. For *bottom three panels,* see TN4.

TN15   *The dollar and structure of the US economy*

Methodology

1. The projections shown in figures 2.3 and 2.4 are based on a regression analysis in which the variable concerned has been disaggregated into an "exposed" and a "sheltered" sector of the economy and regressed on the aggregate. For prices, subcomponents of the CPI were regressed on the total CPI. Similarly, wages in the "exposed" and "sheltered" sectors were regressed on the overall wage level. In the case of profits, employment, and output, the *share* of the "exposed" sector in the total was regressed on the total for each variable.

2. The equations are estimated from quarterly data over a period extending from 1960:1 to 1981:1. The results were then used to forecast through 1985:1, based on actual movements of the explanatory variable. All variables are expressed in first differences of logarithms. The secular tendency in the dependent variable is captured by the constant; since there is little reason to suppose that these structural trends were linear, it is likely that a more sophisticated specification of the time trend would have improved the quality of the results (and the DW statistics).

Prices

3. The dependent variables in equations (1) and (2) are subcomponents of the consumer price index for wage earners *(CPIW)*. The index for all commodities *(PC)* corresponds to the "exposed" sector in figure 2.4 and that for all services *(PS)* corresponds to the "sheltered" sector.

(1) $PC_t = -0.0014 + 1.02\,CPIW_t$, and $\bar{R}^2 = 0.94, DW = 1.41.$
          (3.1)   (37.2)

(2) $PS_t = 0.0028 + 0.94\,CPIW_t.$ $\bar{R}^2 = 0.83, DW = 1.42.$
          (3.8)   (20.2)

4. The projections shown in figure 2.3 are based on equations (3) through (8). The explanatory variable in each case is the consumer price index for urban consumers *(CPIU)*. The dependent variables are subcomponents of the *CPIU*: commodity components for the "exposed" sector, and service components for the "sheltered" sector. The former include apparel *(AP)*,

footwear *(FW)*, and goods for home repair and maintenance *(HG);* the latter include medical care *(MC)*, professional services *(PS)*, and entertainment *(EN)*. These equations are estimated over the period 1967:2 to 1981:1.

(3) $AP_t = 0.0054 + 0.28\,CPIU_t;$ $\bar{R}^2 = 0.15, DW = 1.17;$
      (3.3)   (3.2)

(4) $FW_t = 0.0060 + 0.40\,CPIU_t;$ $\bar{R}^2 = 0.32, DW = 1.07;$
      (4.5)   (5.1)

(5) $HG_t = 0.0056 + 0.59\,CPIU_t;$ $\bar{R}^2 = 0.15, DW = 1.61;$
      (1.6)   (3.3)

(6) $MC_t = 0.0114 + 0.51\,CPIU_t;$ $\bar{R}^2 = 0.31, DW = 1.11;$
      (5.9)   (5.1)

(7) $PS_t = 0.0084 + 0.54\,CPIU_t;$ $\bar{R}^2 = 0.38, DW = 0.91;$
      (4.7)   (5.9)

(8) $EN_t = 0.0089 + 0.28\,CPIU_t.$ $\bar{R}^2 = 0.13, DW = 1.32.$
      (4.9)   (3.0)

Employment

5. The dependent variable in equation (9) is the share of manufacturing in total private nonagricultural employment *(EM)*. This corresponds to the "exposed" sector in figure 2.4; the share of the "sheltered" sector (non-manufacturing) is obtained by inference. Total private nonagricultural employment *(ET)* is the explanatory variable.

(9) $EM_t = -0.0015 - 0.37\,ET_t.$ $\bar{R}^2 = 0.25, DW = 2.19.$
      (1.0)   (5.4)

Profits

6. In equation (10) the dependent variable is the share of manufacturing *(MP)* in total nonfinancial profits. This corresponds to the "exposed" sector in figure 2.4; the "sheltered" sector, as in the case of employment, is obtained by inference. Total nonfinancial profits *(TP)* is the explanatory variable.

(10) $MP_t = -0.0042 - 0.24\,TP_t.$ $\bar{R}^2 = 0.13, DW = 2.60.$
       (0.9)   (3.6)

Output

7. Changes in real GNP (GNP) were used to explain the share of goods in GNP *(SG)* measured in 1972 prices. Somewhat surprisingly, projections based on equation (11) suggest that the share of goods in GNP rose more rapidly in the current recovery (by about 2 percentage points) than might have been expected from historical experience.

$$(11) \quad SG_t = -0.0056 + 0.65\, GNP_t. \qquad \bar{R}^2 = 0.57, DW = 2.13.$$
$$ (7.0) \quad (10.5)$$

Wages

8. The dependent variables in equations (12) and (13) are, respectively, hourly earnings of production workers in manufacturing *(WM)*, and hourly earnings of production workers in service industries *(WS)*. The explanatory variable is hourly earnings of production workers in private, nonagricultural establishments *(WT)*. These equations are estimated over the period 1967:1 to 1981:1.

$$(12) \quad WM_t = -0.0030 + 1.21\, WT_t. \qquad \bar{R}^2 = 0.66, DW = 1.79.$$
$$ (1.4) \quad (10.4)$$

$$(13) \quad WS_t = 0.0089 + .53\, WT_t. \qquad \bar{R}^2 = 0.05, DW = 3.01.$$
$$ (1.8) \quad (2.0)$$

Again, somewhat surprisingly, manufacturing wages appear to have increased more rapidly (by 2 percent cumulatively through 1985:1) than projections based on equation (12) would indicate.

Source: DRI data base.

TN16   *Monetary and fiscal multipliers*

1. *Monetary multipliers* derived from national models under fixed and flexible rates are shown in table A:

T A B L E A   **Monetary multipliers**[a]

	Fixed rates	Flexible rates
United States	.17	.23
Japan	.19	.52
Germany	n.a.	.17
United Kingdom	.08	.22

Source: Chan-Lee and Kato (1984, tables 8 and 10).
a. Average deviation of GNP from baseline in the two years following a 1 percent change in "policy controlled" interest rates

2. As should be expected, these multipliers are systematically higher under flexible exchange rates because higher or lower interest rates move the exchange rate in the direction that adds to the positive or negative effect of the change in interest rates on domestic demand. In the context of the scenarios analyzed in this study, however, the multiplier under *fixed* rates is the most relevant. This is because in these scenarios the path of the dollar exchange rate has been projected independently, and, indeed, it is the movement in the exchange rate which drives the interest rate changes discussed in the text (rather than the other way around, as in the model simulations in table A).

3. On the basis of the above figures, and after reviewing other sources [Oudiz and Sachs (1984); Yoshitomi (1984)], the typical monetary multiplier under fixed rates has been taken in this study as 0.1 in the first year and 0.25 in the second year for both the United States and the ROECD area.

4. In the cooperative scenario the relevant *fiscal multipliers* are those which assume an accommodating monetary policy (table B). In the case of fiscal stimulus by an individual country acting alone, part of the additional demand spills abroad. This is more marked for the European countries than for the United States and Japan (first column) because imports are larger in relation to GNP. Joint action therefore has a much stronger impact than individual

action—nearly double in the 1983 version of the OECD's Interlink model (compare first two columns).

T A B L E B   **Fiscal multipliers[a]**

	Individual action	Joint action[b]	
	1983[c]	1983[c]	1985[d]
United States	1.7	n.a.	n.a.
Japan	1.8	n.a.	n.a.
Europe	1.2[e]	2.2	1.5
ROECD	. .	. .	1.6
OECD	1.5[e]	2.9	1.8

Source: 1983 version of Interlink, Larsen, Llewellyn, and Potter (1983), table A1. 1985 version of Interlink, data supplied by the OECD Secretariat.

a. Increase in GNP above baseline by the third year following expansionary fiscal action equivalent to 1 percent of GNP, with accommodating monetary policy and fixed exchange rates.
b. Increase in GNP above baseline in Europe by the third year if all European countries take action simultaneously, and similarly if all countries in the ROECD or OECD area take action simultaneously.
c. 1983 version of Interlink.
d. 1985 version of Interlink.
e. Weighted average of multiplier for each country taking action in isolation ("unlinked").

5. There has been a fairly general tendency for estimates of fiscal multipliers to be lowered over the last few years. In some cases this reflects a re-specification of the models along the monetarist, rational expectations and neoclassical lines [e.g. Minford (1984) and, to a lesser extent, the UK Treasury's model]. More generally, however, it reflects the fact that when the data from the mid-1970s onwards have been included, estimates of the fiscal multiplier have come out lower (compare second and third columns) because investment demand has tended to respond less strongly to aggregate demand, especially in Europe. In the author's view this should be attributed more to low profitability and high real interest rates than to an erosion of the effectiveness of fiscal policy due to a sudden access of rational expectations. (There is also a problem of joint correlation since the shift to restrictive fiscal policies in Europe coincided with a sharp rise in real interest rates.)

6. Profits have improved quite significantly in Europe in the early 1980s (chapter 6). Interest rates will come down once the dollar's decline gathers momentum, even without a change in monetary policies. Thus, in the cooperative scenario it seems reasonable to assume a fiscal multiplier for joint action in the ROECD area of at least 2.0, rather than the 1.6 incorporated in the 1985 version of the OECD Interlink model. In addition, there should be a further stimulus to GNP from the easing of monetary policy postulated in this scenario in the second phase of the dollar's decline (chapter 7).

TN17   *Estimates of the foreign private dollar portfolio*

The dollar portfolio

1. Table 3.5 gives summary estimates of the outstanding dollar-denominated assets held by the foreign private sector. The figures include both assets issued by the United States and held by non-US residents and estimates of dollar-denominated assets issued and held by non-US residents. They exclude all interbank claims.

2. The detailed estimates are shown only for 1983 in the table below. Estimates for 1978 and 1980 are only roughly comparable because of changes in coverage; for 1984 they are based on incomplete data.

3. In the table below, the first three lines are taken from the "International Investment Position of the United States in 1983," *Survey of Current Business,* vol. 64, no. 6, June 1984. They include assets held by foreign banks and other financial intermediaries. Line four is taken from IMF, *International Financial Statistics* (IFS), March 1985.

4. There are three sources for dollar liabilities by banks to nonbanks. *World Financial Markets* of the Morgan Guaranty Trust, essentially using original BIS data, provides a total for Eurocurrency liabilities to nonbank US residents and nonresidents and gives the dollar-denominated share in *total* Eurocurrency

liabilities. This latter share applied to the relevant nonbank portion yields a figure of $388. An alternative estimate was made based on IFS cross-border deposits of nonbanks (i.e. excluding residents of the country of deposit outside the United States), to which the same dollar share was applied as above, and to which BIS figures make it possible to add an estimate of dollar-denominated deposits by these excluded residents, yielding a total of $410 billion. Averaging the results of these two approaches gives the compromise estimate shown in line 6.

5. The cumulative figures for dollar-denominated bonds issued abroad were supplied by Townsend-Greenspan Inc. It was arbitrarily assumed that one-quarter may be held by US residents.

TABLE A   **1983 estimates of foreign nonbank dollar portfolio** (billion dollars)

US Treasury securities	34
Other US securities	115
Other US nonbank liabilities	25
Nonbank deposits with US banks	59
Total in United States	233
Eurocurrency liabilities to nonbanks (compromise estimate)	400
Eurodollar bonds and international dollar bonds	120
Total	750

Household financial savings

6. While it is difficult to estimate total portfolios, i.e. the stock of financial assets at any point of time, it is relatively easy to derive plausible orders of magnitude for the flow of net financial savings generated in the household sector. The net financial savings of the household sector are available in the OECD national accounts. For the average of the six major ROECD countries for which data are available since 1960, household financial savings oscillated between 6 percent and 8.8 percent of GNP, averaging 8 percent from 1981–84. Similar data are not available for many non-OECD countries, so the estimates for the rest of the world were grossed up from the ROECD figures. Estimates at current prices and exchange rates have been converted to constant 1975 exchange rates using the ratio of current price GNP at current and constant 1975 exchange rates.

7. Since most ROECD countries' household financial savings had been largely wiped out by wartime and early postwar inflation, and given the magnitude of the price rise since then, it appears not unreasonable to make an estimate of the total household financial portfolio using the perpetual inventory method. This was done by cumulating annual household financial savings since 1960. This method underestimates the current portfolio since it does not allow for valuation changes from rising share prices. The resulting estimates show the ratio of the household portfolio to GNP rising through the 1960s and 1970s to about 1.0 in 1984. This compares with ratios to GNP for the private sector's *total* portfolio, including financial intermediaries, ranging from 0.7 to 3.1 for the countries shown in table A of TN25.

TN18   *Estimates of the US savings deficiency at 6 percent unemployment*

1. The impact of a decline in the inflow of foreign savings into the United States will depend to an important extent on what happens to the domestic US investment-savings balance over the next few years. Table A brings together information relevant to forming a judgment on this issue. The first three lines summarize the main elements of this balance during the last three periods during which unemployment was at a cyclical trough. The level of unemployment at periods of "high employment" rose—in good part for demographic reasons—from around 4 percent in the 1960s to around 6 percent by the end of the 1970s. Over the same period, there was a progressive deterioration in the private sector's investment-savings balance. This was, however, more or less exactly offset by an improvement in the financial position of the state and local governments. These two opposite trends are causally related in that the bulk of the growing state and local government surpluses represent an accumulation of pension and other trust fund reserves that reduce the need for private retirement savings (CBO 1984c, p. 29).

2. These trends suggest that at high employment (unemployment at 6 percent) the private sector and the state and local governments together might be expected to generate surplus savings equivalent to around 0.5 percent of GNP.

TABLE A   **US investment-savings balance at periods of high employment,
1960–88** (financial balance as percentage of GNP)

Period	Unemployment (percentage)	Private sector	State and local	Federal[b] Cyclical	Structural	Total	Total domestic = foreign[c]
High employment							
1965–69	3.8	+0 6	0.0	. .[d]	. .[d]	−0.3	+0.3
			+0.6				
1972–74	5.4	+0.1	+0.9	+0.4	−1.3	−0.9	+0.1
			+0.8				
1978–79	5.9	−0.7	+1.3	+0.3	−1.3	−1.0	−0.4
			+0.6				
Recent periods							
1980:4–1981:3	7.4	+0.8	+1.3	−1.1	−0.9	−2.0	+0.1
			+2.1				
1984:3	7.3	+0.4	+1.3	−1.3	−3.6	−4.9	−3.2
			+1.7				

Source: De Leeuw and Holloway (1983); deLeeuw (1982), and *Survey of Current Business.*
a. Includes statistical discrepancy.
b. NIPA basis. Structural position measured at 6 percent unemployment.
c. Public plus private sector: a minus sign indicates an *inflow* of foreign savings.
d. Measured at 4.5 percent unemployment the cyclical component was +0.7 and the structural component −1.0.

3. The cyclical component of the budget deficit, by definition, equals zero when GNP is at its 6 percent trend rate level. In the two periods of high employment in the mid- and late 1970s, however, GNP was somewhat above this level, yielding a small positive figure for the cyclical component (fourth column). In the first two periods, the total federal deficit, taking the cyclical and structural components together, was somewhat more than financed by the rest of the economy, but by 1978–79 about half of it was financed by a small inflow of foreign savings (last column).

4. The last two lines cover two recent periods when unemployment was around 7½ percent. They illustrate the typical inverse relation between savings balances in the public and private sectors at different levels of

economic activity discussed in chapter 1. A rough rule of thumb suggests that for each percentage point that unemployment exceeds 6 percent, the cyclical component of the budget deficit exceeds zero by 1 percentage point of GNP. More specifically, for each 1 percent GNP falls below the "6 percent trend rate GNP," the cyclical component of the budget deficit increases by approximately 0.4 percentage points of GNP, and unemployment rises by 0.4 percentage points. That there should be a close relationship between the two is inherent in the concept and method of construction of the cyclical component; but the fact that it is approximately one-for-one appears to be a fluke.

5. Other things being equal, the counterpart to a cyclical deficit will be found in lower investment relative to savings in the private sector. Thus, in both recent periods when unemployment was just over 7 percent, the combined surplus savings of the private sector and state and local governments exceeded its high employment "norm" by 1.5 to 2 percentage points.

6. There is a striking difference, however, in the last three columns. By 1984, the structural deficit, and hence the total federal deficit, had risen by around 3 percentage points, and this was fully reflected in an equivalent savings deficiency for the economy as a whole, financed by a large-scale inflow of foreign savings. As discussed in chapter 1, while these figures for financial balances reflect, ex post, an economic identity, there can be little doubt that one line of causality during this period was running from the rising structural deficit to the inflow of foreign savings.

7. Summing up. With unemployment at 6 percent there should be a surplus of private savings equal to around 0.5 percent of GNP. For each percentage point that unemployment exceeds 6 percent, the actual budget deficit would exceed the structural deficit by about 1 percent of GNP, but in terms of the overall domestic investment-savings balance this should be roughly offset by more surplus savings in the private sector. Thus, whatever the level of economic activity, the structural budget deficit can only exceed 0.5 percent of GNP to the extent that there are corresponding capital inflows; otherwise there will be an ex ante savings deficiency and crowding out of private investment. It is this relationship that has been used in making the estimates shown in the bottom half of table 5.1.

TN19   *The CBO's baseline projections: assumptions about the dollar*

1. In its baseline projections, the CBO (1985a) assumes that the dollar declines in 1985 by an amount such that its average level in 1985 is the same as in 1984. For the subsequent years, it implicitly assumes that the dollar stays at this level. It is interesting to consider the consistency of this assumption with the CBO's projection for the investment-savings balance over these years (table III-1). In contrast to the rather similar analysis shown in table 5.1 and TN18, table A, the inflow of foreign savings is obtained as a *residual*, after deducting the budget deficit from an estimate of surplus savings in the private sector based on historical trends. This yields an estimate of the foreign savings needed by the US economy averaging 2.4 percent of GNP over the next six years. This happens to be very close to the average inflow in the soft-landing scenario discussed in chapter 4. But the analysis of that scenario showed that such a level of capital inflows would be quite insufficient to maintain the dollar at the level projected by the CBO. Thus, in that scenario, the dollar declines by over 35 percent. In other words, either the inflows of foreign savings will have to be much larger than projected by the CBO, or the dollar would have to decline much more sharply, in which case its assumptions about inflation and interest rates would no longer be valid.

TN20   *The federal budget deficit in the hard-landing scenario*

1. The CBO (1985a, table II-10) has made estimates of the federal budget deficit on unchanged policies ("current services") in its "low-growth" scenario which for fiscal years are as follows (in billion dollars):

1985	*1986*	*1987*	*1988*	*1989*	*1990*
220	232	298	384	412	425

2. The level of GNP in 1988 is very similar in this scenario to that in this study's hard-landing scenario, but both the inflation and interest rates are higher in the latter. Using the ready reckoner provided by the CBO (1985a, table II-11), this would raise the estimated deficit in 1988 to around $425 billion (8.8 percent of GNP). By 1990, however, with faster growth and lower interest rates, the deficit would come down to around $410 billion in the hard-landing scenario instead of continuing to rise.

TN21   *Projecting other exchange rates from changes in the effective dollar exchange rate*

1. Regression analysis shows that there has been, for most currencies, a fairly stable pattern of behavior that can be decomposed into two components: *first,* a trend factor reflecting the tendency of each currency to appreciate or depreciate over time against the dollar because of differences in inflation rates and other factors affecting its competitivity and structure of its balance of payments; and, *second,* a coefficient reflecting how it moves relative to the dollar *when the dollar is moving against all other currencies,* reflecting, in particular, the relative closeness of the country's bilateral trading relations with the United States compared to other countries (TN8), the importance of its financial markets, and whether it is floating or linked in some way to other currencies (as, for example, in the EMS).

2. The method used, suggested by Paul Armington, consisted first of estimating, for each of the currencies represented in the MERM index for the US dollar *(US$M),* a regression equation using the quarterly *US$M* for 1970–84 as the independent variable and the respective cross-rates *(CR)* to the dollar (expressed as dollars per unit of foreign currency) as the dependent variable. These equations were estimated in the form:

(1) $\log CR_{it} - \log CR_{it-1} = a_i - b_i (\log US\$M_t - \log US\$M_{t-1}) + e,$

where i = currency
   t = quarter
   a = estimated constant term (a time trend)
   b = estimated coefficient
   e = error term.

TABLE A   **Regression results for dollar exchange rates**[a]

Country	a	b	$\bar{R}^2$	Country	a	b	$\bar{R}^2$
Austria	0.0071 (2.5)	−1.44 (14.5)	0.78	Belgium	0.0004 (0.2)	−1.50 (16.9)	0.83
Canada	−0.0033 (1.6)	−0.03 (0.5)	0.01	Denmark	−0.0029 (1.2)	−1.38 (17.1)	0.83
France	−0.0051 (1.8)	−1.41 (14.5)	0.78	Germany	0.0070 (2.4)	−1.49 (14.9)	0.79
Italy	−0.0159 (4.9)	−1.09 (9.7)	0.61	Japan	0.0095 (2.4)	−1.16 (8.5)	0.55
Netherlands	0.0045 (1.7)	−1.40 (15.3)	0.80	Norway	−0.0006 (0.2)	−1.14 (12.7)	0.73
Sweden	−0.0061 (1.6)	−1.05 (7.8)	0.51	Switzerland	0.0135 (3.8)	−1.58 (12.6)	0.73
United Kingdom	−0.0088 (2.1)	−1.02 (6.9)	0.45	Australia	−0.0032 (0.8)	−0.61 (4.5)	0.25
Finland	−0.0047 (1.6)	−0.90 (8.8)	0.57	Ireland	−0.0113 (3.4)	−1.18 (10.3)	0.64
Spain	−0.0127 (2.7)	−0.93 (5.6)	0.35				

Source: IMF data base.
a. Estimated over 1970:2 to 1984:4; t-statistic in parentheses.

3. The results are summarized in table A. With the exception of Canada, the b coefficient is significant at the 95 percent level for all countries. The time-trend coefficient is small and not significant for the Norwegian kroner and Belgian franc. For the other countries, this coefficient is quite large. That it is not significant at the 90 percent level for Australia, Denmark, Sweden, Finland (and Canada) reflects the fact that, often because of some form of pegging, the movements were step-like rather than continuous through time. The fit is generally quite good except for Canada and Australia. Chow tests showed no significant structural change in the coefficients (at the 1 percent level) between 1970:2–1978:4 and 1979:1–1984:4 for any country.

4. To make the projections in tables 6.3 and 6.4, a number of the coefficients with the lowest level of significance were adjusted to ensure that a change

in the *US$M* would produce an equivalent change in the weighted cross-rates of all other currencies, by imposing the following constraints on the estimated coefficients:

The weighted sum of the coefficients in the set of regressions equals unity:

(2) $\displaystyle\sum_{i=1}^{17} w_i b_i = -1.$

where w_i = weight of cross-rate i in *US$M*.
The weighted sum of the constants in the set of regressions equals zero:

(3) $\displaystyle\sum_{i=1}^{17} w_i a_i = 0.$

5. These conditions were met by setting the a coefficients to zero for the four currencies with the lowest t-statistic (Belgium, Norway, Australia, and Denmark); and by adjusting the b coefficients in proportion to each country's weight in the US MERM index. In no case (with the exception of Canada) did these adjustments exceed 1.5 standard errors.

6. With these modified equations, it was possible to project how cross-rates would change for a given change in the *US$M* using the following equation:

(4) $CR_{iN} = CR_{io}\, e^{(a_i N - b_i D)},$

where CR_N = cross-rate after N quarters
$\quad CR_o$ = initial cross-rate
$\quad N$ = number of quarters
$\quad D$ = total change in *US$M* (log *US$M_N* /*US$M_o*).

7. In making the projections shown in table 6.3 for the "relative" adjustment of exchange rates, the time-trend coefficient a_i was set to zero. All the MERM currencies were projected, and then the country's MERM weights were used to calculate the corresponding changes in its effective exchange rate. In projecting the dollar cross-rates shown in table 6.4, the number of quarters was set at 14.

8. In both sets of projections, the Canadian cross-rate is set exogenously, for reasons described in the text. The Canadian dollar is assumed to appreciate by 15, 20, and 25 percent against the US dollar in the cooperative, soft-landing, and hard-landing scenarios, respectively; these changes imply virtually no change in Canada's effective exchange rate.

TN22   *Differential impact of the hard-landing scenario on the rest of the OECD area*

1. The 1982 weights of Europe, Japan, and other OECD countries (Canada, Australia, and New Zealand) in the GNP of ROECD area are, respectively, two-thirds, just under one-quarter, and one-tenth.

Net exports

2. In the hard-landing scenario, the US current account swings from a deficit equivalent to 3 percent of US GNP to a surplus of 1.5 percent. At 1982 weights, ROECD GNP was about 1.5 times that of US GNP. Thus the improvement of 4.5 percentage points in the US current balance would be equivalent to about 3 percent of ROECD GNP, as shown in table 6.1.

3. The impact would be quite sharply differentiated among other OECD countries. As compared with their shares in ROECD GNP, Canada, and especially Japan, benefited much more than Europe from the deterioration in the US current balance, and the reverse seems likely in the event of a sharp improvement. On this basis, the respective shares in the total decline in ROECD net exports might be: Europe, between 40 percent and 50 percent, Japan, 35 percent and 45 percent, and other OECD countries, around 15 percent. Related to their GNP, this would give a decline in net exports equivalent to around 2 percent of GNP for Europe, and around 4.5 percent for Japan. If this seems large for Japan, the *increase* in Japanese net exports (volume) from 1980 to 1984 was equivalent to over 5 percent of GNP. It is possible, however, that Japan's great competitive strength may enable it to cushion the impact—in which case the other countries would be hit harder.

GNP

4. The normal foreign trade multiplier for both Europe and Japan may be around 2.5. In the D&D model, however, this has been reduced to 1.9 to allow for the positive impact on domestic demand of lower interest rates linked to the dollar's decline (TN1). This latter effect could be more important for Japan both because Japanese real interest rates are particularly high by historical standards, and because, with more buoyant domestic demand,

lower interest rates could well have a stronger positive impact. Another consideration affecting Japan relates to export prices. Given large profit margins on export sales, especially to the US market, Japanese exporters will likely respond to a decline in the dollar by cutting profit margins rather than by raising prices. This would dampen the negative impact on the volume of exports at the expense of a sharper decline in profits. In the short run, therefore, the negative impact on domestic demand might be less than suggested by the normal multiplier. Over time, however, the decline in profits from exports could have a significant impact on investment for a country as export-oriented as Japan.

5. Putting these various elements together, the direct and indirect effects of declining net exports might reduce the 1990 level of GNP between 4 percent and 5 percent in Europe and between 7 percent and 8 percent in Japan from what it would otherwise have been.

Unemployment

6. For Europe, recent experience suggests that for each percentage point that GNP growth falls below 3 percent, unemployment rises by 0.4 percent to 0.5 percent. With domestic demand rising at 2.5 percent, and constant net exports, unemployment would continue to rise by about 0.25 percentage points a year. Using the same arithmetic, the shortfall of GNP resulting from the direct and indirect impact of declining net exports could raise unemployment by 2 to 2.5 percentage points by 1990. At the same time, however, the growth of the population of working age will slow down sharply after 1985. Nevertheless, unemployment could well rise to above 14 percent in the hard-landing scenario (unless there was a marked productivity slowdown).

7. In Japan, slow growth has a less clear-cut and smaller impact on registered unemployment because of the system of lifetime employment and other special features of the labor market. According to Hamada and Kurosaka (1984), for each percentage point that GNP growth falls below 4.5 percent, registered unemployment rises by around 0.1 to 0.2 percentage points. Thus, in the hard-landing scenario, unemployment could rise from 2.7 percent at the end of 1984 to 4 percent or more in 1990.

TN23   *Impact of different scenarios on the developing countries*

1. A projection model based on Cline (1984) was used to assess the impact on developing countries of macroeconomic assumptions embodied in the baseline, hard-landing, and cooperative scenarios. Using 1984 data, the model projects the trade, current account positions, and debt ratios of developing countries through 1990, based on alternative assumptions about the dollar, OECD growth, interest rates, and terms of trade.

2. Several modifications in the Cline model have been made. In all but the cooperative scenario, the D&D simulations assume a constant real trade balance for developing countries. Thus, LDC export volumes increase with OECD growth, while import volumes are constrained to leave the real balance on goods and nonfactor services unchanged. This differs from Cline's formulation, in which import volumes respond to the assumed developing-country growth rate. In the cooperative scenario, it is assumed that 20 percent of the counterpart of the shift in US net exports in 1989–90 is to be found in the developing countries.

3. Changes in the terms of trade for developing countries are determined exogenously in the three scenarios (box 6.1). In the baseline, the terms of trade (excluding oil) show modest deterioration through 1987 (-2.4 percent cumulatively), then remain stable. In the hard landing, the terms of trade deteriorate sharply in 1987 and do not stabilize until 1990 (-7.8 percent cumulative change). In the cooperative scenario, initial deterioration is followed by modest improvement through 1990 ($+0.4$ percent cumulative change). Nonoil export volumes increase by 40 percent in the baseline, 18 percent in the hard landing, and 55 percent in the cooperative scenario. Combining terms of trade and volume changes, the purchasing power of exports increases by 37 percent in the baseline, 9 percent in the hard landing, and 55 percent in the cooperative scenario.

4. Exports and imports of oil are assumed unchanged in volume terms. Special assumptions are made concerning oil prices. In the baseline and cooperative scenarios, oil is valued at $27 per barrel in 1985 and $26 thereafter. The hard-landing scenario incorporates a significant further decline: to $24 in 1985 and $20 in 1986–90.

5. Interest payments on outstanding debt (except for the portion at fixed interest) are based on the London Interbank Offer Rate (LIBOR), which is assumed to be 1.5 percent above the Treasury-bill rate shown in TN2, table A, in each of the scenarios.

TABLE A   **Ratio of net debt to exports of goods and services**

Seven major developing-country borrowers	1984	1986	1988	1990
Baseline	2.11	1.98	1.71	1.45
Hard-landing scenario	2.11	2.09	1.84	1.57
Deviations from baseline due to				
OECD growth[a]		.04	.39	.43
Dollar		−.17	−.58	−.63
LIBOR		.07	.11	.08
Oil price		.18	.22	.24
Cooperative scenario	2.11	1.88	1.36	1.07
Deviations from baseline due to				
OECD growth[a]		−.03	−.06	−.06
Dollar		−.10	−.31	−.33
LIBOR		.02	.03	.00
Indebted developing countries	*1984*	*1986*	*1988*	*1990*
Baseline	1.27	1.29	1.24	1.18
Hard-landing scenario	1.27	1.30	1.24	1.18
Deviations from baseline due to				
OECD growth[a]		.03	.31	.38
Dollar		−.12	−.42	−.49
LIBOR		.03	.05	.03
Oil price		.06	.07	.08
Cooperative scenario	1.27	1.21	.96	.78
Deviations from baseline due to				
OECD growth[a]		−.02	−.05	−.13
Dollar		−.07	−.24	−.26
LIBOR		.01	.01	.00

Source: IMF, *World Economic Outlook,* and simulations of D&D model. For details, see TN2.
a. Including both the impact on the volume of developing-country exports and their terms of trade, on the assumptions about what happens to developing-country trade balances described in the text.

6. The model does not incorporate any individual country detail. The debt and trade data (derived from the IMF *World Economic Outlook* and World Bank *World Debt Tables*) refer to seven "major borrowers" (Brazil, Mexico, Argentina, Venezuela, Korea, Indonesia, and the Philippines) and to the "indebted developing countries" as a group. In 1984 their debts were $360 billion and $828 billion, respectively.

TN24   *Prices, wages, and unemployment*

1. A very extensive literature exists on the relation between prices, wages, and unemployment. Regrettably, the conclusions reached often differ significantly on the points of central importance to this study. This can be illustrated by comparing the results of three recent in-depth cross-country studies by Grubb (1984), Coe and Gagliardi (1985), and Beckerman and Jenkinson (1985), referred to below as G, CG, and BJ.

2. The most startling difference lies in the role played by unemployment. For the median country in a 19-country group, G finds that a 1 percentage point decline in unemployment raises wage inflation by 1.19 percent. CG get a median wage-inflation coefficient of 0.40 percent for a 10-country group (compared with 1.16 for G's results for the same 10 countries). BJ, using pooled time series and cross-section for 13 countries, find no statistically significant relation between unemployment and wage inflation at all!

3. It seems clear that these differences arise primarily from differences in the estimated impact of *prices* on wages, since, generally speaking, the higher the coefficient found for prices, the lower is the coefficient for unemployment. CG find a larger feedback of prices on wages than G. BJ's results go much further in suggesting that *import* prices, via their impact on the general price level, have played the key role, and that their main determinant, for the OECD area as a whole, has been large fluctuations in world commodity prices.

4. In some respects, these results are not as inconsistent as they appear. G finds that "import prices are a very significant determinant of consumer prices . . . and a quite significant determinant of wages," (p. 25) and that commodity prices (and exchange rates) are an important determinant of import prices. Moreover, G also finds that, if *all* OECD countries reduced unemployment simultaneously, inflation would rise more than twice as much than if one country did so by itself. This is consistent with BJ's central thesis that it is not so much a country's own unemployment that affects its inflation rate as changes in the level of activity in the OECD area as a whole, through its impact on world commodity prices. But this leaves open the question of whether and by how much a country's own unemployment affects its own rate of inflation. In this respect it is disquieting that when BJ added a price acceleration term to the equations used by Layard et al. (1984), they not

only got a better fit, but also found that for six of the seven countries the coefficient on unemployment was no longer statistically significant (BJ 1985, appendix B).

5. CG do not deal explicitly with the role of commodity prices, import prices, and exchange rates. But the fact that they do show a rapid and full feedback from prices to wages (less so in the United States) does suggest that, if shocked for a large change in commodity prices and /or exchange rates, or both, these effects would tend to dominate those coming from changes in the level of unemployment.

6. Other relevant points in these studies are:

• G finds wage inflation sensitive to both levels and changes in unemployment, CG only to levels (and BJ to neither).

• Both CG and G find little evidence that unemployment has less effect on wage inflation when it is unusually high ("nonlinearity"). But CG find two important exceptions: in both Germany and Japan a decline in unemployment from the present unusually high unemployment would raise inflation a good deal less than if employment were closer to normal (table 12), and to a lesser extent the same applies to Austria and the Netherlands.

• Neither CG nor G find a strong tendency for wages to "catch up" from a previous lag of real wages behind productivity.

• Using pooled data BJ find a significant influence from productivity; CG only find this for Germany.

TN25   Budget deficits, public debt, and interest rates

1. Important research is underway at the OECD on the determinants of interest rates using cross-country data. At the time of writing the latest publications were by Atkinson and Chouraqui (1985) and Muller and Price (1984b), referred to below as AC and MP.

2. As MP point out, the most frequent result found in a review of the literature on this subject is a *negative* correlation between interest rates and

the size of the budget deficit or changes in public debt. The explanation is relatively straightforward: interest rates fall and budget deficits rise when activity declines, and vice versa.

3. MP, building on work by others, show that, in addition to cyclical factors, at least four domestic factors have a significant impact on interest rates: expected inflation, monetary policy, the relation of the budget deficit to the *flow* of private savings, and the level or rate of change in public debt in relation to wealth or GNP. These appear as significant variables both for the United States (1958–83) and for a pooled cross-section and time series analysis for 15 other OECD countries (1975–83). The important point is that the deficit and debt variables have been put into the equations in a cyclically adjusted and forward-looking form, and that once this is done they have a *positive* rather than a negative sign. It is comforting to have this confirmation of the common sense view that, over time (and abstracting from cyclical factors), large budget deficits and high or rising levels of public debt do tend to raise interest rates. Indeed, contrary to the views often expressed by some members of the Reagan administration, MP's results suggest that for the United States "the debt and deficit variables together account for a large proportion of the rise in the long-term rate between 1979 and 1983" (p. 19).

4. MP also tried, with less success, to pick up the influence of international capital flows on interest rates. For the ROECD countries, they did find a significant influence from US interest rates, but the coefficient was fairly low (0.2). They thus found that the main reason for the rise in ROECD interest rates from 1979 to 1983 was of domestic origin, notably from both the deficit-savings flow and government debt variables (table 11).

5. The present author has doubts about these results. For ROECD countries, the three key features of the relatively short period covered by MP were (a) a strong rise in real interest rates, (b) a strong rise in debt-GNP ratios, and (c) a marked swing from a weak to a very strong dollar. Given the degree of joint correlation between (b) and (c), there is bound to be a serious identification problem. In the author's view, MP may well not have picked up the strength of the causal relationship running from (c) to (a) arising from the expectational-monetary policy factors and the special role of the dollar discussed in chapter 2. Moreover, because of the joint correlation, a specification that gave more weight to the strong dollar would, ipso facto, be likely to yield a lower coefficient on the debt-GNP term. This question obviously has important implications for policy. Unfortunately, resources

were not available to test alternative hypotheses. In practice, however, it may not be possible to resolve the issue empirically unless and until the dollar weakens significantly.

6. Reviewing the other possible explanations for high real interest rates such as improved profitability, uncertainty about future rates of inflation, and financial deregulation, AC conclude that they "can neither be rejected or supported on the basis of empirical evidence" (p. 41).

7. The analysis of the possible fiscal constraint in ROECD countries in chapter 6 follows recent work in giving emphasis to cyclically adjusted and forward-looking measures of deficits and debt.

8. Following de Leeuw and Holloway (1983), the analysis uses *mid-cycle* structural budget positions, as calculated by the OECD. The reason for this is the assumption that financial markets are not greatly influenced by or concerned about purely cyclical fluctuations in deficits and debt and that the longer term trend of debt will be determined not by the "high employment" structural deficit, but by the average deficit over the course of the cycle.

9. Net interest payments have been deducted to yield a "primary" (mid-cycle) structural deficit. As suggested by other analysts (CBO 1985a, and Chouraqui and Price 1985), the primary deficit is the most relevant concept when analyzing debt-GNP ratios in terms of stocks and flows. In particular,

TABLE A   **Private-sector financial assets and public debt**

	Year	Ratio of private-sector financial assets to GNP	Share of government debt in private-sector financial assets (percentage)	
			Central government	General government
Germany	1981	3.10	4.7	10.1
United States	1982	2.98	5.8	. .
Canada	1981	2.98	12.7	17.9[a]
Sweden	1981	2.21	9.0	12.5
Belgium	1980	1.89	26.8	43.5
Japan	1982	1.31	24.1	35.2
United Kingdom	1982	1.09	. .	46.8
Australia	1979	0.70	. .	25.4

Source: Chouraqui and Price (1983, table C2).
a. 1979.

in a "normal" world where interest rates equal the growth of nominal GNP, the interest rate component of the budget deficit grows at the same rate as nominal GNP; it therefore has no effect on the debt-GNP ratio, whatever its level, and it is only the primary budget position that affects this ratio.

10. In making intercountry comparisons it seems best to measure public debt net rather than gross because of the great differences between countries in the amount of financial intermediation by the public sector (table B). This would also seem to be conceptually correct in that any factors in the debt calculus that are unfavorable to the public sector as a borrower (for example, high real interest rates) should be favorable to it as a lender. Against this it can be argued that public-sector intermediation may either lower interest rates via economies of scale, or raise them by creating a privileged class of borrowers, but both effects seem likely to be second order in the present context. MP obtained very similar regression results using either net or gross debt.

11. It is assumed that the increase in debt is equal to the actual budget deficit. In practice, a whole series of stock-flow adjustments are needed (Commission of the European Communities 1984, p. 133). One of these adjustments is highly relevant in the context of this study. Where the public sector has borrowed abroad significantly in foreign currencies, the debt-GNP ratio, measured in the domestic currency, rises when the currency of its creditor country appreciates. This has been a major factor since 1980 for countries whose public sector borrowed heavily in dollars, and no doubt largely explains why the "stock-flow" adjustment accounted for a 10.6 percentage point rise in the debt-GNP ratio for Belgium between 1980 and 1983, and for as much as a 23.4 point rise for Denmark (Commission of the European Communities 1984, table 6.7).

12. Using these definitions, the forward-looking debt calculus shown in chapter 6 was formulated, with invaluable help from Paul Armington, as follows. Assuming that the present primary deficit (x) remains unchanged, then the debt-GNP ratio (d_t) in some future year (t) is related to the present debt-GNP ratio (d_o) as follows:

(1) $d_t = g^t d_o + (1 + \sum_{j=1}^{t-1} g^{t-j}) x,$

where g is 1 plus the interest rate minus the growth rate. By rearranging terms, we obtain equation (2), used to derive "iso-danger" lines. An "iso-danger" line represents all combinations of x and d_o under which the debt-GNP ratio would reach some given "critical" level (D) over some given number of years (T) for a given difference between the interest rate and the growth rate (G):

$$(2) \quad d_o = D /G^T - x \sum_{j=1}^{T} (1 /G^j).$$

13. Such iso-danger curves all have a positive intercept on the debt ratio axis and a negative slope, i.e. the larger the deficit or the higher the debt-GNP ratio, the greater the danger. An increase in G, i.e. in the interest rate relative to the growth rate, shifts the curve downward and to the left, increasing the danger for all countries whatever their deficit or debt-GNP ratio. An increase in T flattens the slope (and reduces the debt ratio intercept) and thus alleviates the danger for countries with low debt ratios and large primary deficits relative to those with high debt ratios but lower primary deficits.

14. A common critical value of D is assumed for all countries because it provides a common measure of the future burden of public debt service in relation to the taxable base (GNP), and hence also of the danger that

TABLE B   **Major fiscal indicators (general government) for three countries**
(percentage of GNP)

	Year	Germany	Japan	United Kingdom
Gross debt	1983	41.1	66.5	54.0
Net debt	1983	21.8	26.3	47.7
	1984	23.1	27.4	50.2
Structural balance[a]	1984	+0.9	−1.7	+0.9
Mid-cycle structural balance[b]	1984	−0.8	−2.4	−1.2
Net interest payments[c]	1985	1.7	1.9	4.6
Actual balance[d]	1984	−2.3	−2.6	−4.0
	1985	−1.5	−1.4	−3.6
	1986	−1.3	−0.5	−2.9

Source: Muller and Price (1984b), updated by OECD Secretariat.
a. Zero gap between potential and actual GNP.
b. Average gap over the cycle between potential and actual GNP (Muller and Price, annex 3).
c. Estimated by the OECD Secretariat from gross interest payments and ratio of net to gross debt.
d. Estimates and forecasts from *OECD Economic Outlook, no. 37,* June 1985, table 2.

unwillingness to raise the necessary taxes will lead to monetization of the debt. The choice of a critical value of D of 1.0 and of T of 20 years is, of course, entirely arbitrary.

15. An alternative approach, based more heavily on portfolio balance analysis, would be to assume a common critical value of the share of public debt in total financial wealth. Unfortunately, data on financial wealth are available for relatively few countries and even then there are serious problems of comparability. The figures shown in table A suggest that, for many industrial countries, the ratio of private-sector financial assets to GNP lies in the range of 2 to 3. The lower figure for Japan may reflect a lag in the evolution of its financial markets; in contrast to most other countries, the total debt-GNP ratio has been rising rapidly. In the United Kingdom and Australia, on the other hand, the low total debt-GNP ratios may well reflect the heavy "inflation tax" paid by lenders to both the public and private sectors during the 1970s, as interest rates lagged behind inflation. Reluctance to take up government debt because of this unhappy experience could well have increased the fiscal constraint associated with a given level of public debt in these countries.

16. Between 1971 and 1984, this inflation tax would, other things being equal, have reduced the UK public debt-GNP ratio in the United Kingdom by as much as 24 percentage points. Over the same period, there was no net "inflation tax" in the United States, while in Germany and Japan this factor would have raised the public debt-GNP ratio by 3 and 5 percentage points, respectively (Muller and Price 1984a, table A3.4). Thus, for the United Kingdom, it may well be the ratio of public debt to total debt, rather than to GNP, which is most relevant; different iso-danger lines, based on this criterion, are therefore shown in figure 6.5. The criteria are the conditions under which the share of public debt in total debt would reach 50 percent in 20 years under the assumption that total debt rises in line with GNP.

17. The size of primary surplus or deficit that, with a given initial debt-GNP ratio, would be required to keep the debt-GNP ratio constant under different growth and interest rate assumptions can be obtained by solving equation (1) for $d_t = d_0$:

$$(3) \quad x = d_o (1 - g).$$

This equation has been used to calculate for Germany, Japan, and the United Kingdom the size of the actual primary surplus or deficit, as a percentage of

GNP, those countries would have to run to keep their net debt-GNP ratios constant in the baseline ($g = 1.02$) and the cooperative scenario ($g = 0.98$):

	Germany	Japan	United Kingdom
Baseline	+0.5	+0.6	+1.0
Cooperative	−0.5	−0.6	−1.0

These are only very rough estimates. In particular, the calculation assumes that all government debt is rolled over every year (this is not only not the case but varies considerably among countries with different techniques of debt management), and that there are no stock-flow adjustments, i.e. changes in net debt are equal to current fiscal balances.

18. These figures can be read in conjunction with the expected primary balances in these countries on the basis of present fiscal policies. According to OECD projections of actual balances and net interest payments (table B), Germany, Japan, and the United Kingdom would run in 1986 primary *surpluses* equivalent to 0.4, 1.4, and 1.7 percent, respectively. Combining the two sets of figures, debt-GNP ratios could be kept constant at their 1984 levels in the cooperative scenario with negative shifts (ex post) in primary balances equivalent to 0.9, 2.0, and 2.7 percent of GNP for Germany, Japan, and the United Kingdom, respectively. However, the 1986 projection for the United Kingdom is based on oil revenues corresponding to a $27 oil price and current production levels which may overstate the likely improvement in the budgetary situation; using the 1984 position would lower the latter figure to 1.6 percent.

TN26   Cyclically adjusted pretax profits and rates of return

1. *Data.* Gross operating surplus, pretax, as percentage of gross value added *(P)* and as percent of gross capital stock *(R)*, in manufacturing. Europe aggregate is for eight countries only: France, Germany, Italy, United Kingdom, Belgium, Denmark, Finland, and Sweden.

Source: OECD National Accounts, vol. 2, 1970–82, with additional data supplied by the OECD Secretariat.

2. For Europe and Japan, the cyclical adjustment is based on a regression of *P* and *R* on their trend (five-year moving average) values *(TP* and *TR)* and deviations from trend (seven-year moving average) of industrial production *(DIP)*:

(1) $P_{EUR} = -3.67 + 1.12\,TP_{EUR} + 0.20\,DIP_{EUR};$ $\bar{R}^2 = 0.90, DW = 1.33.$
          (1.3) (12.0)   (3.4)

(2) $R_{EUR} = -0.65 + 1.05\,TR_{EUR} + 0.18\,DIP_{EUR};$ $\bar{R}^2 = 0.95, DW = 1.42.$
          (0.8) (16.5)   (5.3)

(3) $P_{JAP} = -4.17 + 1.08\,TP_{JAP} + 0.26\,DIP_{JAP};$ $\bar{R}_2 = 0.98, DW = 1.66.$
          (2.2) (2.7)   (5.0)

(4) $R_{JAP} = -2.69 + 1.09\,TR_{JAP} + 0.35\,DIP_{JAP}.$ $\bar{R}^2 = 0.98, DW = 1.53.$
          (2.4) (26.9)   (4.6)

3. Cyclical adjustment of the US data is more difficult. The best fit was found using deviations of the change in GNP (1972 prices) from a 3 percent trend *(DGNP)*. The figures for 1975 were treated as outliers:

(5) $P_{US} = 0.31 + 0.98\,TP_{US} + 0.58\,DGNP_{US},$ and $\bar{R}^2 = 0.94, DW = 1.87;$
          (0.1)   (8.1)   (11.5)

(6) $R_{US} = 0.44 + 0.97\,TR_{US} + 0.54\,DGNP_{US}.$ $\bar{R}^2 = 0.98, DW = 1.85.$
          (0.5) (19.9)   (9.6)

4. For a more sophisticated cyclical adjustment of US rate of return data using different figures see Bosworth (1985, table 4).

TN27 *A note on the real wage problem*

1. There are several different and sometimes conflicting strands in the literature on the real wage problem, often reflecting the different backgrounds of the economists concerned. Continental European economists tend to see it in a broad historical perspective, giving as much emphasis to the sociological as to the more strictly economic aspects [Giersch (1981) and Giersch and Kirkpatrick (1985), Attali (1981), Aglietta (1977)]. Another school puts the emphasis on supply-side shocks, notably the rise in energy prices [McCracken et al. (1977) chapter five, Bruno and Sachs (1979), Sachs (1983)]. British economists, after a slow start (with the honorable exception of Samuel Brittan), have now plunged into the debate, and have been trying to integrate the real wage thesis with their earlier preoccupation with the expectations-augmented Phillips curve and the NAIRU. [Grubb et al. (1982), Layard and Nickell (1985)]. A characteristic of most of the literature is that more attention is paid to developments in labor markets that could have affected wage bargaining, than to developments in product markets which could explain why price-setters accepted lower profit margins (Tobin 1983).

2. It is now generally agreed that analysis in terms of the "real wage gap," as pioneered by the OECD Secretariat, can be misleading. The case of Japan vividly illustrates the difficulty of choosing an appropriate base period in which real wages and the rate of return on capital are assumed to have been normal. Most studies pick up Japan as suffering from a real wage problem in the 1970s because of the sharp fall—from very high levels—in profit shares and rates of return (figure 6.6). A more plausible interpretation is that up to the early 1970s Japan was suffering (or benefiting) from "disequilibrium" profits (*OECD Economic Outlook,* no. 37, June 1985, p. 30).

3. An equally important point is that supply-side adjustment, or non adjustment, to "excessive" real wages, involves movement along the production function. Thus, in particular, the disappearance of a real wage gap can signify two quite different things: either the growth of real wages has slowed down enough to make it possible to employ all those who wish to work at the going real wage; or the capital stock has been reduced and adjusted to the high real wage through scrapping and labor saving investment, leaving a permanently higher level of "classical" unemployment (Dornbusch et al. 1983, p. 13).

4. Unfortunately, there are serious conceptual and measurement problems involved in estimating production functions, so that estimates of "disequilibrium real wages" based on this approach are subject to a wide margin of uncertainty. Using this approach, Artus (1984) found a positive real wage gap in 1982 in France, Germany, the United Kingdom—and Japan, but not in Canada, Italy, or the United States. Broadly similar results have apparently been found by the OECD Secretariat (Yoshitomi 1985a).

5. A further problem that has received less attention in the literature is that the rate of return required on new investment may have risen because of increased risk premia. As Malinvaud (1982, p. 11) put it: "The often heard objective to restore the profit rate to its pre-1974 level has no strong justification . . . the whole economic environment and prospect of economic growth has changed since 1974." Unfortunately, difficulties abound in trying to measure such risk premia. The implication for policy, however, seems clear. Faster growth should help to reduce risk premia; but in order to achieve it, the more that profit margins can be increased, the better.

6. Simulations showing that a cut in real wages unaccompanied by action to boost demand may have only a small (and in some cases negative) impact on employment include the Commission of the European Communities (1984, pp. 179–187), the NIESR (1985, pp. 41–52), and Wharton (1985, pp. 39–55). It is worth noting that the Commission's simulations show that a cut in real wages in one country alone has more positive impact on its employment than when cuts are also made in other countries, since in the former case some of the benefits are simply made at the expense of other countries—a good example of the zero-sum game aspect of the international side of the real wage problem.

References

Aglietta, Michel. 1977. *Régulation et crises capitalistes: le cas des Etats-Unis.* Paris: Calmann Lévy.

Andersen, P. S. 1984. *Real Wages, Inflation and Unemployment.* BIS Working Paper, no. 9. Basle, Switzerland: Bank for International Settlements, July.

Artus, Jacques R. 1984. "The Disequilibrium Real Wage Rate Hypothesis: An Empirical Evaluation." *IMF Staff Papers,* vol. 31, no. 2 (June).

Atkinson, Paul, and Jean-Claude Chouraqui. 1985. *Real Interest Rates and the Prospects for Durable Growth.* OECD Working Papers, no. 21. Paris, May.

Attali, Jacques. 1981. *Les Trois Mondes.* Paris: Arthème Fayard.

Bach, Christopher L. 1983. "US International Transactions, Fourth Quarter and Year 1982." *US Survey of Current Business,* vol. 63, no. 3 (March).

Baker, James A., III. 1985. Statement before the Senate Budget Committee, 20 February. Washington: US Treasury Department.

Bean, Charles R. 1985. *Exchange Rates, Risk Premia and New Information: A Note.* Centre for Economic Policy Research Discussion Paper, no. 53. London, February.

Beckerman, Wilfred. 1985. "How the Battle Against Inflation Was Really Won." *Lloyds Bank Review,* no. 7 (January).

Beckerman, Wilfred, and Tim Jenkinson. 1986. "Commodity Prices, Import Prices and the Inflation Slowdown: A Pooled Cross-Country Analysis." *Economic Journal,* forthcoming.

Benderly, Jason, and Burton Zwick. 1984. "The Role of and Real Asset Returns in Explaining the Normal Level of Interest Rates: The 1970s versus the 1980s." Kidder, Peabody & Co. Economic Research Report. New York, September.

Bergsten, C. Fred. 1976. "Increasing International Economic Interdependence: The Implications for Research." *American Economic Review,* vol. 66, no. 2 (May).

———. 1984. "The Case for Leaning with the Wind." *Financial Times,* 24 October, p. 19.

———. 1985. "The Second Debt Crisis is Coming." *Challenge,* vol. 28, no. 2 (May/June).

Bergsten, C. Fred, and William R. Cline. 1985. *The US–Japan Economic Problem.* POLICY ANALYSES IN INTERNATIONAL ECONOMICS 13. Washington: Institute for International Economics.

Bilson, John F. O. 1984. *Macroeconomic Stability and Flexible Exchange Rates.* Cambridge, Mass.: National Bureau of Economic Research Program in International Studies, November.

Black, Stanley W. 1984. *Changing Causes of Exchange Rate Fluctuations.* Brookings Discussion Paper in International Economics, no. 12. Washington: Brookings Institution, January.

Blanchard, Olivier J. 1984. "Current and Anticipated Deficits, Interest Rates and Economic Activity." *European Economic Review,* no. 25.

Blanchard, Olivier J., and Lawrence H. Summers. 1984. "Perspectives on High World Real Interest Rates." *Brookings Papers on Economic Activity* 2.

335

Blanchard, Olivier, Rudiger Dornbusch, Jacques Drèze, Herbert Giersch, Richard Layard, and Mario Monti. 1985. *Employment and Growth in Europe: A Two-Handed Approach.* CEPS Papers, no. 21. Brussels: Centre for European Policy Studies.

Bloomfield, Arthur I. 1943. "The Mechanism of Adjustment of the American Balance of Payments: 1919–1929." *Quarterly Journal of Economics,* vol. 57 (May).

———. 1950. *Capital Imports and the American Balance of Payments 1934–1939: A Study in Abnormal International Capital Transfers.* Chicago: University of Chicago Press.

Bosworth, Barry P. 1984. *Tax Incentives and Economic Growth.* Washington: Brookings Institution.

———. 1985. "Taxes and the Investment Recovery." *Brookings Papers on Economic Activity* 1.

Brender, Anton. 1985. "Avec 400 milliards de dollars de plus." *La Tribune de l'Economie,* 26 January.

Brender, Anton, P. Gaye, and V. Kessler. 1984. "Le Bloc Monétaire international du modèle SIMULO." *Recherches Economiques et Sociales,* no. 10 (2nd trimester).

Bruno, Michael, and Jeffrey D. Sachs. 1979. *Supply versus Demand Approaches to the Problem of Stagflation.* Maurice Falk Institute for Economic Research Discussion Paper, no. 796. Jerusalem: MFIER.

Capra, James, and Allen Sinai. 1985. *Deficit Prospects—Half Empty or Half Full?* Economic Studies Series, no. 14 (October). New York, NY: Shearson Lehman Brothers.

Chan-Lee, James, and Hiromi Kato. 1984. "A Comparison of Simulation Properties of National Econometric Models." *OECD Economic Studies,* no. 2 (Spring).

Chan-Lee, James, and Helen Sutch. 1985. *Profits and Rates of Return in OECD Countries.* OECD Working Papers, no. 20. Paris, May.

Chouraqui, Jean-Claude, and Robert W. R. Price. 1984. "Medium-Term Financial Strategy: The Co-ordination of Fiscal and Monetary Policy." *OECD Economic Studies,* no. 2 (Spring).

———. 1985. "Budget Deficits in Europe and the United States: Fiscal Policy Asymmetry and the Sustainability of the Current Recovery." Paper for the conference on Europe and the Dollar, 4–5 June, Turin, Italy. Paris: OECD. Processed.

Cline, William R. 1984. *International Debt: Systemic Risk and Policy Response.* Washington: Institute for International Economics.

Coe, David T., and Francesco Gagliardi. 1985. *Nominal Wage Determination in OECD Economies.* OECD Working Papers, no. 19. Paris, March.

Commission of the European Communities. 1984a. *Annual Economic Report 1984–1985.* Brussels, November.

Congressional Budget Office (CBO). 1984a. *Baseline Budget Projections for Fiscal Years 1985–1989,* February.

———. 1984b. "The Effects of Changes in Interest Rates on Different Sectors of the US Economy." Staff Memorandum, June. Processed.

———. 1984c. *The Economic and Budget Outlook: An Update.* August.

———. 1985a. *The Economic and Budget Outlook: Fiscal Years 1986–1990.* Report to the Senate and House Committees on the Budget, part I. February.

———. 1985b. *The Economic and Budget Outlook: An Update.* August.

Council of Economic Advisers. 1984. *Economic Report of the President.* Washington, February.

Data Resources, Inc. 1983. *Data Resources of the US Economy Review.* Lexington, Mass., July.

De Larosière, Jacques. 1982. "Restoring Fiscal Discipline." Speech given to the American Enterprise Institute, 16 March. Washington: IMF.

De Leeuw, Frank. 1982. "The High-Employment Budget: Revised Estimates and Automatic Inflation Effects." *US Survey of Current Business,* vol. 62, no. 4 (April).

———. 1984. "Conflicting Measures of Private Savings." *US Survey of Current Business,* vol. 64, no. 11 (November).

De Leeuw, Frank, and Thomas M. Holloway. 1983. "Cyclical Adjustment of the Federal Budget and Federal Debt." *US Survey of Current Business,* vol. 63, no. 12 (December).

DeMenil, George, and Anthony M. Solomon. 1983. *Economic Summitry.* New York, NY: Council on Foreign Relations.

Dornbusch, Rudiger. 1976. "Expectations and Exchange Rate Dynamics." *Journal of Political Economy,* vol. 84, no. 6 (December).

———. 1980. "Exchange Rate Economics: Where Do We Stand?" *Brookings Papers on Economic Activity* 1.

Dornbusch, Rudiger, Giorgio Basevi, Olivier Blanchard, Willem H. Buiter, and Richard Layard. 1983. *Macroeconomic Prospects and Policies for the European Community.* CEPS Papers, no. 1. Brussels: Centre for European Policy Studies.

Emerson, Michael, ed. 1984. *Europe's Stagflation.* New York, NY: Oxford University Press.

Emminger, Otmar. 1985a. Summary of remarks to the joint conference organized by the National Foreign Trade Council and the Group of Thirty, 30 January. New York, NY: National Foreign Trade Council.

———. 1985b. *The Dollar's Borrowed Strength.* Group of Thirty Occasional Papers 19. New York, NY.

Fama, Eugene F. 1984. "Forward and Spot Exchange Rates." *Journal of Monetary Economics,* vol. 14, no. 3.

Federal Reserve Board. 1984. *The U.S. Economy in an Interdependent World: A Multicountry Model.* Washington: Federal Reserve.

Feldman, Robert A. 1982. "Dollar Appreciation, Foreign Trade, and the US Economy." Federal Reserve Bank of New York, *Quarterly Review,* vol. 7, no. 2 (Summer).

Feldstein, Martin S. 1983a. "Domestic Saving and International Capital Movements in the Long Run and the Short Run." *European Economic Review,* vol. 21 (March/April).

———. 1983b. Remarks to the Chamber of Commerce International Forum, 14 September, Washington.

Feldstein, Martin S., and Charles Horioka. 1980. "Domestic Savings and International Capital Flows." *Economic Journal,* vol. 90, no. 358.

Frankel, Jeffrey A. 1980. "Tests of Rational Expectations in the Forward Exchange Market." *Southern Economic Journal,* vol. 46 (April).

———. 1984. *The Yen/Dollar Agreement: Liberalizing Japanese Capital Markets.* POLICY ANALYSES IN INTERNATIONAL ECONOMICS 9. Washington: Institute for International Economics.

Frankel, Jeffrey A., and Kenneth Froot. 1985. *Using Survey Data to Test Some Standard Propositions Regarding Exchange Rate Expectations.* National Bureau of Economic Research Working Paper, no. 1672. Cambridge, Mass.: NBER.

Frenkel, Jacob A. 1976. "A Monetary Approach to the Exchange Rate: Doctrinal Aspects and Empirical Evidence." *Scandinavian Journal of Economics,* vol. 78 (May).

———. 1981. "Flexible Exchange Rates, Prices, and the Role of 'News': Lessons from the 1970s." *Journal of Political Economy,* vol. 89, no. 4.

Froot, Kenneth. 1985. "Exchange Rate Survey Data: The Roles of Expectational Errors, the Risk Premium and Measurement Error." Division of International Finance, Board of Governors of the Federal Reserve System, Washington. Processed.

Giersch, Herbert. 1981. "Aspects of Growth, Structural Change, and Employment—A Schumpeterian Perspective." In *Macroeconomic Policies for Growth and Stability: A European Perspective*, edited by Herbert Giersch. Tübingen: Mohr, for Institut für Weltwirtschaft.

————. 1984. *Real Exchange Rates and Economic Development*. Kiel Institute of World Economics Working Paper, no. 218, November.

Giersch, Herbert, and Grant Kirkpatrick. 1985. "Wage Rigidity and Macroeconomic Equilibrium in the Federal Republic of Germany—A Long-Term Perspective." Paper presented to the Conference on Wage Rigidity, 19–20 April, University of the South, Tennessee. Kiel, Federal Republic of Germany: Institut für Weltwirtschaft. Processed.

Goldstein, Morris, and Mohsin S. Khan. 1983. "Income and Price Effects in Foreign Trade." In *Handbook of International Economics*, edited by Peter B. Kenen and Ronald W. Jones. Amsterdam: North Holland.

Golub, Stephen S. 1983. "Oil Prices and Exchange Rates." *Economic Journal*, vol. 93, no. 371 (September).

Government of Denmark. 1985. *Denmark's External Debt Management System*. Department of the Budget, Paper No. 43. Copenhagen: Ministry of Finance.

Greene, Margaret L. 1984. *US Experience with Exchange Market Intervention: September 1977–December 1979*. Board of Governors of the Federal Reserve Staff Studies no. 128 Washington, October.

Group of Five. 1985. Announcement of the Ministers of Finance and the Central Bank Governors of France, Germany, Japan, the United Kingdom and the United States. New York, NY, 22 September. Processed.

Group of Ten. 1985a. "The Functioning of the International Monetary System: A Report to the Ministers and Governors by the Group of Deputies." Tokyo, June. Processed.

————. 1985b. *Communiqué of the Ministers and Governors of the Group of Ten*. Tokyo, 21 June. Processed.

Group of Twenty-four. 1985. *The Functioning and Improvement of the International Monetary System*. Report for the 1985 joint Fund-Bank meetings. Washington: IMF.

Grubb, David T. 1984. *Wage Inflation and Unemployment: A Multi-Country Empirical Investigation*. Centre for Labour Economics Working Paper No. 681. London School of Economics.

Grubb, David T., R. Jackman, and Richard Layard. 1982. *Causes of the Current Stagflation*. Centre for Labour Economics Discussion Paper No. 96 (revised), July. London: London School of Economics.

Gutowski, Armin. 1984. "Where is the Dollar Going?" *Intereconomics*, no. 3 (May/June).

Hamada, Koichi, and Yoshio Kurosaka. 1984. "The Relationship between Production and Unemployment in Japan: Okun's Law in Comparative Perspective." *European Economic Review*, vol. 25.

Hamermesh, D. S. 1985. "The Demand for Labor in the Long Run." In *Handbook of Labor Economics*, edited by O. Ashenfelter and Richard Layard. Amsterdam: North Holland, forthcoming.

Harberger, Arnold C. 1980. "Vignettes on the World Capital Market." *American Economic*

Review. Papers and Proceedings of the 92nd Annual Meeting of the American Economic Association, vol. 70, no. 2 (May).

Hill, Peter. 1984. *Real Gross Product in OECD Countries and Associated Purchasing Power Parities*. OECD Working Papers, no. 17. Paris, December.

Hodrick, Robert J., and Sanjay Srivastava. 1984. "The Covariation of Risk Premiums and Expected Future Spot Exchange Rates." *Journal of International Money and Finance*, vol. 3.

Holloway, Thomas M. 1984. "The Economy and the Federal Budget: Guides to the Automatic Effects." *US Survey of Current Business*, vol. 64, no. 7 (July).

Hooper, Peter. 1976. *Forecasting US Export and Import Prices and Volumes in a Changing World Economy*. International Finance Discussion Paper, no. 99. Washington: December.

———. 1985. *International Repercussions of the US Budget Deficit*. Brookings Discussion Paper in International Economics, no. 27. Washington: Brookings Institution.

Houthakker, Hendrick S., and Stephen P. Magee. 1969. "Income and Price Elasticities in World Trade." *Review of Economics and Statistics*, vol. 11, no. 2 (May).

Hulten, Charles R., and James W. Robertson. 1983. *Corporate Tax Policy and Economic Growth: An Analysis of the 1981 and 1982 Tax Acts*. Urban Institute Discussion Paper. Washington: Urban Institute, October.

International Energy Agency. 1984. *Energy Prices and Taxes, Fourth Quarter 1984*. Paris: OECD.

International Monetary Fund (IMF). 1984. *The Exchange Rate System: Lessons of the Past and Options for the Future*. Occasional Paper, no. 30. Washington, July.

———. 1985. *World Economic Outlook*. Washington, April.

Isard, Peter. 1980. *Factors Determining Exchange Rates: The Roles of Relative Price Levels, Balances of Payments, Interest Rates and Risk*. International Finance Discussion Paper, no. 171. Washington: IMF, December.

Isard, Peter, and Lois Stekler. 1985. "US International Capital Flows and the Dollar." *Brookings Papers on Economic Activity* 1.

Islam, Shafiqul. 1984. *Deficits and the Dollar: Can Theory Explain the Facts?* Federal Reserve Board of New York Research Paper, no. 8423, October.

Japan Economic Institute. 1984. "The Corporate Tax Debate in Japan and the United States." *Report*, no. 45A. Washington, November.

Jurgensen, Phillippe. 1983. Report of the Working Group on Exchange Market Intervention. Versailles: Working Group on Exchange Market Intervention established at the Versailles Summit of the Heads of State and Government 4, 5, and 6 June, 1982. March. Processed.

Kindleberger, Charles P. 1969. "Politics of International Money and World Language." *Essays in International Finance*, no. 74. Princeton, NJ: Princeton University Press.

———. 1978. *Manias, Panics, and Crashes: A History of Financial Crises*. New York, NY: Basic Books, Inc.

King, Mervyn A., and Don Fullerton. 1984. *The Taxation of Income from Capital*. Chicago, Ill.: University of Chicago Press.

Krugman, Paul R. 1985. *Is the Strong Dollar Sustainable?* National Bureau of Economic Research Working Paper, no. 1644. Cambridge, Mass.: NBER.

Kubarych, Roger M. 1984. "Financing the US Current Account Deficit." Federal Reserve Bank of New York, *Quarterly Review*, vol. 9, no. 2 (Summer).

Kuznets, Simon. 1966. *Modern Economic Growth: Rate Structure and Spread*. New Haven, Conn.: Yale University Press.

Larsen, Flemming, John Llewellyn, and Stephen Potter. 1983. "International Economic Linkages." *OECD Economic Studies*, no. 1 (Autumn).

Lawrence, Robert Z. 1984. *Can America Compete?* Washington: Brookings Institution.

Layard, Richard, Giorgio Basevi, Olivier J. Blanchard, Willem H. Buiter, and Rudiger Dornbusch. 1984. *Europe: The Case for Unsustainable Growth*. CEPS Papers, no. 8/9. Brussels: Centre for European Policy Studies.

Layard, Richard, and S. Nickell. 1985. "The Causes of British Unemployment." *National Institute Economic Review*, no. 111 (February).

Lever, Harold, Lord of Manchester. 1985. "The Dollar and the World Economy: The Case for Concerted Management." *Lloyds Bank Review*, no. 157 (July).

Lindbeck, Assar, and Dennis J. Snower. 1985. "Wage Rigidity, Union Activity and Unemployment." Paper presented at the Conference on Wage Rigidity, Employment and Economic Policy, 19–20 April, University of the South, Tennessee. Stockholm, Sweden: Institute for International Economic Studies.

Llewellyn, John. 1983. "Resource Prices and Macroeconomic Policies: Lessons from Two Oil Price Shocks." *OECD Economic Studies*, no. 1 (Autumn).

Malinvaud, Edmond. 1982. "Wages and Unemployment." *Economic Journal*, vol. 92 (March).

Marris, Stephen. 1984. "Managing the World Economy: Will We Ever Learn?" *Essays in International Finance*, no. 155. Princeton, NJ: Princeton University Press.

———. 1985. "The Decline and Fall of the Dollar: Some Policy Issues." *Brookings Papers on Economic Activity* 1.

McCracken, Paul, et al. 1977. *Towards Full Employment and Price Stability*. Paris: OECD.

McKinnon, Ronald I. 1984. *An International Standard for Monetary Stabilization*. POLICY ANALYSES IN INTERNATIONAL ECONOMICS 8. Washington: Institute for International Economics.

McNamar, Robert T. 1984a. Statement before the Senate Subcommittee on International Finance and Monetary Policy. Washington: Department of the Treasury, 6 June.

———. 1984b. Remarks before the Financial Executives Institute, New Orleans, La., 8 October. *Treasury News*. Washington: Department of the Treasury.

Meese, Richard A., and Kenneth Rogoff. 1983. "Empirical Exchange Rate Models of the Seventies—Do They Fit Out of Sample?" *Journal of International Economics*, vol. 14 (February).

Micossi, Stefano, and Tommaso Padoa-Schioppa. 1984. *Can Europeans Control Their Interest Rates?* CEPS Papers, no. 17. Brussels: Centre for European Policy Studies.

Minford, Patrick. 1984. "The Effects of American Policies—A New Classical Interpretation." In *International Economic Policy Coordination*, edited by Willem H. Buiter and Richard C. Marston. Cambridge, United Kingdom: Cambridge University Press.

Ministry of International Trade and Industry (MITI). 1985. *Report on Japanese Macroeconomic Policy*. Report by a private advisory committee to the Director General, Industrial Policy Bureau. Tokyo: MITI.

Morgan Guaranty Trust Company. 1984a. *World Financial Markets*. February, New York, NY.

———. 1984b. *World Financial Markets*. September, New York, NY.

———. 1985. *World Financial Markets*. March/April, New York, NY.

Mortensen, Jorgen. 1984. "Profitability, Relative Factor Prices and Capital/Labour Substitution." *European Economy*, no. 20.

Muller, Patrice, and Robert W. R. Price. 1984a. *Structural Budget Deficits and Fiscal Stance.* OECD Working Papers, no. 15. Paris, July.

———. 1984b. *Public Sector Indebtedness and Long-Term Interest Rates.* Paper prepared for the World Bank–Brookings Workshop on the International Consequences of Budgetary Deficits in the OECD. Paris: OECD, September.

National Association of Manufacturers (NAM). 1985. *U.S. Trade, Industrial Competitiveness and Economic Growth.* Washington, August.

National Institute of Economic and Social Research (NIESR). 1985. *National Institute Economic Review,* no. 112 (May).

Niskanen, William A. 1984. "Midyear Economic Outlook." Testimony before the Joint Economic Committee of the US Congress. Washington: Council of Economic Advisers, 8 August. Processed.

Noguchi, Yukio. 1985. "Tax Structure and Saving-Investment Balance." Paper prepared for symposium on US-Japan Economic Problems sponsored by the Institute for International Economics and the Japan Center for International Trade and Finance, Hakone, Japan, April 25–26. Kunitachi, Tokyo: Hitotsubashi University Department of Economics. Processed.

Ohkawa, Kazushi, and Miyohei Shinohara, eds. 1979. *Patterns of Japanese Economic Development: A Quantitative Appraisal.* New Haven, Conn., and London: Yale University Press.

Oliveira-Martins, Joaquim, and Colette Leroy. 1984. "Les désajustements mondiaux de balances des paiements." *CEPII Economie Prospective Internationale,* no. 17 (1er trimestre).

Organization for Economic Cooperation and Development (OECD). Department of Economics and Statistics. 1983a. *OECD Interlink System, Structure and Operation.* Paris, August.

———. 1983b. *Revenue Statistics of OECD Member Countries, 1965–1982.* Paris.

———. 1983c. *National Accounts 1953–1982,* vols. 1 and 2. Paris.

———. 1985. *OECD Employment Outlook.* Paris, September.

———. *OECD Economic Outlook,* various issues. Paris.

———. *OECD Economic Surveys* of Member Countries, various issues. Paris.

Oudiz, Gilles, and Jeffrey D. Sachs. 1984. "Macroeconomic Policy Coordination among the Industrial Economies." *Brookings Papers on Economic Activity* 1.

Parkin, Michael, and Robin Bade. 1982. *Modern Macroeconomics.* Oxford, United Kingdom: Philip Allan Publishers, Ltd.

Penati, Alessandro, and Michael Dooley. 1984. "Current Account Imbalances and Capital Formation in Industrial Countries, 1949–81." *IMF Staff Papers,* vol. 31, no. 1 (March).

Penner, Rudolph G. 1985. Statement before the Senate Committee on the Budget. Washington: Congressional Budget Office, 6 February.

Perry, George L. 1983. "What Have We Learned about Disinflation?" *Brookings Papers on Economic Activity* 2.

Petersen, Peter G. 1986. *Deficits, Debts, and Demographics* (provisional), forthcoming.

Pigott, Charles, John Rutledge, and Thomas D. Willett. 1984. "Estimating the Inflationary Effects of Exchange Rate Changes." In *Exchange Rates, Trade, and the US Economy,* edited by Sven W. Arndt, Richard J. Sweeney, and Thomas D. Willett. Cambridge, Mass.: Ballinger Publishing Co.

Price, Robert W. R., and Jean-Claude Chouraqui. 1983. "Public Sector Deficits: Problems and Policy Implications." *OECD Economic Outlook Occasional Studies,* Paris: OECD, June.

Putnam, Robert D., and Nicholas Bayne. 1984. *Hanging Together: The Seven Power Summits.* Cambridge, Mass.: Harvard University Press.

Rivlin, Alice M. 1984. *Economic Choices.* Washington: Brookings Institution.

Roosa, Robert V. 1985. Statement prepared for the Senate Finance Committee. New York: Brown Brothers Harriman & Co., 23 April.

Sachs, Jeffrey D. 1979. "Wages, Profits and Macroeconomic Adjustment." *Brookings Papers on Economic Activity* 2.

———. 1980. "The Current Account and Macroeconomic Adjustment in the 1970s." *Brookings Papers on Economic Activity* 1.

———. 1983. "Real Wages and Unemployment in the OECD Countries." *Brookings Papers on Economic Activity* 1.

———. 1985. "The Dollar and the Policy Mix: 1985." *Brookings Papers on Economic Activity* 1.

Shafer, Jeffrey R., and Bonnie E. Loopesko. 1983. "Floating Exchange Rates After Ten Years." *Brookings Papers on Economic Activity* 4.

Shultz, George P. 1985. "National Policies and Global Prosperity." Address before the Woodrow Wilson School of Public and International Affairs, 11 April, Princeton University, Princeton, NJ. US Department of State, press no. 70.

Simon, Matthew. 1960. "The United States Balance of Payments, 1861–1900." In *Trends in the American Economy,* edited by William N. Parkin. Vol. 24, *Studies in Income and Wealth.* Princeton, NJ: Princeton University Press.

Solomon, Robert. 1985a. "Financing the US Current Account Deficit in 1985." *R.S. Associates International Economic Letter,* vol. 5, no. 2 (February).

———. 1985b. *The United States as a Debtor in the 19th Century.* Brookings Discussion Paper in International Economics, no. 28. Washington: Brookings Institution, May.

———. 1985c. *Effects of the Strong Dollar.* Brookings Discussion Paper in International Economics, no. 35. Washington: Brookings Institution, September.

Spitäller, Erich. 1980. "Short-Run Effects of Exchange Rate Changes on Terms of Trade and Trade Balance." *IMF Staff Papers,* vol. 27, no. 2 (June).

Sprinkel, Beryl W. 1981. Statement before the Joint Economic Committee of the US Congress. Washington: Department of the Treasury, 4 May. Processed.

———. 1984. Statement before the House Commitee on Ways and Means, Subcommittee on Trade, 29 March.

Stern, Robert M., Jonathan Francis, and Bruce Schumacher. 1976. *Price Elasticities in International Trade: An Annotated Bibliography.* London: Macmillan Press for the Trade Policy Research Center.

Sturm, Peter. 1983. "Determinants of Saving: Theory and Evidence." *OECD Economic Studies,* no. 1 (Autumn).

Tanzi, Vito, ed. 1984. *Taxation, Inflation, and Interest Rates.* Washington: IMF.

Tanzi, Vito, and Eytan Sheshinski. 1984. Study in progress, reported in *IMF Survey,* vol. 13, no. 22.

Tobin, James. 1983. "The Macroeconomic Impasse of the 1980s: Locomotives Who Can't or Won't." Harry G. Johnson Memorial Lecture, University of Chicago, 3 November. New Haven, Conn.: Yale University. Processed.

US Department of Commerce. Bureau of Economic Analysis. *Survey of Current Business,* various issues.

US Treasury Department. 1984. Office of the Assistant Secretary for Economic Policy. *The Effect of Deficits on Prices of Financial Assets: Theory and Evidence.* Washington, March.
———. 1985. "Report to the Congress on the Functioning of the International Monetary and Financial System and the Role and Operation of the International Monetary Fund." Washington, 15 March. Processed.
United Kingdom Treasury. 1985. *The Relationship Between Employment and Wages.* London: Her Majesty's Treasury.
Volcker, Paul A. 1985a. Statement before the Joint Economic Committee of the US Congress, 5 February. Washington: Federal Reserve. Processed.
———. 1985b. Statement before the Senate Committee on Banking, Housing, and Urban Affairs, 20 February. Washington: Federal Reserve. Processed.
———. 1985c. Remarks before the 13th American-German Biennial Conference, Dallas, Texas, 30 March. Washington: Federal Reserve. Processed.
———. 1985d. Statement before the House Subcommittee on Domestic Monetary Policy. Washington: Federal Reserve, 17 July. Processed.
Wallich, Henry C. 1984. "Why is Net International Investment so Small?" *International Capital Movements Debt and Monetary System.* Essays in Honor of Wilfried Guth. Mainz, Germany: V. Hase & Koehler.
———. 1985. "International and Domestic Aspects of Monetary Policy." Remarks upon receiving the Distinguished Achievement Award of the Money Marketeers of New York University, 28 May. Washington: Federal Reserve Board. Processed.
Wallich, Henry C., and K. Friedrich. 1982. "Cyclical Patterns in the US Balance of Payments." *Economies et Sociétés,* vol. 16, no. 4–5 (April/May).
Wharton Econometric Forecasting Associates. 1985. *Could Europe Grow Faster? Alternative Global Scenarios.* Philadelphia, Pa.: Wharton Econometrics, May.
Williamson, John. 1985. *The Exchange Rate System.* 2nd ed., rev. POLICY ANALYSES IN INTERNATIONAL ECONOMICS 5. Washington: Institute for International Economics.
Witteveen, H. J. 1984. "The Netherlands Budget for 1985." Presented at the Ambassador's Luncheon, 2–5 October, Amsterdam. Amsterdam: Rotterdam Bank N.V.
Woo, Wing T. 1984. "Exchange Rates and the Prices of Nonfood, Nonfuel Products." *Brookings Papers on Economic Activity* 2.
Wyplosz, Charles. 1984. "International Aspects of the Policy Mix in Six OECD Countries." Paper presented at World Bank–Brookings Workshop, Institut Européen d'Administration des Affaires, Fontainebleau, France. Processed.
Yoshitomi, Marasu. 1984. "The Insulation and Transmission Mechanisms of Floating Exchange Rates Analyzed by the EPA World Econometric Model." Paper prepared for delivery at the EPA symposium, Tokyo, 13–15 March. Tokyo: Government of Japan, Economic Research Institute, Economic Planning Agency.
———. 1985a. "International Consequences of Different Wage Rigidities under Oil Crises and Disinflation." Paper prepared for a symposium on Wage Rigidity, Employment and Economic Policy, University of the South, Tennessee, 19–20 April. Paris: OECD, March.
———. 1985b. *Japan as Capital Exporter and the World Economy.* Group of Thirty Occasional Papers, no. 18. New York, NY.
Zaidi, Iqbal Mehdi. 1985. "Saving, Investment, Fiscal Deficits, and the External Indebtedness of Developing Countries." *World Development,* vol. 13, no. 5 (May).

Other Publications from the Institute

POLICY ANALYSES IN INTERNATIONAL ECONOMICS SERIES

The Debt of Low-Income Africa: Issues and Options for the United States
Carol Lancaster

International Aspects of United States Tax Policy: An Overview
Daniel J. Frisch

Europe, the Dollar, and 1992
Stephen Marris

The United States as a Debtor Country
C. Fred Bergsten and Shafiqul Islam

Pacific Area Trade: Threat or Opportunity for the United States?
Bela Balassa and Marcus Noland

Trade Liberalization and International Institutions: What More Could Be Done?
Jeffrey J. Schott

Reciprocity and Retaliation: An Evaluation of Aggressive Trade Policies
Thomas O. Bayard

Third World Debt: A Reappraisal
William R. Cline

The Politics of International Monetary Cooperation
C. Fred Bergsten, I. M. Destler, C. Randall Henning, and John Williamson

The Taxation of Income from International Financial Investment
Daniel J. Frisch

Energy Policy for the 1990s: A Global Perspective
Philip K. Verleger, Jr.

The Outlook for World Commodity Prices
Philip K. Verleger, Jr.

EC 1992: Implications for the World Economy
Jeffrey J. Schott